The New Complete
MEDICAL
and HEALTH
ENCYCLOPEDIA

EDITED BY
Richard J. Wagman, M.D., F.A.C.P.
Assistant Clinical Professor of Medicine
Downstate Medical Center
New York, New York

AND BY
the J. G. Ferguson Editorial Staff

Volume One

J. G. FERGUSON PUBLISHING COMPANY/CHICAGO

Editor

Richard J. Wagman, M.D., F.A.C.P.
Assistant Clinical Professor of
  Medicine
Downstate Medical Center
New York, New York

Contributors to The New Complete Medical and Health Encyclopedia

Consultant in Surgery

N. Henry Moss, M.D., F.A.C.S.
Associate Clinical Professor of
  Surgery
Temple University Health Sciences
  Center and Albert Einstein
  Medical Center;
Past President, American Medical
  Writers Association;
Past President, New York Academy
  of Sciences

Consultant in Gynecology

Douglass S. Thompson, M.D.
Clinical Professor of Obstetrics and
  Gynecology and Clinical Associate
  Professor of Community Medicine
University of Pittsburgh School of
  Medicine

Consultant in Pediatrics

Charles H. Bauer, M.D.
Clinical Associate Professor of
  Pediatrics and Chief of Pediatric
  Gastroenterology
The New York Hospital-Cornell
  Medical Center
New York, New York

Consultants in Psychiatry

Julian J. Clark, M.D.
Assistant Professor of Psychiatry
              and
Rita W. Clark, M.D.
Clinical Assistant Professor of
  Psychiatry
Downstate Medical Center

Consulting Editor

Kenneth N. Anderson
Formerly Editor
Today's Health

Bruce O. Berg, M.D.
Associate Professor
Departments of Neurology and
  Pediatrics
Director, Child Neurology
University of California
San Francisco, California

D. Jeanne Collins
Assistant Professor
College of Allied Health Professions
University of Kentucky
Lexington, Kentucky

Anthony A. Davis
Vice President and Education
  Consultant
Metropolitan X-Ray and Medical
  Sales, Inc.
Olney, Maryland

Peter A. Dickinson
Editor Emeritus
Harvest Years/Retirement Living

Gordon K. Farley, M.D.
Associate Professor of Child
  Psychiatry
Director, Day Care Center
University of Colorado Medical
  Center

Arthur Fisher
Group Editor
Science and Engineering
Popular Science

Edmund H. Harvey, Jr.
Editor
Science World

Helene MacLean
Medical writer

Ben Patrusky
Science writer

Stanley E. Weiss, M.D.
Assistant Attending Physician, Renal
  Service
Beth Israel Hospital and Medical
  Center, New York

Jeffrey S. Willner, M.D.
Attending Radiologist
Southampton Hospital
Southampton, New York

Contents

Volume I

Volume II

Volume III

Volume IV

INTRODUCTION

The NEW COMPLETE MEDICAL AND HEALTH ENCYCLOPEDIA is designed to give you clear, accurate answers to your questions about health care. Thorough discussions of major diseases such as cancer and heart problems are included, along with facts about many other less serious diseases and physical problems and how they are treated.

Many people today want to take an active part in their own treatment. This usually takes the form of asking your physician to present the treatment options available to you, then making a decision about which course to follow. Let's assume that your physician is in tune with this approach and willing to relinquish some of the authority doctors traditionally have assumed to tell patients what to do. You will need information to ask intelligent questions and to understand the alternatives being discussed. This set of books will give you that information.

Fortunately, research in medicine is continually advancing. The NEW COMPLETE MEDICAL AND HEALTH ENCYCLOPEDIA has been revised in this edition to include material on recent advances in medicine and health care.

Becoming ill and being treated are only part of the picture in health care today. More and more, professionals and lay people are putting the emphasis on preventive medicine, doing everything possible to stay well and healthy. To help you and your family stay in the best possible condition, the editors have included detailed information on food and nutrition, dieting, care of skin and hair, dental health, exercises, and physical fitness. The section on exercises includes not only detailed instructions, but also diagrams of how to perform each exercise.

Families often have questions about children's health. Parents, stepparents, and grandparents want to know what is normal and expected from a child at various ages in terms of physical, mental, and emotional development. Therefore, the editors have included two chapters, one on younger children, and the other on teenages, that discuss everything from the common cold to stuttering, from creativity to sexual maturation.

Older people, too, have special health concerns. Senior citizens or their families will want to read the information on diet, daily habits, mental health, activities to pursue during retirement, nursing homes, and retirement homes for the aging.

Generic drugs have been in the spotlight increasingly in recent years. For your convenience in sorting out which drug is equivalent to which, the editors have included a chapter on 100 commonly prescribed generic drugs. The chapter includes information on brand names and the action that each drug has in the body.

These are just a few of the subjects covered in this encyclopedia. How can you make the best possible use of these books? First and foremost, do not use this information to treat yourself or anyone else except temporarily in an emergency. (Please note the chapter on Medical Emergencies.) If any symptom of disease is present, no one can take the place of a trained professional.

Use the NEW COMPLETE MEDICAL AND HEALTH ENCYCLOPEDIA for background information on a host of topics, as a handy guide to first aid, and as a reference on where to get further information.

Get acquainted with these books by looking through the table of contents in each volume. Then, to locate a specific topic of interest, consult the A-Z Index Reference Guide in volume-4. It includes brief descriptions and definitions on hundreds of medical and health topics and terms.

1

Your Body

The Skeleton

Say "skeleton" to children and you probably conjure up in their minds a rickety structure of rigid sticks, or, to the more fanciful child, a clickety-clacketing collection of rattling bones cavorting under a Halloween moon. A look at almost any anatomical drawing of the human skeletal system bears out the child's image: dry sticks of bones, stripped of skin and flesh, muscle and tendon—a grotesque caricature of a living human being.

Our living bones are something quite different. They are rigid, yes, but not entirely so: they also may bend a little and grow and repair themselves; and they are shaped and fitted so that—rather than the herky-jerky motions of a wooden puppet—they permit the smooth grace and coordination power displayed by an accomplished athlete or a prima ballerina.

Our bones do not do just one thing but many things. Some bones, like the collarbone or *clavicle*, mainly give support to other body structures. Others, like the skull and ribs, encase and protect vulnerable organs. Still others, like the *metacarpus* and *phalanges* that make up our hands and fingers, give us mechanical advantages—leverage and movement. There are even bones, the tiny *ossicles* in the middle ear, whose vibrations enable us to hear.

Finally, to think of bone simply as a structural member, like a solid steel girder in a skyscraper, ignores the fact that bone is living tissue. It is one of the busiest tissues in our bodies, a chemical factory that is continually receiving, processing and shipping a wide variety of mineral salts, blood components, and a host of other vital materials.

How the Bones of the Skeletal System Fit and Work Together

Medical textbooks name a total of 206 bones making up the skeletal system of the normal, adult human being. The words "normal" and "adult" are significant. A newborn baby normally has 33 vertebrae making up its backbone (also called *spinal column* or simply *spine*); but by the time a person reaches adulthood, the number of individual vertebrae has shrunk to 26.

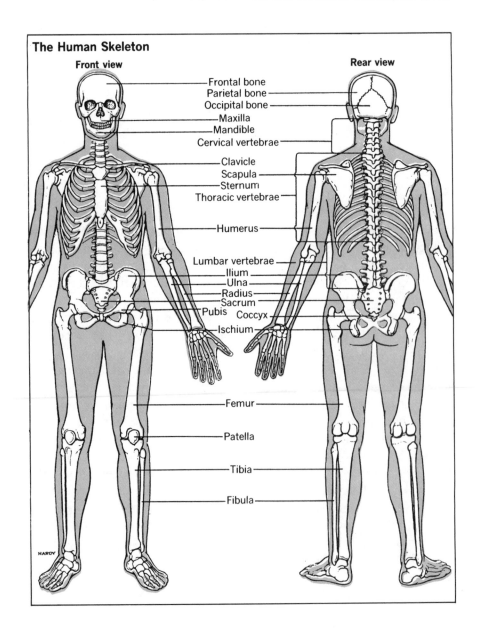

The Human Skeleton

Front view   Rear view

Frontal bone
Parietal bone
Occipital bone
Maxilla
Mandible
Cervical vertebrae

Clavicle
Scapula
Sternum
Thoracic vertebrae

Humerus

Lumbar vertebrae
Ilium
Ulna
Radius
Sacrum
Pubis   Coccyx
Ischium

Femur

Patella

Tibia

Fibula

HARDY

The explanation: during the growth process, the nine bottom vertebrae fuse naturally into just two. In like fashion, we "lose" some 60 bones as we grow up. Some otherwise perfectly normal adults have "extra" bones or "missing" bones. For example, although the normal number of ribs is 12 pairs, some adults may have 11; others may have 13 pairs.

Even a practicing physician might be hard-pressed to identify each of our 200-plus bones and describe its function. An easier way to gain a general understanding of the various functions, capabilities—and weaknesses, too—of our bones is to visualize the skeletal system as a standing coatrack, say, about six feet high.

Call the central pole the backbone. About ten inches down from its top (the top of your skull) is a horizontal crossbar (your shoulders—collarbones and shoulder blades), approximately a foot-and-a-half across. Sixteen or so inches below the bottom of the top crossbar is another, shorter crossbar, broader and thicker—the *pelvic girdle*. The coatrack with its two crossbars is now a crude model of the bones of the head and trunk, collectively called the *axial skeleton*. Its basic unit is the backbone, to which are attached the skull at the top, then the bones of the shoulder girdle, the ribs, and at the bottom, the bones of the pelvic girdle.

By hanging down (or appending) members from the two ends of the top crossbar, and doing the same at the lower crossbar, we would simulate what is called the *appendicular skeleton*—arms and hands, legs and feet.

Now, make the coatrack stand on its new legs, cut off the central pole just below the lower bar (if you wish, calling it man's lost tail), and you have the two main components of the skeletal system, joined together before you. Let us look at each more closely.

The Axial Skeleton

Within the framework of the axial skeleton lie all the most vital organs of the body. People have gone on living with the loss of a hand or a leg—indeed, with the loss of any or all of their limbs. But nobody can live without a brain, a heart, a liver, lungs, or kidneys—all of which are carried within the framework of the axial skeleton.

The Skull

The bones of the skull have as their most important function the protection of the brain and sense organs. There are also, of course, the jawbones that support the teeth and gums and which enable us to bite and chew our food.

Most of the skull appears to consist of a single bone—a hard, unbroken dome. Actually, the brain cage or *cranium* consists of eight individual platelike bones which have fused together in the process of growth. At birth, these bones are separated, causing the soft spots or *fontanelles* we can readily feel on a baby's head. As the baby's brain enlarges, the bones grow along their edges to fill in the fontanelles, finally knitting to-gether in what are called *suture lines,* somewhat resembling inexpertly mended clothes seams. Along the suture lines, the skull bones continue to grow until the individual's mature skull size is reached.

Teeth

The hardest substance in the human body is the *enamel* that covers the exposed surface of a tooth. Below the gum, the tooth's outside surface is composed of somewhat softer *cementum*. Beneath enamel and cementum is a bonelike substance, called *dentin,* which covers the soft interior of the tooth, called *pulp*. Pulp is serviced by blood vessels and nerves through the root or roots of the tooth. The passageway of nerves and blood vessels that lead up through the tooth from the gum sockets is called a *root canal*. Tooth and gum are stuck to each other by a tough, adhesive tissue called *periodontal* (or peridental— "surrounding the tooth") *membrane.* See Ch. 22, *The Teeth and Gums,* for further information on teeth.

The Backbone

At the base of the skull, the backbone begins. The skull is supported by the topmost *cervical* (neck) vertebra. The curious thing about a backbone is that the word has come to suggest something solid, straight, and unbending. The backbone, however, just isn't like that: it consists of 26 knobby, hollowed-out bones—*vertebrae,* rather improbably held together by muscles, ligaments, and tendons. It is not straight when we stand, but has definite backward and forward curvatures; and even some of its most important structures (the disks between the vertebrae) aren't made of bone, but of cartilage.

All in all, however, the backbone is a fairly well designed structure in terms of the several different functions it serves—but with some built-in weaknesses. For a discussion of backache, see Ch. 23, *Aches, Pains, Nuisances, Worries.*

The Vertebrae

Although they will have features in common, no two of our 26 vertebrae are exactly alike in shape, size, or function. This is hardly surprising if we consider, for example, that the cervical vertebrae do not support ribs, while the *thoracic* vertebrae (upper trunk, or chest) do support them.

But for a sample vertebra, let us pick a rib-carrying vertebra, if for no other reason than that it lies about midway along the backbone. If viewed from above or below, a thoracic vertebra, like most of the others, would look like a roundish piece of bone with roughly scalloped edges on the side facing inward toward the chest and on the side facing outward toward the surface of the back, and would reveal several bony projections. These knobby portions of a vertebra—some of which you can feel as bumps along your backbone—are called *processes*. They serve as the vertebra's points of connection to muscles and tendons, to ribs, and to the other vertebrae above and below.

A further conspicuous feature is a hole, more or less in the middle of the typical vertebra, through which passes the master nerve bundle of our bodies, the spinal cord, running from the base of the skull to the top of the pelvis. Thus, one of the important functions of the backbone is to provide flexible, protective tubing for the spinal cord.

Between the bones of one vertebra and the next is a piece of more resilient cartilage that acts as a cushion or shock absorber to prevent two vertebrae from scraping or bumping each other if the backbone gets a sudden jolt, or as the backbone twists and turns and bends. These pieces of cartilage are the intervertebral disks—infamous for pain and misery if they become ruptured or slipped disks.

Regions of the Backbone

The backbone can be divided into five regions, starting with the uppermost, or *cervical* region, which normally has seven vertebrae. Next down is the *thoracic* (chest) section, normally with 12 vertebrae. From each vertebra a rib extends to curl protectively around the chest area. Usually, the top ten ribs come all the way around the trunk and attach to the breastbone (or *sternum*); but the bottom two ribs do not reach the breastbone and are thus called floating ribs. The thoracic section also must support the shoulder girdle, consisting of the collarbones (*clavicles*) and shoulder blades (*scapulas*). At the end of each shoulder blade is a shoulder joint—actually three distinct joints working together—where the arm connects to the axial skeleton.

Below the thoracic vertebrae come the five vertebrae of the *lumbar* section. This area gets a good deal of blame for back miseries: lower back pain often occurs around the area where the bottom thoracic vertebra joins the top lumbar vertebra. Furthermore, the lumbar region or small of the back is also a well-known site of back pain; indeed, from the word "lumbar" comes *lumbago*, medically an imprecise term, but popularly used to describe very real back pain.

Below the lumbar region are two vertebrae so completely different from the 24 above them—and even from each other—that it seems strange they are called vertebrae at all: the *sacrum* and the *coccyx*. These two vertebrae are both made up of several distinct vertebrae that are present at birth. The sacrum is a large bone that was once five vertebrae. The coccyx was originally four vertebrae—and, incidentally, is all that remains of man's tail in his evolution from the primates.

The Pelvic Girdle

The sacrum is the more important of these two strange-looking vertebrae. It is the backbone's connection to the *pelvic girdle,* or pelvis. On each side of the sacrum, connected by the sacroiliac joint, is a very large, curving bone called the *ilium,* tilting (when we stand) slightly forward and downward from the sacrum toward the front of the groin. We feel the top of the ilium as the top of the hip—a place mothers and fathers often find convenient for toting a toddler.

Fused at each side of the ilium and slanting toward the back is the *ischium,* the bone we sit on. The two *pubis* bones, also fused to the ilium, meet in front to complete the pelvic girdle. All the bones of the pelvis—ilium, ischium, and pubis—fuse together so as to form the hip joint (*acetabulum*), a deep socket into which the "ball" or upper end of the thighbone fits.

The Appendicular Skeleton

The bones of the appendages—arms, hands, and fingers; legs, feet, and toes—allow human beings to perform an astonishing array of complex movements, from pushing themselves through the physical rigors of the Olympic decathlon to creating an elaborate piece of needlework. The key points in the appendicular skeleton, as indeed, in the axial skeleton, are where the ends or edges of bones lie close together and must work with or against one another in order to achieve coordinated movement. These key points are the *joints*—not really bones at all but the non-bony spaces between bones.

The Joints

A typical joint consists of several different structures. First, there are the bones themselves—two, three, four, or more almost touching in the area of the joint—with their ends or edges shaped to fit in their respective niches. Between the bones of an appendage joint (as between the vertebrae of the back) is the smooth, resilient material called *cartilage* that allows the bones to move over one another without scraping or catching. At the joint, the bones, with their layer of cartilage between them, are held together by tough bonds of muscle. *Bursas,* tiny sacs containing a lubricating fluid, are also found at joints; they help to reduce the friction between a joint's moving parts.

The Hip and Knee

The hip joint must not only support the weight of the head and trunk, but must allow for movement of the leg and also play a part in the constant balancing required to maintain upright posture. Similar stresses and strains, often literally tending to tear the joint apart, are placed on every joint in the body.

The notoriety of athletes' bad knees attests to the forces battering at the knee joint, the largest in the human body. Sports involving leaping or sudden changes in direction, such as basketball, are especially hard on the knee. However, the fact that there are not more disabled sports heroes speaks well for the design of the knee joint. The same can be said of the ankle joint and the joints of the foot and toes.

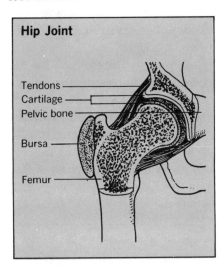

Hip Joint

Tendons
Cartilage
Pelvic bone
Bursa
Femur

The Shoulder, Elbow, and Wrist

The counterpart of the hip joint in the upper trunk is the shoulder joint. Free of weight-bearing responsibilities, the shoulder has a system of three interconnected joints that allow it and the arm far more versatile movements than the hip and leg.

The elbow connects the upper arm bone (*humerus*) with the two bones of the lower arm (*radius* and *ulna*). Like the knee, it is basically a hinge joint, which allows the lower arm to be raised and lowered. The elbow is also constructed to allow some rotation by the hand; likewise, the knee joint allows us to waggle the foot.

Of all our body parts, the wrist, hand, and fingers are perhaps the most elegantly and finely jointed—witness the performance of a concert pianist—and our ankles, feet, and toes probably the most subject to everyday misery.

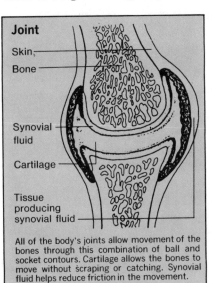

Joint

Skin
Bone

Synovial fluid

Cartilage

Tissue producing synovial fluid

All of the body's joints allow movement of the bones through this combination of ball and socket contours. Cartilage allows the bones to move without scraping or catching. Synovial fluid helps reduce friction in the movement.

Bone as Living Tissue

Our bones, like all our tissues, change as we grow up, mature, and finally grow old. There are changes in the chemical activity and composition of bone representative of each stage of life.

In young children, the ends and edges of bones are mainly cartilage, forming a growing surface on the bone that is gradually replaced by hard bone as full size is attained. The bones of a child are more pliable and less likely to break than those of a full-grown adult.

Similarly, as an adult ages, the bones turn from a resilient hardness to a more brittle hardness. This accounts for the much greater danger of broken bones in older people.

These changes with age are an indication of the great amount of chemical activity going on within bone. We sometimes forget that our bones are amply supplied and penetrated by blood vessels. There is a constant building up and breaking down, an interchange of materials between blood and bone.

The Composition of Bone

A living bone does not have a single uniform composition, but instead is composed of several different kinds of tissue. To begin with, there are actually two types of bone tissue in the same bone: compact and spongy. In addition, bone is sheathed in a tough membranous tissue called the *periosteum,* interlaced with blood vessels. Finally, within most of the larger and longer bones of the body, as well as in the interior of the skull bones and vertebrae, are two more kinds of tissue: red marrow and yellow marrow.

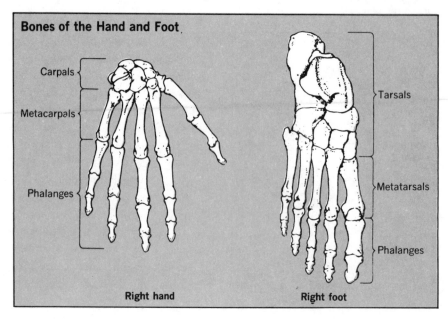

Bones of the Hand and Foot

Carpals

Metacarpals

Phalanges

Tarsals

Metatarsals

Phalanges

Right hand

Right foot

Marrow

Within the spongy bone areas, *red marrow* produces enormous numbers of red blood cells, at a rate of millions per minute. These are needed for growth as well as for replacement of red cells, which also die in enormous numbers. Children's bones contain greater proportions of red marrow than adults'. With age, *yellow marrow,* composed mainly of fat cells, begins to fill the interior bone cavities formerly occupied by red marrow.

Calcium

Bone also serves as a storage and distribution center for one of the most important elements in our body. Calcium, in the form of calcium phosphate, is the basic chemical of bone tissue, but this element also must always be present in the bloodstream at a certain level to ensure normal heartbeat, blood clotting, and muscle contraction. When the calcium level in the blood is deficient, the bones release some calcium into the bloodstream; when the blood has a surplus of calcium, the bones reabsorb it.

Fractures

Like most other tissues, broken bone can repair itself, and it is a remarkable process to observe. It is a process, however, that will proceed even if the ends are not aligned or set—an important reason why any suspected fracture should be checked by a physician.

A break in a bone causes a sticky material to be deposited by the blood around the broken ends. This material begins the formation of a kind of protective, lumpy sleeve, called a *callus,* around the broken ends. Mainly cartilage, the callus hardens into spongy bone, normally within a month or two. Then, the spongy bone begins to be reduced in size by bone-dissolving cells produced in the marrow, while at the same time the spongy bone in the area of the break is beginning to be replaced by hard bone.

Depending on the particular bone involved and the severity of the fracture, the broken bone can be completely healed within four to ten months.

Potential Trouble Spots

Essentially there are two kinds of things that can go wrong with the skeletal system and cause trouble.

Mechanical Difficulties

A healthy bone's main mechanical functions—support, movement, protection—can be impaired. This can happen as a result of a physical injury resulting in a fracture or dislocation.

The stack of vertebrae called the backbone is vulnerable to a number of painful conditions from top to bottom, especially in the region of the lower back. Unfortunately, man seems to have evolved relatively quickly from a four-footed creature, and his backbone is not ideally suited for standing and walking on two feet. Back troubles become increasingly common with age.

Areas where bones interact are also very susceptible to injury because of the stresses and strains they undergo even in people who are not especially active. Normal wear and tear also takes its toll on our bones and joints; for example, the bones' structure or their alignment at a joint may be altered slightly with age, making one bone or another prone to slipping out of the joint causing a dislocation. In any case, it is not advisable to make the same demands on our skeletal system at 40 as we did at 20. Joints are also the site of arthritis.

Disease

Second, and generally more serious if untreated, the interior bone tissues themselves may become infected and diseased. This can lead as a secondary effect to impairment of the bones' mechanical functions. *Osteomyelitis,* for example, a bacterial infection of bony tissues, can destroy large portions of bone unless antibiotics are started at once.

Fortunately, disorders of the skeletal system generally reveal themselves early and clearly by pain. Any severe or lingering pain of the joints or bones should be reported to a physician. For example, some people may feel that aching feet are unavoidable—and a little undignified. But a foot is not meant to hurt, nor is any part of the skeletal system. Consulting a physician could prevent much present and future misery. See also Ch. 7, *Diseases of the Skeletal System.*

The Muscles

Some 600 muscles of all sizes and shapes are attached to the framework of the skeletal system. Altogether these muscles make up nearly half of a normal adult's weight. They hold the skeleton together and, on signals originating in the brain, empower its various parts to move. Everywhere throughout the skeletal system, muscles work together with bones to protect the body's vital organs and to support and move its parts.

Skeletal Muscle

Such muscles are called, collectively, *skeletal muscle*. They are also called *voluntary muscles* because, for the most part, we can choose when we want them to act and what we want them to do—drive a car, kick a football, turn a page, jump a brook, ride a bicycle. Skeletal muscle also goes by two other names, based on its appearance under a microscope—striped and striated.

Skeletal, voluntary, striped, striated—all refer to the same general type of muscle. To avoid confusion, the term used throughout this section is skeletal muscle.

Muscles of the Abdomen and Thorax

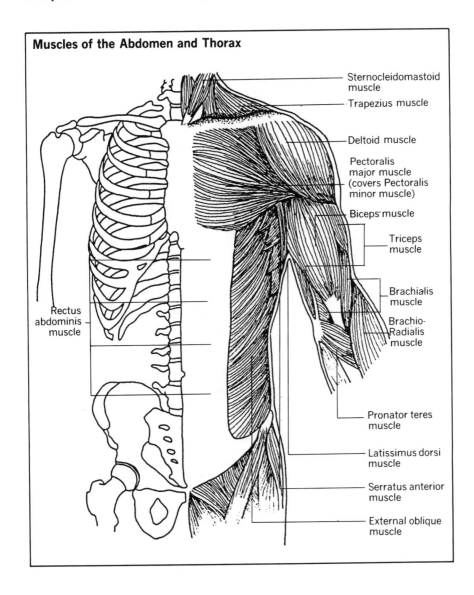

Sternocleidomastoid muscle

Trapezius muscle

Deltoid muscle

Pectoralis major muscle (covers Pectoralis minor muscle)

Biceps muscle

Triceps muscle

Brachialis muscle

Brachio-Radialis muscle

Rectus abdominis muscle

Pronator teres muscle

Latissimus dorsi muscle

Serratus anterior muscle

External oblique muscle

Smooth Muscle

There are two other general types of muscle. One is called *smooth muscle* because, under the microscope, it lacks the clearly defined stripes of skeletal muscle. Smooth muscle has another name, *involuntary muscle,* so called because the brain does not voluntarily control its actions. Smooth muscle is responsible for movements such as the muscular action that moves food and waste along the digestive tract, or the contraction and dilation of the pupil of the eye, as well as countless other involuntary movements of the sense and internal organs—with the exception of the heart.

Muscles of the Back

Trapezius muscle

Infraspinatus muscle

Deltoid muscle

Rhomboid muscle

Teres major muscle

Triceps muscle

Latissimus dorsi muscle (covers spinal erector muscle)

External oblique muscle

Internal oblique muscle

Gluteus maximus muscle

Cardiac Muscle

The third and last general type of muscle is confined to the heart area, and is called *cardiac muscle*. (Cardiac means having to do with the heart.) It is involved in the rhythmic beating and contractions of the heart, which are not under conscious control, and cardiac muscle is therefore termed involuntary.

Structure of the Muscles

Each of the three kinds of muscle shares certain structural similarities with one or both of the others. All are made up of bundles of varying numbers of hair-thin fibers. In skeletal and smooth muscles, these fibers are lined up side by side in the bundle, while in cardiac muscle the fibers tend more to crisscross over one another. Skeletal muscle and cardiac muscle

Muscles, Their Locations, and Exercises that Strengthen Them		
Muscle	**Location**	**Movement**
Trapezius	Upper back and each side of neck	Shoulder-shrugging and upward-pulling movements
Deltoids	Shoulders	Arm raising and overhead pressing
Pectorals	Chest	Horizontal pressing and drawing arms across body
Latissimus dorsi	Wide back muscle stretching over back up to rear Deltoids	Pulling and rowing movements
Serratus	Jagged sawtooth muscles between Pectorals and lattissimus Dorsi	Pullover and Serratus leverage movements
Spinal erectors	Lower length of spinal column	Raising upper body from a bent-over position
Biceps	Front portion of upper arm	Arm bending and twisting
Forearms	Between wrist and elbow	Reverse-grip arm bending
Triceps	Back of upper arm	Pushing and straightening movements of upper arms
Rectus abdominals	Muscular area between sternum and pelvis	Sit-up, leg-raising, knee-in movements
Intercostals	Sides of waist, running diagonally to Serratus	Waist twisting
External oblique abdominals	Lower sides of waist	Waist twisting and bending
Buttocks	Muscular area covering seat	Lunging, stooping, leg raising
Leg biceps	Back of thighs	Raising lower leg to buttocks, bending forward and stretching
Frontal thighs	Front of thighs	Extending lower leg and knee bending
Calves	Lower leg between ankle and knee	Raising and lowering on toes

are both striped, that is, they show darker and lighter bands crossing over a group of adjacent fibers, while smooth muscle lacks these distinct cross-bands.

Both involuntary muscle types, smooth and cardiac, are controlled by signals carried by the autonomic nervous system. Signals that result in movements of the skeletal muscles are carried by a different nerve network, the central nervous system. The individual fibers in a muscle bundle with a particular function all react simultaneously to a signal from the nervous system; there is no apparent time lag from fiber to fiber.

How the Skeletal Muscles Work

The great range and variety of functions served by skeletal muscles can be suggested by naming just four: the diaphragm, used in breathing; the muscles that make the eye wink; the deltoid muscle that gives the shoulder its shape; and the tongue.

As with the bones, the body tends to make its greatest demands on muscle tissue in the area of the joints and the backbone. A smoothly functioning joint requires that bone, cartilage, and muscle all be sound and able to work together effectively.

Tendons and Ligaments

We often hear the words tendon and ligament used in the description of the knee or another joint. These are actually two types of skeletal muscles, distinguished as to their function.

A *tendon* can be described as a tight cord of muscle tissue that attaches other skeletal muscle to bone. For example, the Achilles tendon running down the back of the calf, the strongest tendon in the body, connects the muscles of the calf with the bone of the heel. A *ligament* is a somewhat more elastic band of muscle fibers that attaches bone to bone.

A tendon is not always evident in the connection of muscle to bone. Various groups and shapes of muscle fibers may be similarly employed, forming connective tissue without the formation of tendon.

Various associated tissues between or around skeletal muscles serve to reduce the wear and tear of

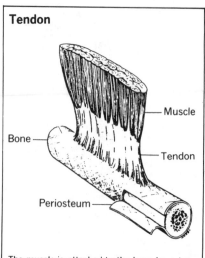

Tendon

Muscle

Bone

Tendon

Periosteum

The muscle is attached to the bone by a tendon. The fibers of the tendon interlace with the fibers of the periosteum, forming a strong bond.

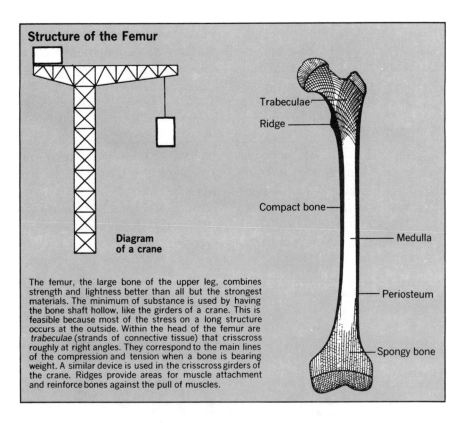

Structure of the Femur

Diagram of a crane

The femur, the large bone of the upper leg, combines strength and lightness better than all but the strongest materials. The minimum of substance is used by having the bone shaft hollow, like the girders of a crane. This is feasible because most of the stress on a long structure occurs at the outside. Within the head of the femur are *trabeculae* (strands of connective tissue) that crisscross roughly at right angles. They correspond to the main lines of the compression and tension when a bone is bearing weight. A similar device is used in the crisscross girders of the crane. Ridges provide areas for muscle attachment and reinforce bones against the pull of muscles.

Trabeculae
Ridge
Compact bone
Medulla
Periosteum
Spongy bone

friction in areas such as a joint, where muscle, bone, and cartilage may rub against one another. For example, the tendons that pass along the back of the hand from the wrist to the fingertips, as well as many other muscle groups throughout the body, are enclosed in lubricated sheaths. The muscle-sheathed *bursas,* lined inside with lubricating fluid, are also found in areas subject to friction, such as where a tendon passes closely over a bone.

Man's upright posture and two-legged locomotion subject the backbone to heavy stresses. It is buttressed, however, with scores of tightly packed bundles of muscle attached to either side of the spinal column.

Flexors and Extensors

Most of us probably first used the word "muscle" when, as children, we watched an older child or adult flex an arm and proudly display the bump of muscle between the crook of elbow and shoulder. This biceps muscle works together with the triceps muscle on the underside of the arm. The arm is bent at the elbow by contraction of the biceps, which makes this muscle get shorter and thicker; in this position, called *flexion,* the triceps muscle is relaxed. To return the arm to its normal straight position, called *extension,* the biceps relaxes and the triceps contracts. In this bit of muscle teamwork, the biceps, which bends the arm at the elbow joint, is called the *flexor,* while the triceps straightens the arm and is called the *extensor.* Similar flexor–extensor action can be observed at many body joints, including the fingers.

Smooth Muscle

Beginning about midway down the esophagus, layers of smooth muscle line the walls of the 25 feet of digestive tract, extending into the stomach and through the intestines. These muscles keep the stomach and intestinal walls continually in motion, constricting and relaxing to push food along. Smooth muscle also effects the opening and closing of important valves, called *sphincters,* along the digestive tract.

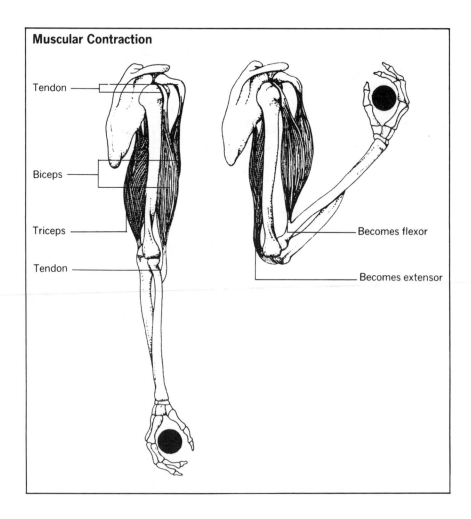

Muscular Contraction

Tendon

Biceps

Triceps

Tendon

Becomes flexor

Becomes extensor

How Muscles Reduce Stress on Bones

Bones are prevented from bending under normal stress by a system of braces, in which ligaments play an important role. But the main braces are the muscles. The diagrams above show the arm attached to the shoulder blade with the hand supporting a weight. Without muscles *(left)*, the weight would pull unevenly on the humerus, which would bend, thus compressing one side of the bone and stretching the other side. *(Middle)* Addition of a single-jointed muscle (as the brachialis) reduces the stress on the lower end of the humerus. *(Right)* Addition of a two-jointed muscle (as the biceps) also reduces the stress on the upper part of the humerus. There is now no shearing stress that is liable to break the bone, only a compression.

Trouble Spots

The functions and failures of the skeletal muscles are closely allied to those of the skeletal system. The same areas are vulnerable—joints and back—and the same rule holds: severe or persistent muscle pain is a cause to consult your physician.

Hernia

One type of disorder associated exclusively with a weakness or abnormality of muscle is a rupture or *hernia*. This is the protrusion of part of another organ through a gap in the protective muscle. A likely area for a hernia to appear is in the muscles lining the abdomen, although hernias may occur in any other part of the body where there is pressure against

Muscle Action in Forearm Movement

Muscles usually work in pairs to produce movement of a part of the body. Contraction of the biceps bends, or flexers, the arm. The biceps is a flexor muscle. Contraction of the triceps extends the arm. The triceps is an extensor muscle.

a muscle wall that is not as strong as it should be. Weight control and a sensible program of exercise—abdominal muscles being particularly liable to slackness—are good preventive measures against hernia.

Atrophy of Muscle Tissue

Muscle tissues are likely to *atrophy* (shrink and weaken) if they are not used for too long a time. Thus, illness or injuries that cause paralysis or an extended period of immobility for the body or a part of it must be followed

All our muscles, in fact, benefit from regular exercise; but you don't have to exhaust yourself physically every day to reach and maintain the desirable plateau physicians describe as good muscle tone.

by a medically supervised program of physical therapy to rebuild the weakened muscles. See also Ch. 8, *Diseases of the Muscles and Nervous System.*

Skin, Hair, and Nails

Perhaps no other organ of the human body receives so much attention both from its owner and the eyes of others as the skin and its associated structures—hair and nails.

Vanity is hardly the issue. The simple facts are that skin is the last frontier of our internal selves, the final boundary between our inside and outside, and our principal first line of defense against the dangers of the outside world. It shows, not always clearly, evidence of some internal disorders; and it shows, often quite

clearly, the evidence of external affronts—a bump, a cut, a chafe, an insect bite, or an angry reaction to the attack of germs.

In personal encounters, the unclothed portion of our skin is one of the first things other people observe, and—if we happen to have some unsightly scratch, rash, or blemish—the last thing by which we wish to be remembered. Of all our organs, the skin is the most likely candidate for a program of self-improvement.

The Organ Called Skin

It is always a little surprising to hear, for the first time, the skin referred to as a single organ. This is not to say it is a simple organ; on the contrary, it

is an exceedingly complex and varied one. However, despite variations in appearance from part to part of the body, our entire outer wrapper (the

Anatomy of the Skin

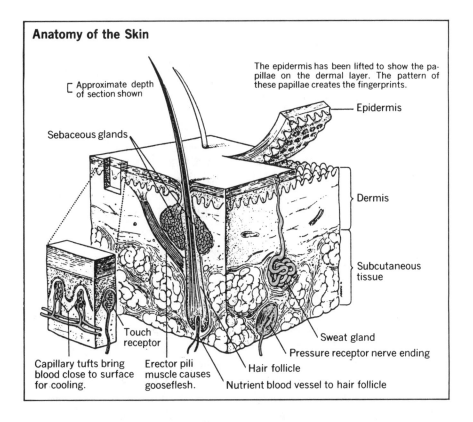

[Approximate depth of section shown

The epidermis has been lifted to show the papillae on the dermal layer. The pattern of these papillae creates the fingerprints.

Sebaceous glands

Epidermis

Dermis

Subcutaneous tissue

Touch receptor

Sweat gland

Pressure receptor nerve ending

Capillary tufts bring blood close to surface for cooling.

Erector pili muscle causes gooseflesh.

Hair follicle

Nutrient blood vessel to hair follicle

more technical word is *integument*) is similarly constructed.

One might object: "But my nails and hair certainly look different from the skin on my nose!" This is perfectly true, but nails and hair are extensions of the skin, and wherever they occur are composed of similar tissues: the nail on a little toe is made of the same material as the hair.

Functions of the Skin

The skin has three main functions, and its different outward appearance on different parts of the body reflects to some extent which of these functions a certain area of skin primarily serves. The three main functions are protection (from germs or blows), temperature control (e.g., through perspiration, to aid in keeping the body's internal organs near our normal internal temperature of 98.6° F.), and perception. Nerve endings in the skin give us our sensations of touch, pain, heat, and cold. Associated with the skin's important role in temperature regulation is its function as an organ of excretion—the elimination, via perspiration, and subsequent evaporation of water and other substances. Skin is also the site of the body's natural production of vitamin D, stimulated by exposure to sunlight.

Anatomy of the Skin

Skin has three more or less distinct layers. The outermost is called the *epidermis;* the middle, the *dermis;* and the innermost, *subcutaneous* (under- skin) tissue. The epidermis may also be called *cuticle;* and the dermis either *corium* or *true skin.*

The Subcutaneous Layer

The subcutaneous layer is really a rather vague border zone between muscle and bone tissues on one side, and the dermis on the other, a kind of springy, fatty padding that gives bounce and a look of firmness to the skin above it. With age, the fatty cells of the subcutaneous layer are not con- tinually replaced as they die, and this layer tends to thin out. The result is wrinkles, which form where the outer layers of skin lose their subcutaneous support, much like the slipcover of a cushion that has lost some of its stuffing.

The Dermis

The dermis is serviced by the multitude of tiny blood vessels and nerve fibers that reach it through the subcutaneous tissue. In addition, many special structures and tissues that enable the skin to perform its various functions are found in the dermis: *sebaceous* (skin oil) glands and sweat glands; minuscule muscles; and the roots of hairs encased in narrow pits called *follicles.*

The topmost layer of the dermis, interconnecting with the epidermis above it, resembles, under a microscope, nothing so much as a rugged, ridge-crossed landscape carved with valleys, caves, and tunnels. The basic forms of this microscopic terrain are cone-shaped hills called *papillae;* between 100 and 200 million of them are found in the dermis of an adult human being.

Because the dermal papillae serve as the bedrock for the surface layer of skin, the epidermis, we can understand why there is really no such thing as smooth skin; even the smoothest patch of a baby's skin appears ridged and cratered under a magnifying glass.

The distribution of papillae in the skin falls into certain distinctive patterns that are particularly conspicuous on the soles of babies' feet and on the fingertips, and give each of us our unique finger, toe, and footprints. The mathematical possibility of one person having the same fingerprints as another is thought to be about one in 25 billion. The papillae ridges on the fingertips also make it easier for us to pick up and handle such things as needles or pencils or buttons.

Finally, because there are relatively more papillae concentrated at the fingertips than on most other areas of the body, and because papillae are often associated with dense concentrations of nerve endings, the fingertips tend to be more responsive to touch sensations than other parts of the body.

The Epidermis

The bottom layer of the epidermis, its papillae fitted into the pockets of the layers of the dermis beneath it, is occupied by new young cells. These cells gradually mature and move upward. As they near the surface of the skin, they die, becoming tough, horny, lifeless tissue. This is the outmost layer of the epidermis, called the *stratum corneum* (horny layer), which we are continually shedding, usually unnoticed, as when we towel off after a bath, but sometimes very noticeably, as when we peel after a sunburn.

A suntan, incidentally, is caused by the presence of tiny grains of pigment, called *melanin,* in the bottom layers of epidermis. Sunlight stimulates the production of melanin, giving the skin a darker color. A suntan fades as the melanin granules move to the surface and are shed with dead skin cells.

Fingerprint

The pattern of ridges in a fingerprint reflects the contours of the papillae (conelike bumps) of the upper layer of the dermis, just below the epidermis.

Hair and Nails

Certainly the most noticeable of the specialized forms of skin are our hair and nails. What we see of them is really a dead tissue, called *keratin,* similar to the dead skin cells that are continually being shed by our bodies, but much more firmly packed together. However, hair and nails both originate in cells that are very much alive—as anyone who has plucked a group of hairs or suffered the pain of a torn-out nail knows very well. Growth occurs in this living region, with new cells pushing the dead, hard hair and nail stalks upward, then dying themselves and being replaced from below.

The bottom end or root of a hair is lodged, as noted above, in a *follicle,* a hollow resembling a rounded bottle with a long, narrow neck slanting toward the skin's surface. Each follicle is supported by the little hummock of a papilla, and is serviced by tiny oil glands that lubricate the shaft (or neck) through which the hair pushes toward the surface.

The follicles of the long hairs of the scalp, groin, and armpits may be found deep in the subcutaneous layers of the skin; others are no deeper than the top layers of dermis. Attached to a follicle are microscopic muscle fibers that, if stimulated by cold or emotional factors, can contract around the follicle; the result is goose-flesh or sometimes even the sensation that our hair is standing on end.

A nail's living, growing part is found beneath the whitish half moon, or *lunula,* at its base. The lunula is sometimes obscured because a layer of epidermis (cuticle) has grown over it. Except at its very top (the part we can trim without pain), the nail is firmly attached to the ridged upper layer of the dermis, a region richly laced with tiny blood vessels.

Oil Glands

The skin's oil-producing (or *sebaceous*) glands are almost always associated with hair follicles, into which they seep their oils (or *sebum*). The oily substance works its way up toward the surface, lubricating both the hair and outer layers of epidermis, which need continual lubrication in order to stay soft and flexible. Also, skin oils serve as a kind of protective coat against painful drying and chapping.

Sweat Glands and Blood Vessels

While everybody is aware that the amount we perspire is related to the temperature around us, not everybody is aware that the countless tiny blood vessels in our skin—some 15 feet of them coursing beneath every square inch of skin—also react to changes in outside temperatures. Working together, and both controlled by an automatic "thermostat" in our brain, sweat glands and blood vessels have the all-important role of keeping our internal organs near their normal 98.6° Fahrenheit temperature.

The trick in maintaining an internal body temperature near normal is to conserve body heat when it is colder outside and to lose heat when it is warmer. Blood circulating near the surface of the skin is warmed (gains heat) or cooled (loses heat) according to the outside temperature.

The skin's myriad blood vessels constrict when the outside temperature is colder. This means that less blood can come into contact with the colder outside air, and therefore the overall temperature level of the blood remains warmer than if the blood vessels had not become constricted. On the other hand, when the body needs to lose heat—for example, during and after a vigorous tennis match—the skin's blood vessels dilate. This accounts for the "heat flush" or reddening of skin that light-skinned people exhibit when very heated.

Sweat glands aid in temperature regulation by secreting moisture, which, evaporating on the skin's surface, cools the skin and therefore the blood flowing beneath it. Moisture that does not evaporate but remains as liquid on the skin or runs off in rivulets is not efficient in cooling. Humid air tends to prevent evaporation, while moving air or wind aids it. Sweat that evaporates as soon as it reaches the skin's surface usually goes unnoticed. Fresh sweat has no odor; but if it remains without evaporating, bacteria begin to give it the odor known medically as *bromhidrosis*.

There are some two million sweat glands in the skin. Each consists of a coiled, corkscrewlike tube that tunnels its way up to the surface of the skin from the dermis or from the deeper subcutaneous layer.

Potential Trouble Spots

All of us are very conscious of the condition of our skin and worry when something seems to be wrong with it. The temptations to worry too much, to overtreat, to take the advice of a well-meaning friend, to use the wrong (but heavily advertised) product are very great. Knowing about the properties of the skin and what medical knowledge has to say about skin problems can help to avoid mistakes in caring for it. See Ch. 21, *Skin and Hair.* For a discussion of adolescent skin problems, see also Ch. 3, *The Teens.*

The Nervous System and the Brain

Most of us have heard often enough that the brain, acting as control center for a communication network we call our nervous system, is an incredible computer, weighing a mere three pounds. Its form and functions, however, are often described as being so much more intricate and complex than any existing or imagined computer that thorough knowledge of the brain seems very remote. This is certainly true. But it doesn't prevent us from knowing some general things about the brain and nervous system, or what its most significant parts are and how they work.

Basically, the nervous system has just two functions: first, getting information (impulses, signals, messages) from outside or inside the body to where it can be acted upon, usually in the brain; and secondly, feeding back information (for example, to the muscles) so that the indicated action can be taken. Thus, nerves can be divided by their function into two general types, each following a separate pathway. Those that receive information—for example, from our senses—and pass it along are called *sensory,* or *afferent* (inward-traveling). Those that relay information back, with a directive for action, are called *motor,* or *efferent* (outward-traveling).

The brain and the spinal cord can be considered as the basic unit of the *central nervous system.* All sensory and motor information comes or goes from this central core. The spinal cord is the master nerve tract (or nerve trunk) in our body and consists of millions of nerve fibers bundled together, somewhat like many small threads making up a large rope.

Like the spinal cord, all the lesser nerves, shown as single cords in a typical anatomical drawing, are made up of hundreds of thousands of individual fibers. Each fiber is part of a single nerve cell, or *neuron.* Neurons—there are 12 to 15 billion of them in our brain alone—are the basic structural units of the brain and nervous system, the tubes and transistors and circuits of which our personal computer is built.

The Brain

The appearance of the brain within the skull has been described as a huge gray walnut and a cauliflower. The inelegance of such descriptions is the least of many good reasons why we should be happy our brains are not exposed to public view.

Brain tissue—pinkish gray and

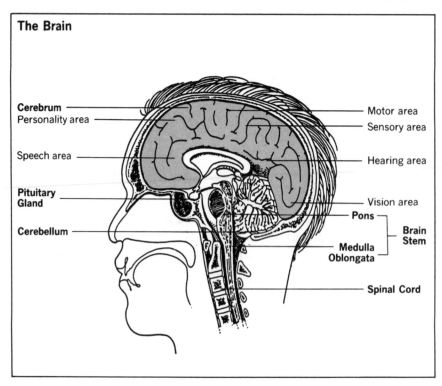

The Brain

Cerebrum
Personality area

Speech area

Pituitary Gland

Cerebellum

Motor area

Sensory area

Hearing area

Vision area

Pons

Brain Stem

Medulla Oblongata

Spinal Cord

white—is among the most delicate in our body, and the destruction of even a small part may mean lasting impairment or death. Its protection is vital and begins (if we are so fortunate) with a mat of hair on the top, back, and sides of our skull. Next comes the resilient layer of padding we call the scalp, and then the main line of defense—the rounded, bony helmet of skull.

The brain's armor does not stop with bone. Beneath are three strong, fibrous membranes called *meninges* that encase the brain in protective envelopes. Meninges also overlie the tissue of the spinal cord; infection or inflammation of these membranes by bacteria or viruses is called *cerebrospinal meningitis.*

Between two of the meninges is a region laced with veins and arteries and filled with *cerebrospinal fluid.* This fluid-filled space cushions the brain against sudden blows and collisions. The cerebrospinal fluid circulates not only about the brain but through the entire central nervous system. Incidentally, chemical analysis of this fluid, withdrawn by inserting a hypodermic needle between vertebrae of the spinal column (a spinal tap), can provide clues to the nature of brain and nervous system disorders.

The Cerebrum

What we usually mean by "brain" is that part of the brain called the *cerebrum.* It is the cerebrum that permits us all our distinctly human activities—thinking, speaking, reading, writing.

Only in man does the cerebrum reach such size, occupying the interior of our entire dome above the level of the eyes.

The surface of the cerebrum is

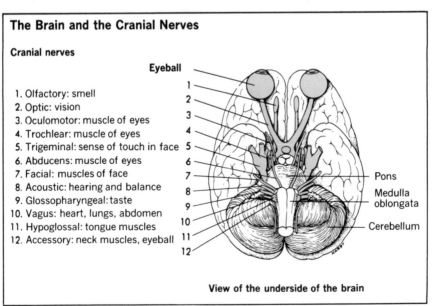

The Brain and the Cranial Nerves

Cranial nerves

Eyeball

1. Olfactory: smell
2. Optic: vision
3. Oculomotor: muscle of eyes
4. Trochlear: muscle of eyes
5. Trigeminal: sense of touch in face
6. Abducens: muscle of eyes
7. Facial: muscles of face
8. Acoustic: hearing and balance
9. Glossopharyngeal: taste
10. Vagus: heart, lungs, abdomen
11. Hypoglossal: tongue muscles
12. Accessory: neck muscles, eyeball

Pons

Medulla oblongata

Cerebellum

View of the underside of the brain

wrinkled, furrowed, folded and in-folded, convoluted, fissured—anything but smooth. This lavishly wrinkled outer layer of the cerebrum, about an eighth of an inch thick, is called the *cerebral cortex*. From its grayish color comes the term "gray matter" for brain tissue. There is a pattern among its wrinkles, marked out by wider, or deeper fissures, or furrows, running through the brain tissue. The most conspicuous fissure runs down the middle, front to back, dividing the cerebrum into two halves, the left hemisphere and the right hemisphere. The nerves from the left half of the body are served by the right hemisphere, and the right half of the body by the left hemisphere, so that damage to one side of the brain affects the other side of the body.

The Lobes of the Cerebrum

Smaller fissures crisscross the cerebrum and mark out various specific areas of function called *lobes*. The frontal lobes, one on the left hemisphere and one on the right in back of our eyes and extending upward behind the forehead, are perhaps the most talked about and the least understood by medical researchers. The specific functions of most other lobes in the cerebrum, such as the two occipital lobes (centers for seeing), the olfactory lobes (centers for smelling), and the temporal lobes (centers for hearing) are much better known.

The Brain Stem

The cerebrum, like a large flower obscuring part of its stalk, droops down around the *brain stem*. Thus, while the brain stem originates just about in the middle of our skull, it does not emerge completely from the folds of the cerebral hemispheres until it reaches the back of the neck. Then it soon merges into the spinal cord.

Associated with this portion of the brain—roughly speaking, between the cerebrum and the spinal cord— are centers that take care of the countless necessary details involved in just plain existing, and structures (such as the *medulla oblongata* and the *pons*) that serve also as traffic control points for the billions of nerve impulses traveling to and from the cerebrum. The largest of these "lesser brains" is the *cerebellum*, whose two hemispheres straddle the brain stem at the back of the head.

The Cerebellum

The cerebellum is the site of balance and body and muscle coordination, allowing us, for example, to "rub the tummy and pat the head" simultaneously, or tap the foot and strum a guitar, or steer a car and operate the foot pedals. Such muscle-coordinated movements, though sometimes learned only by long repetition and practice, can become almost automatic—such as reaching for and flicking on the light switch as we move into a darkened room.

But many other activities and kinds of behavior regulated by the part of the brain below the cerebrum are more fully automatic: the control of eye movement and focusing, for example, as well as the timing of heartbeat, sleep, appetite, and metabolism; the arousal and decline of sexual drives; body temperature; the dilation and constriction of blood vessels; swallowing; and breathing. All these are mainly functions of the *autonomic nervous system,* as opposed to the more voluntary actions controlled by the *central nervous system.*

The Body's Nervous Systems

Simply speaking, the human body has only one nervous system, and that is all the nerve cells, nerve cords, nerve centers (both voluntary and involuntary) in the body. It is helpful, however, though quite arbitrary, to divide our nerves into the central and autonomic nervous systems. This division tends to obscure the countless interconnections and interplay between the two systems. For example, where do you place the control of breathing or blinking? Such actions are automatic except when we choose to regulate them.

The Central Nervous System

The central nervous system, as noted above, includes the brain and the spinal cord. It also includes all the nerves of conscious response and voluntary action that link up with the brain and spinal cord.

Twelve pairs of *cranial nerves* originate within the brain and emerge at its base. These include the very important nerves that connect with our sense organs, nerve bundles that control the facial and neck muscles, and the *vagus* (or tenth cranial nerve) that serves the heart, lungs, stomach, intestines, esophagus, larynx, liver, kidneys, spleen, and pancreas. The vagus nerve, although anatomically part of the central nervous system, controls bodily functions that are mainly automatic.

Spinal nerves branch out from the spinal cord as it snakes its way through the vertebrae of the spinal column. All the major nerve cords that wrap around the trunk and reach the arms and hands, legs and feet, originate from spinal nerves.

The cranial nerves and the spinal nerves, together with all those nerves lying outside the confines of the brain and spinal cord, are sometimes referred to as the *peripheral nervous system.* This term can be confusing, however, because it is also used to include all the nerves of the autonomic nervous system, next discussed.

The Autonomic Nervous System

The muscles served by the central nervous system are all of one general type (striated), while the muscles served by the autonomic system are called involuntary or smooth. The autonomic nerves regulate body activity without our conscious control—for example, as we sleep. They are rather elegantly divided into two categories: *sympathetic* and *parasympathetic* nervous systems. These are distinguishable primarily by their op-

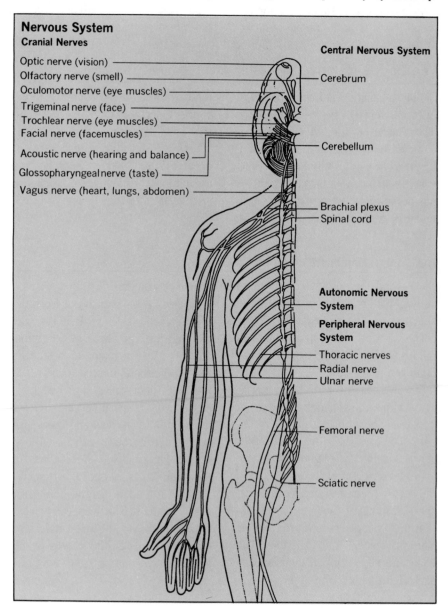

Nervous System
Cranial Nerves

Optic nerve (vision)
Olfactory nerve (smell)
Oculomotor nerve (eye muscles)
Trigeminal nerve (face)
Trochlear nerve (eye muscles)
Facial nerve (facemuscles)
Acoustic nerve (hearing and balance)
Glossopharyngeal nerve (taste)
Vagus nerve (heart, lungs, abdomen)

Central Nervous System

Cerebrum

Cerebellum

Brachial plexus
Spinal cord

Autonomic Nervous System

Peripheral Nervous System

Thoracic nerves
Radial nerve
Ulnar nerve

Femoral nerve

Sciatic nerve

posite effects on the body organs. For example, impulses along parasympathetic nerve trunks dilate blood vessels, slow the heartbeat rate, and increase stomach secretions, while the sympathetic system constricts blood vessels, increases rate of heartbeat, and inhibits stomach secretions.

The Neuron—What Nerves Are Made Of

A nerve cell is a grayish blob of tissue from which protrude several short gray fibers, *dendrites,* and one longer whitish fiber, an *axon.* Both the dendrites and the axon resemble ropes with their ends splayed and frayed. Dendrites register impulses coming into the central blob of the neuron (perhaps from a neighboring neuron's axon); an axon picks up the incoming impulses and carries them away.

Both units are equally important for normal nerve functioning, but the axon is far more showy as an anatomical structure. All nerve cords are made up of the single strands of many axons, which may reach lengths of several feet. In other words, if we could stretch out certain neurons in our body—for example, those making

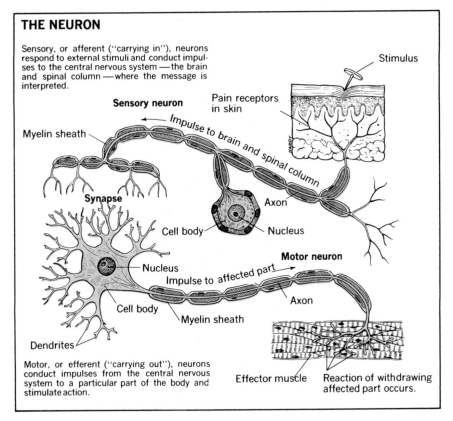

THE NEURON

Sensory, or afferent ("carrying in"), neurons respond to external stimuli and conduct impulses to the central nervous system —the brain and spinal column —where the message is interpreted.

Stimulus

Sensory neuron

Pain receptors in skin

Myelin sheath

Impulse to brain and spinal column

Synapse

Axon

Cell body

Nucleus

Motor neuron

Nucleus

Impulse to affected part

Cell body

Axon

Myelin sheath

Dendrites

Motor, or efferent ("carrying out"), neurons conduct impulses from the central nervous system to a particular part of the body and stimulate action.

Effector muscle   Reaction of withdrawing affected part occurs.

up the sciatic nerve that runs from the small of the back to the toes—their axon "tails" would make them three or four feet long.

Myelin

A normal axon usually has a fatty coating of insulation called *myelin*. An axon severed into two pieces cannot grow together again; but if the myelin sheath is pretty much intact, a surgeon can sometimes restore nerve function by sewing the two ends together, or replace the nerve with one from another part of the body. The part of the severed axon connecting to the central portion usually remains alive in any case—which is why a person can often retain the sensation of feeling in an amputated part.

Certain serious and progressively disabling diseases involve the gradual loss (*demyelination*) of this coating, causing paralysis, numbness, or other loss of function in an organ; a demyelinated nerve fiber is not able to carry impulses to and from the brain. Two such diseases are multiple sclerosis and "Lou Gehrig's disease" (amyotrophic lateral sclerosis).

Effects of Aging

Once we reach maturity, the number of our nerve cells begins to decrease, because our bodies cannot manufacture new neurons to replace the ones that die in the normal process of living. (Other kinds of tissue are continually replenished with new cells.) This has some relation to senility, but the loss of a few million out of many billions of brain and nerve cells has little effect on mental powers unless the losses are concentrated in one area.

Synapse, Ganglion, and Plexus

When a nerve impulse, traveling away from the neuron's central part, reaches the ends of an axon, it meets a gap that it must jump to get to the tentaclelike dendrites of the next neuron. This gap is called a *synapse*.

At certain points in the body a great many nerve cell bodies and branches are packed closely together, with a resulting profusion of interwoven axons, dendrites, and synapses. Such a concentration of nervous tissue is called a *ganglion*, or *plexus*. A blow or jolt to such an area can be extremely painful and even stupefying—affecting as it does a whole network of nerves—as anyone who has been hit in the solar plexus or learned the pressure points of karate knows.

The Movement of Impulses along Nerve Fibers

There is really no exact counterpart in the mechanical world for how an impulse moves along a nerve fiber and then jumps across a synapse to the next nerve. Nor is this movement completely understood by scientists. Suffice it to say that it is somewhat like an electrical current moving along in a chemical environment that allows the impulse to travel, in discreet little jumps, at a speed of about 200 miles per hour—quite slowly when we compare it to the speed of light or electricity: 186,000 miles per second. This speed serves us quite well in most situations, but there are times when we wish human beings' nerves could act more quickly—on the high-way, for example, or when a cherished vase starts to topple off the mantelpiece.

One of the simplest and quickest kinds of reactions to an outside stimulus is one that bypasses the brain. We don't really think to pull our hand away from a piping hot radiator. This is called a *spinal reflex*. What happens is that the sensory nerve endings in the finger pick up the "too hot" impulse from the radiator; the impulse then travels to the spinal cord where it activates the motor nerve pathway back to the burned finger, carrying the message, "Jerk your finger away!"

When to Suspect Trouble

Our entire existence as human beings depends so much on the normal functioning of our brain and nervous system that any real brain or nervous disorder or disease is a very serious matter. A sprained joint or cut foot can spell doom for an animal that depends on speed and mobility for survival; but the same injury is often not much more than a painful inconvenience to us. Impairment of our brain or nervous system is far more of a threat to our survival.

Multiple sclerosis and meningitis have been mentioned as serious disorders affecting the nerves, others are Parkinsonism, shingles, encephalitis, and brain tumors. The possible presence of one of these disorders is reason enough not to shrug off any of the following signs and symptoms: recurrent headaches, intense pain of unknown cause, tremors, numbness, loss of coordination, dizziness, blackouts, tics, cramps, visual difficulties, and loss of bowel and bladder control. Also, any person who has remained unconscious for more than a few minutes should be taken to a physician as soon as possible. This applies even when the person has regained consciousness and says he feels fine.

Our complex emotions, of course, are linked to the functioning of our brain and nervous system. A mind free of undue anxiety, guilt, and frustration functions better than a mind racked with worries and conflicts, and is a much more efficient and reliable leader of the body. See also Ch. 8, *Diseases of the Muscles and Nervous System*. For a discussion of mental and emotional health, see Ch. 36.

The Circulatory System, the Heart, and Blood

When the heart stops beating—that is to say, stops pumping blood—for longer than a couple of minutes, we stop living. But the heart, fortunately, is extremely sturdy. It is also simple in construction, capable of operating at a great many different speeds, in many cases self-repairing if damaged, and probably the one continuously operating automatic pump that we could, with any confidence, expect to last 70 years or longer.

These simple facts tend to be forgotten today, in what is probably the most heart-conscious era in history. True, heart disease, along with cancer, is statistically one of today's major killers. But we should remember two circumstances: not until about 50 years ago did deaths from heart disease begin to be accurately recognized and reported; second, with longer and longer life spans, it becomes more likely that a nonstop vital organ like the heart will simply wear out. Heart transplants, open heart surgery, and artificial heart parts—often reported sensationally in the public media—have also conditioned us to think of our hearts as terribly vulnerable, rather delicate, a bit inadequate to their tasks, and quite open to improvement.

Advances in heart surgery do, indeed, hold greater promise for persons whose hearts had been considered, until now, irreversibly damaged or diseased. But the great attention accorded such miracles of medicine tends to obscure the humdrum, day-in-day-out, low-key drama performed for a lifetime by a healthy, uncomplaining heart.

The Heart and Circulatory Network

Perhaps the best way to put the heart in perspective is to place it where it belongs, at the hub of the body's circulatory system. This hollow, fist-sized lump of sinewy tissue is located behind the breastbone, centered just about at the vertical midline of our chest. It is connected into a closed system of flexible tubes, called blood vessels, ranging down from finger-thick to microscopically slender, that reach into every cavern, crevice, and outpost of our body—a network of some 70,000 miles.

The heart has essentially one function—to push blood, by pumping action, through this enormous network of blood vessels. We have about six quarts of blood in our body, pumped at the rate of about five ounces every time the heart beats (normally about 72 times a minute for an adult), which we feel as our pulse. The blood circulates and recirculates through the blood vessels, pushed along by the pumping of the heart.

Arteries and Veins

The blood vessels are generally described as *arterial*, referring to the *arteries* that carry blood away from the heart; or *venous*, referring to the

The Circulatory System

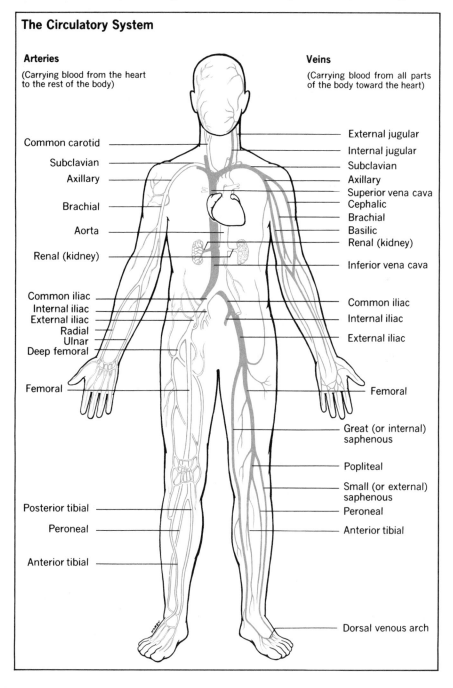

Arteries

(Carrying blood from the heart to the rest of the body)

Common carotid
Subclavian
Axillary
Brachial
Aorta
Renal (kidney)
Common iliac
Internal iliac
External iliac
Radial
Ulnar
Deep femoral
Femoral
Posterior tibial
Peroneal
Anterior tibial

Veins

(Carrying blood from all parts of the body toward the heart)

External jugular
Internal jugular
Subclavian
Axillary
Superior vena cava
Cephalic
Brachial
Basilic
Renal (kidney)
Inferior vena cava
Common iliac
Internal iliac
External iliac
Femoral
Great (or internal) saphenous
Popliteal
Small (or external) saphenous
Peroneal
Anterior tibial
Dorsal venous arch

veins through which blood seeps and flows back toward the heart to be re-pumped. A large artery such as the *aorta* branches into smaller arteries, and these eventually into still smaller vessels called *arterioles,* and the arterioles, finally, into the smallest blood vessels, the *capillaries.* These in turn open onto other capillaries, which are the starting point for the return of blood to the heart.

The microscopic capillaries typically form a kind of cat's cradle connection, sometimes called a capillary bed, at the transition zone where arterial blood becomes venous blood.

The returning blood moves from the capillaries to small veins called *venules* (the counterparts of arterioles) and through successively larger veins back to the heart.

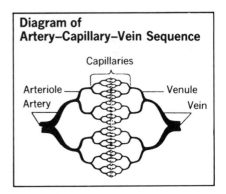

Diagram of Artery–Capillary–Vein Sequence

Blood and Our Internal Fluid Environment

What makes this fairly rudimentary collection of plumbing so absolutely indispensable to life is the fluid it pumps—blood. If any part of the body—cell, tissue, or major organ—is denied circulating blood and the substances it carries with it for longer than a few minutes, that part will fail. It is the job of the heart and the blood vessels to get blood to all the body's far-flung tissues, where it both picks

up and deposits substances.

Blood is really a kind of fluid tissue. About 80 percent of its volume is water, and blood's indispensable, life-sustaining power is owed in great part to its watery base, which permits it both to flow and to take up and carry materials in solution. All our tissues and organs have a kind of give-and-take arrangement with the circulating blood.

Carrier of Oxygen

Perhaps the most critical of these give-and-take transactions occurs in the lungs; it is this transaction that if interrupted by heartbeat stoppage for more than a few minutes causes death by oxygen starvation of vital tissues. Before a unit of blood is pumped out by the heart to the body, it picks up

in the lungs the oxygen that we have inhaled and which every cell in the body needs to function. The blood then transports the oxygen, delivering it to other parts of the body. By the time a given unit of blood has made a tour of the blood vessels and returned to the lungs, it has given up most of its oxygen and is laden instead with carbon dioxide, the principal waste product of living processes.

The venous blood releases its carbon dioxide, to be exhaled by the lungs.

Distributor of Nutrients

Food, or more accurately the nutrient molecules needed by cells, are also transported throughout the body by the blood. In the digestive tract, food is broken down into tiny submicroscopic pieces that can pass through the tract's walls (mainly along the small intestine) and be picked up by the blood for distribution around the body.

One of the specialized, small-volume transportation jobs handled by the blood is to pick up hormones from the endocrine glands and present these chemical messengers to the organs they affect.

Composition of Blood

Blood is a distinctive and recognizable type of tissue, but this does not mean it is a stable, uniform substance with a fixed proportion of ingredients. Quite the opposite is true; its composition is ever changing in response to the demands of other body systems. Other organs are constantly pouring substances into the blood, or removing things from it. Blood in one part of the body at a given moment may be vastly different in chemical makeup from blood in another part of the body.

Despite its changing makeup, blood does have certain basic components. A sample of blood left to stand for an hour or so separates into a clear, watery fluid with a yellowish tinge and a darker, more solid clump. The clear yellow liquid is called *plasma,* and accounts for about 55 percent of the volume of normal blood. The darker clump is made up mainly of the blood's most conspicuous and populous inhabitants, the red cells that give blood its color.

Plasma

It is the plasma that enables our blood to carry out most of the transportation tasks assigned it. Being over 90 percent water, the plasma has water's property of being able to carry substances both in solution and in suspension. (A substance in solution is one, like salt, that must be removed from water by chemical or physical action, such as boiling; while a substance in suspension—such as red blood cells within whole blood in a standing test tube—separates out more readily, particularly when its watery carrier has been contained and its flow stilled.)

Red Blood Cells

Red blood cells (or *erythrocytes*) numbering in the trillions are carried in suspension by the plasma. In turn, the red blood cells carry the single most important substance needed by the body's cells—oxygen. For such an important task, the red blood cell looks hardly adequate. As it matures, this cell loses its nucleus. Lacking a nucleus, it is sometimes not even called a cell but a red blood *corpuscle.* What gives red blood cells their special oxygen-carrying ability, and also their color, is their possession of a complex iron-protein substance called *hemoglobin.*

Hemoglobin

Molecules of hemoglobin have the property of loosely combining with oxygen where it is plentiful, as in the lungs. They can then hold on to oxygen until they reach an area where oxygen has been depleted by the demands of living processes. There— usually in the fine tubes of the capillaries—hemoglobin's hold on oxygen is challenged by the demands of other cells, and the red cells give up their oxygen. The hemoglobin of red cells develops an immediate affinity for carbon dioxide, the waste product of cell metabolism, and the red blood cells then carry this carbon dioxide back to the lungs for exhalation.

Hemoglobin's ability to carry oxygen is not unique. Water, and therefore plasma, also have this ability. Hemoglobin's specialness lies in how much oxygen it can carry. Hemoglobin increases by more than 50 times the oxygen-carrying capacity of our blood.

White Blood Cells

White blood cells have many different shapes and sizes, all going under the general scientific name of *leukocytes.* They are typically larger than red blood cells, but far less numerous. If we accept an estimate of 25 trillion as the number of living red blood cells in our body, then the number of white blood cells might be generously estimated at around 40 billion, a ratio of one white cell to about 600–700 reds.

According to their shape, size, and other characteristics, white blood cells have been divided into various categories such as lymphocytes, monocytes, and granulocytes. But as a group these blood cells are distinguished by their common propensity for attacking foreign bodies that invade our tissues, whether these invaders be sizable splinters or microscopic bacteria. White blood cells move in force to the site of an infection, do battle with the intruding agents, and frequently strew the area with the wreckage of the encounter— a collection of dismantled alien bacteria and dead white cells, which we know as pus.

Platelets

Platelets, also called *thrombocytes,* initiate some of the first steps in the complex biochemical process that leads to the clotting of blood. They thus help to spare us from bleeding to death from a slight injury. Platelets are the most rudimentary and diminutive of the major blood components. Like mature red blood cells, they lack nuclei, but are only one-quarter as big. By no stretch of the imagination can they be called blood cells. Rather, they are blood elements—bits of cell substance with a recognizable size and shape, circulating with the blood.

The Proportions of Blood Cells

All the several types of blood cells and subcells in a healthy body occur in proportions that, though never precisely fixed and unchanging, are recognized as having normal upper and lower limits. If a particular type of cell shows a sudden increase or decrease in population, so that its proportion relative to other blood cells shows a variation markedly outside its normal range, some infection, disease, or disorder must be suspected.

In addition to occurring in certain normal-range proportions, each type of cellular blood component has a typical shape, appearance, and set of chemical and physical properties. Variations from these norms occur in many diseases.

The analysis of blood samples (usually taken from the finger or arm) and their inspection under a microscope have proved invaluable in diagnosing illness and disease, often before a person feels any symptoms whatsoever. This is why a thorough medical checkup should always include taking a sample of your blood. It is then up to the physician to decide which of the dozens of tests should be made on your blood in the medical laboratory. One common test is a *blood count,* in which the number of a certain type of cell in a given unit of your blood can be estimated, and then compared to the normal number in the same amount of blood.

Blood Groups and Rh Factors

The identification of *blood groups* and *Rh factors* is another aspect of blood analysis. The four most common blood groups are called A, B, AB, and O, classifications based on chemical differences that may be incompatible if one group is mixed with another. Thus, it is absolutely essential before a person receives a blood transfusion to know both his own blood type and the type of the blood he is to be given. Blood group O is considered the safety for transfusion, and people with type O blood are sometimes called "universal donors." It is a wise practice to carry, along with your other important cards, a card giving your own blood type. The blood of a donor, however, is always *cross-matched* (checked for compatibility) with the blood of the person who is to receive it in order to avoid transfusion reactions.

Blood Cell Manufacture and Turnover

Most types of blood cells, both red and white, are manufactured in the red marrow of bones. The rate and quantity of total production is staggering; estimates range from one to five million red blood cells per second. This prodigious output is necessary because blood cells are disintegrating, having served their useful lives, in the same enormous numbers every second. The normal life span of a red blood cell is about four months, which means that four months from now every blood cell in your body will have died and been replaced with new cells.

The Liver As a Producer of Red Blood Cells

The red bone marrow is backed up by several other tissues that can, if called upon, turn out blood cells in quantity or serve as specialized producers of certain blood cells and blood elements. One such organ is the liver, which, before and after birth and into childhood, is a site of red blood cell production. In an emergency, such as severe internal hemorrhage, the liver sometimes reverts to its earlier function of manufacturing red cells. The liver also serves as a kind of salvage yard for the iron from dead red cells. It stores the iron for later combination into hemoglobin and passes off the rest of the red blood cell fragments as part of the bile pigments that empty into the duodenum of the small intestine.

The Spleen As a Producer of Blood Cells

Certain white blood cells, in particular the lymphocytes, are produced at a variety of locations in the body—for example, by the lymph nodes, by little clumps of tissue called *Peyer's patches* in the intestinal tract, and by the spleen.

The spleen plays a number of interesting secondary roles in blood cell production. Like the liver, it can be pressed into service as a manufacturer of red blood cells and serve as a salvage yard for iron reclaimed from worn-out red blood cells. A newborn baby is almost totally dependent on its spleen for the production of red blood cells, with a little help from the liver. In an adult, however, a damaged or diseased spleen can be surgically removed, with little or no apparent effect on the health or life span of the person, provided the patient's bone marrow is in good functioning order.

Movement of Blood Cells through the Capillaries

A blood cell must be able to slip through the microscopic, twisting and turning tunnels of the capillaries that mark the turn-about point in the blood cell's round-trip voyage from the heart. Blood cells, therefore, must be small (the point of a pin could hold dozens of red blood cells), and they must be jellylike in order to navigate the tight tortuous, capillary channels without either blocking the channel or breaking apart themselves. A red blood cell is further adapted to sneaking through the capillaries by its concave-disk shape, which allows it to bend and fold around itself. Nevertheless, so narrow are the passageways within some of the capillaries that blood cells must move through them in single file. If a substantial number of the cells are misshapen, as in sickle-cell anemia, they tend to move sluggishly or clog up the passageway—a condition that can have serious consequences. See also Ch. 9, *Diseases of the Circulatory System.*

Lymph and the Lymphatic System

Of all our body systems, perhaps the most ignored is the lymphatic system, although it forms a network throughout our body comparable to the blood vessels of our circulatory system.

Lymph is a whitish fluid that is derived from blood plasma. As plasma circulates through the body, some of it seeps through the walls of capillaries and other blood vessels. This leakage is of the utmost importance, because the leaked fluid, lymph, supplies the liquid environment around and between individual cells and tissues that is essential for their survival.

The presence of lymph requires a drainage system to keep the fluid moving. If there were no drainage system, two things could happen: the dammed-up lymph could create areas swollen with water in which cells would literally drown, or stagnant pools of lymph could become breeding grounds for infection.

As it moves through the vessels of the lymphatic system, lymph carries away from the tissues the bits and pieces of cells that have died and disintegrated, and also potentially harmful bacteria and viruses.

Lymph and Lymphocytes

Confusion often arises about the connection between the white blood cells called *lymphocytes* and the lymph itself. Lymph is not made up of lymphocytes, although it often carries them; lymph is simply a watery vehicle moving through the lymphatic network. At certain points along this network, the vessels enlarge into clumpy structures called *lymph nodes* (or, misleadingly, lymph glands). Lymph nodes are major manufacturing sites for lymphocytes.

Lymph Nodes

Swollen glands are actually swollen lymph nodes, where a small army of lymphocytes is doing battle against invading bacteria or other harmful microscopic organisms. The lymph nodes, more than a hundred of them distributed around the body, serve as defense outposts against germs approaching the interior of the body. Those in the neck, groin, and armpits most frequently exhibit the pain and swelling that may accompany germ-fighting.

Circulation of Lymph

Lymph circulates without any help from the heart. From the spaces between cells, it diffuses into lymph capillaries which, like the venous capillaries, merge into larger and larger vessels moving inward toward the heart. The lymph moves—even upward from the legs and lower part of the body—because the muscles and movements of the body are constantly kneading and squeezing the lymph vessels. These vessels are equipped with valves that prevent back-flow. This is not so very different from the way venous blood makes its way back to the heart.

Eventually, master lymph vessels from the head, abdomen, and torso join in the thoracic lymph duct, which then empties into large neck veins that carry lymph and venous blood, mixed together, back to the heart.

The Heart at Work

The structure and performance of the heart, at first glance rather complicated, assume a magnificent simplicity once we observe that this pulsating knot of hollow, intertwining muscle uses only one beat to perform two distinct pumping jobs.

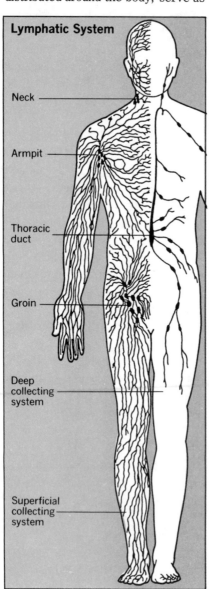

Lymphatic System

Neck

Armpit

Thoracic duct

Groin

Deep collecting system

Superficial collecting system

The heart has a right side (your right) and a left side (your left), divided by a tough wall of muscle called a *septum*. Each side has two chambers, an upper one called an *atrium* (or *auricle*), and a lower one called a *ventricle*.

How the Heart Pumps the Blood

Venous blood from the body flows into the right atrium via two large veins called the *superior vena cava* (bringing blood from the upper body) and the *inferior vena cava* (bringing blood from the lower part of the body). Where the blood enters the right atrium are valves that close when the atrium chamber is full.

Then, through a kind of trapdoor valve, blood is released from the right atrium into the right ventricle. When the right ventricle is full, and its outlet valve opens, the heart as a whole contracts—that is, pumps.

To the Lungs

The blood from the right ventricle is pumped to the lungs through the pulmonary artery to pick up oxygen. The trapdoor valve between the right atrium and ventricle has meanwhile closed, and venous blood again fills the right atrium.

Having picked up oxygen in the lungs, blood enters the left atrium through two pulmonary veins. (They are called veins despite the fact that they carry the most oxygen-rich blood, because they lead *to* the heart; just as the pulmonary artery carries the oxygen-poorest blood away from the heart, to the lungs.) Like the right atrium, the left atrium serves as a holding reservoir and, when full, releases its contents into the left ventricle. A valve between left atrium and ventricle closes, and the heart pumps.

How Blood Circulates through the Heart

Pulmonary vein

Arteries to head and arms

Superior vena cava

Pulmonary artery

Right atrium

Left atrium

Left ventricle

Inferior vena cava

Right ventricle

Aorta carries blood to abdomen and legs.

Blood from the head and arms enters the right atrium from the superior (i.e., upper) vena cava. Blood from the torso and legs enters from the inferior (i.e., lower) vena cava. The blood, controlled by a valve, passes to the right ventricle. It is then pumped into the pulmonary artery, which divides into two vessels, one leading to each lung. After being enriched with oxygen, the blood is brought back to the left atrium via the pulmonary veins, is admitted by a valve into the left ventricle, and is pumped through the aorta to be distributed to all parts of the body.

Both atria contract at the same time, forcing blood into the ventricles. Then both ventricles contract (while the atria relax), forcing blood into the great arteries. This period of contraction is called systole, and is followed by a period of relaxation called diastole.

To the Body

Blood surges through an opening valve of the left ventricle into the aorta, the major artery that marks the beginning of blood's circulation throughout the body. The left ventricle, because it has the job of pumping blood to the entire body rather than just to the lungs, is slightly larger and more muscular than the right ventricle. It is for this reason, incidentally, that the heart is commonly considered to be on our left. The organ as a whole, as noted earlier, is located at the center of the chest.

The Heart's Own Circulatory System

Heart tissue, like that of every other organ in the body, must be continually supplied with fresh, oxygen-rich blood, and used blood must be returned to the lungs for reoxygenation. The blood inside the heart cannot serve these needs. Thus the heart has its own circulation network, called *coronary arteries* and *veins,* to nourish its muscular tissues. There are two

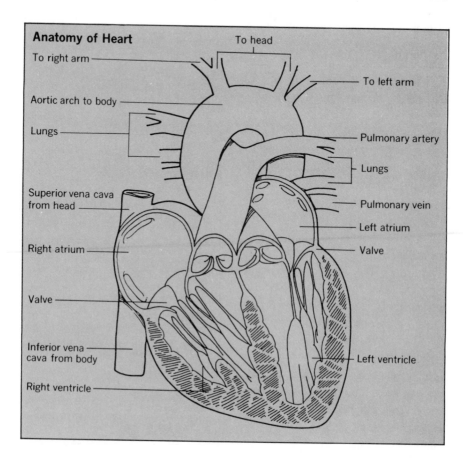

Anatomy of Heart

To head
To right arm
To left arm
Aortic arch to body
Lungs
Pulmonary artery
Lungs
Superior vena cava from head
Pulmonary vein
Left atrium
Right atrium
Valve
Valve
Inferior vena cava from body
Left ventricle
Right ventricle

major arteries on the surface of the heart, branching and rebranching eventually into capillaries. Coronary veins then take blood back to the right atrium.

Structure of the Heart

The musculature of the heart is called cardiac muscle because it is different in appearance from the two other major types of muscle. The heart muscle is sometimes considered as one anatomical unit, called the *myocardium.* A tough outer layer of membranous tissue, called the *pericardium,* surrounds the myocardium. Lining the internal chambers and valves of the heart, on the walls of the atria and ventricles, is a tissue called the *endocardium.*

These tissues, like any others, are subject to infections and other disorders. An infection of the endocardium by bacteria is called *bacterial endocarditis.* (Disease of the valves is also called *endocarditis,* although it is a misnomer.) An interruption of the blood supply to the heart muscle is called a *myocardial infarction,* which results in the weakening or death of the portion of the myocardium whose blood supply is blocked. Fortunately, in many cases, other blood vessels may eventually take over the job of supplying the blood-starved area of heart muscle.

Heartbeat

The rate at which the heart beats is controlled by both the autonomic nervous system and by hormones of the endocrine system. The precise means by which the chambers and valves of the heart are made to work in perfect coordination are not fully understood. It is known, however, that the heart has one or more natural cardiac pacemakers that send electrical waves through the heart, causing the opening and closing of valves and muscular contraction, or pumping, of the ventricles near the normal adult rate of about 72 times per minute.

One particular electrical impulse (there may be others) originates in a small area in the upper part of the right atrium called the *sinus node.* Because it is definitely known that the contraction of the heart is electrically activated, tiny battery-powered devices called *artificial pacemakers* have been developed that can take the place of a natural pacemaker whose function has been impaired by heart injury or disease. Through electrodes implanted in heart tissue, such devices supply the correct beat for a defective heart. The bulk of the device is usually worn outside the body or is implanted just under the skin.

The fact that both ventricles give their push at the same time is very significant. It allows the entire heart muscle to rest between contractions—a rest period that adds up to a little more than half of a person's lifetime. Without this rest period, it is more than likely that our hearts would wear out considerably sooner than they do.

Blood Pressure

A physician's taking of blood pressure is based upon the difference between the heart's action at its period of momentary rest and at the moment of maximum work (the contraction or push). The split-second of maximum work, at the peak of the ventricles' contraction, is called the *systole*. The split-second of peak relaxation, when blood from the atria is draining into and filling up the ventricles, is called the *diastole*.

Blood pressure measures the force with which blood is passing through a major artery, such as one in the arm, and this pressure varies between a higher *systolic* pressure, corresponding to the heart's systole, and a lower *diastolic* pressure, reflecting the heart's diastole, or resting phase. The device with which a physician takes your blood pressure, called a *sphygmomanometer*, registers these higher and lower figures in numbers

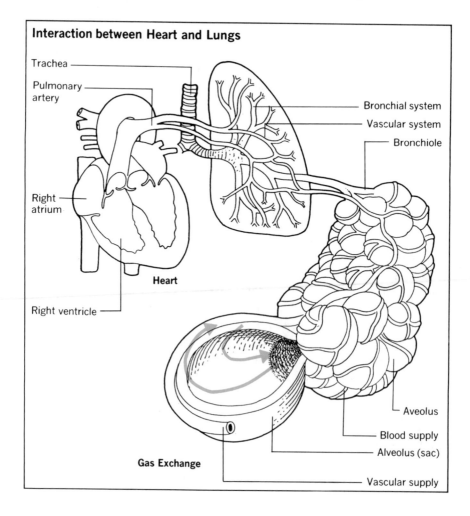

Interaction between Heart and Lungs

Trachea

Pulmonary artery

Bronchial system

Vascular system

Bronchiole

Right atrium

Heart

Right ventricle

Aveolus

Blood supply

Alveolus (sac)

Gas Exchange

Vascular supply

equivalent to the number of millimeters the force of your arterial blood would raise a column of mercury. The higher systolic force (pressure) is given first, then the diastolic figure. For example, 125/80 is within the normal range of blood pressure. Readings that are above the normal range—and stay elevated over a period of time—indicate a person has high blood pressure, or hypertension.

Hypertension has no direct connection with nervous tension, although the two may be associated in the same person. What it does indicate is that a heart is working harder than the average heart to push blood through the system. See also Ch. 9, *Diseases of the Circulatory System* and Ch. 10, *Heart Disease.*

The Digestive System and the Liver

A physician once remarked that a great many people seem to spend about half their time getting food into their digestive tracts and the other half worrying about how that food is doing on its travels. The physician was exaggerating, but he made his point.

The digestive tract has essentially one purpose: to break down food, both solid and fluid, into a form that can be used by the body. The food is used as energy to fuel daily activities or to nourish the various tissues that are always in the process of wearing out and needing replacement.

A normally functioning digestive tract, dealing with a reasonable variety and quantity of food, is designed to extract the maximum benefit from what we eat. Urine and feces are the waste products—things from which our body has selected everything that is of use.

Our digestive system's efficiency and economy in getting food into our bodies, to be utilized in all our living processes, can be attributed basically to three facts.

First, although the straight-line distance from the mouth to the bottom of the trunk is only two or three feet, the distance along the intestinal tract is about 10 times as great—30 feet—a winding, twisting, looping passageway that has more than enough footage to accommodate a number of ingeniously constructed way stations, checkpoints, and traffic-control devices.

Second, from the moment food enters the mouth, it is subjected to both chemical and mechanical actions that begin to break it apart, leading eventually to its reduction to submicroscopic molecules that can be absorbed through the intestinal walls into the circulatory system.

Finally, each of the three main types of food—carbohydrates, fats, and proteins—receives special treatment that results in the body deriving maximum benefit from each.

Sensing the Right Kind of Food

Lips, eyes, and nose are generally given scant notice in discussions of the digestive process. But if we consider digestion to include selection of food and rejection of substances that might do us harm, then all three play very important roles.

The sensitive skin of our lips rep-

resents one of our first warning station that food may be harmful if taken into the mouth. It may tell us if a forkful of food is too hot or warn us of a concealed fishbone.

Our eyes, too, are important selection-rejection monitors for food. What else keeps us from sitting down

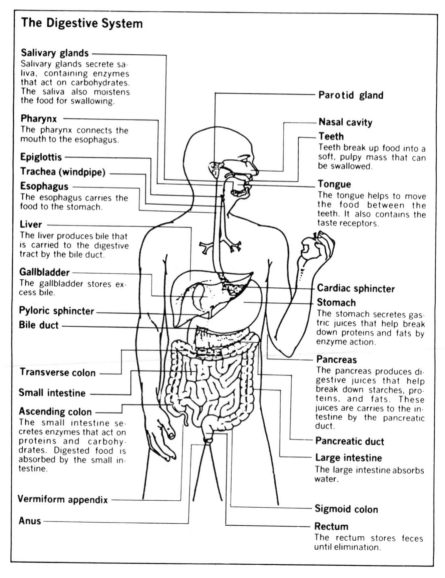

The Digestive System

Salivary glands
Salivary glands secrete saliva, containing enzymes that act on carbohydrates. The saliva also moistens the food for swallowing.

Pharynx
The pharynx connects the mouth to the esophagus.

Epiglottis

Trachea (windpipe)

Esophagus
The esophagus carries the food to the stomach.

Liver
The liver produces bile that is carried to the digestive tract by the bile duct.

Gallbladder
The gallbladder stores excess bile.

Pyloric sphincter

Bile duct

Transverse colon

Small intestine

Ascending colon
The small intestine secretes enzymes that act on proteins and carbohydrates. Digested food is absorbed by the small intestine.

Vermiform appendix

Anus

Parotid gland

Nasal cavity

Teeth
Teeth break up food into a soft, pulpy mass that can be swallowed.

Tongue
The tongue helps to move the food between the teeth. It also contains the taste receptors.

Cardiac sphincter

Stomach
The stomach secretes gastric juices that help break down proteins and fats by enzyme action.

Pancreas
The pancreas produces digestive juices that help break down starches, proteins, and fats. These juices are carries to the intestine by the pancreatic duct.

Pancreatic duct

Large intestine
The large intestine absorbs water.

Sigmoid colon

Rectum
The rectum stores feces until elimination.

to a crisp salad of poison ivy, or, less facetiously, popping a moldy piece of cake into our mouth?

As mammals' noses go, man's is a very inferior and insensitive organ. Nevertheless, we make good use of our sense of smell in the selection and enjoyment of foods. The nose adds to our enjoyment of favorite food and drink not only before they enter the mouth, but also after, because stimulation of the olfactory cells in the nasal passages combines with the stimulation of the taste cells on the tongue to produce the sensation-and-discrimination gradations of taste.

The Mouth:
Saliva, Teeth, and Tongue

By the time food leaves the mouth and is pushed down into the gullet (or esophagus), it has already received a sampling of all the kinds of punishment and prodding that will be provided by the 30-foot tube that lies ahead of it. The chances are slim that any piece of food will end that journey in the same condition it started, but if it did it would have traveled those 30 tortuous feet at the rate of something less than two feet per hour. Normally, the elapsed time is between 17 and 25 hours.

As in the rest of the digestive tract, the mouth puts both chemical and mechanical apparatus to work on a bite of food. Saliva supplies the chemical action. Teeth and tongue, backed up by powerful sets of muscles, are the mashers, crushers, and prodders.

Saliva

The mere presence of food in our mouth—or even the smell, memory, or anticipation of it—sends signals to our brain, and our brain in turn sends messages back to a system of six salivary glands: one pair, called the *sublingual glands,* located under the tongue toward the front of the mouth; another pair, the *submaxillary* (or *submandibular*) glands, a bit behind and below them; and the largest, the *parotid glands,* tucked in the region where jaw meets neck behind the ear lobes.

Saliva is mainly composed of water, and water alone begins to soften up food so that it can pass more smoothly down the esophagus toward encounters with more powerful chemical agents.

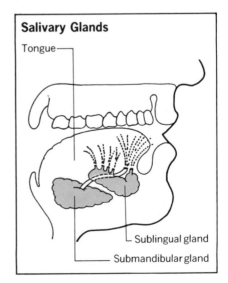

Salivary Glands

Tongue

Sublingual gland

Submandibular gland

There is also a very special substance in saliva, an enzyme called *ptyalin,* whose specific job is to begin the breakdown of one of the toughest kinds of food our digestive system has to handle—starches. Starch is a kind of carbohydrate, the group of foods from which we principally derive energy; but in order for the body to utilize carbohydrate, it must be broken down into simpler forms, which are called simply sugars. Ptyalin, then, begins the simplification of carbohydrate starch into carbohydrate sugar.

Saliva also does a favor or two for the dominating structures of the mouth—the tongue and teeth. Without its bathing action, the tongue's taste cells could not function up to par; and because it has a mild germicidal effect in addition to a simple rinsing action, saliva helps protect our mouth and teeth from bacterial infection.

Teeth

The role of the teeth in digestion can be summed up in one word: destruction. What the wrecker's ball is to a standing building, our teeth are to a lump of solid food. They do the first, dramatic demolishing, leaving smaller fragments to be dealt with and disposed of in other ways.

Starting from the center of the mouth, we have two incisors on either side, top and bottom, followed by a canine, a couple of premolars, and three molars, the most backward of which (it never appears in some people) is the curiously named "wisdom" tooth, so called because it commonly appears as physical maturity is reached, at about 20 years of age.

Our teeth equip us for destroying chunks of food by a gamut of mechanical actions ranging from gripping and puncturing to grinding and pulverizing. The teeth in front—canines and incisors—do most of the gripping, ripping, and tearing, while the premolars and molars at the back of the jaws do the grinding.

The Tongue

The surface of the tongue is not smooth, but has a finely corrugated look and feel. This slightly sandpapery surface results from the presence of thousands of tiny papillae, little pyramid-shaped bumps. When we are young, the walls of a single papilla may contain up to 300 taste cells, or buds. As we get older, the maximum number of taste buds per papilla may decline to under 100.

There are four kinds of taste cells, distinguished by the type of taste message each sends to the brain: salty, sweet, sour, and bitter. Each of the four types is a narrow specialist in one type of taste. However, simultaneous or successive stimulation of all four types (combined almost always with information picked up by our sense of smell) can produce a tremendous variety of recognizable tastes—although perhaps not so many as some gourmets or wine-tasters might have us believe.

All four types of taste buds—salty, sweet, sour, and bitter—are found associated with papillae in all areas on the surface of the tongue; but there tend to be denser populations of one or the other kinds of taste cells in certain places. For example, salty and sweet cells predominate at the tip of the tongue and about halfway back along its sides; sour cells are more numerous all the way back along the sides; bitter buds are densest at the back of the tongue.

In addition to its tasting abilities, the tongue is a very versatile, flexible, and admirably shaped bundle of muscle. Not only can it flick out to moisten dry lips and ferret out and dislodge food particles in the oral cavity, but it also performs the first mechanical step in the all-important act of swallowing.

Swallowing

Swallow. You'll find that you feel the top of your tongue pressing up against the roof of your mouth (hard palate). You may never have thought about it consciously, but the pressing of the tongue against the hard palate pre-vents food from slipping to the front of your mouth—and also gives the food a good shove up and to the back of your mouth. At this point, the *soft palate* (from which the teardrop-shaped piece of tissue called the

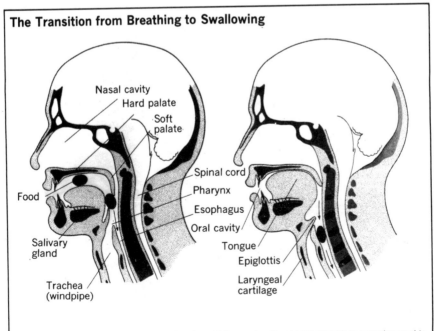

The Transition from Breathing to Swallowing

Nasal cavity
Hard palate
Soft palate
Spinal cord
Food
Pharynx
Esophagus
Oral cavity
Salivary gland
Tongue
Epiglottis
Laryngeal cartilage
Trachea (windpipe)

(Left) The soft palate begins to move upward to close off the nasal cavity, and the epiglottis to move downward to close off the trachea. (Right) By the time the food has passed into the esophagus, the trachea and the nasal cavity are completely shut off.

uvula hangs down) slips up to cover the passageway between mouth (oral cavity) and nasal cavity, nicely preventing the food from being misdirected toward your nose.

Once past the soft palate, the food is in the *pharynx,* a kind of anatomical traffic circle with two roads entering at the top, those from the mouth and nasal cavity, and two roads leading away from the bottom, the *trachea* (windpipe) and the *esophagus* or food tube.

The Epiglottis

A wedge of cartilage called the *epiglottis* protrudes from the trachea side, the side toward the front of the neck. When we are breathing, the epiglottis is flattened up against the front wall of the pharynx, allowing free movement of air up and down the trachea. Simultaneously, the epiglottis helps to close off the entrance to the esophagus; a good part of the esophagus-closing work is done by a bundle of sinewy, elastic tissue we associate primarily with speech—the tissue of the vocal cords, otherwise known as the voice box or *larynx.* The laryngeal tissue is connected to the epiglottis above it, and supplies the epiglottis with most of its muscle for movement.

During the movement of a swallow, the larynx exerts an upward force against the epiglottis that serves to block off the trachea. At the same time, the larynx relaxes some of its pressure on the esophagus. Result: food enters the esophagus, where it is meant to go, and not the windpipe, which as we all know from having had something "go down the wrong way," produces an immediate fit of coughing.

Once we have swallowed, we lose almost completely the conscious ability to control the passage of food along the intestinal tract. Only when wastes reach the point of elimination do we begin to reassert some conscious control.

Peristalsis

The mechanical action called *peristalsis,* affected by muscles in the walls of all the organs of the gastrointestinal tract, first comes into play in the esophagus. Two layers of muscles intermesh in the intestinal walls: the inner layer encircles the esophagus in a series of rings; the outer layer stretches lengthwise along the tube. These two sets of muscles work in tandem to produce the basic action of persistalsis, called a *peristaltic wave.*

The alternative contraction and relaxation of the muscles—closing behind swallowed food and opening in front of it—combine to move both liquid and solid food (medical term, *bolus*) along the digestive tract. Gravity, in a sense, is left behind once food enters the esophagus. Because of peristalsis, we can swallow lying down or even standing on our heads; and astronauts are able to eat in near zero-gravity or under weightless conditions.

Peristalsis has another important function besides moving food through the body. The constricting and relaxing muscles serve also to knead, churn, and pummel the solid remains of the food left after our teeth have done their best.

Digestive Sphincters

If you think about it, the gastrointestinal tract has to be equipped with a number of gates that can open or shut, depending on the amount of food that is passing through. Otherwise, the food might push through so fast that little nourishment could be extracted from it: we would feel hungry one minute and glutted the next. The gastrointestinal tract is thus equipped at critical junctures with a number of muscular valves, or *sphincters*, which, usually under the direction of the autonomic nervous system, can regulate the movement of food through the digestive tube. Another function of a sphincter is to prevent backflow of partially digested food.

The muscles of a sphincter are often described as "pursestring muscles" because the way they draw together the sides of the digestive tube is roughly similar to drawing up the strings of a purse. The first of these pursestring valves occurs at the *cardia*, the opening where the esophagus meets the stomach, and is called the *cardiac sphincter*, from its location almost directly in front of the heart. (But there is no physical connection.)

Another important muscle ring is the *pyloric sphincter*, at the opening called the *pylorus*, located at the other end of the stomach, at the connection between stomach and small intestine. The release of waste from the rectum is controlled, partly voluntarily, by an *anal sphincter*, located at the *anus*, which marks the end of the tract.

The Stomach

About ten inches down the esophagus, the food we swallow must pass the cardiac sphincter. Then the food, by now fairly well diced and mashed, passes into the stomach.

Inelegant as it sounds, the stomach is best described as a rough, leatherskinned balloon. When empty, its skin shrivels around itself like a deflated balloon; but when "pumped up" by a hearty meal, the stomach becomes a plump, J-shaped bag about a foot long and six inches wide, holding about two quarts of food and drink.

The Passage of Food through the Stomach

Although its food-processing function tends to get more attention, the stomach's role as a storage reservoir is equally important. A moderate, well-rounded meal with a good blend of carbohydrates, proteins, and fats takes usually a minimum of three hours to pass out of the pyloric sphincter into the small intestine—more if the meal is heavy in fats and rich foods. Thus, a meal that might take us 15 minutes to eat, may take up to 20 times as long to pass from the stomach into the small intestine. This decelerating of food's rate of passage has two very significant results: first, it allows time for the food-processing activities within the stomach; and second, it releases food (in a mushy form called *chyme*) in small, well-spaced amounts that can be efficiently handled by the small intestine.

Although the stomach is not an absolutely essential organ—a person can live a full life with part or even all of it removed—it is a tremendous convenience. Without a stomach, frequent, carefully selected, well-chewed small feedings rather than "three square meals a day" are necessary so as not to overburden the small intestine, which can handle only a small quantity of food, well-mashed, at one time. If too much food goes directly to the small intestine, only so much nourishment (carbohydrates, proteins, fats) per meal can be supplied to the body, with the result that we would be weak from hunger after going a few hours without eating.

It will come as no surprise to know that the food processing done in the stomach is both mechanical and chemical. The three layers of crisscrossing muscles in the stomach walls are rarely still. They contract and relax continually, squeezing, pummeling, and mixing the stomach's contents into chyme. So active and relentless is the stomach's muscular activity that it actually "chews up" pieces of food that have been swallowed too hastily.

The Passage of Food through the Alimentary Canal

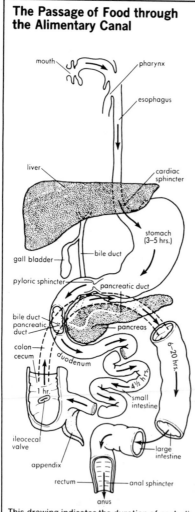

This drawing indicates the duration of each digestive process. Food enters the mouth and is passed through the pharynx and esophagus into the stomach, where it is partly digested. The small intestine completes digestion and absorbs digested food. The large intestine absorbs excess water. Indigestible residue collects in the rectum for later disposal.

Stomach Chemicals

The various chemicals found in the stomach are produced and secreted into the stomach cavity by some 40 million gland cells that line the interior stomach walls. The constant wiggling and jouncing of the stomach helps to mix these chemicals thoroughly into the food. Each of the chemicals is secreted by a special type of cell and has a specific function. They include the digestive enzymes pepsin, rennin, and lipase; hydrochloric acid; and watery mucus.

A look at the special assignments of rennin, pepsin, hydrochloric acid, and mucus—and how they interact with and depend upon one another—provides a good glimpse into the elegant and complex chemical events that occur when the stomach encounters a swallow of food.

Rennin and Pepsin

Rennin, well known to cheesemakers, has essentially one task: to turn milk into milk curds. But the curds are not ready to pass on to the small intestine until they are further dismantled by *pepsin*. Pepsin has other duties as well: one of them is to begin the breakdown of proteins. But pepsin can only begin to split up protein foods after they have been worked on by *hydrochloric acid.*

Hydrochloric Acid

Hydrochloric acid is a corrosive substance and, except in very dilute strengths, could quite literally eat away the lining of the stomach. (This is apparently what happens in cases of gastric ulcers.) Mucus secretions, with the help of fluids in the food itself, dilute the hydrochloric acid to a point where (in a normal stomach) it is rendered harmless. Even so, the normal, healthy condition inside our stomach is slightly acid. The slight acidity of the stomach serves to inhibit the growth of organisms such as bacteria.

The Small Intestine

By the time food-turned-chyme gets through the pyloric sphincter, it has already traveled about two-and-a-half feet: about 6 inches from lips to epiglottis; 10 or 12 inches down the esophagus; and about a foot through the stomach. But at this point it has actually traveled less than one-tenth of the gastrointestinal (GI) tract, and the longest stretch lies just ahead: the 20-plus feet of the small intestine, so named because of its relatively small one-to-two inch diameter. The preparation of food particles to pass through the walls of the GI tract is completed in the small intestine—almost completed, in fact, before the chyme has traveled the first foot of the small intestine. By the time it leaves the small intestine, chyme has given up virtually all its nutrients. In other words, the process called *absorption* or *assimilation* has taken place: the nutrients have left the GI tract for other parts of the body via the circulating blood and lymph. What passes on to the large intestine is principally waste and water.

The small intestine is somewhat arbitrarily divided into three sections: the *duodenum,* the *jejunum,* and the *ileum.*

The Duodenum

Within this horseshoe loop, eight to ten inches long and about two inches in diameter, more chemical interactions are concentrated than in any other section of the GI tract. One of the first jobs in the duodenum is to neutralize the acidity of the chyme. The final steps of digestion, and the absorption of food through the intestinal lining, proceed best in a slightly alkaline environment.

The alkaline juices needed to neutralize the acidity of the chyme come mainly from the liver in the form of bile. Bile produced by the liver but not needed immediately in the duodenum is stored in concentrated form in the gallbladder, a pouchlike, three-inch-long organ. On signal from the autonomic nervous system, the membranous muscular walls of the gallbladder contract, squeezing concentrated, highly alkaline bile into a short duct that leads to the duodenum. Bile components are indispensable for the digestion and absorption of stubborn fatty materials.

Through a duct from the pancreas, a host of pancreatic enzymes, capable of splitting apart large, tough molecules of carbohydrate, protein, and fat, enters the duodenum. These digestive enzymes manufactured by the pancreas are the most powerful in the GI tract.

What triggers the production of bile and pancreatic juice for the duodenum? Apparently, it is a two-step process involving hormones. When the stomach walls secrete hydrochloric acid on the arrival of food, hormones are released; they travel to the liver and pancreas with instructions to step up their production of digestive juices.

Still other strong enzymes are secreted by the walls of the duodenum and join the bile and pancreatic enzymes in the duodenum.

Thus, in the not quite foot-long tube of the duodenum, the final breakdown of food—digestion—reaches a dramatic climax. The nutrients in the food eaten some hours ago have almost all been reduced to molecules small enough to be absorbed through the intestinal walls into the bloodstream. Carbohydrates are reduced to simpler sugars; proteins to amino acids; and fats to fatty acids and glycerol.

Some absorption of these nutrients occurs in the duodenum, but the far greater proportion takes place in the next two, longer sections of the small intestine: the eight- to ten-foot jejunum and the twelve-foot ileum. Likewise, some oversize food molecules that get past the duodenum may be digested further along in their passage through the small intestine.

The Jejunum

As peristalsis pushes the nutrient broth out of the duodenum and into the first reaches of the jejunum, a gradual change in the appearance of the intestinal lining is evident. Greater and greater number of *villi*—microscopic, hairlike structures—sprout from the already bumpy walls of the intestinal lining into the GI tube.

The Villi

The villi (singular, *villus*) have the primary responsibility for absorbing amino acids (from protein), sugars (from carbohydrates), and fatty acids and glycerol (from fats) from the digested contents of the small intestine, and starting them on their way to other parts of the body. What the villi do not remove from the chyme—such as the cellulose fragments of fruits and vegetables—passes on to the large intestine in a thin, watery soup almost completely lacking in nutritional value.

Gland cells near the bottom of a villus secrete various enzymes, mucus, and other substances that perform digestive "mop-up operations" along the whole length of the small intestine.

The Ileum

In this third and final 12-foot section of the small intestine, villi line the walls in such profusion that the intestinal lining resembles, under moderate magnification, nothing so much as a plush, velvety carpet. The greatest numbers of the estimated five or six million villi in the small intestine are found along the lining of the ileum, making it the primary absorption site of the GI tract.

Also adding to the ileum's absorption efficiency is its gradually narrowing diameter (just one inch at its junction with the large intestine), which helps to keep the chyme always in close contact with the swishing villi. The end of the ileum is marked by the *ileocecal valve*, beyond which lies the first bulge of the large intestine, the *cecum*.

Principally because of vigorous peristaltic contractions and relaxations, the walls of the small intestine are always moving like the walls within some spasmodically flexing, nightmarish tunnel. Attached to the intestinal walls, the villi, too, are always in restless motion: waving and thrashing, protracting and retracting, even growing thinner or fatter.

Although the entire distance through the small intestine, from the pyloric sphincter to the ileocecal valve at the junction with the large intestine, is only a bit over 20 feet, the villi give the small intestine's internal lining a relatively gigantic surface area—over 100 square feet. This is about five times the surface area of our body's skin. Of course, the greatly enlarged surface area gives the small intestine lining that much more space in which to absorb nutrients.

The small intestine is supported in the abdomen by a fan-shaped web of tissues called the *mesentery.* Attached at the back of the abdomen, the mesentery connects to the small intestine at various points, and yet allows it some freedom to squirm and sway—much like the V network of ropes that attaches either end of a hammock to a tree. Nerve fibers and blood vessels also reach the small intestine via the mesentery.

The Liver, Gallbladder, and Pancreas

These three organs all share a common function—sending digestive substances to the duodenum—although, except in the case of the gallbladder, it is not their only function. Lying outside the GI tract proper, they nevertheless are indispensable in the processes of digestion and absorption. Digestive fluids from all three converge like tributaries of a river at the common bile duct, and their flow from there into the duodenum is controlled by a sphincter muscle-ring separating the duodenum and common bile duct.

From the liver, bile drips into the *hepatic duct,* which soon meets the *cystic duct* arriving from the gallbladder. Converging, they form one duct, the *common bile duct,* which meets the *pancreatic duct,* carrying enzymatic fluid from the pancreas. Like a smaller river meeting a larger one, the pancreatic duct loses its own name at this confluence and becomes part of the common bile duct, which empties on demand into the duodenum. When the sphincter of the bile duct is closed, bile from the liver is forced to back up into the cystic duct, and eventually into the gallbladder. There it is stored and concentrated until needed, when it flows back down the cystic duct.

The Liver

Four pounds of highly efficient chemical-processing tissues, the liver is the largest solid organ in the body. You can locate it by placing your left hand over your right, lowermost ribs; your hand then just about covers the area of the liver. More than any other organ, the liver enables our bodies to benefit from the food we eat. Without it, digestion would be impossible, and the conversion of food into living cells and energy practically nonexistent. Insofar as they affect our body's handling of food—all the many processes that go by the collective name of nutrition—the liver's functions can be

MUSCLES AND TENDONS

MUSCLES
1. Temporal
2. Mimetic muscles
3. Masseter (a muscle of mastication)
4. Infrahyoid muscles
5. Sternomastoid
6. Omohyoid
7. Deltoid
8. Pectoral muscles
9. Serratus anterior
10. External oblique
11. Rectus abdominus
12. Biceps brachii
13. Flexor digitorum superficialis (sublimis)
14. Gracilis

15. Adductor group
16. Sartorius
17. Rectus femoris
18. Quadriceps femoris
19. Vastus medialis
19a. Vastus lateralis
20. Dorsiflexors
21. Trapezius
22. Infraspinatus
23. Teres major
24. Triceps brachii
25. Latissimus dorsi
26. Rhomboideus major
27. Gluteus medius
28. Gluteus maximus

29. Digital extensors
30. Hamstring muscles
31. Gastrocnemius
32. Plantar flexors

TENDONS
33. Rectus sheath
34. Flexor retinaculum of carpal tunnel
35. Patellar tendon
36. Retinaculum of tarsal tunnel
37. Tendons of long digital extensors
38. Tendon of tibialis anterior
39. Lumbodorsal fascia
40. Fascia lata
41. Achilles

© C. S. HAMMOND & Co., N Y.

BONES AND LIGAMENTS

BONES
1. Skull
2. Mandible
3. Vertebrae
4. Clavicle
5. Scapula
6. Manubrium
7. Body of sternum
8. Xiphoid process
9. Ribs
10. Humerus
11. Radius
12. Ulna
13. Sacrum
14. Ilium
15. Coccyx
16. Femur
17. Patella
18. Tibia
19. Fibula
20. Carpals
21. Metacarpals
22. Phalanges
23. Metatarsals
24. Tarsals
25. Heel

LIGAMENTS AND JOINTS
26. Capsule of shoulder
27. Sternoclavicular
28. Capsule of elbow
29. Sacroiliac
30. Iliofemoral
31. Wrist
32. Capsule of knee
33. Ankle
34. Pubic symphysis
35. Intervertebral discs

© C. S. HAMMOND & Co., N. Y.

**ANTERIOR LUNGS, LIVER,
AND SMALL INTESTINE**

9. Larynx
10. Thyroid gland
11. Trachea
12. Lung (Right superior lobe)
13. Lung (Right middle lobe)
14. Lung (Right inferior lobe)
15. Lung (Left superior lobe)
16. Lung (Left inferior lobe)
17. Diaphragm
19. Liver (Right lobe)
20. Liver (Left lobe)
21. Falciform ligament
22. Gall bladder
29. Jejunum
30. Small intestine
35. Transverse colon
40. Taenia

POSTERIOR LUNGS, LIVER, AND SMALL INTESTINE

9. Larynx
10. Thyroid gland
11. Trachea
12. Lung (Right superior lobe)
13. Lung (Right middle lobe)
14. Lung (Right inferior lobe)
15. Lung (Left superior lobe)
16. Lung (Left inferior lobe)
17. Diaphragm
18. Principal bronchi
19. Liver (Right lobe)
20. Liver (Left lobe)
21. Falciform ligament
22. Gall bladder
29. Jejunum
30. Small intestine
31. Ileum
35. Transverse colon
40. Taenia coli
41. Cystic duct
42. Portal vein
43. Hepatic artery
44. Hepatic vein

© C. S. HAMMOND & Co., N. Y.

ANTERIOR CIRCULATORY SYSTEM

17. Diaphragm
23. Esophagus
37. Sigmoid colon
38. Rectum
44. Hepatic vein
49. Superior mesenteric artery
53. Common carotid artery.
54. Internal jugular vein
55. Subclavian artery
56. Subclavian vein
57. Aortic arch
58. Aorta
60. Heart
61. Pulmonary arteries
63. Superior vena cava
64. Inferior vena cava
65. Coronary arteries
66. Coeliac trunk
68. Inferior mesenteric artery
69. Renal artery
70. Renal vein
71. Common iliac artery
72. Common iliac vein
73. Femoral artery
74. Femoral vein
75. Internal iliac artery
76. Internal iliac vein
77. Kidneys (r. and l.)
78. Suprarenal glands (r. and l.)
79. Ureters (r. and l.)

© C. S. HAMMOND & Co., N. Y.

POSTERIOR CIRCULATORY
SYSTEM

17. Diaphragm
23. Esophagus
37. Sigmoid colon
38. Rectum
53. Common carotid artery.
54. Internal jugular vein
55. Subclavian artery
56. Subclavian vein
57. Aortic arch
58. Aorta
60. Heart
61. Pulmonary arteries
62. Pulmonary veins
63. Superior vena cava
64. Inferior vena cava
69. Renal artery
70. Renal vein
71. Common iliac artery
72. Common iliac vein
73. Femoral artery
74. Femoral vein
75. Internal iliac artery
76. Internal iliac vein
77. Kidneys (r. and l.)
79. Ureters (r. and l.)

© C. S. HAMMOND & Co., N. Y.

ANTERIOR INTERIOR RIB CAGE AND SPINE

5. Ribs
85. Cervical vertebrae
86. Thoracic vertebrae
87. Lumbar vertebrae
87a. Transverse process of vertebra
88. Sacrum
89. Coccyx
90. Intervertebral discs
91. Scapula
92. Humerus
93. Head of humerus
94. Ilium
95. Femur
96. Head of femur

© C. S. HAMMOND & Co., N. Y.

**POSTERIOR RIB
CAGE AND SPINE**

   5. Ribs
  85. Cervical
       vertebrae
  86. Thoracic
       vertebrae
  87. Lumbar
       vertebrae
  88. Sacrum
  89. Coccyx
  91. Scapula
  92. Humerus
  93. Head of
       humerus
  94. Ilium
  95. Femur
  96. Head of
       femur

© C. S. HAMMOND
    & Co., N. Y.

roughly divided into those that break down food molecules and those that build up or reconstitute these nu-trients into a form that the body can use or store efficiently.

Breaking Down Food Molecules

Bile, as we have seen, assists in the destruction of large food molecules in the small intestine, enabling absorption of nutrients by the villi. Bile acts to increase alkalinity, breaking down big fat molecules; stimulates peristalsis; and prevents food from putrefying within the digestive tract. Unusable portions of the bile, destined to be eliminated as waste, include excess cholesterol, fats, and various components of dead disintegrated cells. Pigments from dead cells in bile give feces its normal, dark, yellow-brown color. Other cell fragments in bile, especially iron from disintegrated red blood cells, are reclaimed from the intestines and eventually make their way via the bloodstream to other parts of the body, where they are built into new cells.

Reconstituting Nutrients

Oddly enough, the liver rebuilds some of the proteins and carbohydrates that the bile has just so effectively helped to break down in the digestive tract. But this is really not so strange as it sounds. The types of proteins and carbohydrates that can be used by man for cell-rebuilding and energy are usually somewhat different in fine structure from those in food. Thus, the liver receives the basic building blocks of proteins and carbohydrates—amino acids and sugars—and with them builds up molecules and cells that can be utilized by the human body. The amino acids and sugars reach the liver through the *portal vein,* which is the great collection tube for nutrient-carrying blood returning from capillaries along the stomach and small intestine.

Glycogen and Glucose

In the liver, sugars from the small intestine are converted into a special substance called *glycogen;* amino acids are made available as needed for building new cells to replace the cells that are always naturally dying in a healthy normal body. Glycogen, simply speaking, is the liver's solution to a difficult space and storage problem. The form of carbohydrate the body can use best is a sugar called *glucose,* but the liver isn't large enough to store the necessary amount of glucose. The answer is glycogen, a tidy, compact sugar molecule that the liver can store in great quantities. When a call comes from any part of the body for glucose, the liver quickly converts some glycogen to glucose and releases it into the bloodstream. By this mechanism, healthy blood sugar levels are maintained.

The liver also builds up human fats from fatty acids and glycerol, packs them off to storage, then reverses the process when necessary by breaking down body fats into forms that can serve as fuel to be burned by the body for energy.

Other Functions

In addition to its functions closely related to digestion and nutrition, the liver also serves as a storehouse and processor of vitamins and minerals—it is, in fact, the manufacturer of vitamin A. It can remove many toxic substances from the blood and render their poisons harmless. It picks up spent red blood cells from the circulation and dismantles them; and it continually manufactures new blood elements.

The liver is also a manufacturing site for *cholesterol,* a substance belonging to the class of body chemicals called steroids. Above-normal levels of cholesterol in the blood have been linked to hardening of the arteries and heart disease; but cholesterol in the proper amounts is needed by almost every tissue in the body. Some brain and spinal tissues, for example, have cholesterol as one of their main structural components.

With all these vital chemical activities and more, the liver might be expected to be a most delicate and fragile organ. In a sense it is: minor liver damage from one cause or another is thought to be fairly common. But what saves our lives (and us) is that we have a great deal more of it than we need for a normal healthy life. Before symptoms of a liver deficiency appear, more than 50 percent of the liver cells may be destroyed. Furthermore, the liver has a great capacity for regeneration, rebuilding diseased tissues with new liver cells.

The Gallbladder

Bile stored in the gallbladder is much more concentrated and thicker than bile that is fresh from the liver. This allows the three-inch gallbladder to store a great deal of bile components. But the thickening process can also create problems in the form of extremely painful gallstones, which are dried, crystallized bile. Fortunately, the entire gallbladder can be removed with little or no lasting ill effect. All that is missing is a small storage sac for bile.

The Pancreas

This manufacturer of powerful digestive enzymes, only six inches long, resembles a branchlet heavily laden with ripe berries. Its important role in digestion is often overshadowed by the fact that it also manufactures the hormone *insulin.* The pancreas cells that manufacture digestive enzymes are completely different from those that manufacture insulin. The latter are grouped into little clusters called the *islets of Langerhans,* which are

discussed under *The Endocrine Glands* in this chapter.

The Large Intestine

The large intestine, also called the large bowel, is shaped like a great, lumpy, drooping question mark— arching, from its beginning at the ileocecal valve, over the folds of the small intestine, then curving down and descending past more coiled small intestine to the anus, which marks the end of the GI tract. From ileocecal valve to anus, the large intestine is five to six feet in length.

The junction between the ileum and the *cecum,* the first section of the large intestine, occurs very low in the abdomen, normally on the right-hand side. The cecum is a bowl-like recep-tacle at the bottom of the colon, the longest section of the large intestine.

Just below the entrance of the ileum, a dead-end tube dangles down from the cecum. This is the *appendix vermiformis* (Latin, "worm-shaped appendage") commonly known as the appendix. Three to six inches long and one-third inch in diameter, the appendix may get jammed with stray pieces of solid food, become infected, swell, and rupture, spewing infection into the abdominal cavity. This is why early diagnosis of *appendicitis* and removal (*appendectomy*) are critically important.

Sections of the Colon

The colon is divided into three sections by pronounced *flexures,* or bends, where the colon makes almost right-angle changes of direction. Above the bowl of the cecum, the *ascending colon* rises almost vertically for about a foot and a half.

Then there is a flexure in the colon, after which the *transverse colon* travels horizontally for a couple of feet along a line at navel height. At another flexure, the colon turns vertically down again, giving the name of *descending colon* to this approximately two feet of large intestine. At the end of the descending colon, the large intestine executes an S-shaped curve, the *sigmoid flexure,* after which the remaining several inches of large intestine are known as the *rectum.*

Some people confuse the terms rectum and anus: the rectum refers specifically to the last section of the large intestinal tube, between sigmoid flexure and the anal sphincters, while the anus refers only to the opening controlled by the outlet valves of the large intestine. These valves consist of two ringlike voluntary muscles called anal sphincters.

Any solid materials that pass into the large intestine through the ileocecal valve (which prevents backflow into the small intestine) are usually indigestible, such as cellulose, or substances that have been broken down in the body and blood in the normal process of cell death and renewal, such as some bile components. But

what the cecum mainly receives is water.

Functions of the Large Intestine

The principal activity of the large intestine—other than as a channel for elimination of body wastes—is as a temporary storage area for water, which is then reabsorbed into the circulation through the walls of the colon. Villi are absent in the large intestine, and peristalsis is much less vigorous than in the small intestine.

As water is absorbed, the contents of the large intestine turn from a watery soup into the semisolid feces.

Meanwhile, bacteria—which colonize the normal colon in countless millions—have begun to work on and decompose the remaining solid materials. These bacteria do no harm as long as they remain inside the large intestine, and the eliminated feces is heavily populated with them. Nerve endings in the large intestine signal the brain that it is time for a bowel movement.

The Peritoneum

Lining the entire abdominal cavity, as well as the digestive and other abdominal organs, is a thin, tough, lubricated membrane called the *peritoneum*. In addition to protecting and supporting the abdominal organs, the peritoneum permits these organs to

slip and slide against each other without any harm from friction. The peritoneum also contains blood and lymph vessels that serve the digestive organs. See Ch. 11, *Diseases of the Digestive System.*

The Respiratory System and the Lungs

The heart, by its construction and shape, tells us a great deal about the lungs and respiration.

Interaction between Heart and Lungs

The heart is divided vertically by a wall called a septum into right (your right) and left parts. The right part is

smaller than the left: its muscles only have to pump blood a few inches to the lungs, while the muscles of the left half have to pump blood to the whole body.

The function of the right half of our heart is to receive oxygen-poor blood from the veins of the body. Venous blood empties into the top-right chamber, or right atrium, of the heart, and the right ventricle pumps that oxygen-poor blood (via the pulmonary artery) to the lungs, where the blood, passing through minute capillaries, picks up oxygen.

From the lungs, the oxygen-rich blood flows back into the heart's left atrium via the pulmonary veins; and from the left atrium, the oxygen-rich blood drains into the left ventricle, from whence it is pumped via the aorta to the body.

The blood pumped to the lungs by the right ventricle is oxygen-poor blood; it has given up its oxygen to the cells that need it around the body. But this "used blood" is rich in something else—carbon dioxide. As the body's cells have taken oxygen, they

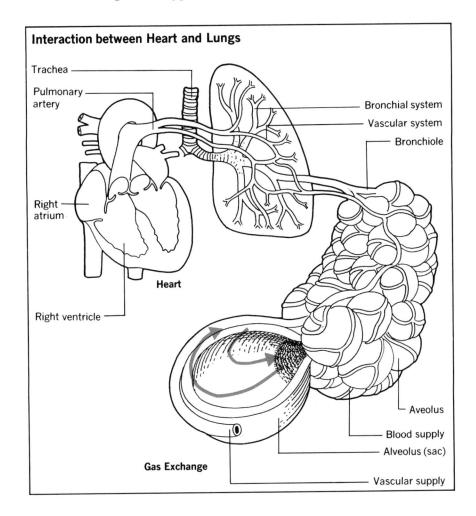

Interaction between Heart and Lungs

Trachea

Pulmonary artery

Bronchial system

Vascular system

Bronchiole

Right atrium

Heart

Right ventricle

Aveolus

Blood supply

Alveolus (sac)

Gas Exchange

Vascular supply

have given up carbon dioxide to the circulating blood. For both oxygen and carbon dioxide, the "carrier" has been *hemoglobin,* a complex iron-protein substance that is part of our red blood cells.

Capillaries and Alveoli

The pulmonary artery carrying this lung-bound blood soon branches into smaller and smaller vessels, and eventually into microscopic capillaries that reach into every crook and crevice of the lungs.

In the lungs, the walls of the capillaries touch the walls of equally microscopic structures called *alveoli* (singular, *alveolus*). The alveoli are the smallest air sacs of the lungs. These tiny, expandable air cells are the destination of every breath of air we take. Estimates of the total number of alveoli in both our lungs vary between 300 million and a billion—in any case, we normally have several hundred million of them.

The Alveoli
Bronchiole
Pulmonary artery
Pulmonary vein
Cross section of alveolus
Capillaries on alveolus

The branches of the pulmonary tree terminate in the alveoli, grapelike clusters of air sacs covered by capillaries, where the gaseous exchange occurs.

Carbon Dioxide and Oxygen Exchange

Where they meet, the membranous walls of both a capillary and an alveolus are both about as thin as any living tissue can be—a thickness that is only the width of one cell. Under such conditions, the carbon dioxide carried by the hemoglobin in our blood to the lungs diffuses (as tiny gaseous "bubbles") across both the wall of a capillary and the wall of an alveolus.

Once inside the sac of the alveolus, carbon dioxide is ready to be exhaled from the body by "breathing out." One indication of just how well this system works is the fact that the air we exhale has roughly 100 times more carbon dioxide than the air we breathe in.

At the same time that hemoglobin dumps carbon dioxide at the interface of the capillary and alveolus walls, it picks up the oxygen made available from inhaled fresh air that has reached the alveoli. The molecular oxygen bubbles cross the membranes in the same way—but in the opposite direction—as the carbon dioxide.

Hemoglobin in the capillaries picks up the oxygen and carries it via veins leading away from the lungs, to the left atrium of the heart.

Essential Role of Moisture

The alveolar membranes are supplied with a thin film of moisture that is absolutely indispensable to the exchange of gases in the lungs. As in so many of our body's reactions, our evolutionary descent from water-dwelling ancestors is revealed by the wet environment demanded if our lungs are to supply our body with oxygen.

Respiration at the One-Cell Level

Oxygen molecules, then, are carried to the body's cells by the hemoglobin of the arterial blood pumped by the heart's left ventricle. But how does a cell take oxygen from the blood and use it?

Exchange of Gases

The transfer of oxygen from blood to cell is accomplished in much the same way as the exhanges that take place in the lungs. The circulating arterial blood has a surplus of oxygen; the cells have a surplus of carbon dioxide. When the oxygen-rich blood reaches the finest capillaries, only the very thinnest membranous walls (of cell and capillary) separate it from the carbon-dioxide-rich cells. As in the lungs, both these gases (dissolved in water) diffuse through these thinnest of membranes: the oxygen into the cell, the carbon dioxide into the blood for eventual deposit in the alveoli, and exhalation.

Within the cell, the oxygen is needed so that food, the body's fuel, can be burned to produce energy. At the cellular level, the most convenient and common food is a fairly simple carbohydrate molecule called glucose.

Conversion of Carbohydrates into Energy

Energy is locked into a carbohydrate molecule such as glucose in the form of chemical bonds between its atoms. If one of these bonds is broken—say, a bond holding together a carbon and a hydrogen atom—a bit of pent-up energy is released as if, in a stalemated tug of war, the rope suddenly broke and both teams went hurtling off a few feet in opposite directions. This is precisely the effect of respiration within a cell: the cell "breaks the ropes" holding together a carbohydrate molecule. The result is the release of energy—either as body heat or to power other activities within the cell.

It is useful—but a somewhat misleading oversimplification—to consider cellular respiration as a type of burning, or combustion. When a typical cell burns food, a carbohydrate molecule (glucose) together with molecules of oxygen are changed into carbon dioxide and water. During this change, chemical energy is released—energy that has been trapped, as we have seen, in the carbohydrate molecule. That complex, energy-rich molecule has been dismantled into the simpler molecules of carbon dioxide (CO_2) and water (H_2O). Oxygen is necessary here just as it is in fiery combustion. But the energy released here, instead of rushing out as heat and flame, is used to power the living activities of the cell.

This description of cellular respiration is all right in principle, but the trouble is this: if it all happened at once—if carbohydrate was so abruptly dismantled, split up at one stroke to water and carbon dioxide—such a great amount of energy would be released that the cell would simply burn itself up. As one biologist has said, the cell would be in exactly the same position as a wood furnace built of wood.

What protects the cell is its army of enzymes. These remarkable protein molecules combine briefly with energy-containing food molecules, causing them to break down bit by bit, so that energy is released gradually rather than all at once.

Carbon Dioxide—Precious Waste

In most of our minds, oxygen tends to be the hero of respiration and carbon dioxide the villain or at least the undesirable waste gas. This isn't really a fair picture. While it is true that too much carbon dioxide would act as a poison in our body, it is also true that we must always have a certain amount of the gas dissolved in our tissues. If we did not, two potentially fatal events could occur. First, our blood chemistry, especially its delicate acid-alkali balance, would get completely out of control. Second—and something of a paradox—the body's whole automatic system of regulating breathing would be knocked out.

It is the level of carbon dioxide in the bloodstream that controls our breathing. This level is continuously being monitored by the autonomic nervous system, specifically by the lower brain's "breathing center" in the medulla at the top of the spinal cord. When the level of carbon dioxide in our body goes above a certain level, signals from the medulla force us to breathe. Almost everybody has played, "How long can you hold your breath?" and knows that, past a certain point, it becomes impossible *not* to breathe. When you are holding your breath, the unexhaled carbon dioxide rapidly builds up in your system until the breathing center is besieged with signals that say "Breathe!" And you do.

Our Big Breathing Muscle: The Diaphragm

What gets air into and out of our lungs? The answer may seem as obvious as breathing in and out. But except for those rare instances when we consciously regulate our breathing pattern—which physicians call "force breathing"—we do not decide when to inhale and when to exhale. And even when we do force-breathe, it is not primarily the action of opening the mouth and gulping in air, then blowing it out, that gets air down the windpipe and into the alveoli of the lungs. The main work of inhaling and exhaling is done by the contraction and relaxation of the big helmet-shaped muscle on which the lungs rest and which marks the "floor" of the chest or thoracic cavity and the "ceiling" of the abdominal cavity. This muscle is the *diaphragm.*

It is the diaphragm that causes the lungs to swell and fill with fresh air, then partially collapse to expel used gases. The muscles and tendons of the sinewy diaphragm are attached at the back to the spinal column, at the front to the breastbone (*sternum*), and at the lower sides to the lower ribs.

The diaphragm contracts and relaxes on orders from the brain's breathing center, orders that are carried along the pathways of the autonomic nervous system. When the medulla sends messages to the breathing muscles to contract, the diaphragm is pulled downward, en-

Diaphragm

Scapula

Serratus muscles

Spinal column

Internal intercostal muscles

External intercostal muscles

Sternum

Rib

Diaphragm

larging the space filled by the lungs. This creates a temporary partial vacuum, into which air rushes, inflating and expanding the lungs. When the diaphragm relaxes, the lung space is reduced, pushing air out.

Other Breathing Muscles

The diaphragm muscle's leading role in breathing is supported by several other muscles that play minor parts. Among these are the *intercostal muscles* between the ribs that give the rib cage a slight push upward and outward, enlarging the thoracic cavity, and the *serratus muscles*, which are mainly muscular sheaths along the ribs, to which other muscles are attached.

The Trachea and the Lungs

The right lung (your right) is somewhat bigger than the left. The lungs hang in the chest attached to the windpipe or *trachea*.

The Trachea

The trachea itself branches off at the back of the throat, or *pharynx*, where the epiglottis prevents food from entering the trachea and channels swallowed food along its proper route, the esophagus. The top part of the trachea forms the voice box or *larynx*, made up of vocal cords—actually two flaps of cartilage, muscle, and membranous tissue that protrude into the windpipe—whose vibrations in response to air exhaled from the lungs give us our voice.

Below the larynx, the trachea descends five or six inches to a spot just about directly behind your breastbone, where the first of many thousands of branchings into *bronchi, bronchioles,* and alveoli occurs. C-shaped rings of cartilage give the trachea both support and flexibility. Running your finger down the front of your neck, you can feel the bumps made by the cartilage rings.

Above the base of the trachea in midchest the lungs arch on either side like giant butterfly wings, then fall to fill out the bottom of each side of the thoracic cavity.

The Pleural Membranes

Both lungs are encased in moist, clinging, tissue-thin membrane called the *pleura*, which also lines the inside of the thoracic cavity where it comes into contact with the pleural coating of the lungs. The slippery pleural membranes hold tightly to each other, because there is an air lock or vacuum between them, but at the same time are free to slide over each other. The principle is the same as that illustrated by moistening the surfaces of two pieces of plate glass and placing the moistened surfaces together: the two pieces of glass will slide over each other but will resist being pried apart, because a partial vacuum exists between them.

The Pleural Cavity

The vacuum space between the pleura of the lung and the pleura of the thoracic cavity—although it is normally not a space at all—is called the *pleural cavity*. Each lung has its own pleural membrane: that of one lung does not interconnect with the other, so that one pleura may be injured without affecting the other.

It is extremely fortunate for us that the pleural linings both stick fast and can slide along each other's surfaces. Although the lungs are virtually without muscle, they are extremely elastic and in their natural condition are stretched fairly taut, held to the sides of the thoracic cavity by the suction of the pleura.

Collapsed Lung

Should this suction be broken and the pleural linings pull apart, the lung would shrink up like a deflated balloon. Such a condition, caused by the rush of outside air into the pleural cavity, is known medically as *pneumothorax* and causes a lung collapse. Violent injuries such as gun and stab wounds, various lung diseases, and obstructions of the breathing tubes can cause a lung or portion of a lung to collapse.

In the surgical procedure called *artificial pneumothorax,* a physician deliberately injects air between the pleural linings to collapse a portion of a lung. This is done to rest a lung in severe diseases such as tuberculosis, or to control heavy bleeding within the thoracic cavity.

Pleurisy

The intense chest pains called *pleurisy* are caused by inflammation of the pleura. The pleural linings lose their slipperiness and the increased friction stimulates pain receptors in the pleural lining of the chest. There are, however, no pain receptors in the lungs' pleural linings nor in the lungs themselves: this is why pain is not an early warning signal of lung cancer.

The Bronchi

Just behind the breastbone and just in front of the heart, the trachea divides into the right bronchus and the left bronchus, leading respectively to the right and left lungs. These are the primary two *bronchi* or *bronchial tubes.* Each is the main trunk of a bronchial tree that serves its respective lung.

Soon after leaving the trachea, each bronchus branches repeatedly into smaller tubes called *bronchioles,* which in turn branch into alveolar ducts, which terminate finally with the hundreds of millions of microscopic air sacs called alveoli, discussed at the beginning of this section. The alveoli are the site of the all-important exchange of carbon dioxide and oxygen.

Lobes and Segments

The larger right lung has three distinctive sections, or *lobes*—upper, middle, and lower. The left lung has only an upper and lower lobe. The lobes themselves are divided into smaller segments. Medically, these lobes and segments are important because they are somewhat independent of each other and can be damaged or removed surgically, as in operations for lung cancer, usually without damaging the function of adjacent, healthy segments or lobes.

The fact that a lung segment, lobe, or even an entire lung can be removed implies that we have plenty of reserve lung tissue, and this is indeed the case. When we are at rest, we use only about one-tenth of our total lung capacity. The total surface area exposed within our lungs to outside air is, amazingly, 600 square feet. This compares to a mere 20 square feet of skin surface. To appreciate the incredibly intricate, lacelike finery of the lungs' structure, we need only know that those 600 square feet of surface area are contained within two organs that together weigh only two-and-a-half pounds.

Oxygen Requirements

How much air do we breathe, and how much oxygen do we absorb into our body from the air? A normal, moderately active person breathes in and out (a complete respiration or breath cycle) about 18 times a minute; that is, the diaphragm contracts and relaxes 18 times a minute, or something over 25,000 times every day. At about four-fifths of a pint of air per breath cycle, this means that we inhale and exhale about 20,000 pints, or 10,000 quarts, or 2,500 gallons of air every day.

Only a very small proportion of this volume is oxygen that finds its way into our bloodstream: about a pint every minute in normal, quiet breathing, a little over 1,400 pints, or 700 quarts, or 175 gallons of oxygen every day. The amount of oxygen our lungs are capable of delivering to our body, however, varies tremendously: during sleep a person may need only a half-pint of oxygen per minute, half the average, while the lungs of a hard-driving athlete striving to break the mile record can deliver up to five quarts to the bloodstream—ten times the average.

At any given time, there are about two quarts of oxygen circulating in our blood. This is why a stoppage of breathing has an upper time limit of about four minutes before it causes irreversible damage or death. With our body needing about a pint of oxygen every minute for normal functioning, we have about four minutes before we use up the oxygen dissolved in our blood and other tissues.

Pollution Control— Filters, Cleaners, and Traps

Air pollution being what it is these days, it is fortunate that we have several natural devices that serve to filter out and wash away most of the impurities in the air we inhale.

Air gets into the lungs from outside about equally well via the nose or mouth. The mouth offers the advantage of getting more air in at a faster rate—absolutely a must if we have to push our body physically. But the nose has more and better equipment for cleaning air before it reaches the trachea. Via the mouth, air must only pass over a few mucous membranes and the tonsils, which can collect only so many germs and impurities.

Nose Filter System

Air taken in through the nose, however, first meets the "guard hairs" (*vibrissae*) of the nostrils, and then must circulate through the nasal cavity, a kind of cavern framed by elaborate scroll-shaped bones called *turbinates,* and lined with mucus-secreting membranes and waving, hairlike fibers called *cilia.* Foreign particles are caught by the cilia and carried away by the mucus, which drains slowly down the back of the throat.

It would be nice to be able to ascribe an important function to the eight *paranasal sinuses,* four on either side of the nose: the headache and discomfort of sinusitis might then be more bearable. But these "holes in the head" seem to exist simply to cause us trouble; for example—swelling to close the nasal air passages, making it impossible to breathe, as recommended, through the nose.

Filter System beyond the Nose

The cleansing and filtering action started in the nose and mouth does not stop there, but is repeated wherever air travels along the air passages of the lungs. Cilia project inward from the walls of even the tiniest bronchioles of the lungs, and impurities are carried from the alveoli on films of mucus that move ever back toward the trachea for expulsion—as when we cough. See also Ch. 12, *Diseases of the Respiratory System* and Ch. 13, *Lung Disease.*

The Endocrine Glands

Technically speaking, a gland is any cell or organ in our bodies that secretes some substance. In this broad sense, our liver is a gland, because one of its many functions is to secrete bile. So too, is the placenta that encloses a developing baby and supplies it with chemicals that assure normal growth. Even the brain has been shown by modern research to secrete special substances. But lymph glands are not considered true glands and are more correctly called lymph nodes.

Physicians divide the glands into two categories. *Endocrine glands* are

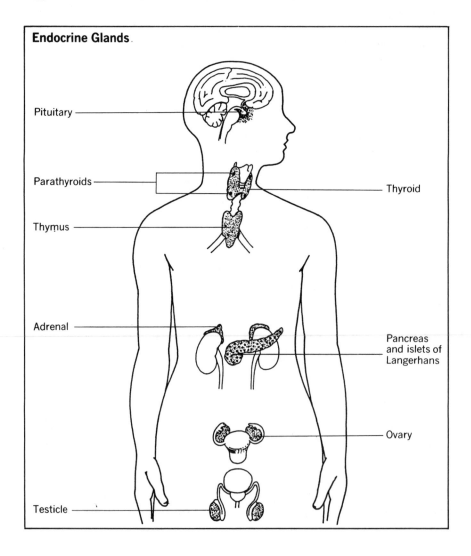

Endocrine Glands

Pituitary

Parathyroids

Thymus

Adrenal

Testicle

Thyroid

Pancreas and islets of Langerhans

Ovary

also known as *ductless glands,* because they release their secretions directly into the bloodstream. *Exocrine glands,* by contrast, usually release their substances through a duct or tube. Exocrine glands include the sebaceous and sweat glands of the skin; the mammary or milk glands; the mucous glands, some of which moisten the digestive and respiratory tract; and the salivary glands, whose secretions soften food after it enters the mouth. The pancreas has both an endocrine and an exocrine function and structure.

Role of the Endocrine Glands

The *endocrine glands* have the all-important role of regulating our body's internal chemistry. The substances they secrete are complex compounds called *hormones,* or chemical messengers.

Together with the brain and nerves, the system of endocrine glands controls the body's activities. The nervous system, however, is tuned for rapid responses, enabling the body to make speedy adjustments to changing circumstances, internal and external. The endocrine glands, with some exceptions, like the adrenal, are more concerned with the body's reactions over a longer period of time—from season to season, as it were. They regulate such processes as growth, levels of metabolism, fertility, and pregnancy.

For a group of tissues that exercise awesome power over our body's well-being, the endocrine glands are surprisingly small and inconspicuous—all of them together would weigh less than half a pound. Nor are they placed with any particular prominence in our body. They tend to be little lumps of tissue attached to or tucked behind grander bodily structures. Their power comes from the hormones they release into the bloodstream.

Scientists have discovered the exact chemical makeup of a number of these complex substances, have extracted several in pure form from living tissue, and have succeeded in making a few synthetically in the laboratory. This avenue of research, called *endocrinology,* has enabled physicians to treat persons suffering from certain endocrine gland disorders.

Hormones have been aptly described as chemical messengers. Their action, while still not completely understood, is that of catalysts. This means that the presence of a hormone (the name comes from a Greek word meaning "arouse to activity"), even in very small quantities, can affect the rate at which a chemical change occurs or otherwise stimulate a reaction, and without itself being affected. The hormone is a promoter, either of a positive or negative sort; it speeds up a process or slows it down.

The endocrine glands form an interdependent family. The functioning or malfunctioning of one can affect all the others.

The Pituitary—Master Gland

The *pituitary* is often called the master gland because the hormones it secretes play an active part in controlling the activities of all the other endocrine glands. This impressive power is wielded from two little bumps at the base of the brain, about midway between the ears at eye level. The two parts, or lobes, are connected by a tiny bridge of tissue, the three structures together being about the size of a small acorn. The lobe lying toward the front of the head is the *anterior lobe;* the one at the back, the *posterior lobe.* Each lobe is really an independent gland in itself, with its own quite distinct activities.

The Pituitary Gland

Posterior pituitary gland

Anterior pituitary gland

The Posterior Lobe and the Hypothalamus

The posterior lobe, so far as is known, does not make any of its own hormones, but serves as a storehouse for two hormones manufactured by the *hypothalamus,* located in the brain's cerebellum. The hypothalamus, apart from having a role in controlling the body's autonomic nervous system, also functions as an endocrine gland, secreting its own hormones, and as a connecting link between the brain's cerebral cortex and the pituitary gland.

The posterior lobe of the pituitary releases the two hormones it receives from the hypothalamus, called *vasopressin* and *oxytocin,* into the bloodstream. Vasopressin plays a role in the fluid balance of the body; oxytocin is thought to pace the onset and progress of labor during childbirth.

The Anterior Lobe

The anterior lobe secretes no less than six known hormones, five of which act as stimulators of hormone production by other endocrine glands. The sixth, identified as *somatotrophin* in medical textbooks, is more popularly known as the *growth-stimulating hormone* or simply as the growth hormone. It controls the rate of growth and multiplication of all the cells and tissues in our bodies—muscle, bone, and all our specialized organs.

Gigantism

In rare instances, during childhood, the pituitary releases too much or too little somatotrophin. If too much is secreted, the result is an overstimulation of growth processes, causing a disorder known as *gigantism.* Victims of this disorder have been known to grow nine feet tall and weigh 500 pounds.

Dwarfism

If too little somatotrophin is secreted, *dwarfism* results. This pituitary-type dwarf, of which Tom Thumb was one, is different from a dwarf suffering from a disorder of the thyroid (another endocrine gland, discussed below). The pituitary dwarf is usually well proportioned despite a miniature size, while the thyroid dwarf typically has short, deformed limbs.

Neither pituitary gigantism nor dwarfism affects basic intelligence. If oversecretion of somatotrophin occurs after full size has been reached—as, for example, because of a tumor affecting the pituitary, the condition known as *acromegaly* occurs. The bones enlarge abnormally, especially those of the hands, feet, and face.

Anterior Pituitary Hormones

Of the five anterior pituitary hormones that regulate other endocrine glands, one affects the adrenal glands, one the thyroid, and the remaining three the sex glands or gonads (the testicles in men and the ovaries in women). Each is identified by a set of initials derived from its full name, as follows:

- *ACTH,* the *a*drenocor*t*icotrophic *h*ormone, affects the production of hormones by the outer "bark" of the adrenal glands, called the *adrenal cortex.*

- *TSH,* the *t*hyroid-*s*timulating *h*ormone, also known as *thyrotrophin,* causes the thyroid gland to step up production of its hormone, *thyroxin.*

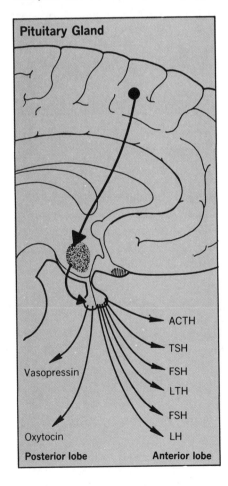

Pituitary Gland

Vasopressin

Oxytocin

Posterior lobe

ACTH
TSH
FSH
LTH
FSH
LH

Anterior lobe

- *FSH,* the *f*ollicle-*s*timulating *h*ormone, spurs production in women of estrogen, a sex hormone produced by the ovaries; and in men, of sperm by the testicles. Follicle here refers to the *Graafian follicles* in the ovary, which contain developing female egg cells whose growth is also stimulated by FSH. Graafian follicles have approximate counterparts in the male—tiny pouches (seminal vesicles) on either side of the prostate gland that store mature sperm cells.

- *LH,* the *l*uteinizing *h*ormone, transforms a Graafian follicle, after the follicle has released a ripened egg cell, into a kind of tissue called *corpus luteum*. The corpus luteum, in turn, produces *progesterone,* a hormone that prepares the mucous membrane lining the uterus (the endometrium) to receive a fertilized egg.

- *LTH,* the *l*actogenic *h*ormone, or *luteotrophin,* stimulates the mother's mammary glands to produce milk; LTH also joins with LH in promoting the production of progesterone by the sex glands.

The last three hormones mentioned—follicle-stimulating, luteinizing, and lactogenic—are sometimes called the *gonadotrophic* hormones because they all stimulate activity of the gonads.

The Adrenal Glands

Resting like skull caps on the top of both kidneys are the two identical *adrenal glands*. Each has two distinct parts, secreting different hormones.

Adrenaline

The central internal portion of an adrenal gland is called the *medulla*. Its most potent contribution to our body is the hormone *adrenaline* (also called *epinephrine*). This is the hormone that, almost instantaneously, pours into our bloodstream when we face a situation that calls for extraordinary physical reaction—or keeps us going past what we think to be our normal limit of endurance.

A surge of adrenaline into the bloodstream stimulates our body to a whole array of alarm reactions—accelerating the conversion of stored foods into quick energy; raising the blood pressure; speeding up breathing; dilating the pupils of the eyes for more sensitive vision; and constrict-

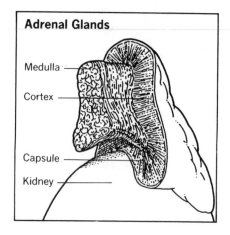

Adrenal Glands

Medulla
Cortex
Capsule
Kidney

ing the blood vessels, making them less vulnerable to bleeding.

Adrenaline provides a good example of the interdependence of the endocrine system. Its production stimulates the secretion of ACTH by the pituitary gland. And ACTH, as noted above, causes the adrenal cortex to accelerate production of its hormones. Some of these adrenal cortex hormones enable the body to call up the reserves of energy it does not normally need. For example, body proteins are not usually a source of quick energy, but in an emergency situation, the adrenal cortex hormones can convert them to energy-rich sugar compounds.

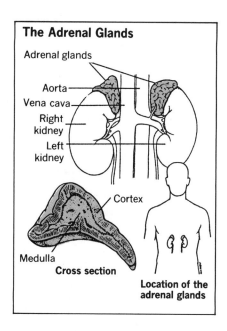

The Adrenal Glands

Adrenal glands
Aorta
Vena cava
Right kidney
Left kidney
Cortex
Medulla
Cross section
Location of the adrenal glands

The Corticoids

There are some 30 different hormones, called the *corticoids,* manufactured in the adrenal cortex—the outer layer of the adrenal. A few of these influence male and female sexual characteristics, supplementing the hormones produced in the gonads. The others fall into two general categories: those that affect the body's metabolism (rate of energy use), and those that regulate the composition of blood and internal fluids. Without the latter hormones, for example, the kidneys could not maintain the water–salt balance that provides the most suitable environment for our cells and tissues at any given time.

Corticoids also influence the formation of antibodies against viruses, bacteria, and other disease-causing agents.

Extracts or laboratory preparations of corticoids, such as the well-known cortisone compounds, were found in the 1950s to be almost "miracle" medicines. They work dramatically to reduce pain, especially around joints, and hasten the healing of skin inflammations. Prolonged use, however, can cause serious side effects.

The Islets of Langerhans

Strewn at random throughout the pancreas are hundreds of thousands of tiny clusters of cells. Each of them, when seen under a powerful microscope, forms an "islet" of its own, similar to the other distinct islets, but markedly different from the pancreatic tissue surrounding it. These

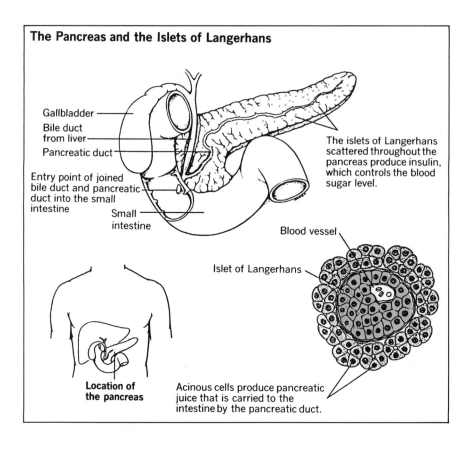

The Pancreas and the Islets of Langerhans

Gallbladder

Bile duct from liver

Pancreatic duct

Entry point of joined bile duct and pancreatic duct into the small intestine

Small intestine

The islets of Langerhans scattered throughout the pancreas produce insulin, which controls the blood sugar level.

Blood vessel

Islet of Langerhans

Location of the pancreas

Acinous cells produce pancreatic juice that is carried to the intestine by the pancreatic duct.

are the *islets of Langerhans,* named after the German scientist who first reported their existence in 1869. Each of these little cell clumps—up to two million or more of them—is a microscopic endocrine gland.

They secrete the hormone *insulin,* and the disease that occurs if they are not functioning properly is *diabetes mellitus.*

Actually, the islets of Langerhans produce not only insulin, but also a

The Pancreas and the Islets of Langerhans

Bile duct

Pancreatic duct

Pancreatic gland (pancreatic juice)

Islet of Langerhans (insulin)

Intestine

Vascular supply

related hormone called *glucagon.* Both regulate the amount of sugar (glucose) that is present in the bloodstream and the rate at which it is used by the body's cells and tissues. Glucose supplies the energy for life and living processes.

When insulin and glucagon are not in sufficient supply, the cells' ability to absorb and use blood sugar is restricted, and much of the sugar passes unutilized out of the body in urine. Because the body's ability to obtain energy from food is one of the very foundations of life, diabetes calls for the most careful treatment.

One of the great advances of twentieth century medicine has been the pharmaceutical manufacture of insulin and its wide availability to diabetics. With regulated doses of insulin, a diabetic can now lead a normal life. See Ch. 15, *Diabetes Mellitus* for a full discussion of this disease.

The Thyroid Gland

The *thyroid gland* folds around the front and either side of the trachea (windpipe), at the base of the neck, just below the larynx. It resembles a somewhat large, stocky butterfly facing downward toward the chest.

Thyroxin

The thyroid hormone, *thyroxin,* is a complex protein-type chemical containing, along with various other elements, a large percentage of iodine. Like a number of other hormones manufactured by the endocrine glands, thyroxin affects various steps in the body's metabolism—in particular, the rate at which our cells and tissues use inhaled oxygen to burn the food we eat.

Hypothyroidism

A thyroid that is not producing enough thyroxin tends to make a person feel drowsy and sluggish, put on weight (even though his appetite is poor), and in general make his everyday activities tiresome and wearying. This condition is called *hypothyroidism.*

Hyperthyroidism

Its opposite—caused by too much secretion of thyroxin—is *hyyperthyroidism.* A hyperthyroid person is jumpy, restless, and may eat hugely without

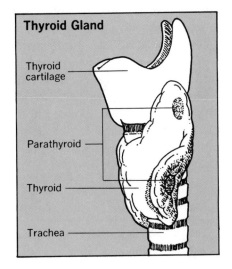

Thyroid Gland

Thyroid cartilage

Parathyroid

Thyroid

Trachea

gaining weight. The difference between the two extremes can be compared to environments regulated by two different thermostats, one set too high and the other set too low.

Although a normally functioning thyroid plays a significant part in making a person feel well, physicians today are less willing than in former years to blame a defective thyroid alone for listlessness or jittery nerves. Thirty or forty years ago it was quite fashionable to prescribe thyroid pills (containing thyroid extract) almost as readily as vitamins or aspirin; but subsequent medical research, revealing the interdependence of many glands and other body systems, made thyroxin's reign as a cure-all a short one.

Of course, where physical discomfort or lethargy can be traced to an underfunctioning thyroid, thyroxin remains an invaluable medicine.

Goiter

One disorder of the thyroid gland—the sometimes massive swelling called *goiter*—is the direct result of a lack of iodine in the diet. The normal thyroid gland, in effect, collects iodine from the bloodstream, which is then synthesized into the chemical makeup of thyroxin. Lacking iodine, the thyroid gland enlarges, creating a goiter. The abnormal growth will stop if iodine is reintroduced into the person's diet. This is the reason why most commercial table salt is iodized—that is, a harmless bit of iodine compound has been added to it.

The Parathyroid Glands

Four small glands, each about the size of a small pea, cling to the base of the thyroid gland, two on each of the thyroid's lobes curving back of the trachea. These are the *parathyroids,* whose main role is to control the level of calcium—as well as other elements needed in carefully regulated amounts by the body—in the bloodstream and tissues. The parathyroids secrete two hormones: *parathormone* when blood calcium is too low; *calcitonin* when the calcium level is too high. These hormones work by controlling the interchange of calcium between bones and blood.

The most common symptom of defective parathyroids is *tetany*—a chronic or acute case of muscle spasms, which can be controlled by administration of synthetic parathyroidlike chemicals or concentrated vitamin D preparations.

The Gonads

The *gonads* refer to both the two male testicles and the two female ovaries. There are four hormones secreted by the gonads: the female sex hormones, *estrogen* and *progesterone;* and the male hormones, *testosterone* and *androsterone.* Each sex merely has a predominance of one or the other pair of hormones. Men have some of the female hormones, and women some of the male hormones.

In both sexes, puberty is signaled by the release of the gonadotrophic hormones (or *gonadotrophins*) of the pituitary gland. These stimulate the production of sex hormones by the sex glands and the subsequent appearance of secondary sexual characteristics. In men, these include the enlargement of testicles and penis, growth of facial, axillary (armpit) and pubic hair, and enlargement of the larynx, resulting in deepening of the voice. Pubescent women also experience pubic and axillary hair growth, in addition to breast growth and changes in the genital tract that give it childbearing capability.

Estrogen and progesterone control the cyclic changes within the uterus that involve the development, ripening, and discharge of the egg (ovulation) to be fertilized; the preparation of the lining of the uterus to receive a fertilized egg; and this lining's subsequent dismantling—all the complex biochemical events that occur as part of every woman's menstrual cycle.

The Thymus and Pineal Glands

These are the least known of the endocrine family; in fact, physicians do not know the function of one of them—the *pineal*—and are not even agreed that it is an endocrine gland. Situated near the hypothalamus, at the base of the brain, this tiny, pinecone-shaped body has follicles that suggest a glandular function and some calcium-containing bits that medical researchers have descriptively dubbed "brain sand."

The *thymus,* only slightly better understood, has the intriguing characteristic of shrinking in size as a person grows up. It is located in the middle of the chest, about midway between the base of the neck and the

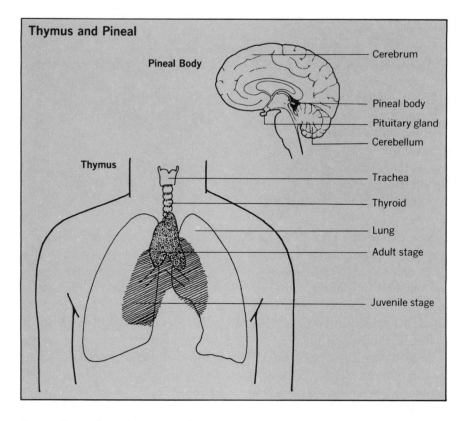

Thymus and Pineal

Pineal Body

Cerebrum

Pineal body

Pituitary gland

Cerebellum

Thymus

Trachea

Thyroid

Lung

Adult stage

Juvenile stage

breast line. There is some evidence that the secretions of the thymus play a role in the body's natural immunity defenses. See also Ch. 14, *Diseases of the Endocrine Glands.*

The Sense Organs

Once upon a time, a grade-school teacher would ask, "How many senses do we have?" And his pupils would confidently chorus back, "Five!" People who displayed a knack for predicting future events, or whose quick reactions seemed to give them a jump over most everybody else, were credited with having a "sixth sense."

Scientists now recognize about twice that number—12 or 13 or more. Man, of course, has not grown a number of new senses in addition to the traditional five: sight, hearing, touch, smell, and taste. What has happened is that scientists have discovered many more specific kinds of sense receptor cells. For example, whereas touch was formerly thought of as just one sense, it has now been divided into no less than five different senses, each having its own special kind of receptor cell in the skin.

We can talk with a little more justification of the five sense organs, the five anatomical structures we associate with our senses—the eyes, ears, nose, tongue, and skin. But here, too, it does seem to be oversimplifying things to thus equate the nose—having only a tiny patch of olfactory (sense of smell) receptor cells—with the marvelously complex arrangement of sensing structures that make up the eye. Moreover, the other sense organs are not nearly so specialized as the eye. For example, a good case could be made for the nose being more valuable as an air purifier than as an organ of smell, or for the tongue being more valuable as an aid in digestion than as a source of the taste sensation.

Suppose we accept the proposition that pain is one of the senses of the skin; how then do we explain a pain from inside our bodies—say, a stomachache or a deep muscle pain? The answer, of course, is that there are pain receptors in many other places besides the skin.

What Is a Sense?

A sense is a nerve pathway, one end of which (the receptor end) responds in a certain way to a certain condition affecting our bodies, and whose other end reaches to a part of our brain that informs our conscious mind of what has happened or is happening. A sense is thus distinguished from the body's countless other nerve pathways by the fact that our brain *consciously* registers its impulses, although the impulses themselves are no different from those of the autonomic nervous system.

While remaining aware of the limitations of the traditional list of five sense organs, let us now analyze what they can do and how they operate:

- The eye (vision): Nerve impulses to the brain are stimulated by light waves, from which the brain forms visual images.

- The ears (hearing): Nerve impulses to the brain are stimulated by sound waves, out of which the brain forms meaningful noise, such as speech. Deep within the ear, also, are structures that give us balance.

- The nose (olfaction): Nerve impulses to the brain are stimulated by airborne chemical substances, moistened within the nasal cavity, from which the brain elicits distinctive smells.

- The tongue (taste): Nerve impulses to the brain are stimulated (in presence of water) by chemical substances in food, from which the brain forms sensations of sweet, salty, sour, bitter, or combinations of these tastes.

- Skin (touch): Nerve impulses to the brain are stimulated by the presence of outside physical forces and changes in the physical environment, including varying temperatures, which the brain registers as feelings of contact, pressure, cold, heat, and pain. (Some medical texts add traction, as when the skin is pulled or pinched, as well as the sensation of tickle.)

The Eye

Rather than take a name-by-name anatomical tour of the eye, let's instead take just three programmed tours of the eye to explore:

● the transformation of light energy into vision;

● focusing, or how the structure of the eye prepares light for transformation into vision; and

● the supporting structures and service units of the eye.

Transforming Light Energy into Vision

If you could look through the opening in the front of your eye (the *pupil*), and see to the very back surface of your eye (as if you could see through the needle valve opening to the inside skin of a basketball), you would see your own *retina*. On your retina are located all the sense receptor cells that enable us to see. There are none anywhere else in the body.

Rods and Cones

A good argument can be made that man's vision is really *two* senses. For on the paper-thin retina are two quite anatomically distinct sense receptors (nerve endings) named, for their appearance under high magnification,

Eye

Fovea (rod)　Macula lutea (cone)

Lacrimal gland
Eyelid
Pupil
Lens
Iris
Cornea
Retina
Chorioid
Sclera
Ocular muscle
Optic nerve
Vascular supply

cones and *rods*. The cones are concentrated at a tiny spot on the retina called the *fovea*.

If the focusing machinery of the eye (cornea, lens, etc.) is working just right, light rays from the outside have their sharpest focus on the fovea. Surrounding the fovea is a yellowish area called the *macula lutea* (Latin, "yellow spot"). Together, the fovea and macula lutea make a circle not much bigger than the head of a pin.

All our seeing of colors and fine details is accomplished by the cones of the fovea and the macula lutea. Beyond the yellowish circumference of the macula lutea, there are fewer and fewer cones: rods become the dominant structures on the retina. It has been estimated that there are something less than 10 million cones on the retina of each eye, but more than 10 times as many rods—100 million of them or more.

Although the tight circle of cones in each eye gives man his ability to do close, detailed work (including reading) and to discriminate colors, the cones are virtually useless in detecting objects that are a bit off center from our direct focus, and furthermore operate only in good lighting conditions or in response to bright light sources.

The rods compensate for the specialized limits of the cones. They take over completely in dim light, and also give us the ability to detect peripheral objects and movements—"out of the corner of the eye." Because the rods are not sensitive to colors, our seeing at night is almost completely in black-and-white.

You can give yourself an interesting demonstration of the interacting functions of your own cones and rods if you walk from bright, sunny daylight into a dimly lit theater. In the bright light, your cones have been picking out sharp images and colors. But once in dimness, the cones become inoperative. For a few moments, in fact, you may see almost nothing at all.

Visual Purple

The momentary interval after the cones stop working but before the rods begin to function is explained by a curious pigment present in the eye called *visual purple*. This substance is manufactured constantly by the rods, and must be present for the rods to respond to dim light—but it is destroyed when exposed to bright light.

Thus, after entering a darkened room, it takes a few moments for visual purple to build up in the retina. One of the principal constituents of visual purple is vitamin A, which is why this vitamin (present in carrots and other yellow produce) is said to increase our capacity to see in the dark.

The Optic Nerve

Every nerve ending is part of a larger unit, a neuron or nerve cell, and the sense receptors called rods and cones are no exception. Like all nerve cells, each rod and cone sports a long nerve fiber or *axon* leading away from the site of reception. In each eye, fibers serving the hundred-million-plus rods and cones all converge at a certain spot just behind the retina, forming the *optic nerve.* There are no rods and cones at the point where the optic nerve exits from behind the retina at the back of the eyeball: that is why everybody has a "blind spot" at that point. An image passing through that spot completely disappears.

From the retina, both optic nerves set a course almost directly through the middle of the brain. Right and left optic nerves converge, their individual fibers partially intertwining a short distance behind the eyes. Then this joint optic nerve trunk proceeds toward the rear of the head, where the *occipital lobes,* the brain's "centers for seeing," are located. Just before reaching the occipital lobes, the optic nerve splits again into thousands of smaller nerve bundles (called *visual radiations*) that disappear into the visual cortex or "outer bark" of the occipital lobes. Only at this point are the bits of light energy that have stimulated our rods and cones transformed into images that our brain can "see."

Focusing and Light Control

Lacking the structures of the retina and their connection to the brain via the optic nerve, we could not see. Lacking reasonably normal functioning of the cornea, lens, and iris, we do not see well.

Good vision depends upon the eye being able to bend incoming light rays in such a way that the image being observed falls directly on the retina— in other words, upon proper focusing.

The bending or *refraction* of light rays is the joint work of two curves, transparent slivers of specialized tissue through which light passes on its way to the retina. These are the *cornea* and the *lens.* Broadly speaking, the degree of curvature and thickness of these two structures determines whether we see well or poorly, are nearsighted or farsighted.

The Cornea and Lens

The cornea, which does the major light-bending, has a virtually fixed curvature and thickness. The lens puts the finishing touches on the focusing. Its thickness and curvature are adjustable—more or less without our conscious awareness—depending on whether we wish to focus on something nearer or farther away.

The lens is made thicker or thinner, a process called *accommodation,* by the relaxing and contracting of tiny, attached *ciliary muscles.* Normally, these muscles do not have to work at all if we are looking at objects more than 20 feet away: but they often are overworked by a great deal of close work.

Focusing

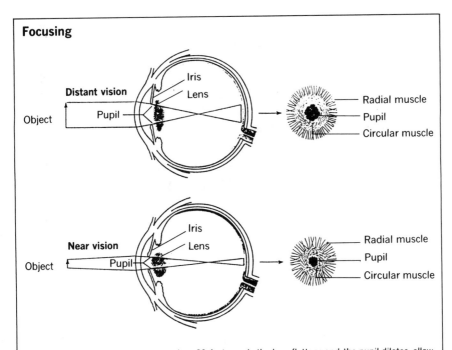

When viewing a distant object (more than 20 feet away), the lens flattens and the pupil dilates, allowing more light to enter the eye. The pupil is dilated by the action of the outer radial muscles of the iris, which contract and thus stretch the previously contracted circular muscles. When viewing a near object, the lens becomes more oval and the pupil contracts as more light enters the eye. This prevents overstimulation of the retina. The pupil is reduced in size by the contraction of the inner circular muscles, which serve to stretch the previously contracted radial muscles.

The Pupil and Iris

Effective focusing in various light conditions also depends upon the diameter of the hole through which light enters the eye. This hole is the *pupil*. Its diameter is controlled automatically—wider in dim light, narrower in bright light—by the muscles of the surrounding *iris*. The iris muscle contains pigment that gives our eyes color (brown, blue, green, etc.). The pupil, opening into the dark interior chamber of the eye, is black. A fully dilated (widened) pupil, as would occur in the dimmest light, illuminates over 15 times more retinal surface than the tiny "pinhole" pupil of an eye exposed to very bright light.

Structural Support and Protection of Eye

Two outer layers protect the eye. The tough outermost layer is the *sclera,* the white of the eye. Underlying the sclera is another layer, the *choroid,* which contains numerous tiny blood vessels that service the sclera and other structures on the eyeball. Both sclera and choroid have concentric openings that allow for the hole of the pupil. The cornea is really

---

Muscles of the Eye

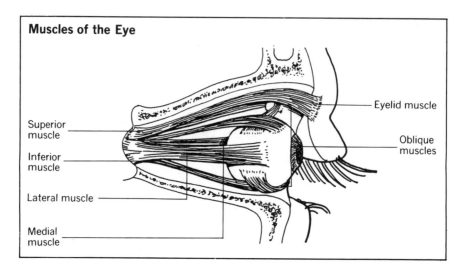

- Eyelid muscle
- Oblique muscles

Superior muscle

Inferior muscle

Lateral muscle

Medial muscle

---

a specialized extension of the sclera, and the iris of the choroid.

Two trapped reservoirs of fluid within the eye are important in maintaining the eye's shape as well as the frictionless operation of its moving parts. These two reservoirs contain fluids called the *aqueous humor* and *vitreous humor.* The tiny space between the cornea and lens, corresponding to the pupil, is called the anterior chamber and is filled with the clear, watery, aqueous humor. The larger interior space behind the lens is called the posterior chamber, and is filled with the vitreous humor.

Muscles for Movement of Eye

In addition to the tiny muscles within the eye that control the opening of the pupil and the shape of the lens, we also have a number of elegant muscles that control the movements of each eyeball, and make both eyeballs move together in unison.

The movements of each eyeball are affected by six muscles attached to its top, bottom, and sides. The teamwork between these muscles—some contracting while others relax—allows the eye to move from side to side, up and down, and at all intermediate angles (obliquely). One of our eyes is always a dominant or leading eye; that is, its movements

Ciliary Muscle Contraction

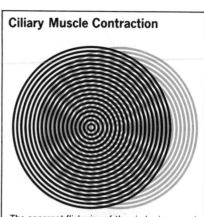

The apparent flickering of the circles is caused by contractions of the ciliary muscles, which control the accommodation (or change in thickness) of the lens for accurate focusing of objects at a variety of distances.

are always followed by the other eye.

Our protective eyelids, of course, are controlled by opening and closing muscles that lie outside the eye proper. These muscles can function both voluntarily and involuntarily.

Lubrication and Hygiene of Eye

Without the moisture provided by tears, our eyeball would scrape excruciatingly on the inside lining (*conjunctiva*) of the eyelid. In addition to lubrication, tears also have a cleansing action, not only because they supply water for washing and rinsing but also because they contain a mild germicide called *lysozyme* that kills bacteria and other potentially harmful microbes.

Tears are produced by the *lacrimal glands* above the eyeball, just under the eyebrow, a bit further toward the temple side than the nose side. They are discharged from several short ducts and spread over the surface of the eyeball by blinking. The *conjunctival sac* at the bottom inner (nose) side of the eye—visible in the mirror as a pinkish flap of tissue—serves as a collecting pool for tears; from there, they drain down a duct into the nasal cavity. This is why somebody who is crying also snuffles and must blow his nose.

There is another tiny drainage network in the eye, located at the interconnection of the cornea and iris, which serves to keep the fluid pressure of the space filled by the aqueous humor within normal limits. Drainage of this area is through microscopic conduits called the *canals of Schlemm*. Improper drainage can cause build-up of pressure, such as occurs in glaucoma, and impairment or loss of vision.

The Ear

Within the tunnels and chambers of the ear lie the two special types of sense receptors that give us, respectively, the sense of hearing and the sense of balance.

The Outer Ear

The *outer ear* includes that rather oddly shaped and folded piece of flesh and cartilage from which earrings are hung, and more important, the external *auditory canal,* a tunnel leading from the ear's opening to the *tympanic membrane,* or *eardrum.*

The Middle Ear

The *middle ear* includes the inner surface of the eardrum and the three tiny, bony *ossicles,* named long ago for their shape (apparently by some blacksmithing anatomist), *the hammer, the anvil,* and *the stirrup;* or in Latin: *the malleus, the incus,* and *the stapes.* These bones respond to the

Ear

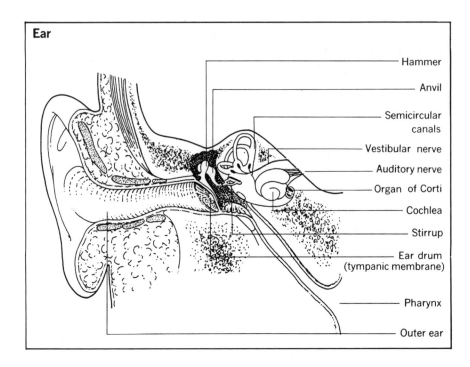

- Hammer
- Anvil
- Semicircular canals
- Vestibular nerve
- Auditory nerve
- Organ of Corti
- Cochlea
- Stirrup
- Ear drum (tympanic membrane)
- Pharynx
- Outer ear

vibrations in the air that are the basis of sound, vibrate themselves, and transmit their vibrations to the inner ear, where the sense receptors for hearing are located, and the *auditory* (or *acoustic*) *nerve* to the brain begins.

The middle ear is connected to the back of the throat (pharynx) by the Eustachian tube. This tunnel between throat and middle ear makes the pres-sure on the inside of the eardrum, via the mouth, the same as the pressure of the atmosphere on the outside of the eardrum. (Thus yawning helps to equalize pressure.) Without it, or if the Eustachian tube becomes clog-ged, the taut membrane of the ear-drum would always be in imminent danger of bursting.

The Inner Ear

The chambers of the *inner ear* are completely filled with fluid, which is jostled by the ossicles "knocking" on a thin membrane called the oval win-dow, separating the middle from the inner ear. Another flexible mem-brane, the round window, serves to restrict the motion of the inner ear fluid when the movement is too stormy.

Organ of Hearing

Within the inner ear is a bony struc-ture coiled like a snail shell about the size of a pea. This is the *cochlea,* the actual Latin word for snail or snail shell. Following the internal spiral of the cochlea is the *organ of Corti,* the true sense receptors for hearing.

The organ of Corti is made up of thousands of specialized nerve endings that are the individual sense receptors for sound. These are in the form of tiny hairs projecting up from the internal membrane lining the cochlea; they wave like stalks of underwater plants in response to the oscillating currents of the inner ear fluid. There are some 20,000 of these hairs within the cochlea, responsive to almost as many degrees of movement of the fluid. These thousands of nerve endings merge at the core of the cochlea and exit from its floor as the nerve bundle of the *auditory nerve.*

Organ of Balance

The organ of balance, or equilibrium, is also behind the oval window that marks the beginning of the inner ear. The principal structure consists of

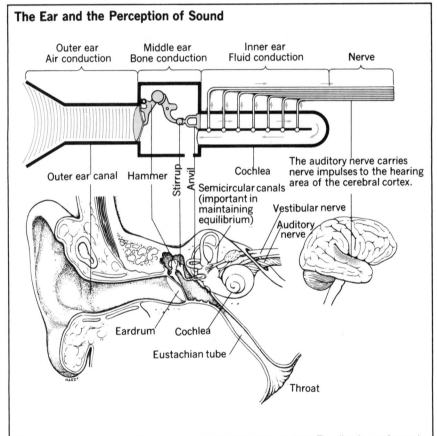

The Ear and the Perception of Sound

Outer ear
Air conduction

Middle ear
Bone conduction

Inner ear
Fluid conduction

Nerve

Outer ear canal   Hammer   Stirrup   Anvil   Cochlea

Semicircular canals (important in maintaining equilibrium)

Vestibular nerve

Auditory nerve

The auditory nerve carries nerve impulses to the hearing area of the cerebral cortex.

Eardrum   Cochlea

Eustachian tube

Throat

The sound waves are funneled through the outer ear canal to the eardrum. The vibrating eardrum sets into motion the three bones of the middle ear. The bones terminate in an opening in the fluid-filled cochlea. The vibrating bones set the fluid in motion. This stimulates nerve endings, which unite to become the auditory nerve. The nerve impulses are carried to the hearing area in the cerebral cortex.

three fluid-filled *semicircular canals* arranged, like the wheels of a gyroscope spinning on a perfectly flat plane or surface, at right angles to each other. When we are in a normal, upright position, the fluid in the canals is also in its normal resting state. But when we begin to tilt or turn or wobble, the fluid runs one way or another in one or more of the canals. This fluid movement is picked up by crested, hairlike nerve endings lining the inside of the canals and relayed as nerve impulses along the *vestibular nerve* to the brain. Then, the brain sends messages to the muscles that can restore our equilibrium.

The term *labyrinth* is sometimes used to refer collectively to the cochlea, semicircular canals and associated structures of the inner ear. The space or cavity within the labyrinth is called the *vestibule,* which gives its name to the vestibular nerve.

How We Hear

Just as our eye has certain special equipment—its focusing apparatus—to prepare light for the retina, so our ear has special equipment to prepare vibrations for reception by the organ of Corti.

This equipment consists of structures that amplify the vibrations reaching the ear, or, more rarely, damping (decreasing) the vibrations caused by very loud or very close occurrences.

Sound waves are really vibrations in the air that reach the eardrum at the narrow end of the funnel-shaped auditory canal. These vibrations set the membrane of the eardrum vibrating ever so slightly. Behind the eardrum, the first ossicle encountered is the hammer, which is attached to the eardrum by a projection descriptively called the hammer-handle.

From the eardrum, vibrations travel up the handle and set the hammer vibrating. The hammer, in turn, sets the anvil vibrating; and the anvil, the stirrup. The stirrup then knocks like an impatient caller on the oval window of the inner ear, and the then vibrating oval window stirs the fluids within the cochlea. This chain of

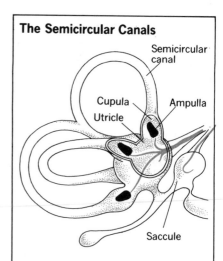

The Semicircular Canals

Semicircular canal

Cupula

Ampulla

Utricle

Saccule

The semicircular canals are swollen at their bases into three ampullae in which receptors are located. When the head moves or accelerates, the fluid within the canals (endolymph), tends to move slower than the head, and the cupula is displaced. This is communicated to the hairlike nerve receptors. Soon the endolymph catches up to the head movement and the cupula returns to its normal position. When movement stops, the endolymph continues to move, the cupula is again displaced, and the nerve receptors are activated until the endolymph ceases to move.

events can account for a tremendous amplification of vibrations—so that we are literally able to "hear a pin drop."

Tiny muscles in the middle ear relax or tighten the eardrum and adjust to changing volumes of sound. For example, a muscle connecting the stirrup and the eardrum relaxes when the stirrup is vibrating violently in the presence of very loud noises. A lax eardrum is less likely to rupture and transmits fewer vibrations to the delicate mechanisms of the middle and inner ear than a taut one. Thus we have to some degree built-in, automatic protection against the assaults of noise pollution—but not nearly enough, according to physicians who are convinced that more and more cases of deafness are caused by the incessant battering of the modern world against our eardrums. Human eardrums are not made to withstand the sound of jet planes taking off, for example.

The Nose and Tongue

The sense receptors on the tongue and within the nasal cavity work very closely together to give us our sense of taste. These five kinds of receptors—the olfactory cell in the nose and the four special cells or taste buds on the tongue for discriminating salty, sweet, sour, and bitter tastes—also have a functional similarity. All are chemical detectors, and all require moisture in order to function. In the nose, airborne substances must first be moistened by mucus (from the olfactory glands) before they can stimulate olfactory cells. In the mouth, the saliva does the wetting.

The general number and distribution of the four types of taste receptors are described earlier in this chapter under "The Digestive System and the Liver." These nerve endings, numbering in the hundreds of thousands, merge into two nerve bundles traveling away from the tongue to the brain's "taste center." The receptors toward the rear of the tongue collect into the *glossopharyngeal nerve;* those at the front and middle are directed along the *lingual nerve.*

Our smell receptors are clustered in an area about a half-inch wide on ceiling of the nasal cavity. This is called, appropriately enough, the smell patch. The nerve endings pass upward through the sievelike *ethmoid bone,* separating the nasal cavity from the brain, and connect to the olfactory bulb, which is the "nose end" of the *olfactory nerve.* At the other end of the olfactory nerve is the "nose brain" or *rhinencephalon*—a tiny part of the cerebrum in man, but quite large in dogs and other mammals whose sense of smell is keener than man's.

Although man's sense of smell is probably his least used sense, it still has a quite remarkable sensitivity. With it we can detect some chemicals

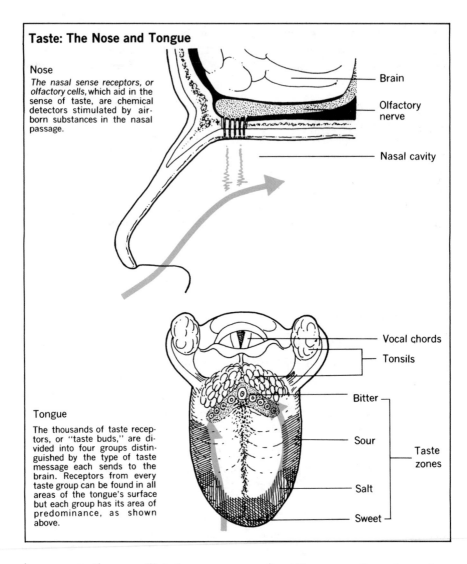

Taste: The Nose and Tongue

Nose
The nasal sense receptors, or olfactory cells, which aid in the sense of taste, are chemical detectors stimulated by air-born substances in the nasal passage.

Brain

Olfactory nerve

Nasal cavity

Vocal chords

Tonsils

Bitter

Tongue
The thousands of taste receptors, or "taste buds," are divided into four groups distinguished by the type of taste message each sends to the brain. Receptors from every taste group can be found in all areas of the tongue's surface but each group has its area of predominance, as shown above.

Sour

Taste zones

Salt

Sweet

in concentrations as diluted as one part in 30 billion—for example, the active ingredient in skunk spray. Also, man's ability to smell smoke and to detect gas leaks and other warning scents has prevented many a tragedy.

Skin

The sensations stimulated by the various types of sense receptors in the skin are described at the outset of this section. It is worth noting, however, at the end of our tour of the sense organs that the senses associated with the skin are really in a class by themselves. Perhaps the most telling indication of their unique place in the hierarchy of senses is the fact that practically our entire central nervous system is given over to handling the impulses transmitted by these receptors. See also Ch. 16, *Diseases of the Eye and Ear.*

The Urinogenital System and the Kidneys

In large part our good health depends on the quality of the body's internal environment. There is a kind of ecological principle at work within us—if one chain threatens to break, one system becomes polluted, one balance is tilted, then the whole environment is in imminent danger of collapsing. The major responsibility for keeping our internal environment clean and unclogged lies with our two kidneys. They are the filters and purifiers of body fluids: the body's pollution-control stations, its recycling plants, and its waste-disposal units.

The Anatomy of the Kidney

The cortex is the darker, outer part of the kidney. The medulla, the inner part, includes the renal pyramids and the straight tubules associated with them.

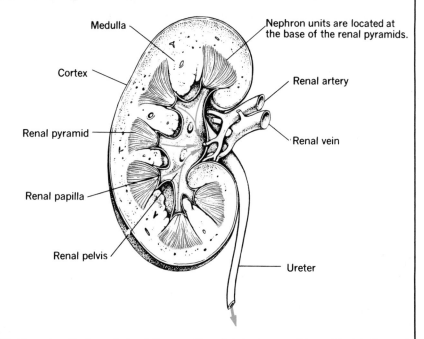

Medulla

Cortex

Renal pyramid

Renal papilla

Renal pelvis

Nephron units are located at the base of the renal pyramids.

Renal artery

Renal vein

Ureter

Urine is produced in the nephrons of the pyramids and drains by way of the papillae into the renal pelvis, which empties into the ureter. The ureter carries the urine to the bladder.

The Kidneys

The kidneys are located just behind our abdominal cavity on either side of the spinal cord, their tops usually tucked just under the bottommost rib. Each of our kidneys is four to five inches long and weighs about half a pound. The right kidney is normally placed a bit below the left, to accommodate the bulky liver lying also on the right side above it. Neither kidney is fixed rigidly; both can shift position slightly. Lying outside the muscular sheath of the abdonimal cavity, the kidneys are more vulnerable than most internal organs to outside blows, but good protection against all but the severest jolts is afforded by surrounding fatty cushions, the big back muscles, and the bone and musculature associated with the spinal column.

As it has with the lungs, the liver, and most other vital organs, nature has supplied us with a large reserve capacity of kidney tissue—a life-giving overabundance in the event of kidney disease or injury. Indeed, normal function of only one-half of one kidney can sustain a person's life.

The kidney's task of purifying our internal environment—that is, our circulating blood—is really a double task. Each kidney must purify the blood that passes through it, sending back into circulation only "clean blood"; and it must dispose of the impurities it has taken from the blood. The latter is accomplished by the urine draining down a tube, or *ureter,* leading from each of the two kidneys to one common urinary *bladder.* Urine is discharged from the bladder down another tube called the *urethra* to the external opening for urination.

How the Kidneys Process Body Fluids

Blood is brought to the kidney by a renal artery, is treated in the kidney's unique microscopic structures, and exists via the renal vein. (*Renal* means associated with the kidneys.)

The sheer volume of blood processed by both our kidneys is prodigious: between 400 and 500 gallons are processed every day.

Internal Structure

Within each kidney are over a million microscopic units called *nephrons.* The nephron is the basic functional unit of the kidney—a little kidney in itself—and is really a superbly engineered and coordinated arrangement of many smaller structures, all working together.

Blood arriving at the kidney from the renal artery is quickly channeled into finer and finer vessels, until finally it flows into a kind of cat's cradle or "ball of wool" structure called a *glomerulus* (composed of intertwining, microscopic vessels called glomerular capillaries). The entire structure of the nephron is built around the microscopic glomerulus (Latin, "tiny

The Nephron

Bowman's capsule

Proximal convoluted tubule

Glomerulus

Renal artery

Renal vein

Distal convoluted tubule

Capillary network

Descending limb

Ascending limb

Collecting tubule

Loop of Henle

The nephron is a microscopic unit that filters out certain products from the blood. Useful products are reabsorbed by the capillary network. The waste product (urine) is carried to the collecting tubule and emptied into the renal pelvis.

ball"). Surrounding the glomerulus, like a hand lightly cupping a ball of wool, is another structure called *Bowman's capsule*. Fluid and dissolved materials filter out of the blood from the glomerular capillaries through the membranes into Bowman's capsule.

Substances in Bowman's Capsule

The fluids and dissolved materials filtering into Bowman's capsule are by no means all wastes and impurities. In fact, some of the substances must soon be reclaimed. Among the waste substances captured by Bowman's capsule and destined for excretion in urine are various nitrogen salts and other waste products of cellular metabolism, as well as actual or potential poisons that have entered or accumulated in the bloodstream. Non-waste substances include needed sugars and salts, and water.

Reclaiming Essential Substances

Before we leave the glomerulus altogether behind, it should be noted that like any capillary bed, this small ball of blood vessels has not only an inflow from the renal artery but also outflow vessels leading eventually back to the renal vein.

From the cupped lips of Bowman's capsule, fluid and dissolved substances from the blood trickle into a single tube called a kidney *tubule*. The outflow vessels from the glomerulus wind closely over and around the tubule, forming a capillary network around it. By this means the non-waste substances are reclaimed and returned to refresh the blood moving away from the nephron.

The tubule itself makes many twists and turns—including one hairpin turn so stunning that it has its own medical name—*Henle's loop*. So much twisting and turning gives the tubule a great deal more surface area than a simple, straight tube would have within the same space, thus increasing the amount of water and dissolved substances that can be recaptured by the encircling capillaries.

If there were no recapturing system in the kidneys, death would probably result from dehydration. Even if that could be avoided, the loss of essential salts and other substances would prove fatal in a short time.

The arithmetic of the situation goes something like this: every day, an estimated 42 gallons of fluid filter out of the glomeruli and into the two kidneys' approximately two and a half million tubules. Dissolved in this 42 gallons—representing about three times the body's weight—are about two-and-a-half pounds of common salt, just one of the many substances in the fluid that our body needs in sufficient amounts. The loss of either water or common salt at a rapid rate would prove fatal in a matter of hours.

But so efficient is the tubule-capillary recapturing system that only an average of less than two quarts of fluid, containing just one-third ounce of salt, pass daily out of the kidneys into the ureter and are excreted as urine. In other words, over 99 percent of both the water and common salt removed from the blood at Bowman's capsules is returned to the blood.

The Kidneys and Blood Pressure

A surprising insight into the critical role played by our kidneys in almost every body function is provided by the relation of blood pressure to kidney function. The blood in the glomerular capillaries must be at higher pressure than the fluid around them, so that the fluid and its dissolved substances can push through the capillary membranes toward Bowman's capsule. If blood pressure in the body falls too low (severe *hypotension*) the formation of urine ceases.

On the other hand, if a portion of the kidney is suffering from anemia due to some disorder, kidney cells secrete *pressor hormones,* which serve to elevate the blood pressure. Thus high blood pressure (*hypertension*) may be a sign of kidney disorder.

The Urinary Tract

From the ends of the million or so tubules in each kidney, urine drains into larger and larger collecting basins (called *calyces,* singular *calyx*) which drain in turn into the kidney's master urine reservoir, the *kidney pelvis.* Then, drop by drop, urine slides down each ureter to the urinary bladder.

Urine is held in the bladder by the contraction of two muscle rings, or *sphincters,* one located just inside the bladder before it meets the urethra, and the other encircling the urethra itself. When about a half-pint has accumulated, nerves convey the urge to urinate to the brain, and the person voluntarily causes the sphincters to relax, emptying the bladder. (In exceptional circumstances, the elastic-walled bladder can hold two or three quarts of urine.) Up to the point where the bladder drains, the male and female urinary tracts are very similar, but after the bladder, any similarity stops.

Female Urethra

The female's urethra, normally about one and a half inches long, is not much more than a short channel by which urine is eliminated from the bladder. Its very shortness often gives it an undesired significance, because it

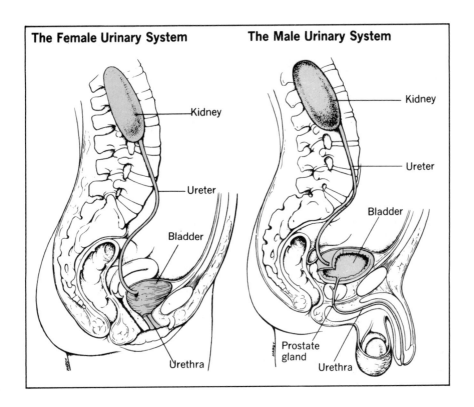

The Female Urinary System

Kidney

Ureter

Bladder

Urethra

The Male Urinary System

Kidney

Ureter

Bladder

Prostate gland

Urethra

represents an easy upward invasion route for bacteria and other infection-causing microbes from the outside. Acute and painful inflammations of the urethra (*urethritis*) and bladder (*cystitis*) are thus common in women. These lower urinary tract infections, however, can usually be halted before spreading further up the urinary tract by the administration of any of several antimicrobial drugs. See Ch. 25, *Women's Health* for more information on these disorders.

Male Urethra

In contrast to the female, the male's urethra is involved with reproductive functions. So closely connected are the male's lower urinary tract and genital organs that his urethra (from bladder to the outside) is properly called the urinogenital (or genitourinary) tract. This is the reason why the medical specialty known as *urology* deals with both the urinary and genital apparatus of men; but with only the urinary tract of women. The urologist's specialty does not extend to the female genital and childbearing organs, which are the concern of the *gynecologist* and *obstetrician*.

However, all the distinctly male sex glands and organs are linked more or less directly into the eight- or nine-inch length of the male urethra.

The Genitals

The Female Reproductive System

As indicated above, the urinary and genital systems of women are dealt with by two different medical specialties. For this reason, the female genitals are discussed elsewhere. For a description and illustration of the female reproductive system, see Ch. 3, *The Teens*. For a description of infections of the female reproductive tract, see Ch. 25, *Women's Health*

The Male Reproductive System

From its emergence below the bladder, the male urethra serves as a conduit for all the male sexual secretions.

Prostate Gland

Directly below the bladder outlet, the *prostate gland* completely enwraps the urethra. The prostate secretes substances into the urethra through ejaculatory ducts; these substances are essential in keeping alive the spermatozoa that arrive from their manufacturing sites in the *testicles* (or *testes*).

Testicles

The two testicles hang down within a wrinkled bag of skin called the *scrotum*. Although the vulnerable position of the testicles remains something of an evolutionary mystery, one clue is that the optimum production of spermatozoa takes place at a temperature some degrees lower than the normal internal body temperature.

Spermatozoa produced in the testicles travel upward toward the urethra through a seminal duct or tube called the *vas deferens* (one from each testicle). (These are the ducts, incidentally, that are tied and cut in the male sterilization procedure known as a vasectomy.) The sperm cells are then stored, until ejaculation, in little reservoirs called *seminal vesicles* which are situated on either side of the urethra in the area just above the prostate gland.

The portion of the male urethra from the bladder to where it emerges from the encircling prostate, having received the emission of both the prostate and the testicles, is called the prostatic or posterior urethra. The remainder, mainly consisting of the conduit running down the middle of the shaft of the penis, ending in the external opening called the *meatus,* is known as the anterior urethra. See also Ch. 17, *Diseases of the Urinogenital System.*

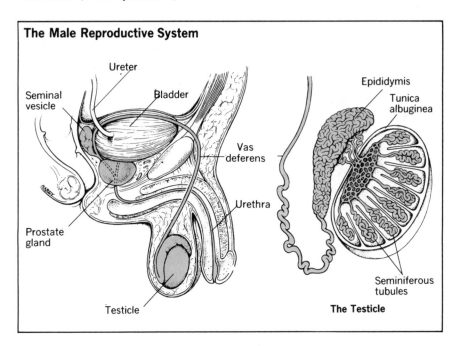

The Male Reproductive System

Ureter

Seminal vesicle

Bladder

Epididymis

Tunica albuginea

Vas deferens

Urethra

Prostate gland

Testicle

Seminiferous tubules

The Testicle

2

The First Dozen Years

Birth, Infancy, and Maturation

Before the Baby Arrives

When a husband and wife decide to have a baby they should both undergo complete physical examinations. This will make it possible to detect and treat abnormalities like diabetes and anemia that might affect the future pregnancy. A pregnant woman should have periodic checkups so that her physician can observe both her progress and that of the growing fetus. Such observation will help to assure a pregnancy and delivery that are free from troublesome complications.

What the Newborn Baby Looks Like

At birth the baby's skin is wrinkled or scaly, and may be covered by a cheesy substance called *vernix caseosa*. During the first two weeks the skin will become quite dry to the touch. The skin of white newborns is red, and sometimes turns yellow during the first few days. Black newborns often are not as dark as they might be later. Their skin becomes just as yellow as that of white babies, but the change is more difficult to observe.

The newborn's head is large in proportion to the rest of its body. The genitals too may seem large, especially in girls. Newborn girls may have swollen genitalia that is a result of *edema* (fluid in the tissues, causing puffiness), but the swelling is usually present for only a few days after birth.

The eyes, slate blue in color, can open and react to light, but are unable to focus. Noises produce a *startle re-*

Newborn Infant

Skull
Because the skull bones are not completely closed at birth, it is possible to see and feel the two most obvious "soft spots" on a baby's head. One is above the brow and the other in back, close to the crown. These *fontanels* close up in the first weeks of life.

Eyes
The eyes appear dark blue and unfocused, with slightly puffy eyelids. Initially, before there is greater muscle control, a baby's eyes may sometimes be turned in a crossed or wall-eyed position.

Skin
The skin is dry and wrinkled especially during the first two weeks of life and some *vernix caseosa* (white prenatal covering) remains. Veins may be visible and downy bodily hair is not uncommon. The bodies of fair skinned babies may temporarily be very ruddy.

Face
The face of the newborn is generally round and pudgy without much definition. Usually it will have a broad, flat nose with very little bridge, a receding chin, and an undersized lower jaw.

Head
The head of a newborn baby normally looks too big for its body. It may appear elongated or lopsided—a temporary condition caused by the physical pressure before birth or during the birth process.

Torso
The torso of a newborn is somewhat startling with its short neck, small sloping shoulders, a round protruding abdomen, and narrow pelvis and hips. The umbilical stump will drop off eventually to form the navel.

Hand
The hands show tissue-paper thin nails on tiny fingers characteristically curled into fists. Finely lined palms and deep bracelet creases at the wrists are also common.

Feet
The feet, though they look quite complete, contain only one real bone at birth, located at the heel. What will later form into bone is now only cartilage. The skin on a baby's feet may be loose and finely lined.

Size
The average newborn is very tiny, weighing in at only six to eight pounds. Its measure from top to toe is usually anywhere from 18 inches to 21 inches.

Legs
The legs are usually drawn up in the prebirth position against the abdomen with knees slightly bent. Extended, the legs measure on the short side compared to the arms and are somewhat bowed.

Genitals
The genitals of both sexes will seem too large in proportion to other parts of the body, particularly in comparison to scale in the adult.

sponse, a complex involuntary reaction marked by a sudden, jerky, arm and leg movement. The newborn cries a great deal, sucks, and may sneeze.

The infant's stomach may look rather large and protuberant, and, of course, it has the stump of the umbilical cord dangling from it. The umbilical cord has been cut and tied near the navel, and will eventually fall off.

If you feel the front and back of the baby's head, you will notice one or two soft spots, called the *anterior* and *posterior fontanelles*. The posterior fontanelle usually closes at the baby's second month of life, and the anterior at 18 months or earlier.

You also may feel many different ridges in the baby's head. These are the borders of the different skull bones, which fuse as the baby gets older. They are present so that the skull can grow as the baby's brain and head continue to grow.

Soon after birth, you may detect a swelling on the baby's head just under the scalp. This is called *caput succedaneum.* It is nothing to worry about, as it dissolves a day or two after birth. Occasionally, another swelling known as *cephalhematoma* may also be present. This, too, disappears, within a few weeks.

The baby's weight will, of course, vary. Most full-term babies weigh between six and eight pounds. Babies of diabetic mothers are often heavier, and may weigh up to twelve pounds.

Some Advice to New Mothers

Unless the new father and mother are really prepared to change some of the conditioned patterns of their relationship, both can be in for a very difficult time. The father suddenly finds himself taking second place in his wife's attentions and affection. The new mother is tired physically and mentally. In-laws and other relatives may infringe on the couple's privacy and interfere with their right to make their own decisions. The new mother may find it hard to reconcile her maternal instinct with her desires as a woman and wife.

All of these problems can be minimized if the mother follows a few commonsense guidelines:

• The new baby is a shared responsibility. Do not shut your husband out of the experience of parenthood. Let him learn to feed the baby, diaper her, hold her, get acquainted with her. Make your husband feel just as important to the baby as you are, and just as important to you as he was before the baby was born.

• Arrange for some kind of assistance in your home, and don't wait until the day you bring the baby home to do it. Plan ahead. You will be physically and emotionally tired after childbirth, no matter how marvelous you may feel when you leave the hospital. During the hospital stay the baby was cared for by a trained staff. At home the burden will fall mainly on you, unless you take steps to get help. If you cannot get your mother or another relative to stay with you, engage a housekeeper or some other trained person. The investment will pay off for you, the baby, and your husband.

- If it is at all possible, arrange to have a separate area for the baby. It is best for a baby not to be kept in the parents' room. Parents must have privacy. If you do not have a bedroom for the baby, section off some spot where you can put a crib and a dressing table to hold the supplies you will need when you feed, change, bathe, and dress her.

- Don't make the baby the focus of attention 24 hours a day. If she fidgets and fusses at times, try not to get nervous. Don't run to her at every whimper so long as you know she has been fed, is dry, and nothing is really wrong. Relax. The baby will be very sensitive to your emotional responses, particularly when you hold her. Through your physical contact you will develop a kind of communication with your baby which she will sense when you pick her up or feed her.

- As important as it is for you and your husband to avoid overhandling the baby, it is more important that family and friends be made to follow a "hands off" policy except at your discretion. A new baby should not be subjected to excessive stimulation. For example, you may notice that if you pick her up and put her back in her crib, and then let someone else hold her a few minutes later, the baby may cry. If you slam a door, the baby's body reacts in the startle reflex, the involuntary reaction previously described. A baby needs a quiet, organized home, free from the kind of upsetting distraction that comes from being surrounded and fussed over by too many people. You and your husband must decide when you want the baby to have visitors and how those visitors are to behave. You must do this even if it causes hurt feelings among your friends and relatives. When the baby is a little older there will be time enough for friends and relatives to admire and play with her.

Feeding the Baby

One of the first questions a mother-to-be must ask herself is how she will feed her baby.

Breast-feeding is certainly the simplest method, and many women believe that a both mother and child get more emotional satisfaction from it than from bottle-feeding. It is also, obviously, less expensive.

Breast-Feeding

Almost any healthy woman who wants to breast-feed her baby can do so. All she needs is the desire and motivation. No special preparation is necessary except, perhaps, some stimulation of the breasts, as prescribed by her physician during pregnancy.

On the other hand, a variety of different factors might necessitate a change from breast to bottle-feeding. Although breast-feeding may be discontinued at any time, some mothers may feel a sense of failure or frustration at being unable to continue having the intimate relationship that so many other mothers enjoy. No harm will come to the baby by being switched to a formula. Once started on a formula, however, it may be difficult to go back to breast-feeding on a regular basis. For a while, at least, the mother will have to stimulate her breasts artificially to increase their milk-producing capacity.

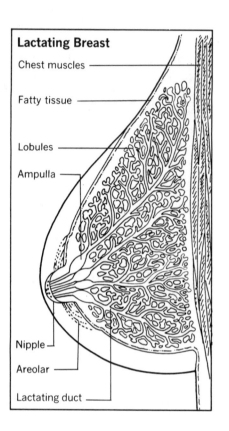

Lactating Breast

Chest muscles

Fatty tissue

Lobules

Ampulla

Nipple

Areolar

Lactating duct

The First Few Days

When a mother first starts to breast-feed, she may be worried that she won't have sufficient milk for the baby. Her breasts are just beginning to fill up with a creamy, yellowish substance called *colostrum*. Transitional and then regular breast milk will not come in for three to five days or longer. Colostrum contains more protein and less fat than breast milk. Secretions of colostrum are small, but during this time the baby does not need very much fluid, and the colostrum will give her adequate nutrition.

Actually, it is important that the milk does not fill the breasts right away because engorgement would be so severe that the baby would not be able to suck well or strongly enough to empty them. During engorgement, the mother's breasts feel extremely tender and full. A good nursing brassiere will lift and support the breasts and alleviate the tender sensation during the one-or-two-day period of the engorgement.

Some Advice to Nursing Mothers

If you do not have enough milk for the first few days, don't worry about it. Let the baby suck on your nipples for three, five, or even ten minutes. Don't keep her on your breasts for twenty or thirty minutes right from the beginning. Start with three minutes the first day, five minutes the second, and so on until you work up to fifteen or twenty minutes. In this way you will toughen your nipples so that your breasts will become accustomed to the baby's sucking. A bland cream may be used to massage the nipple area, particularly if the nipples become sore or cracked.

Be sure to use both breasts. By emptying the breasts, milk production is stimulated; thus an adequate milk supply is dependent upon using both breasts. To avoid any soreness or tenderness, use one breast longer than the other during each nursing period.

Let us assume, for example, that at the first feeding of the day you nurse the baby on the left breast for a long period, then on the right for a short period. During the next feeding the right breast will become the first one on which the baby nurses (for the long period), and the left will be nursed second (for the short period). After a few weeks you should be nursing the baby on the first breast for twenty minutes and on the other for ten minutes.

The Feeding Schedule

Depending on how often the baby wants to feed, you will be wise to adhere to a modified demand schedule. Don't watch the clock and feed the baby every four hours on the dot. You might feed at approximately every fourth hour, which means that you could start a second feeding early—at a three-hour interval—or late—at a five-hour interval. And, needless to say, never wake your baby up at night. She will awaken you.

Bottle-feeding

New parents have a choice between prepackaged formulas and the homemade variety. Either provides the same basic nutritional requirements.

The basic homemade formula for newborns consists of evaporated milk, water, and sugar or one of the sugar derivatives. Twice as much water as evaporated milk is used with one to two tablespoons of sweetening. A similar formula can be made with whole milk in somewhat different proportions. As the baby gets older, the formula will be changed from time to time by your physician.

If one formula does not agree with the baby, it will not help to put her on a similar formula; its ingredients are likely to be virtually the same. You must switch to a radically different formula, such as one containing no milk at all or no carbohydrates. It is up to your physician to advise you which modified formula to try.

As to how much formula should be given at each feeding, let the baby decide. If she is satisfied with two-and-a-half ounces, she is probably getting enough. If she wants up to four-and-a-half ounces, give it to her. The amount is not important as long as your physician feels the baby is in good health.

A final thing to remember about feeding is this: whether you use breast or bottle, you must give your baby the love, warmth, and body contact that she needs. As you feed her, you are not only providing nutritional nourishment for her growing body but giving her emotional and mental food for her developing personality.

The First Six Months

It is extremely important that the baby have regular health supervision. Your baby's physician—whether pediatrician or general practitioner—will check the baby's height and weight on each visit, and make certain she is growing and gaining at a satisfactory rate. Often, the first sign of illness in a baby is a change in her height and weight pattern.

Although no two children develop at the same rate, it is possible to make certain generalizations about their development. See the charts in this chapter showing the growth rates for boys and girls.

By two months a baby often holds her head up when she lies on her stomach or when she is being held up. She recognizes large objects, and she knows her bottle or feeding position. She can probably smile.

Sometime during the second or third month, your physician will start a series of injections against diphtheria, whooping cough, and tetanus (called *DTP*), as well as oral immunizing agents against polio—the *Sabin vaccine*. See the chart in the "Alphabetic Guide to Child Care" under "Immunization" later in this chapter.

The Three-Month Mark

By three months most babies are eating some solids specially processed for babies—fruits, cereals, vegetables, meats—in addition to having formula. They may, of course, still be entirely on breast milk. Your physician will also suggest the use of vitamin supplements, in the form of drops, which can be added to the baby's milk or solid food. All babies need vitamins A, C, and D. Occasionally, vitamin B is also prescribed. If fluorides are not present in your drinking water, they are often added to the baby's vitamins to retard tooth decay.

At Four Months

By four months the baby will look at moving objects. Do not be surprised if her eyes cross. This is a normal condition during early infancy, and may even persist for a year.

At about this time, the baby may also learn to turn over from front to back—an important milestone. Some babies may have developed bald or flat places on the back of the head from lying more or less in one position. At about this time the condition should begin to disappear.

The Second Six Months

At six months most babies smile when they are brought to the physician's office. At one year of age a visit to the physician is more likely to produce tears and screams. The friendly, sociable attitude of the six-month-old gives way to one in which strangers are shunned or mistrusted, and everyone other than mother may qualify as a stranger.

By the sixth month the baby may roll over when placed on her back. She may learn to crawl, sit, pull herself up, and even stand. By a year she may start to walk, although walking unaided does not often occur so soon.

At this stage the baby is full of life and activity. She won't lie still when you change her diaper, and often needs distraction. She cries if you put her down or leave her alone. Unless you are firm and resist running to her first whimper, you may set the stage for spoiling her as she gets older. Of course, if she continues to cry for any considerable length of time—not more than half an hour—make sure there is nothing wrong with her besides her displeasure at your not appearing like a genie because she screams or fusses.

Other Changes

Other changes occur at this age. Where before she had been a good sleeper, she may now not want to go to sleep or she may awaken at night. Let her know that you are nearby, but don't make a habit of playing with her in the middle of the night—not if you value your sleep.

If you should notice, as many parents do at about this time, that your baby seems to be left-handed, do not try to make her right-handed. Each of us inherits a preference for one hand or the other, and it is harmful to try to change it. In any case, you are not likely to know for sure which hand your child prefers until the second year of her life.

In this second six-month period, the baby will probably take some of her milk from a cup. Don't be surprised if she takes juices out of a cup but insists on taking milk from a bottle. If she tries to hold the bottle or cup herself, let her. Of course, it may be wise to keep a mop handy at first, but after few months her skills will improve. In any case, nonbreakable cups are recommended.

Diet and Teeth

The baby's diet is soon expanded to include pureed baby foods. You might even want to try the somewhat lumpier junior foods; as more of her teeth erupt, the baby will enjoy lumpier food more and more. Teething biscuits can be added to the diet, too. By the time she is one year old she will usually have six teeth (incisors), although, because no two children are alike, she may have none at all. By the end of the first year she will have lost some of her appetite, and her rapid weight gain will cease. This is entirely natural in a period when the outside world is taking more and more interest.

As she starts to move around she wants to investigate everything. Keep dangerous objects—detergents, poisons, and medicines, especially baby aspirin—out of her reach. Tell her "no" to emphasize the seriousness of certain prohibitions. She should understand what "no" means by the time she is one-year-old, and will also probably respond to other simple commands.

It is essential that your baby's health supervision be continued without interruption. During the second six months of life she will complete her protection against diphtheria, whooping cough, tetanus (DTP), and polio (Sabin), and be tested for exposure to tuberculosis (the tuberculin test).

Behavioral Development during Infancy

During a child's first year she needs a warm and loving emotional environment in the home. It is during this time that a child establishes what psychiatrists and psychologists call basic trust. That is, she learns to be a trusting individual who feels that her important needs—those of being cared for, fed, and comforted—will be met by other human beings, initially by her mother.

Emotional Needs

Such activities as holding and cuddling the infant, talking to her, and playing with her in an affectionate, relaxed way are important for her emotional growth. Experiments with animals have shown that if the infant animal does not get sufficient cuddling and physical contact from its mother during its early development, it is unable to perform adequately as an adult later in life. It has also been shown that infants growing up in an environment lacking warm, loving, close physical and emotional contact with a mother or a mother-substitute often fail to thrive and may even die.

Fondling and Sucking

During the first year, most of an infant's satisfactions and gratifications are through the skin's perception of being touched—through physical contact with her mother and other caring adults—and through the mouth, especially sucking. Infants have a great need to suck even when they are not hungry, and this sucking should be both allowed and encouraged.

Parents frequently worry that if they respond to a baby's crying by picking her up they will spoil her, and the baby will cry often in order to get attention. In general, it could be said that during its first year an infant cannot be spoiled. When an infant cries she usually does so because she is uncomfortable, hungry, sick, or needs some physical attention.

Social Responses

As she matures, one of a child's tasks is to begin to see herself as separate from the world around her. During early infancy, the infant does not see herself as an individual who is separate from her mother, from other adults, and from the rest of the world. But, gradually, some time within the first year of life, this feeling of separateness and individuality begins to emerge in the developing infant.

One of the important and gratifying events in the early months of a child's life is the smiling responses. For the first time the infant can respond in a social way to other human beings. It is often at this time that the infant's mother and father begin to think of her as a real person and an individual. Thus the smile could be considered one of the infant's first social communications.

Suspicion of Strangers

Somewhere around the age of eight months, an infant who has in the past without complaint allowed anyone to pick her up begins to distinguish her mother from other individuals. When picked up by another the infant usu-

ally cries, acts frightened, and, in general, looks unhappy. This response indicates that she can now tell her mother and other individuals apart—an important and normal step in an infant's development.

Fear of Separation

Some time later, usually around the age of one year, the infant begins to become fearful upon separation from her mother. When her mother walks out of the room or leaves the baby

with a sitter, the child may respond with crying, fear, and anger. This again indicates that the infant can now tell her mother from strangers and does not like being separated from her. Although the response is normal and usually subsides within three to four months, parents should learn to leave the child in the hands of a competent sitter, and walk out without guilt or anger. The child must learn that separations are temporary and that parents do return.

The Second Year: The Toddler Stage

It is during the second year of a child's life that he begins to develop independence and separateness from his mother. Beginning with his growing ability to walk, usually some time early in the second year (age 12 to 16 months), an infant starts to explore the world around him more actively. He experiments with greater and greater distances and increasing independence from his mother.

Toward the end of the second year, children frequently become quite independent, trying to do many things for themselves, and resenting their parents or other well-meaning adults doing things for them. Even if the child is not yet capable of performing the tasks he attempts, he should be encouraged in these early moves toward independence. It is also during the second year that speech begins to develop, with the child's first words usually being "ma ma," "da da," "milk," and the ever-present "no."

Developing Relationships with Mother and Father

It is in this phase of the child's life that he develops a real relationship with his mother. In most homes, mother is the loving, warm, secure comforter in his life, the giver of rewards and disciplinarian of his activities, the center of his life. During this period it is imperative that the child's father spend as much time with his son or daughter as possible, so that the child begins to recognize the difference between his relationship to his mother and father.

In some cases the father, because of the demands of business, may find it impossible to spend enough time with his family. This is an unfortunate fact, but one that can be dealt with positively, because it is the quality of the time a father spends with his child rather than the quantity that is most important.

Testing Himself and the World around Him

The toddler is insatiably curious. He wants to explore and investigate everything. Take him outdoors as much as possible. Let him meet children of his own age so that he can play and learn the beginnings of social contact.

Physically, the toddler tries to do many things apart from walking, running, and climbing—including quite a few things that he can't do. He is easily frustrated and may have a short attention span. (Girls are better than boys in this respect.) Don't be impatient with your toddler; don't punish him for his clumsiness. He has a great many experiences ahead of him, and many skills to learn and develop.

You can now expect a negative reaction to your control. Obviously, you must set limits on your child's behavior—on what is acceptable and what is not, while still giving him the freedom to express his emotions and energies in vigorous physical play.

Make the rules easy to understand so that the child will not become confused about what is expected of him. And do not set up impossible standards.

The Third Year

The third year is extremely important. Children are usually toilet trained, show marked growth in their language abilities, and demonstrate a continuing and growing independence.

Negativism

From two to about three and perhaps beyond, a child is extremely negative. When asked to do anything or when asked about anything, he often responds by saying, "No, no, no, no, no." This saying of the word "no" on the slightest provocation indicates a child's wish to become separate and independent from parents, to do what he wants to do when he wants to do it, and to be free from the control of others.

The child's desire for independence can be respected and encouraged by parents within limits, but this does not mean that a parent must give in to a child on every issue. A parent should try to determine what is really important and not make an issue over petty matters that can best be handled with relaxed good humor.

Language Development and Play

A rapid spurt in language development takes place at this time. A child may increase his vocabulary from about 50 words at the beginning of the third year to an almost countless vocabulary at the end of the third year. It is during this year, too, that children first show marked interest in imaginative play activities. Play, including making up stories, using toy trucks and cars, blocks, dolls, and toy furniture, is vital activity for children and should be encouraged by parents. It is through play that children express their feelings, often feelings that cannot be expressed in ordinary ways. The child also experiences what it feels like to be an adult by playing the role of physician, fire fighter, police officer, teacher, mother or father. In addition, during play children discharge tensions and learn to use their muscles and bodies.

Exploring the Body

From very early infancy, all children show a strong interest in their own and in other's bodies. During infancy this takes the form of playing with his own or his mother's body. A baby puts his fingers in his own mouth, in his mother's mouth, ears, eyes, and pats her on the tummy or on the breast. An infant also explores and touches his own body, including the genital region. This interest is normal and need not be discouraged.

Dental Development

The roots of all 20 primary teeth are complete at the child's third year of life. These teeth, which began erupting between 6 and 7 months of age, are called the *central incisors*. The primary teeth, the last of which usually fall out between the eleventh and thirteenth year, are smaller and whiter than the permanent teeth, of which there are 32. The first permanent tooth erupts between 7 and 8 years of age, while the last, the third molars, or *wisdom teeth*, erupt between the seventeenth and twenty-first year.

The Preschooler

This is the age when many children go to school for part of the day and begin learning how to get along with other children in play and in organized activities. They also begin to meet adults other than their parents.

First Separation from Mother

During the ages of three and four, the preschooler develops increasing interest in the world around him, in children his own age, and in himself. One of the key problems that the preschooler has to deal with is his impending separation from his mother when he becomes old enough to go to school. This can often be made less painful by arranging for the child to spend at first short and then increasingly longer periods of time away from his mother. By using baby-sitters both in the evening and during the day, by later having the child spend three or more half-days a week at a preschool, and lastly by enrolling him in kindergarten for either all day or half a day, five days a week, the mother can ease the child's adjustment to the world outside the home.

Although his first nearly full-time separation from mother is difficult for the child, it may be difficult for the mother as well. Mothers often feel that this initial separation from their child will eventually lead to their child's growing up and leaving home. Parents are often nostalgic and somewhat regretful about their children's first going off full time to school. The child's fearful anticipation of a strange situation can be eased by a mother's anticpating school with the child, talking with him about it and reassuring him regarding his fears of abandonment or separation.

Differences between Boys and Girls

A word might be mentioned here concerning differences between boys and girls. At the age of five most girls are ready to attend kindergarten; they can sit in their seats for long periods of time, pay attention to a teacher, and be interested in a task. Boys, because of their somewhat slower rate of maturity, are often less ready than girls for coping with a classroom situation at the age of five.

A child of five grows at a slower rate than in earlier years, but his body is nonetheless changing. The protruding abdomen and knock-knees of the toddler begin to disappear.

Television

Students of the medium suggest that television offers some worthwhile programs for the young child. At the same time, the experts warn that television watching can, over time, become addictive. A basically passive experience, it may also decrease the quality of family life and raise early obstacles to literacy and learning.

The parent's main task, insofar as television watching is concerned, is to find ways to use "the tube" to help the child develop. Parents can, for example, turn on programs that their child enjoys, that do not frighten or overexcite, and that the toddler can learn from. The television should not be used as an "electronic baby-sitter"; as much as possible, parents should watch when their child does. If a child is 18 months old or older the experts say parents should select the special programs they want their child to see. Television should not, finally, be used as a reward for being good. Such an approach can suggest the TV is more important than interesting games and other worthwhile activities.

Personal Hygiene

Good habits of cleanliness should be established. The child should know that hand-washing before meals is essential even when the hands look clean. He will learn this only if he sees parents do it. As he gets older he should select his own clean clothing and know that dirty clothing should be washed. A daily routine of washing or bathing should be set up, and the child should be encouraged to observe it.

School-Age Children:
Parent–Child Relationships

Beginning around the age of four, boys show a decided preference for their mothers. A boy may, for example, tell his mother that when he grows up he would like to marry her and kick father out of the house. At times he may even suggest that he would work to support her and that life would be much nicer if daddy were not around.

This interest in his mother is often expressed in what may be thought of as sexual ways. That is, the child of this age enjoys his mother's affection, including kissing, hugging, and close bodily contact. This wish to have mother all to himself and to have father out of the picture is called the *Oedipal complex* by psychiatrists and psychologists, after the ancient Greek tragedy, *Oedipus Rex*, in which Oedipus kills his father and marries a woman whom he later discovers to be his mother.

At about this same age, similar emotional developments take place in a girl. She will likely be somewhat seductive, coy, and coquettish with her father, and may talk about marrying father (or a man like father) and having mother out of the picture. This phase of emotional attachment between a girl and her father is called the *Electra complex* after the Greek play, *Electra*.

At these times, both the girl and the boy have a strong, although not always conscious, wish to displace the parent of the same sex and have the opposite-sexed parent all to themselves. Strong conflicts disturb children in this phase of development, for they also realize that they love and need the same-sexed parent to instruct them, to guide them, to provide for them, and to love them.

Identification

Both males and females eventually resolve these conflicts by abandoning their so-called sexual attachment to the opposite-sexed parent, forming a closer attachment to the same-sexed parent and trying to be like that parent. This is not a conscious decision, but one that a child makes without realizing it. This process of *identification* with the parent of the same sex starts very early, perhaps as early as the second year, and continues through adolescence, but it is especially noticable from five to ten.

Much of the energy that had previously been utilized in loving the parent of the opposite sex is now spent in loving the parent of the same sex. The boy follows father around, wants to do whatever he does, and holds as his greatest ambition to be exactly like father when he grows up—even to marrying a woman like the one father did.

The girl during this same period spends the energy that was once expended in love for her father in an attempt to learn to be like mother and perhaps eventually to marry a man resembling in some way her father.

This, however, does not mean that children do not continue to love the opposite-sexed parent; it means only that their primary attachment during these years is to the same-sexed parent. It is this process of identification with the same-sexed parent that facilitates the chief task of the school-age child from 5 or 6 to 11: the task of learning.

Six Years to Adolescence

The years from 6 to 11 have generally been regarded as quiet years as far as emotional development is concerned. Many of the tasks of earlier childhood have been completed, and the relatively stormy years of adolescence have not yet begun. A child's interests begin to turn more and more away from his family and to other children his own age, usually children of the same sex. At this stage, a child's interest in learning is broad and intense.

During this period children begin to be more and more individualistic. Some are solitary, others sociable; some are athletic, others not. One likes only other children, another prefers the company of adults. Some children have imaginary fears that disappear with age or when the fears are discussed with an adult who can explain how or why they originated.

Curiosity about Sex

The child's earlier curiosity about naked people may change to a concern about being clothed and being with people who are clothed. Questions about sex should be answered simply and truthfully.

Adolescence

Adolescence arrives anywhere from 9 to 14 years of age. A girl usually enters adolescence at 10, a boy at about 12.

In female children, there is growth of the breasts and nipples; the pelvis matures, and the external genitalia develop. Axillary (underarm) and pubic hair appear. On the average, girls have their first menstrual period around age thirteen, but it can occur between 10 and 16 years of age. Be sure to explain menstruation to your daughter before the beginning of adolescence.

In male children, the penis and testes develop. Facial, axillary, and pubic hair appear. The voice begins to deepen.

In both boys and girls, there is a rapid growth in height and weight which is related to sexual development. In general the average height of the adolescent is double what is was at age two. See Ch. 3, *The Teens*.

Alphabetic Guide to Child Care

The following Guide is an alpha-
betically arranged list of articles dealing with many of the problems that
confront parents. It includes articles
on physical disorders and ailments of
childhood; behavioral and emotional
problems; and on situations that occur
normally in the life of almost every
child which may cause tension or distress for parents, child, or both. It is
hoped that having information about
such normal developmental tensions
will help to minimize them.

**A note on the cross-refer-
ences:** Where a particular subject is
covered elsewhere within this Guide,
the reference is printed in small capital letters. (For example: See also
TONSILLITIS.) References to sections
in other chapters are printed in italic
type along with the chapter number.
(For example: See "Tonsils and Adenoids" in Ch. 20, *Surgery.*)

Accidents

All children have accidents and injure
themselves. Some do more frequently or more seriously than others. Parents should treat the ones
that are minor and seek immediate
medical attention for ones that are
major. The parents' response to an
injury can greatly determine the
child's response to it. Calm, responsible behavior will keep the child
calmer, even in a serious accident.

For minor injuries such as cuts and
bruises, treatment can be completed
at home. Cuts and scrapes should be
washed thoroughly with warm (not
hot) water and 3 percent hydrogen
peroxide. A skin disinfectant can be
applied, only if the cut is not deep. A
bandage should be applied during the
day to keep dirt out. The cut should
be left uncovered when possible,
though, to allow it to dry and heal.
Once the cut or scrape has scabbed
over, a bandage need not be used,
unless the scab is damaged or tears
off.

Sprains, unless very minor, are difficult to treat at home. It is not likely
that a parent can determine the damage to muscle tissue. Sprains can be
more painful than breaks and can inflict severe damage to ligaments and
tendons. X rays are usually required
to determine the damage done to the
limb.

Minor sprains that show slight
swelling or discoloration of the skin
can be treated by applying ice to the
injured area as soon as possible after
the accident. Keep the limb elevated
for ten to twenty minutes with the ice
pack on the injured joint. Have the
child avoid using the limb for a while.
Once movement can be made without
serious pain, warm water soaks or
baths will help reduce swelling. If pain
persists for more than 24 hours, consult a physician.

Bruises are caused by bleeding under the surface of the skin with no cut to the surface of the skin. Black eyes are bruises under the eye tissue. Minor bruises can be treated with cold water or ice packs to the area hurt. (Eyes should receive only water packs, ice against the eye is not recommended.) As the bruise fades a purple or yellow tint to the skin will remain for a few days or so as the body removes the last of the dried blood from the bruised tissue. Bruises can take several days to fade and heal. If it takes longer, a doctor should be consulted.

Head injuries in children are also common. A sharp blow to the head, or a fall, can trigger vomiting in a child. This, in itself, is not a danger signal. Danger signals are:

- Both pupils in eyes not dilated equally.
- Eyes do not move together when following something.
- Child sleeps immediately, or is hard to waken during a nap. Any child should be awakened every three hours to check, for 24 hours after the accident.
- More than one episode of vomiting.
- Any sign of mental disorder — speech or movement difficulties, dazed focus or attention, or any type of non-response.
- Increasing headache.
- Blood or fluid from nose or ears. If any one of these symptoms appear, contact the local hospital emergency facilities immediately.

For more information, see Ch. 35, *Medical Emergencies,* and "The Emergency Room" in Ch. 20, *Surgery.*

Adenoidectomy

See "Tonsils and Adenoids" in Ch. 20, *Surgery.*

Adenoids, Swollen

The adenoids are clusters of lymph tissue located behind the soft palate where the nasal passages join the throat. Along with the tonsils and lymphoid tissues elsewhere in the body, the adenoids are involved in warding off infection. When they themselves become inflamed because of bacterial or viral invasion, they become swollen. Swelling may also occur because of allergy.

Swollen adenoids may block the air passages sufficiently to cause mouth breathing, which in turn will not only give the child an "adenoidal" look, but will lead to more frequent upper respiratory infection, as well as to eventual malformation of the lower jawbone. Chronic swelling may also block the eustachian tube, causing pain in the ear and increasing the possibility of ear infection as well as of intermittent hearing loss. The child's physician can keep track of the severity of such symptoms during periodic checkups and can evaluate the need for surgery. See also TONSILLITIS. For a description of adenoidectomy, see "Tonsils and Adenoids" in Ch. 20, *Surgery.*

Adopted Children

No matter what their individual differences about child rearing, all specialists agree that an adopted child should be told that she was adopted. It doesn't matter that the adoptive parents have come to feel that the child is completely their own. Biologically, she isn't, and it is her human right to find this out not from a neighbor or schoolmate but from the people she loves and trusts as her parents. The fact of her adoption should be talked about naturally in the child's presence even before she can understand what it means. If she is being raised in a loving atmosphere and feels secure in the acceptance of her adoptive parents, the child isn't likely to be upset by the reality of her situation.

When the child becomes curious about the circumstances of her adoption, or if she wants to know about her "real" mother and father, she should be given no more—and no less—information than the adoption agency provided originally.

A widow or divorced woman who remarries when her children are still very young may be faced with the possibility that her second husband wants to legally adopt the offspring of her first marriage. Far-reaching consequences are involved in such a decision, and it should not be undertaken lightly. The problem should be discussed with a lawyer who can present the facts in a detached way so that the decision will cause the least anguish and fewest unpleasant consequences for everyone.

Aggressiveness

In the rough and tumble of play, some puppies are obviously more aggressive than others, and one of them is clearly determined to be top dog. The same is true of children, especially in any society where energy and enterprise are rewarded.

Aggressive tendencies are natural; the form they take is up to the civilizing efforts of the parents. It is they who have the responsibility of helping a child understand that bullying and bossiness are unacceptable. It seems that because of inheritance, body build, or temperament, some youngsters, whether male or female, are more clearly aggressive than others. It is especially for such children that healthy outlets must be provided for aggression—in the form of toys and playground activities when they are little, and in suitable physical and intellectual endeavors when they get older.

Guilt Feelings

Making a child feel guilty about the strength of his aggressive feelings or thwarting them constantly won't wipe out or destroy the feelings; they'll simply be turned inward, or take the form of nail-biting, or express themselves in some sneaky and antisocial way. Parents who are upset by children's play that simulates violence and who disapprove of toy guns should make their feelings clear without making the youngster feel like a monster because he enjoys them. Aggressiveness that expresses itself in violence and bloodshed—as it so often does in Westerns and in TV programs—should not be the day-in-day-out entertainment to which children are exposed no matter what the parental feelings are.

Boy/Girl Differences

As for a boy who doesn't seem aggressive enough to suit a parent's idea of what a boy should be, or a girl who seems too aggressive to conform to family notions about what "feminine" is all about: these stereotypes are being reexamined and discarded by many people because they are too confining and too rigid to permit the full development of a child's personality. It's no disgrace for a boy to cry, and it should be a source of pride to have a daughter who's determined to be the best math student in the fourth grade.

Allergies

See NUTRITION, and Ch. 24, *Allergies and Hypersensitivities.*

Anger

Anger is a feeling that everyone is familiar with. There are moments when even the most controlled and civilized adult experiences the kind of anger that might become blind rage. A child whose bike has been stolen has a right to her anger; a child whose baby brother has broken a valuable doll is justifiably angry. Some youngsters seem to be angry all the time because they feel they're always being pushed around by adults. (Many adults are always angry because they feel they're

being pushed around by other adults.) Almost continuous anger seems especially common among some children of six, seven, and eight. Their theme song is "It isn't fair" and they get to be known as injustice-collectors, angry at their friends, siblings, teachers.

Means of Expressing Anger

When parents know that a child's anger comes from a healthy feeling of outrage or because of confusion, they should allow the anger to be expressed—in words or tears. But it does have to be made clear that smashing things in a fit of rage or having a tantrum is unacceptable. A child at the mercy of powerful feelings of rage can be frightened by them and should be helped to understand and control them. It's also a comfort to children to know that grown-ups get terribly angry from time to time, but that part of growing up consists in being able to handle one's feelings and in learning how to express them in the right way at the right time. Thus, a father who is in a rage with his boss will find ways of letting him know that he feels an injustice has been done rather than swallow his anger at work and let it out against his wife or children as soon as he comes home.

Animal Bites

See "Animal Bites" in Ch. 35, *Medical Emergencies.*

Anxiety

Children become chronically anxious when their parents constantly criticize them for failing to measure up to some unachievable standard of perfection. Likewise, parents become anxious about being parents when they criticize themselves for failing to measure up to some unachievable standard of perfection.

Anxiety is one of the most widespread and most debilitating stresses from which people of all ages suffer in the United States, chiefly because many Americans have been victimized by the notion that everybody can be everything. Thus, a parent will expect a little child to be good, bright, neat, polite, aggressive enough to complete adequately but not so aggressive that the other children don't like him, relaxed and cheerful at the same time that he's supposed to do all his chores and the homework and remember to be nice to his baby-sister. What child burdened with such expectations isn't going to feel anxious about fulfilling them so that he can gain his parents' love and approval?

Parents may waste emotional energy feeling anxious because they think they're inadequate mothers or fathers, perhaps because they lose their tempers from time to time or because they're often too tired to play with their toddler and stick him in the playpen just to keep him out of trouble. A child will also be made chronically anxious if he's always being threatened with punishment, or if he's made to feel that he's bad when he's trying to be good but doesn't know how. The way to keep anxiety at a minimum is to have achievable goals. Is the child healthy, moderately well-

behaved, cheerful, and inspiring no complaints from his teachers? Are you as a parent helping him to be healthy, moderately well-behaved, cheerful, and cause no trouble at school? If pressure on the child is small, and he still seems anxious, counseling may be considered.

Asthma

Asthma, also known as *bronchial asthma*, is a respiratory disturbance in which breathing becomes difficult and labored and is accompanied by a wheezing sound. It is a chronic disorder in which the bronchial tubes suddenly contract or go into spasm, thus cutting off the passage of air from the windpipe to the lungs. Spasms are accompanied by secretion of mucus into the air passages and a swelling of the bronchial tubes, causing the intake and outflow of air to be further obstructed. The disorder may be triggered by a variety of factors; in children it is associated chiefly with allergy and emotional stress. In some cases, asthma may accompany a bacterial or viral infection of the nose or throat.

The Asthma Attack

It can be very frightening to witness a child's first asthma attack, because judging from the sounds and the effort involved in breathing, the child seems to be suffocating. Call the child's pediatrician promptly. Until the physician can be consulted for emergency treatment, parents should try to be calm and reassuring. Immediate symptoms can be alleviated by prescribed medicines given orally or by injection, or by placing the child in a moist environment, such as in the bathroom with the shower turned on (but not *in* the shower). Otherwise, the child should be kept in bed in a humidified room. The condition itself should be carefully assessed by the physician to decide whether desensitization to a particular food or pollen is necessary, whether a pet has to be given away, or whether the child's emotional needs are being neglected. Chronic asthma should not go untreated because frequent and acute attacks can affect general health. Medicines now available can sometimes prevent acute attacks if taken daily by inhalation when one is well.

Autism

See under MENTAL ILLNESS.

Baby-sitters

Families who can always count on a grandparent or an older child to look after the little ones in their absence are spared the complications and expense of hiring baby-sitters. However, many parents must rely on their own resources, especially when both parents work. In such situations the sitter has become an indispensable adjunct of the family.

Instruction in Baby-sitting

All aspects of the sitter's responsibilities and privileges should be covered. Does the sitter do the dinner dishes? May local phone calls be made? May the refrigerator be raided? The potential employees should be encouraged to ask all the questions they feel uncertain about. Instructions should include a list of hourly rates with all variants: base rate per hour; increase in rate after midnight; increase per number of children to be looked after, and so on.

Cooperative Sitting

For families who want to get out occasionally but can't afford the extra expense of a sitter, a cooperative parents' pool is a good solution. Each month, one participating parent is responsible for keeping track of who had been sitting for whom, how many hours are owed and how many have been "paid for" and so on. The advantage of this arrangement is that mothers or fathers sit for each others' children and no money changes hands. If such a cooperative pool is worked out, remember that the more accurately the records of time asked for and given are kept, and the more businesslike the arrangements, the longer the system will work and the less friction there will be. Each group should decide for itself what the maximum number of participants should be, and as the group becomes too large to function efficiently, it can split into two separate pools.

Provide for Emergencies

Parents should always leave clear and explicit instructions about possible emergencies with baby-sitters and if possible should leave a telephone number where they can be reached. As the children become opinionated about hired sitters, their wishes should be taken into account. When your own youngsters begin to be hired as sitters themselves, you should keep track of where they're working and when they'll be escorted home. Meet the family for whom they will be sitting, *before* the first sitting.

Beds

Infants should not be left on a full size bed to nap. Because the mattress does not fit snugly against the frame or the wall, a child risks becoming wedged between the mattress and the solid object and suffocating. Crib mattresses are designed to fit tightly against the frame, avoiding the risk of suffocation. To further protect an infant from suffocation, he should not be given a pillow while napping or sleeping. An infant who rolls over and is unable to lift his head may suffocate in the pillow.

Bedtime

From babyhood on, the routine of bedtime should be as relaxed as possible for both parent and child. Little babies love to be chanted to (even off-key) or talked to in a gentle tone of voice (even though they don't understand the words) or rocked a bit in their crib. Some little ones seem to resist and fight falling asleep: they fuss and whimper, and then, as though they had been bewitched in the middle of a cry—off they go, all of a sudden. Toddlers may want to hear the same story every night for months, or may cling to the bedtime bottle for quite a while after they've begun to use a cup in the daytime.

Keeping things peaceful at bedtime doesn't mean giving in to the child's pressures or whims. It generally involves keeping one's voice calm, pleasant, and firm: "It's bedtime, and you tell me which story to read to you tonight." The youngster who keeps calling out after having been tucked in—for water, for a last hug, for a last question, for a last trip to the bathroom—isn't determined to make a nuisance of herself; she's just a little scared and wants to make absolutely sure that you're still there. If the family tradition calls for prayers at bedtime, the tone should be cheerful. No child can be expected to relish, "And if I die before I wake I pray the Lord my soul to take" as an accompaniment to sleep.

In a crowded family where siblings share a bedroom, compromises have to be made about the bedtime hour: the younger ones may stay up a little later than they otherwise would, and the older ones may go to bed a little earlier—but they have the pleasure of each other's company. Adjustments in the bedtime hour should be made from time to time not because of a child's wheedling, but because you decide that the occasion calls for it.

Bedwetting

See "Bedwetting" in Ch. 17, *Disease of the Urinogenital System*.

Behavior Problems

See AGGRESSIVENESS, ANGER, DELINQUENCY, DESTRUCTIVENESS, DISHONESTY, DISOBEDIENCE.

Birthmarks

See "Pigment Disorders and Birthmarks" in Ch. 21, *Skin and Hair.*

Biting

Some children learn that their strongest weapon when angry is their teeth. They may bite siblings, friends, and occasionally parents. Because of the enormous risk of infection from the bite, and because it can inflict extreme pain to the person bitten, biting should be strongly discouraged by any child.

Blindness

See DISABLED CHILD.

Booster Shots

See IMMUNIZATION.

Boredom

Babies are usually too hungry or too sleepy—or too cranky—to be bored. Toddlers have so much to investigate around the house that boredom is not likely to be one of their problems. As a child gets older and complains about having nothing to do, you might get him involved in a household chore by saying, "Let's . . ." rather than "Why don't you" or "How would you like to." "Let's tidy the cans on the pantry shelf" or "Let's make some cookies" can make a three-year-old feel useful and interested.

Rainy Days

If you're too busy for a cooperative effort and there's a long rainy day ahead, provide for it in advance by keeping a "boredom box" in the closet and renewing its contents from time to time: wrappings saved from gifts; bits of material; boxes of various sizes; discarded magazines to be cut up; old clothes for dress-up activities, and the like.

Coping with Boredom Can be Productive

A child who is never allowed to be bored because his parents or older siblings feel that they have to entertain him or play with him is deprived of the possibility of calling on his own resources and learning how to amuse himself. The fact that an only child may have to live through stretches of boredom often contributes to his exploring his own abilities in a creative way. Sometimes just asking a child to "Tell *me* a story" can work wonders. Some parents solve the recurrent problem of boredom by organizing informal play groups of three or four children; others find a nursery school the best solution.

Convalescence

An older child who is recovering from an illness that has kept him out of school and isolated him from his friends may require some special project to work on in addition to catching up on his homework. A period of protracted convalescence is a good time to introduce a new hobby or craft such as model-making or clay sculpture that may solve the boredom problem for years to come.

Brain Damage

Brain damage refers to an organic defect of the brain—that is, tissue destruction—caused by an injury to the nervous system occurring before, during, or after birth. Such injury can be caused by toxic chemicals as well as by physical trauma. It can result in any of a variety of neurological disorders, such as cerebral palsy or other impairment of motor coordination, mental retardation, convulsive seizures, hyperkinesis, or perceptual difficulties.

Minimal Brain Damage

Minimal brain damage (or, more formally, *minimal brain dysfunction*) refers to a condition of some children who suffer from a motor or perceptual impairment that may affect their ability to learn or use language, interfere with memory, or make it difficult for them to control their attention. Some learning disabilities are attributed to minimal brain damage. See also DYS-LEXIA.

Brothers and Sisters

Rivalry and jealousy and bickering are inevitable among brothers and sisters; companionship, a helping hand, and good times together are part of the picture too. Parents can keep resentments and quarrels at a minimum by not playing one child off against the other or by refraining from holding up one child as an example of virtue to another. In an atmosphere of equal recognition, brothers and sisters will love and respect each other most of the time and fight only occasionally. Special privileges granted on the basis of such distinctions as "Well, he's the oldest" or "She's the youngest" or exceptions made because "He's a boy" or "She's only a girl" can cause resentments that last a lifetime.

Burns

See "Burns" in Ch. 35, *Medical Emergencies.*

Camps

There seems to be no end to the diversity of camps available for summer enrollment. Most urban and suburban communities have day camps in which children may be accepted for certain minimum periods. They range from expensive groups that offer sightseeing trips, swimming instruction, and other special attractions to groups that cost very little and function more or less like day-care centers. "Sleepaway" camps run by organizations such as the Scouts and the 4-H Clubs are comparatively cheap and will register a child for a week rather than for a month or for the entire summer. Camps subsidized by community funds or private endowment are available for urban children from poor families.

Special Camps

The proliferation of special camps has been a blessing to the parents of handicapped children: those with diabetes, muscular dystrophy, learning disabilities, obesity, and other problems need no longer be deprived of a camping experience with their peers. In many cases, particularly for overweight youngsters, the summer experience can be a major health contribution.

In general, an effort should be made to choose a camp that suits the tastes and temperament of the child. A youngster who hates competitive sports is likely to have a miserable time in a camp that emphasizes team spirit. Instead, he may enjoy a place that offers lots of nature study, hiking, and animal care. A child eager to improve his swimming would be better off at a camp with better-than-average water sport facilities rather than one that concentrates on arts and crafts and offers only a nearby pond for all water activities. Information about camps that have official standing can be obtained by writing to The American Camping Association, 5000 State Rd., 67 N, Martinsdale, IN 46151.

Cancer

Rare as it may be and affecting only one child in about 7,000 each year, cancer still claims the lives of more children between the ages of one and fourteen than any other single disease. Among the cancers that more commonly affect children in their early years are the following: *acute lymphocytic leukemia,* in which white blood cells proliferate in the bone marrow in such great quantities that they disrupt normal blood production; *neuroblastoma,* which may occur in any part of the body but characteristically involves a tumorous growth in the sympathetic nerve tissues of the adrenal glands; *brain* or *spinal cord tumor; Hodgkin's disease,* or cancer of the lymph nodes; *Wilms' tumor,* a rare kidney cancer that accounts for about one-fifth of all childhood cancers; *retinoblastoma,* an eye tumor that is probably hereditary and is most frequently encountered in children under four; and *bone cancer* that may attack the long bones of the forearm and leg during the growing years. Many of these cancers can now be arrested, and some can be cured if symptoms are detected early enough. See Ch. 18, *Cancer,* for further information about cancer.

Early Symptoms

Early detection is best accomplished by calling to a physician's attention any of the following symptoms that last for more than a few days: continued crying or pain for which there appears to be no explanation; intermittent nausea and vomiting; the development of lumps or swellings in or on any part of the child's body; stumbling or walking unsteadily; a loss of appetite and general lassitude; any marked change in bowel or bladder habits; any unexplained discharge of blood, whether in the stool or urine, or in heavy nosebleeds, or any marked slowness of bleeding to stop after an injury.

Celiac Disease

Celiac disease, officially known as *malabsorption syndrome*, is the designation for a group of congenital enzyme deficiencies in which certain nutriments are not properly absorbed from the intestinal tract. *Celiac* means having to do with the abdomen. Celiac disease is characterized by frothy, bulky, and foul-smelling stools containing undigested fats. Diarrhea may alternate with constipation, the child has severe stomach cramps, and the abdomen becomes conspicuously bloated. If the disease is untreated, anemia results, and the child's growth is impaired. Early symptoms should be brought to a physician's attention so that a correct diagnosis can be made based on laboratory investigation of the stools. Treatment consists of a special, gluten-free diet under a physician's continuing supervision. *Gluten* is a protein component of wheat and rye; special breads, cookies, etc., must therefore be used. If the diet is strictly adhered to, full recovery can be expected although it may take over a year.

Cerebral Palsy

Cerebral palsy is the general term for a group of abnormal conditions commonly associated with a brain disorder that causes the loss or impairment of muscle control. Approximately one child in about 7,000 suffers from some degree of this disability. Damage to the nervous system that results in cerebral palsy may have occurred before birth, during delivery, or in rare cases, as a consequence of accident, injury, or severe illness during infancy or childhood. Because symptoms vary widely, each individual case is assessed for proper treatment by a team of therapists under the supervision of a specialist, usually a pediatrician. One of the most important aspects of treatment involves parental understanding of the fact that it is essential that they help the child to help himself as much as possible. Guiding the youngster towards self-acceptance and independence requires the patience, persistence, and resourcefulness of the entire family, and may require a certain amount of group therapy and counseling. For a discussion of symptoms and treatment, see "Cerebral Palsy" in Ch. 8, *Diseases of the Muscles and Nervous System*.

Cheating

See DISHONESTY.

Checkups

Medical and dental checkups are essential to everyone's health, but they are especially important for the growing child. An infant should be examined by a physician every month for the first six months, and less frequently after that. The pediatrician usually recommends a schedule for immunization and future checkups. If possible, parents should try to maintain continuity with the same physician so that when an illness occurs, the child sees the physician as an old friend rather than a threatening stranger. Continuity also gives the physician a total picture of the child in sickness and in health and enables him to diagnose variations from the normal with more accuracy. Parents who cannot afford the services of a private physician can be assured of good infant and child care at a local child-health station or at the well-baby clinic of a nearby hospital. Between checkups, it's a good idea for parents to keep a running list of questions or problems they would like to discuss with the doctor at the next visit.

Chicken Pox

Chicken pox cannot be prevented at this time. It does not usually cause any severe complications in a child, but it can be serious in an adult. It is highly infectious and spreads rapidly.

Chicken pox is caused by a virus. Its incubation period is two to three weeks. Symptoms include those of the common cold, a fever, general malaise, and a rash.

The rash, which may be either mild or severe, is different from that produced by measles or by rubella. The measles rash is red and blotchy. Chicken pox has bunches of blisters close together. These blisters are filled with fluid, and there is a reddened area around each lesion. As new blisters appear, the older ones become encrusted. The rash may affect the mouth, nose, ears, vagina, penis, or scrotum. In an older child

the symptoms may be more severe than in a younger one, and may be accompanied by headache and vomiting.

Treatment

The only way to treat chicken pox is symptomatically. The rash is very itchy, and an affected child must be prevented from scratching. Otherwise, he may develop a secondary infection and be left pitted and scarred.

Treatment involves the use of lotions, such as Calamine, applied locally to the pox to relieve the itching. If the child is old enough, it's a good idea to let him paint it on himself. Your physician may also prescribe medicine to be taken orally to help the child stop scratching the blisters. In a few days, the rash clears up, the lesions dry, and the crusts fall off.

Child Abuse and Neglect

Child abuse and neglect have been defined in various ways.

In 1962, Dr. C. Henry Kempe, chief pediatrician at the University of Colorado Medical Center, coined the term *battered child syndrome*. According to Dr. Kempe's definition, the victim of battering is "any child who [has] received *nonaccidental* injury or injuries as a result of acts or omissions on the part of his parents or guardians." Under the Child Abuse Prevention and Treatment Act (Public Law 93-247), passed by Congress in 1974 and amended in 1978, child abuse and neglect are defined as the physical or mental injury, sexual abuse or exploitation, negligent treatment, or maltreatment of a child under the age of 18 by a person who is responsible for the child's welfare under circumstances which indicate that the child's health or welfare is harmed or threatened thereby.

Abuse and neglect clearly take many forms. *Physical abuse* may involve punching, scalding, suffocating, headcracking, and stomping. *Sexual abuse* can mean intercourse, incest, rape, sodomy, or impairing of a minor's morals (see SEXUAL ABUSE). *Physical neglect* occurs when parents or parent surrogates fail to provide the essentials of a normal life. These include food, clothing, shelter, care, and supervision. Under *emotional abuse or neglect* authorities include parental failure to provide love and proper direction, parental rejection, and deprivation of mothering.

Incidence

Figures on the incidence of child abuse and neglect are difficult to confirm. Many such cases are never reported. At least one agency, the National Center on Child Abuse and Neglect, a federal agency, has concluded that more than one million children are maltreated each year. Another estimate indicates that some 3,000 children die annually in New York City alone as a result of physical abuse.

Most of the abuse victims are three years old or younger. Some authorities believe that the cases of neglect are far more numerous than those of actual abuse.

Control

Approaches to control of the problem of child abuse and neglect have been both legislative and social. Laws passed by all 50 states require physicians and other professionals to report suspected cases of child abuse. In increasing numbers the states also require reports from nurses, teachers, counselors, social workers, clergymen, law enforcement officers, attorneys, and coroners. Some states provide for penalties, including fines up to $1,000 or prison sentences of as much as one year, for persons mandated to report but failing to do so.

Control measures have focused in addition on the rehabilitation of abusive parents and protection of abused children. The National Center on Child Abuse and Neglect, established in 1974 as part of the Children's Bureau of the federal Office of Child Development, receives funding that makes possible protective services for the short-term care of endangered children outside the home. The Center also provides counseling for parents, foster-care payments, and other services.

On the principle that the abusive parent must be treated if child abuse and neglect are to be controlled, various organizations have instituted parent-oriented programs. Parents Anonymous sponsors therapy sessions in which abusive parents can meet to help themselves and each other. "Helplines" operating in many communities offer aid and counseling to parents who have abused a child but are afraid to contact a social service or other agency. A number of other agencies and groups provide emergency, counseling, outreach, and related services to parents or parent surrogates. Some helplines have workers available to visit homes in life-threatening situations.

Other groups and agencies take a multidisciplinary approach. Alliance, a division of Catholic Charities, brings together existing community agencies that work together in teams to treat child abuse and neglect cases. Hospital-based treatment programs may include a physician, nurse, social worker, and consulting psychiatrist. Lay therapists may visit homes under other programs, and "foster grandparents" over 65 years of age may be recruited to care for battered children who have been hospitalized.

Sources of Help

Persons seeking help or advice on abused and neglected children can look in their communities' yellow pages under the heading "Social Services Organizations." A number of organizations that offer assistance are listed in the SEXUAL ABUSE section. Others include:

- Parents Anonymous, 1733 South Sepulveda, Ste. 270, Los Angeles, CA 90045; 213/410-9732.

- American Association for Protecting Children (a division of the American Humane Association), 9725 E. Hampden Ave., Denver, CO 80231; 303/695-0811.

- Parents without Partners, 8807 Colesville Rd., Silver Springs, MD 20910; 301/588-9354.

- Parents United, P.O. Box 952, San Jose, CA 95108; 408/279-1957.

Cholesterol

Cholesterol poses two types of problems in children. The first is a lack of cholesterol in children whose parents have kept them from infancy on low cholesterol diets. Parents should keep in mind that the body requires some cholesterol to function correctly and that the protein derived from meat and eggs is almost essential to growing bodies. Children who are not fed meat, dairy products, or eggs need to have the protein, amino acids, and other nutrients replaced by either pills or a very well balanced diet. Certain vitamins cannot be found in a vegetarian diet, such as one type of vitamin B. Children on restrictive low-fat, low-cholesterol diets can suffer growth failure and malnutrition unless the diet is supervised by a doctor.

The second problem is an extremely elevated cholesterol level. Although general testing of children for high cholesterol is not recommended, one statistic that proved reliable in spotting 9 out of 10 children with raised levels was the amount of television watched. Children who watched two or more hours of television a day were more likely to have cholesterol levels exceeding 200 mg. More importantly, less than half of those children who had raised levels and watched two hours of television came from families who had a history of high cholesterol. This means that these children are not from high-risk families, but they still manage to increase their cholesterol because of their eating patterns and lack of exercise in their daily routine. The flag that points to the problem is excessive TV viewing. Snacking while watching TV, and not exercising, are the suspected culprits.

Circumcision

Circumcision is a surgical procedure in which the foreskin, or *prepuce*, that covers the cone-shaped tip of the male infant's penis is removed. The Book of Genesis speaks of circumcision as a religious rite. Once relatively common in the United States, the procedure has become more rare. The American Academy of Pediatrics has stated that "routine circumcision of the newborn infant lacks medical justification."

Usually performed a few days after birth, the procedure takes only a few minutes and can be done in various ways. A scalpel may be used, for example. Possible complications include excessive bleeding, infection, and urinary obstruction resulting from contraction of the skin at the base of the foreskin. But complications are infrequent.

The parents of the newborn male infant should decide whether to have their son circumcised or not. They may first consult their obstetrician or pediatrician. In most cases, decisions are made on the basis of family, religious, or cultural traditions. However, many family health insurance policies today provide no coverage for the procedure.

Cleft Palate and Cleft Lip

A *cleft palate* is a split in the roof of the mouth sometimes extending to the lip and into the nose. The split is caused by the failure of the two sides of the face to unite properly during prenatal development. The condition occurs in about 1 out of 1,000 births and is sometimes associated with a foot or spine deformity. It is in no way related to mental retardation.

An infant born with a cleft palate cannot suck properly unless a special device, called an *obturator*, is inserted into the split to close it against the flow of air. Where this is undesireable, feeding may be done with a spoon or a dropper.

Because the condition eventually causes speech distortion, it should be corrected at about 18 months of age, before the child begins to talk. The surgery consists of reconstructing the tissue. Sometimes, even at this early age, the child may need some corrective speech therapy following the operation.

If the split occurs only in the lip, commonly called a *harelip*, surgery may be recommended when the infant weighs about 15 pounds, usually at the age of 12 to 15 months. When the operation is performed this early, there is no danger of speech impairment, and the result is only a thin scar.

Clothing

Standards have been set up by the U.S. government for infants' and children's sleepwear to be flame retardant or flame resistant. This does not mean that the material will not burn— even flame retardant material will burn when fire is held against the cloth. The difference is that when the flame is removed, the retardant material ceases to burn. Nontreated material will continue to burn and fuel further flames.

Until recently this meant that sleepwear for small children had to be non-natural fibers. Synthetic material could be coated so that it would not continue to burn after the flame was removed. Cotton does continue to burn and increases the likelihood of serious injuries to a child in case of fire. However, recent improvements in chemical treatment of cotton have provided the clothing industry with flame retardant cotton. Always check clothing labels to see if the cotton is treated. If it is not labeled as flame retardant or flame resistent, it should not be considered for sleepwear.

Labeling should be checked on all clothing that will be used as sleepwear. Often times, manufacturers will produce clothing for infants that looks like sleepwear but is labeled daywear or playwear in order to avoid the need for flame retardant treatment of the cloth. If the clothing is not marked flame retardant, or is not specifically labeled as sleepwear, it should not be used to clothe a sleeping child.

Clubfoot

Clubfoot is a bone deformity characterized by an inturning or outturning of the foot. An orthopedist must put the clubfoot and part of the leg into a cast to correct the condition. If casting does not cure the abnormality, orthopedic surgery may be necessary.

Occasionally, a benign and easily correctable condition involving a child's legs may have been produced by the position the baby was in while still in the uterus.

The mother can help to correct the condition by daily passive exercises of the baby's feet. She does this by turning the feet correctly for a few minutes every day. To maintain the corrected position, the application of plaster is sometimes necessary. Such a procedure requires the attention of an orthopedic surgeon.

Colic

During the first three or four months, many babies have occasional attacks of *colic*, a general term applied to infantile digestive discomfort. After feeding, the baby may cry out in pain and draw up her arms and legs. Her abdomen may feel hard. Apart from making sure the baby is as comfortable as can be, there's not much that can be done for colic. You must try not to let the baby's crying make you a nervous wreck, for your nervousness will be communicated to the baby, which will only create a vicious circle of increasing tension. Usually colic tapers off at about the third month. If the baby's colic attacks are very frequent or persistent, consult your pediatrician.

Color Blindness

Color blindness is a genetic inability to distinguish between certain colors, most commonly between red and green. This defect, which is characteristically male, is inherited through the mother. That is, a woman whose father was color blind can pass the trait to her son without herself suffering the defect. About 8 million people in the United States have the red/green form of color blindness which can neither be cured nor corrected. Many of them are scarcely aware of their deficiency. Parents who suspect that their child may have this minor disability can arrange for simple testing.

Common Cold

By recent count, there are about 150 different viruses that cause common cold symptoms, and because not a single one of them can be treated effectively by medicines, coping with a cold seems to be part of the human condition. Parents who are sniveling, sneezing, and coughing should ask the physician what precautions to take when handling the baby.

Young children with stuffy noses and breathing difficulties should be kept indoors, near a humidifier or steam kettle if the air is especially dry. Nose drops should not be given unless the physician says so. Older children may not want to miss school because of a cold. If they do go, they should be given lots of liquid when they get home and steered in the direction of an afternoon nap. Colds in and of themselves are unavoidable and not serious, but the proper precautions should be taken to prevent complications, such as an ear infection or a sore throat.

Competitiveness

See AGGRESSIVENESS.

Conscience

See GUILT AND CONSCIENCE.

Constipation

Parents who are anxious about the frequency of their own bowel movements or who are excessively refined in their attitudes towards defecation are pretty sure to transmit these feelings to their children unless they make some effort not to. Concerns of this kind are one sure way of constipating a child. Actually, if a child is eating a proper diet, getting enough exercise, and drinking a sufficiency of liquids, constipation is not likely to be a problem.

Frequency of Bowel Movements

Not everyone has a bowel movement every day. On the other hand, some people routinely have more than one movement a day. There is considerable variation among normal patterns of bowel movements. This should be borne in mind before parents conclude that their child is constipated. Children need to be assured that they are not necessarily abnormal if they deviate from the one-a-day pattern.

However, any abrupt change in the normal pattern of bowel movements should be noted, and if it persists contact a physician. Frequent small movements can be a sign of constipation.

A youngster on a light diet because of illness, or one who is dehydrated because of a fever, may suffer from mild constipation that will clear up when he recovers. If constipation becomes chronic, don't resort to enemas or laxatives on your own; discuss the problem with your physician who will want to check on other symptoms that might indicate an intestinal disorder.

Cradle Cap

This condition is marked by yellowish crusts on the baby's scalp. It is usually harmless, and can be taken care of by regular shampooing. Occasionally, a special soap as well as a very fine comb may be helpful.

Crib Death

See SUDDEN INFANT DEATH SYNDROME.

Crossed Eyes (Strabismus)

Do not be alarmed if your baby's eyes do not focus. Crossed eyes are a common condition that usually corrects itself somewhere between the ages of six and twelve months. If crossing of the eyes persists after one year, an ophthalmologist (eye specialist) should evaluate the baby's vision.

If a real problem does develop, one eye—or each eye alternately—may cross, turn outward, or focus below or above the other. Frequently the reason for "turning" is that there is a larger refractive error in one eye than in the other. Eyeglasses will often correct this condition.

Occasionally, eye muscle weakness is the cause of crossed eyes. This is most often true of premature children. The weakness of some muscles causes overaction of other muscles.

Eyeglasses will often prevent the need for eye surgery. Sometimes, however, surgery will be necessary to straighten the eyes. Either before or after surgery the eyes may need further attention in the form of eye drops, a patch to cover one eye, or glasses.

Croup

Croup, a most harassing and terrifying experience for new parents, is a spasm of the windpipe or trachea, especially involving the larynx. When such a spasm occurs, an affected child has great trouble in breathing and produces a cough that sounds like the bark of a dog. In some cases, the child can't breathe at all.

An attack of croup is an emergency. The younger the child, the more dangerous it is. You must get the baby's airway open. The best thing to do is to take the child into the bathroom, shut the door, and turn on the hot water of the shower full force, or of the bathtub and sink if you don't have a shower. The idea is to fill the room with hot steam in order to loosen the mucus plug in the baby's trachea, thus enabling him to cough up the mucus.

Get to your physician as soon as possible so that more effective treatment can begin. If the croup is viral in origin, antibiotics may not help; but when the infection is caused by bacteria, your physician will put the child on one of the antimicrobial agents. If your child is subject to croup, it is a good idea to invest in a hot or cold air vaporizer and use it whenever he has congestion resulting from a cold.

In a really severe emergency, when the windpipe closes completely, a *tracheostomy* must be performed so that the throat can be opened and an airway inserted. A tracheostomy should be performed in a hospital, but if for some reason it is performed elsewhere, the child should be hospitalized as quickly as possible.

Curiosity

If we weren't born curious, we'd never learn a thing. Even before a child can walk and talk, curiosity motivates a good part of her behavior: putting things into her mouth, poking at things, pointing at people, and as the natural urge to speak becomes stronger, holding things up or bringing them to mother or father in order to find out what they're called.

Respecting Curiosity

A parent who respects the child's curiosity will be attentive to it and satisfy it as part of the ongoing learning experience. It doesn't take any extra time when a toddler is sitting in your lap to say the words for the parts of your face (and hers) as she touches them, or the words for her articles of clothing as she tries to help put them on. Dealing with the "why" stage of curiosity is more complicated, especially because in many instances, the child is asking "Why?" for the sheer joy and sense of power of being able to do so.

Many parents who don't know anything about mechanics or astronomy have developed a sense of security by heading for the children's shelves at the local library and reading the simplest books on the subject that interest their preschool children so that they can answer some of their questions. Of course, no one can answer all the questions that a child might ask during an average day. Some should be answered by mother, some by father, and some will have to wait. There's no harm in telling a four-year-old child who wants to know why the wind makes a whistling sound that she'll find out about such things when she goes to school. That's a much better answer than "Don't ask so many questions." Questions should always be listened to even if the answers aren't readily available.

As the child reaches the age of eight and can do a certain amount of reading, it's a good idea to invest in a fairly simple encyclopedia. With such a source of information available, it's possible to respond to some questions with "Let's go find the answer together."

Each family must decide for itself where the line is to be drawn between legitimate curiosity and unacceptable snoopiness or nosiness as children get older and become interested in such matters as how rich the neighbors are, or "What were you and mommy fighting about when I was falling asleep last night?"

Cystic Fibrosis

Cystic fibrosis is an inherited disease in which the child cannot handle the normal secretions of the respiratory tract. There is a lack of ciliary action—the beating movement by the hairs of the cells lining the bronchial tubes of the lungs. Thick mucus collects at the base of the lungs, obstructing the smaller air passages and causing labored breathing and chronic cough.

Respiratory Complications

Bacteria multiply in the accumulated lung secretions, predisposing the patient to chronic bronchitis and other respiratory infections, such as pneumonia. Lung tissue changes can result eventually in severe, permanent damage to the lungs.

Digestive Complications

The abnormally thick, viscous mucus produced by the cystic fibrosis patient tends to obstruct the ducts or openings of the mucus-secreting glands. When such mucus obstructs the pancreas, it interferes with its ability to supply important digestive enzymes to the intestinal tract, thus leading to poor digestion and malabsorption of a number of important nutrients. A child with cystic fibrosis may therefore be poorly nourished in spite of an adequate diet.

Other Complications

Tissue changes in the lungs can restrict blood flow to the heart, leading to increased blood pressure and chronic heart strain. Loss of large amounts of salt through malfunctioning sweat glands can become a very serious problem for youngsters in hot weather, causing dehydration and heat exhaustion. Laboratory tests usually find an abnormally high concentration of salt in the sweat of cystic fibrosis patients. (Indeed, the skin of a cystic fibrosis patient is apt to taste salty.) Some tissues may show three times the normal concentration of sodium and twice the normal levels of potassium.

Treatment

There is no known cure for cystic fibrosis. Treatment includes the use of humidifiers and inhalation medication in the form of aerosols to loosen secretions. Another method used is *postural drainage*—lying facedown with the head lower than the feet to let gravity help loosen secretions. Antibiotics are used to control infections; special diets with reduced fat intake and added nutrients are prescribed to compensate for abnormal digestive function. Other medical techniques are utilized in individual cases to maintain normal heart and lung function.

The discovery of the defective gene involved in triggering cystic fibrosis is expected to improve diagnostic testing for the genetic disorder. The subsequent discovery of the cell malfunction that blocks the making of a protein will also enable scientists to improve treatment of the disease with aerosol inhalers and with mucus-thinning medication. Several drugs are being tested with success on patients.

Once considered strictly a disease of early childhood, an increasing number of cases of cystic fibrosis have been detected in recent years among adolescents and adults. Symptoms of the disease, including respiratory difficulty with chronic coughing, may resemble those of an allergic reaction.

How the Disease Is Inherited

Cystic fibrosis is transmitted to a child only when both parents are carriers of the trait. When only one parent carries the trait, however, some of the children can become carriers. Through marriage with other carriers, they may then become the parents of a child afflicted with the disorder.

Information on new treatment techniques, the location of treatment centers, and genetic counseling may be obtained from the national headquarters of the Cystic Fibrosis Foundation, 6931 Arlington Rd., Ste. 200, Bethesda, MD 20814.

Daydreaming

See FANTASIES.

Deafness

Major advances have been made in recent years in educating and socializing incurably deaf children who are normal in all other ways. Starting with a proper assessment of the child's degree of deafness at the earliest possible time and the fitting of a hearing aid are two crucial considerations. The child's instruction in lipreading and the use of her own vocal equipment are professionally supervised, and the rest of the family is very much involved in the whole process. Nowadays an important advance in speech therapy is the use of a feedback system that make it possible for the youngster to be self-corrective. Parents seeking information about special schools and services, summer camps, and other facilities can write to the following agencies: Alexander Graham Bell Association for the Deaf, 3417 Volta Place, N.W., Washington, D.C. 20007; American Speech-Language-Hearing Association, 10801 Rockville Pike, Rockville, MD 20852. See also HEARING.

Death

Some children's first experience of death is the loss of a grandparent; others may have to confront the fact of death for the first time when a beloved pet dies. A child wants to know where people or animals go when they die. Parents should be as honest as possible in answering such questions and tell their offspring what they themselves truly believe. Those parents who believe that there is life after death should say so; those who do not should say that they do not. Whatever one's beliefs, there are better ways to phrase them than "Grandma is in heaven watching you" or "People who are naughty go to hell when they die."

Death of a Parent

A child who has to cope with the death of a parent may be so disoriented that his behavior will seem odd to the adults around him. He may pretend that the death never happened; others may protect themselves from the shock by burying their feelings and never talking about the dead parent. Still others may feel rage at having been abandoned. Many youngsters are overwhelmed by guilt, feeling that in some magic way they caused the death because from time to time they secretly wished it. In cases where the bereft child cannot cope with the loss, it may be advisable to provide some help in the form of psychiatric therapy.

Delinquency

Juvenile delinquents are minors who are guilty of breaking the law or who are engaged in associations and activities considered harmful to children's morals, such as running errands for gamblers, acting as a lookout during a robbery, or sniffing glue for kicks.

Swiping a candy bar or a comic book at the age of ten doesn't define a child as a hardened delinquent, but where such behavior becomes chronic, it's a sign that something is wrong that needs to be corrected. With the guidance of a therapist, it may turn out that the child alone is not entirely responsible for his delinquent tendencies. See also DESTRUCTIVENESS, DISHONESTY, DISOBEDIENCE.

Dental Care

The proper attitude toward dental care is best instilled not by lectures or warnings, but by example. Parents who themselves go regularly to the dentist for checkups, who take care of their teeth by keeping them clean with routine brushing and the use of dental floss, can do more for their child's dental health than those who depend on stern warnings to shape the attitudes of their children. Parents can hardly expect their offspring to be heroic about dental visits when they themselves scarcely ever go unless they have a toothache.

Start Early

Dental care can begin by having the toddler accompany the parent to the dentist so that his baby teeth can be inspected and he can be given a special toothbrush of his own with instructions about how to use it. In communities where the water supply is not fluoridated, the dentist may recommend an ongoing program of fluoride application to the teeth themselves. Some families find that a pediatric dentist who specializes in children's dentistry can deal with a frightened or anxious child more expertly than the family dentist. Other families use the services of the dental clinics that are part of the dental schools of large universities.

No matter who is in charge of the family's dental health, it is important that professional attention is given to the child's dental development at every stage: fillings for decay in the first teeth, routine cleanings and checkups, and preventive orthodontics where advisable. Another aspect of dental care involves keeping the consumption of sweets to a minimum, and making sure that the child's daily diet contains the proper nutrients for building healthy teeth. See also ORTHODONTICS. For full discussion, see Ch. 22, *Teeth and Gums*.

Destructiveness

"It was an accident!" is a common cry when a child destroys a valuable object because of carelessness. And it probably was an accident. Parents who don't want precious bric-a-brac or other delicate possessions broken had better put them out of the reach of curious and clumsy little fingers. Young children should not be punished because their toys always seem to be destroyed; better to give them playthings that are sturdy and comparatively indestructible.

The child who is destructive unwittingly should not be spoken to in the same way as one would speak to a boy who willfully breaks his sister's doll or a girl who spitefully tears her brother's model-making manual. De-structiveness born of anger ("I was so furious, I smashed a dish") may happen rarely, but when it does, it should be commented on as an unsuitable way of dealing with the problem that caused the anger in the first place. When destructiveness gets out of hand or involves group activities amounting to vandalism, parental action should be taken with the guidance of a professional counselor.

Developmental Disability

Any disability that interferes with a child's normal development is a *developmental disability*. The term has been used more specifically, however, to refer to mental retardation, cerebral palsy, epilepsy, and autism.

Diabetes

No one knows why some children develop diabetes. Diabetes is a noncontagious disease that results from the body's inability to produce enough insulin for the normal metabolism of sugar. The diabetic child is thus improperly nourished because the sugar that should be incorporated into the tissues is excreted in the urine. Finding sugar in the urine facilitates early diagnosis. Also, because this disorder causes a disturbance in the metabolism of fat, there is an increase of fat in the blood, detectable in a routine blood count. Juvenile onset diabetes can be more volatile that adult onset diabetes. Control is usually though injectable insulin.

Insulin treatment has undergone some improvements in the past few years. Human insulin is now readily available; beef-pork insulin was common in usage before. There is less likely to be an allergic reaction to human insulin produced through genetic reproduction. Also, doses can be adjusted to the individual though the mix of fast-acting and slow-acting preparations.

Early Signs

Parents who are themselves diabetic will be alert to any symptoms in their offspring. The disease occurs more frequently in children where there is a family history of diabetes. However, because the disorder may occur in children where there is no previous family history of diabetes, alertness to the following signs is advisable: an abnormally frequent need to urinate; an excessive desire for fluids; itching of the genitals; general listlessness; frequent boils and carbuncles; slow healing of cuts and bruises.

If a diagnosis of diabetes is made by the physician, the child may be hospitalized for a few days for a series of definitive tests, and all the members of the family will be educated in the best way to supervise the child's diet and daily routine so that serious complications can be avoided. Professional guidance is also available to ensure that the youngster's emotional adjustment is a healthy one. For a full discussion see Ch. 15, *Diabetes Mellitus.*

Diaper Rash

See RASHES.

Diapers

Some controversy has built up in the past few years over which is more ecologically sound—cloth diapers or paper diapers. Paper diapers in landfills take more than one hundred years to deteriorate. Even if the plastic lining is removed, it is believed that the paper will deteriorate only weeks faster than if the diaper left intact. Effective recycling of paper diapers does not yet exist, and it may be years before the material can be sanitized to the point of recyclability.

Cloth diapers, on the other hand, require strong soaps and chemicals to clean. To insure the sterility and whiteness of the cloth, bleach and harsh detergents are used. These go into the water supply and affect the plant and animal life. The energy used for hot water to wash the diapers also adds to the environmental cost.

Many parents try to use paper diapers only while traveling or in places where having a soiled diaper to carry or clean would be extremely inconvenient. This infrequent use of paper diapers allows for the occasional convenience of the throwaway while reducing paper waste.

Some parents believe that cloth diapers cause more diaper rash; other parents believe that the sealed paper diaper causes more diaper rash. The biggest cause of diaper rash is excessive moisture against the baby's skin, which can be avoided by frequent diaper changes, for whatever diaper used. Excessive use of powders and creams can also increase the problem because of the pasty substance that forms when these encounter moisture.

Diarrhea

Diarrhea, or loose and watery bowel movements, is common in babies because they are more sensitive to certain intestinal germs than older children. They may also be reacting to a change in their formula or to the roughage in a newly introduced fruit or vegetable. In older children, diarrhea may occur not only as a symptom of bacterial or viral infection, or because of food poisoning, but also as an allergic response, or because of overexcitement or anxiety.

Diarrhea in an infant should always be brought to a doctor's attention if it continues for more than 24 hours. The same holds true for an older child, especially when there are also symptoms of cramps, fever, or aches and pains in the joints. Persistent diarrhea from any cause, because it can lead to serious dehydration especially in infants, requires prompt medical attention.

Diphtheria

Diphtheria is a severe and contagious bacterial infection, often fatal if untreated. Once one of the most threatening of all childhood diseases, there are now fewer than 1,000 cases a year in the United States because of widespread and effective immunization.

The first symptoms—fever, headache, nausea, and sore throat—may be confused with the onset of other disorders. However, there is a manifestation of diphtheria that is uniquely its own: patches of grayish yellow membrane form in the throat and grow together into one large membrane that interferes with swallowing and breathing. The diphtheria bacteria also produce a powerful toxin that can eventually cause irreversible damage to the heart and nerves. Diagnosis is usually verified by laboratory identification of the bacteria in a throat culture.

If diphtheria does occur, it is best treated in a hospital. The prompt prescription of antitoxin serum and antibiotics results in recovery in practically all cases. See IMMUNIZATION.

Disabled Child

Whether a handicap is hereditary or acquired, mental or physical, temporary or permanent, it is always a condition that prevents a child from participating fully on an equal footing in the activities of her own age group. But how fully she can participate and her attitude toward her disability are usually a reflection of the attitudes of her parents, teachers, and the community. Of primary importance is an assessment at the earliest possible age of the extent to which the handicap can be decreased or corrected.

Exactly how deaf is the deaf child? Can surgery repair a rheumatic heart? Is a defect of vision operable? Is the child with cerebral palsy mentally retarded or is the seeming mental malfunction a reversible effect of the physical condition? Parents should investigate all the available services offered by voluntary organizations and community groups that might help them and their child. See Ch. 36, *Voluntary Health Agencies*.

One promising development in recent years is the attempt to integrate handicapped children, whenever possible, into the mainstream of education rather than segregate them in special classes. School systems in various parts of the United States are placing deaf, blind, physically disabled, and emotionally disturbed youngsters into classrooms with their nonhandicapped peers and providing them with essential supportive services at various times during the school day. The experience of dealing with nonhandicapped children will provide them with a more realistic preparation for their adult lives.

Discrimination

See PREJUDICE.

Dishonesty

Nobody is honest about everything all the time, and that goes for children as well as adults. It's unrealistic to expect a child never to lie about anything.

Little children like to make things up and can't be held strictly accountable for some of their tall stories when they're still at an age at which fact and fantasy are not clearly distinguished. A colorful exaggeration needn't call for an accusation of lying. It's better to respond with, "That's an interesting story," or "You're just imagining."

Lying and Punishment

As youngsters get older, they should feel secure enough to tell the truth about having been naughty, knowing that although they may be punished, they will get approval for having told the truth. Children shouldn't be so fearful of their parents that dishonesty is their only protection against a beating.

Cheating

Children who are pressured beyond their ability to perform are the ones likeliest to cheat; so are those for whom winning has been held up constantly as a transcendent value. A child who has been caught cheating at school is usually punished by the authorities. If the incident is discussed at home, the parents might reexamine their values before adding to the child's burdens. A youngster who cheats regularly at games will suffer the natural punishment of exclusion by his peers.

Stealing

Young children who embark on group enterprises of stealing "for fun" — whether it's taking candy from the corner market or shoplifting from a department store — needn't be viewed as case-hardened criminals unless the stealing becomes habitual. A nine-year-old who swipes a candy bar once or twice and regrets it belongs in a different category from one who is hired as a lookout for older delinquents. Children usually have respect for other people's property when they have property of their own that they value and don't want anyone else to take.

Disobedience

Father gets a parking ticket because he forgot about alternate sides of the street on Wednesdays; mother has a whipped cream dessert in spite of her physician's orders not to. Are mother and father disobedient? When Junior comes home from the playground at five instead of obeying orders to come home at four, is his disobedience any worse than theirs? Genuine forgetfulness, negligence, or occasional breaking of a rule is only human. Willful chronic disobedience is another matter.

Some children with a strong urge toward independence may test out many parental rules by disobeying them on purpose. A child who has been ordered not to spend any time with another child because the families are feuding, may, by flouting the order, be telling his parents that he has a right to choose his own friends. Where disobedience affects a youngster's health or safety or morals, it's time for parental action, not necessarily in the form of punishment, but in taking stock of the situation to find out why the child won't obey.

Divorced Parents

See "Separation and Divorce" in Ch. 5, *The Middle Years.*

Dreams and Nightmares

Children go through periods of having "bad dreams" or nightmares that wake them up in the middle of the night in a state of terror and bewilderment. It won't do to say, "It's just a dream." To a young child who is just beginning to grasp the difference between what's real and what isn't, nightmare can be extremely threatening. If the child wants to describe the dream after she collects herself, she should be allowed to do so even at 3:00 A.M. She may amplify and exaggerate a little bit, but that's only to let you know that she's been very brave through it all. Parental patience is called for; with a certain amount of reassurance, the child can usually be led back to bed and to sleep.

Youngsters whose sleep is regularly interrupted by nightmares or who are in the grip of the same nightmare may be feeling anxious about a daytime activity or may be feeling guilty about some undiscovered naughtiness. A tactful chat can sometimes reveal what the trouble is so that it can be disposed of during waking hours.

Night Terrors

Some children may have occasional nightmares — often called *night terrors* — in which they scream or tremble in terror. They may sit up in bed while still asleep, or even walk around. Their terror is certainly real, but the parents should remember that the cause of it is purely imaginary. Accordingly, they have no reason to be alarmed; in spite of the child's appearance, she is not in any danger, and no drastic action is called for.

Simply comfort the child, who frequently will be disoriented and confused in a half-awake state, until she can go back to sleep. She will probably have no recollection of the episode the next morning.

If night terrors occur only occasionally, there is no cause for concern, although it might be a good idea to check on the television shows your child is watching before bedtime. If there is a great deal of tension in the household, that could be a contributing cause. If night terrors are persistent or frequent, however, a physician should be consulted. See also SLEEPWALKING.

Dyslexia

Dyslexia is a condition in which an otherwise average or intelligent child suffers from a complex of motor-perceptual disabilities that interfere with the orderly processing and acquisition of language. The disability that results in an inhibition of symbol recognition essential for learning how to read, write, and spell is thought to originate in some form of brain circuitry malfunction that may have been caused by injury or by genetic defect. Recent researchers have established some connection between dyslexia and a faulty pathway between the lower brain—the cerebellum—and the inner ear, causing the dyslexic child to suffer from a mild and permanent form of motion sickness that interferes with learning.

Symptoms

The symptoms of dyslexia vary considerably and may include: garbled or disordered development of speech during the early years; an inability to learn the relationship between sounds and symbols for purposes of reading aloud; an inability to learn how to spell or how to organize written expression; confusion about serial order, as in naming the days of the week or in number concepts; unusual difficulty in doing simple repetitive tasks.

If a parent suspects that a child is suffering from dyslexia, a diagnosis should be made on the basis of tests administered by trained professionals. The child's pediatrician or the school guidance counselor should be consulted about where such tests are best given and assessed. Should the child be diagnosed as dyslexic, an appropriate remedial program or an accredited special school can help surmount some of the learning difficulties.

Earache

Earache is one of the most common complaints of childhood.

As Secondary Infection

Earache is often attributable to bacterial infection of the middle ear and should be treated promptly by a physician. Because the eustachian tube that connects the back of the throat with the middle ear is shorter and wider in a child than in an adult, it affords easier entry to bacteria. Infections of the ear may thus occur as the result of a sore throat or a postnasal drip. Infectious mucus from the nose is often forced into the middle ear by way of the eustachian tube because young children are inclined to sniff it back rather than to blow it out. And when a child is mastering the technique of noseblowing, he should be told that neither one nor both of the nostrils should be pressed closed in the process. Rather, both nostrils should be blown out gently at the same time, and with the mouth open. If gentle blowing doesn't clear the nostrils, the nose should be wiped as necessary.

Recognizing Earache in an Infant

Earache in an infant may be combined with fever and the kind of crying associated with sharp pain. A toddler may indicate the source of discomfort by pulling at the earlobe. Until the pediatrician can prescribe proper medication, discomfort can be relieved by applying a heating pad to the involved ear and giving the child a non-aspirin pain reliever.

Other Causes

Earache may also accompany teething or tooth infection, or it may be the result of pressure caused by water that has been trapped in the ear after swimming or bathing. In small children, an earache may be a sign that the youngster has stuffed a bean or a tiny plastic object so far into his ear that it won't come out as easily as it went in. If you suspect such an occurrence, avoid poking and prodding in an attempt to remove the object. The child should be taken to a physician or to a hospital so that the object can be removed with the proper instruments and the ear examined and treated for possible injury.

Consequences of Neglect of Earache

An earache should always be brought to a physician's attention without delay because untreated middle ear infections can lead to irreversible hearing loss. The leading cause of mild hearing loss in toddlers is believed to be *serous otitis media*, or serous infection of the middle ear. This condition is specifically an inflammation of the middle ear with an accumulation of fluid behind the eardrum. When the condition is chronic or improperly treated during the first three years, it may impair hearing permanently and as a consequence lead to a failure to develop normal language skills. Occasionally the physician may have to make a small opening in the eardrum to drain the fluid, a procedure known as a *myringotomy*. Other treatments may include the insertion of a synthetic tube into the eustachian to expand constricted areas and allow drainage of the inner ear through the auditory tube. The isthmus of the auditory tube is the narrowest point in the canal and may close during swelling or inflammation. To drain the ear properly the tube should be reopened to avoid further infection. See also HEARING.

Eczema

See under RASHES.

Education

See SCHOOL.

Epilepsy

Epilepsy in childhood most commonly takes the form of petit mal or psychomotor episodes.

Petit Mal Seizures

Petit mal episodes are characterized by brief lapses of consciousness, sometimes occurring many times a day. The child does not fall down but simply stops what he is doing and may appear to stare absently.

Psychomotor Seizures

Psychomotor episodes are characterized by the performance of some activity during a brief lapse of consciousness. The child may walk around in circles, or sit down and get up in a purposeless way. During this type of seizure the child may babble nonsensically or chant the same word over and over. Such an attack may last no more than a few minutes, and when the child recovers he is likely to have no memory of its occurrence.

In many instances, parents who expect a certain amount of bizarre behavior from their youngsters may not realize that a form of epilepsy is the cause. Should such incidents occur frequently, they should be called to the attention of the physician who may think it advisable to have the child examined by a neurologist.

A parent witnessing a *grand mal* or convulsive epileptic seizure for the first time may be unduly alarmed and take measures that may harm the child rather than help. For a description of emergency measures during a grand mal seizure, see Ch. 35, *Medical Emergencies*. For a full discussion of epilepsy, see Ch. 8, *Diseases of the Muscles and Nervous System*.

Exercise

Some children seem to sit around a great deal; others are on the move from morning until bedtime. A youngster might be listless or lethargic because there's something the matter that needs to be investigated by a physician. This type of sitting around is quite different from playing with dolls for hours at a time or looking at picture books instead of running around. A young child who really cannot sit still at all may have a problem that needs diagnosing by a physician, too. Practically all children are found between these extremes.

Exercise as a Developmental Need

Toddlers must be allowed to get the exercise necessary for the development of their bodies. They shouldn't be confined in a playpen for most of the day. Three- and four-year-olds who don't go to a nursery school and have no play equipment in their backyard (if they have a backyard), should be taken whenever possible to a local park or playground that has swings, slides, seesaws, jungle gyms, or other devices that are safely designed and installed. Most schools have some kind of supervised gym activity or a free time for yard play, and if they don't, they should. If this scheduled exercise is insufficient for a nine- or ten-year-old, inquiries can be made about athletic facilities at a local YMCA, settlement house, church, or fraternal organization.

Choice of Activities

As children get a little older, they should be permitted to choose the exercise that appeals to them unless there's a good reason for its being forbidden. A girl who wants to join a sandlot baseball team shouldn't be forced to go to a ballet class, and a boy inspired by the dancing he's seen on TV shouldn't be discouraged if the family can afford the lessons. Exercise needn't be synonymous with competition unless the youngster wants it to be. See also "Physical Fitness" in Ch. 3, *The Teens*.

Eyeglasses

Now that infants and youngsters have periodic eye checkups with their physicians, and regular tests are given to all students, more children are wearing glasses than in former years. In addition to *strabismus* (crossed eyes), the three major eye problems encountered in children are *myopia* (nearsightedness), *hyperopia* (farsightedness), and *astigmatism*.

Myopia

The *myopic* or nearsighted child cannot see distant objects well but can see close objects clearly. A very young child so afflicted may stumble and fall easily. An older child attending school may make errors in copying because she has difficulty in making out the words and figures written on the chalkboard. She may be called a behavior problem or may even be said to be mentally retarded. Most cases of myopia can be helped with glasses.

Hyperopia

The *hyperopic* (also called *hypermetropic*) or farsighted eye is shorter from front to rear than the normal eye, and if not corrected will often hinder close work like reading. When a farsighted child reads she often complains of blurring of the printed page, sleepiness, and headache. Farsightedness is often associated with crossed eyes and is usually correctable with glasses.

Astigmatism

In *astigmatism* or distorted vision, there is an uneven curvature of the cornea or lens surface of the eye. This condition causes some light rays to focus further back than others and produces a blurred, distorted image on the retina.

Either a farsighted or nearsighted eye can be *astigmatic;* the abnormality can usually be corrected by properly prescribed eyeglasses.

Fantasies

Every normal child has fantasies, some highly pleasurable, some fearful and frightening. Young children sometimes have a hard time sorting out what they imagine from what's real; this may be especially true when a nightmare interferes with sleep.

Many children quite consciously say, "Let's pretend" or "Let's make believe" when they embark on a dress-up activity; others simply and straightforwardly act out their fantasies by playing games of violence with toy guns. An only child may create a fantasy companion with whom she has conversations; a child who is encouraged to draw may give shape to her fantasies in pictures that mean a lot to her but not much to anyone else.

Daydreaming

Some children infuriate their energetic parents by sitting around and daydreaming (with one sock on and one off) instead of doing their chores. Whatever form fantasies may take, they are an inevitable part of growing up and should be respected, unless they become the equivalent of a narcotic escape from reality rather than a means of enriching it. When a child's fantasy life appears to be turning into a substitute for his real one, the time has come to consult a psychiatric authority.

Fears and Phobias

Babies are fearful about being dropped, and they're frightened by a sudden loud noise. (You *can* make babies cry by saying, "Boo!" When they get older and catch on, they'll think it's fun to be scared.) Toddlers are taught to be afraid of a hot stove, and as children get a little older, they develop night fears that become bad dreams. Many parents transmit, de-

liberately or unknowingly, some of their fears to their children: fear of dogs, or thunder and lightning, or infection by germs.

Only a thin line separates sensible caution from anxiety. Where a threat of punishment is involved, an anxiety may develop that can last a lifetime. Parents should control the impulse to say such things as, "Don't eat that, it's going to make you sick" or "Don't climb so high, you're going to fall" or "Don't play in the mud; the germs will make you sick." Or, worse yet, "If you do that, the bogey man will get you" or "God will punish you."

Phobias

If fears are often legitimate and usually outgrown through reassuring experiences, phobias are deep-seated unconquerable fears. Many adults suffer from them; two of the most common are *claustrophobia*, the fear of being in an enclosed place, and *acrophobia*, the fear of heights. *Phobia* is a clinical term and shouldn't be used to describe a youngster's aversion to school at a particular time, or his apprehension about elevators and escalators. If parental reassurance can help a child overcome fears of this type, they need not be classed as phobias.

Fever

As every parent knows, babies can run very high fevers. In itself, a rectal temperature of 103° F or 104° F is not necessarily cause for alarm. (Normal rectal temperature is about ½° F to 1° F higher than the oral norm of 98.6° F.) Of course, you should take the immediate step of calling your pediatrician to find out what's causing the fever.

If a baby's fever goes over 104° F, the infant may experience convulsions. To avoid this possibility, he may be bathed with cool water or with equal parts of water and alcohol. (The alcohol is not necessary.) If convulsions do occur, protect the baby from injuring himself by seeing that his head and body don't strike anything hard. The convulsion, though frightening, is usually brief and ends of its own accord. Get in touch with your physician without delay.

Although the mechanism that results in fever is not precisely understood, the elevation in temperature is almost always a sign that the child's normal body processes are being disturbed. A child old enough to talk can let you know that his throat is sore or that he has an earache.

Possible Causes

Fever is often the sign of the onset of an infectious disease such as measles or influenza; it usually accompanies severe sunburn; it may be a warning that the infection of a local cut is spreading through the rest of the body. When it comes suddenly and rises quickly, along with cramps or diarrhea, it may indicate a gastrointestinal infection or food poisoning. No matter what a child's age, if temperature by mouth rises above 101° F, a physician should be informed of the fever and accompanying symptoms.

Treatment

Until a diagnosis is made and treatment prescribed, the feverish youngster should be put to bed and kept on a diet of light foods and lots of liquids. If the elevated temperature is combined with stiff neck, aching joints, or headache, nonaspirin medication can be given for relief according to dose instructions indicated.

Fluoridation

Although it has been unequivocally established that fluoridated drinking water is the best safeguard against tooth decay, many parts of the United States continue to resist this public health measure, thus placing a special burden on the parents of preschool children. Families in such communities are strongly urged to consult their dentist or the closest dental clinic connected with a university's college of dentistry for advice on the appropriate measures to be taken to protect their children's teeth. A consultation of this nature is advisable as soon as the baby shows signs of teething, because the fluoride treatments should begin as early as possible.

In many areas where the water supply remains unfluoridated, programs in the public schools supply youngsters with fluoride tablets every day. Although this method of applying the chemical is less effective than its availability in the drinking water, it is a step in the right direction. Concerned parents can make an effort to initiate such programs where none exists by contacting state public health officials.

Foot Care

Unless the child's pediatrician indicates the need for corrective or orthopedic shoes, parents need have little concern for pigeon toes or bowed legs or flat feet. If a shoe salesman suggests remedial footwear, his suggestions should be discussed with a physician before complying with them. A good general rule to follow about the fit of shoes is that they should be about three-quarters of an inch longer than the foot itself. For a child whose feet have a tendency to perspire heavily, sweat socks made of cotton or wool are to be preferred to those made of synthetics. Blisters that form on the instep, heel, or any other part of the foot because of ill-fitting footwear must be treated promptly to avoid serious infection.

Friends

Everyone needs friends. Some children need only one; others seem to enjoy having several. A three-year-old who is just beginning to learn about sharing may be more relaxed playing with just one other child; a ten-year-old may like the hurly-burly of a group of friends to get together with when school is out.

Parents Please Stay Out

Parents should try to steer clear of squabbles between children. One day, Nancy and Harriet are best friends, the next, bitter enemies, because of some real or imagined outrage. Left to their own devices, the children will probably patch things up. If parents get involved, the situation gets magnified out of all proportion. It's not unusual in such situations for the two sets of parents to stop speaking to each other and the two little girls to go back to being best friends again.

Keeping Bad Company

What's to be done about "unsuitable" friends? Some parents may think a particular child is unacceptable because she's too aggressive or too foul-mouthed. If your child seems fond of her nonetheless, voice your opinions, but don't forbid the youngster from coming to the house. Any attempt to break up the friendship is likely to be resisted until your child learns from experience that your judgment was the right one. Children who are discouraged from bringing their friends home because they make a mess or make too much noise are actually deprived of feeling at home in their own house.

Friendships between girls and boys may begin in nursery school and continue for years afterward. Although the tone of the friendship may change, the closeness can be very valuable if it doesn't exclude other relationships.

Frostbite

See Ch. 35, *Medical Emergencies*.

Guilt and Conscience

Children often feel as guilty about bad thoughts as they do about bad deeds. After being angry, a child may feel as badly about having had a fleeting wish to hurt his mother as he would have felt had he actually hurt her. A child should be helped to understand that his thoughts are his own, that his thoughts cannot harm anybody, and that he will not be punished for his thoughts. He should understand that it is only actions of certain kinds that cannot be allowed and that will result in a reprimand or punishment. In other words, a child should not be made to feel guilty for angry or aggressive thoughts toward other members of his family, but only for angry and aggressive acts.

A parent might say to a child, "I understand that you really disliked your brother when you hit him, in fact, even hated him and would have liked to hurt him. It's okay for you to be angry with him, but I am not going to let you hurt him." A clear distinction should be made between hostile feelings and hostile behavior.

Headaches

Children get headaches just as adults do. The difficulty in diagnosing and treating them comes from the differ-

ent symptoms that children experience. It is believed that up to 10 percent of preadolescents suffer from migraine headaches.

Symptoms of headaches in children include aggression, agitation, vomiting, nausea, visual problems, insomnia, and profuse sweating. Causes are the same as they are in adults: tension, stress, eye strain, migraine, or emotional or physical problems. For a child experiencing frequent or severe headaches, a physician should be consulted to eliminate the possibility of an underlying physical disorder, such as near or farsightedness. Once the doctor has determined that no physical disorder exists, treatment of the psychological cause should be considered. Undue pressure from home or the school can create as much stress on a child as an adult experiences in the workplace.

Medication of children should be taken only under the supervision of a qualified doctor. Children respond to certain medications much differently than adults, and care must be taken in administering the types and quantities of drugs. Also treatment of any child with aspirin should be supervised because of the risk of Reye's Syndrome.

Diagnosis and treatment of children with headaches is difficult. Parents should continue to seek treatment for their children until they are satisfied that the problem has been addressed and is being remedied.

Health Records

It may seem somewhat troublesome to keep orderly health records for every member of the family, but the accumulated information can be extremely helpful if it can be supplied at a moment's notice to a physician or a hospital. Chronologically arranged facts can also provide the material eventually needed by summer camps and school applications and insurance policies.

A notebook containing essential data about past illnesses, accidents, allergies, surgery, and other facts can be extraordinarily helpful and time-saving in supplying a physician with a medical history that simplifies diagnosis and treatment. Such a notebook should have separate sections for immunizations and booster shots and their dates; annual weight and height progress; illnesses with dates and special notations; accidents with dates and any permanent consequences; hospitalization and reason; individual problems relating to allergies, hearing, vision, speech, and the like. Visits to physician and dentist should be recorded, and the blood type entered in a conspicuous place. If possible, parents should also provide a summary at the back of the notebook of their own major illnesses, disabilities, and surgical history.

Hearing

Approximately half of all adult hearing problems are thought to have originated in childhood. About five out of every hundred children reveal some hearing disability when screening tests are given. Total deafness among children is uncommon, and where it does exist, its symptoms become manifest to parents and physicians alike during infancy.

Partial Hearing Loss

Partial hearing disability, on the other hand, is common, and is likely to be overlooked until it may be too late to correct its consequences.

A physician begins to suspect a hearing problem when the mother of a young baby tells him that the child does not react to her voice, to noises, or to other auditory stimuli. As the child gets older, he may not speak properly. Because he has never heard speech, he cannot imitate its sound and may fail to develop normal language skills. Sometimes these children, like visually handicapped children, are mistakenly called mentally retarded or are classified as suffering from hyperkinesis or brain dysfunction. Often the undetected hearing disability stemmed from a middle ear infection that was treated inadequately or not treated at all.

Language Problems

A hearing loss of 15 decibels is considered sufficiently large to produce language problems for a very young child, causing a major handicap in the acquisition of language skills. Specialists therefore recommend that parents ask that their physician test a baby's hearing, especially during and after an ear infection. If a compensatory hearing aid is necessary, the baby should be supplied with one immediately. Speech will not develop normally—that is, the language function of the brain will be impaired—unless the essential sounds of language can be perceived during the first two years of life.

Just as glasses or surgery can help eye problems, simple hearing aids, the surgical removal of excessive lymphoid tissue blocking the eustachian tube, or special instruction in lip reading can often help a hearing problem and open up a new world for the child afflicted with a hearing disability.

Heart Disease

See RHEUMATIC FEVER. See also "Congenital Heart Disease" in Ch. 10, *Heart Disease.*

Hernia

A *hernia* is a condition in which part of an organ protrudes through a weak spot or other abnormal opening in the wall of a body cavity. There are three types of hernias that may occur in children.

Umbilical Hernia

The most common is an *umbilical hernia*, in which there is a protrusion of some of the contents of the abdomen through an opening in the abdominal wall at the navel where the umbilical cord was attached. When the baby cries or strains, the protrusion becomes more obvious, and when the baby is at rest, the bulge recedes. An umbilical hernia usually disappears by the time a child reaches the second year. Because it represents no danger to any of the body functions, the condition need be no cause for concern. It is very common in non-Caucasian children.

Inguinal Hernia

The second most common type of hernia in childhood is known as an *indirect inguinal hernia,* occurring frequently in boys. At birth it may have the appearance of a marble located under the skin at the groin. In time, it may descend into the scrotum that encloses the testicles. This type of hernia is usually corrected by simple surgery that repairs the weakened musculature. The weak muscles are often present on both sides.

Hiatus Hernia

Another congenital hernia is known as a *hiatus hernia* (or *diaphragmatic hernia*) in which part of the stomach protrudes upward through the part of the esophagus that opens into the diaphragm. In some cases, this structural defect is self-healing. Surgical correction is advised only if the hernia interferes with respiration. See also Ch. 11, *Diseases of the Digestive System.*

Hospitalization

Most children at some time in their first 15 years of life require at least one hospitalization, ranging in time from a few days to many months. This can be a frightening experience and may leave permanent emotional scars on a child. Parents can do many things to make the experience less harmful.

Preparing the child for the hospital stay may be the most important task for the parent. There are many books available for different age groups on going to the hospital. Authorities generally agree that parents should:

- Try to answer all the questions the child asks. If you have no answer, try to find one.

- Be as honest as possible. The child will want to know why he or she has to go to the hospital, what will be done there, how long it will take, and whether it will hurt.

- Be reassuring. The child should know that he or she will receive good care and that the hospital visit will be temporary.

- Explain what the hospital is and what it is like — with wheeled carts, people in uniform, and so on.

- Using sheets as gowns, role-play to make it clear that under the gowns will be helping people.

- Let the child know when they will be in the hospital and how long they will stay.

Most hospitals today try to work with parents to make the child feel at home and to allay the child's fears. Many hospitals offer rooms so that parents can "room in" — and stay near the young patient. A playroom may be available. Hospital staff members may hold parent-nurse sessions to introduce mothers and fathers to the hospital's schedule, locations of facilities, and other details. Parents of a child who has to be hospitalized can, by learning as much as possible and cooperating with the staff, help alleviate a child's natural fears of separation, of mutilation, and of the strange new situation.

Fear of Separation

Hospitalization for an operation or an illness affects different children at different stages of their development in different ways. Very young children may be particularly worried about separations from their mothers. Parents can help with this fear by assuring the child that separation will not be permanent.

If at all possible, the child's mother or another member of the family should stay with the child during much of the hospital stay. During an extended hospitalization, of course, this may become difficult or impossible. Barring accidents, children should always be forewarned of a hospitalization; if they are not, they may feel they were deceived by their parents and lose trust in them.

Fear of Mutilation

Children of about 4 to 10 or 11 may be more worried about possible damage or mutilation of their bodies than about separations from their families. They often have fears that parts of their bodies may be cut out or that in some way they may be permanently harmed. They may feel that when they come back from the hospital they will not be the same as they were when they went in. Matter-of-fact reassurance by the parents can be most helpful in alleviating these fears.

Fear of the Strange

Both younger children and older children aged 10, 11, or 12 may fear the new or strange, such as the anesthetic that goes with an operation. The child should be allowed to talk out fears. Simple explanations usually help. A child can, for example, understand that when you get sick taking medicine can sometimes make you better. At other times an operation, or surgery, is the only thing that will help. In the hospital, physicians or nurses may have to make tests to find out what is wrong. One such test is the X ray, which is simply a "picture" of a part of the child's body.

The parent can prepare the child for the operating room and for the operation. Everything in this special place, for example, must be kept perfectly clean, so nurses and physicians wear long-sleeved gowns. They also wash carefully before the operation begins. They wear sterile gloves so that they can touch patients without passing on germs. They also wear masks, shoe coverings, and caps. They may make a small opening in the patient's skin so that they can take out or get rid of whatever is making the child sick. The physicians and nurses use stitches, or sutures, to pull the skin edges together and allow healing to begin. Some stitches may be under the skin; these simply melt, or dissolve, by themselves.

A dressing may be placed over the part of the child's body that was opened up. These pieces of soft cloth protect the skin opening and keep out germs. When the dressing comes off, a white scar may remain. The scar will not open up and it will not hurt. It will be a sign that the child was sick, got well, and came home.

Hostility

See ANGER.

Hyaline Membrane Disease

Hyaline membrane disease, now technically called the *respiratory distress syndrome*, is a disorder that affects approximately 50,000 newborn babies each year, and until recently was fatal for about half of them. The disorder occurs especially among premature infants, those born by caesarian section, and those with diabetic mothers. In premature infants, the immaturity of the lungs may result in a collapse of the air space within the lungs themselves when the first breath is exhaled. Each new breath then becomes a greater struggle, and with the spread of lung collapse, exhaustion and asphyxiation may occur.

A treatment known as *continuous positive airway pressure* is now being successfully used in many of the special hospital units equipped for newborns with disabilities. The therapy involves a pressure chamber that forces high-oxygen air into the lungs and keeps these air spaces open. The method has already prevented thousands of infant deaths. Newborns who need this assistance acquire the ability to breathe normally in about a week.

Hyperkinesis

Hyperkinesis is a behavioral disorder diagnosed in a large number of schoolchildren—more often boys than girls—who are unable to concentrate and who are overactive and excitable. These characteristics cause them to become disruptive in the classroom as well as disturbing to their families. There are indications that this disorder manifests itself in infancy, when the physician might describe an excessively fretful and restless baby as *hypertonic*, and prescribe medication to calm him down.

For reasons not yet understood, it has been found that the symptoms of hyperkinesis often respond to antidepressants or stimulants, and as a result, a significant number of otherwise unmanageable youngsters are being treated medically. Although the medication enables them to conform to classroom situations, it may have the negative effect of appetite loss; to avoid sleep difficulties, the medication is never given in the evening.

Hyperkinesis appears to run in families, although there is some evidence that imperceptible brain damage may be one of its causes. Parents of a clinically hyperkinetic child—not one who is simply rambunctious—should seek advice about proper treatment from the psychiatric and neurological staffs of the nearest teaching hospital or from specialists recommended by the family physician.

Imagination

See FANTASIES.

Immunization

Recently developed vaccines against measles, mumps, and rubella (German measles) should eventually wipe out these diseases in the same way that smallpox has been eliminated practically everywhere in the world. Routine immunization follows a schedule of shots administered with minor variations by most pediatricians and child care clinics. Severe reactions are rare, but should they occur, they should be reported to the physician promptly.

Keeping Records

Records should be kept of the child's immunization history so that booster shots can be given at proper intervals. Because families move from one place to another, changing physicians as they relocate, it saves a great deal of time and trouble if immunization data is written down rather than committed to memory. See HEALTH RECORDS.

DTP Injections

DTP stands for diphtheria, tetanus, and pertussis (or whooping cough). DTP injections are usually given in the muscles of the mid-thigh or upper arm, at intervals of one month, sometimes longer. To prevent fever or other severe reactions, the two- to five-month-old baby should receive one grain of baby aspirin within a few hours after the injection. If she nev-

Recommended Schedule for Active Immunization of Normal Infants and Children

Recommended Age	Vaccine[a]	Comments
2 months	DTP, OPV	Can be initiated earlier in areas of high incidence
4 months	DTP, OPV	2-month interval desired for OPV to avoid interference
6 months	DTP	OPV optional for areas where polio might be imported (e.g., some areas of southwestern United States)
12 months	TB test	May be given simultaneously with MMR at 15 months (see text)
15 months	Measles, Mumps, Rubella; DPT, OPV	MMR preferred
24 months	Hemophilus b polysaccharide vaccine	
24 months	Hemophilus b	Hemophilus b polysaccharide vaccine for Hemophilus influenza type b
4–6 years	DTP, OPV	

[a] *DTP*—diphtheria and tetanus toxoids with pertussis vaccine. *OPV*—oral, attenuated poliovirus vaccine contains poliovirus types 1, 2, and 3. *Tuberculin test*—mantoux (intradermal PPD) preferred. Frequency of tests depends on local epidemiology. The Committee recommends annual or biennial testing unless local circumstances dictate less frequent or no testing (see tuberculosis for complete discussion. *MMR*—live measles, mumps, and rubella viruses in a combined vaccine (see text for discussion of single vaccines versus combination). *Td*—adult tetanus toxoid (full dose) and diphtheria toxoid (reduced dose) combination.

[b] Up to the seventh birthday.

ertheless develops fever or has other severe reactions, your physician may have to give lower doses, and therefore give more than three injections. Very rarely is a severe reaction reported with smaller doses of the vaccine. If there is such a reaction, no further injections of pertussis vaccine will be given.

Occasionally, redness or a lump appears at the site of the injection. This is a local reaction. It is harmless and will disappear within a few weeks. If it does not, consult your physician.

It is recommended that a booster or recall shot be given at one-and-a-half and at three years of age. Another recall injection of only TD (tetanus-diphtheria toxoid) is given at six years and at twelve years.

DTP Reactions

Adverse reactions to the DTP vaccine have been reported in a few cases. The reactions ranged from permanent neurological damage to such mild symptoms as persistent crying and unusual sleepiness. Crying may be high-pitched and may continue as long as three hours or more. Sleepiness may resemble a shocklike state. Some children may run temperatures of 105° F or higher. In cases of suspected adverse reactions to DTP or any other vaccine, a pediatrician or family physician should be called immediately.

Parents may want to discuss their children's medical histories with their family physicians or pediatricians before taking a child in for an inocculaton. The American Academy of Pediatrics suggests that children with personal histories of convulsions or allergic reactions to DTP or other vaccines should not be given the DTP vaccine. The same is true of children born prematurely.

Independence

Many parents feel that the most memorable moment in a child's progress towards independence comes when he takes his first steps alone. Upright and walking! Most children accomplish this by going independently from the secure arms of one adult to the waiting arms of another. As youngsters move toward greater independence, they will do so with confidence if they can start out from a secure foundation of rules and limits, and return to the security of acceptance and understanding should they come to grief.

The Toddler Stage

The toddler relishes the independence of being able to explore the house or the playground but he won't go very far before he returns to check

in with the person in charge of him so that he can start out all over again. He voices his independence, too: "no" to naps; "no" to outings; "no" to a bath. This is the phase during which parents must be wary of asking "Would you like to" or "Do you want to" instead of just proceeding with the business at hand. Patience is required for the self-assertive fumblings and clumsy efforts at self-feeding and putting clothes on. Assistance should be subtle and tactful, not hurried and bossy: "Baby do, daddy help," is the general idea.

School Age

As the child moves into the larger arena of school and friendships, "I'm not a baby any more" may become a complaint if he wants more freedom than he's permitted to have. At this stage, he begins to learn that responsibility goes hand-in-hand with freedom and independence. Old enough to ride the bike farther and farther from home means taking on the responsibility of keeping it in good repair and obeying all the traffic rules.

Influenza

See "The Common Cold, Influenza, and Other Viral Infections" in Ch. 12, *Diseases of the Respiratory System.*

Insect Stings and Bites

When a child is bitten or stung by an insect, he often complains about the pain or the itching, but with the application of a lotion or salve to relieve discomfort and a bandage to prevent infection, the incident is soon forgotten. There are times, however, when a sting or a bite may require emergency treatment.

It has been estimated that about four children out of every 1,000 have serious allergic reactions to the sting of a hornet, wasp, bee, yellow jacket, or the fire ant. A child who has sustained multiple stings, or whose body, tongue, or face begins to swell because of a single sting should be taken to the hospital immediately. Tests can clearly distinguish between those children who are highly sensitive to stings and those who are not.

Preventive Measures

A physician should be consulted about the advisability of testing youngsters who are going off to camp for the first time or who are planning long hikes. Rather than curtail the activities of a child who turns out to have an acute sensitivity, it may make sense to plan a series of desensitization treatments against the particular venom. For children who are very allergic to insect stings, an emergency kit containing adrenaline is now available and should always be carried.

Mosquitoes

Every effort should be made to eradicate mosquitoes by eliminating their breeding places. A mosquito bite can be a serious threat to a child's health because these insects transmit several diseases. Where mosquitoes are a problem, infants and children should be protected against them by screens, netting, and the application of repellents.

Ticks

Families that travel and those that have pets should guard against the possibility of infection by disease-bearing ticks. A species of tick known as *Ixodes dammini* can transmit an illness called Lyme disease while another common tick may carry Rocky Mountain spotted fever.

Rashes may appear as symptoms of infection by either tick. The Lyme disease rash may be circular and hot to the touch. It may have a diameter as wide as 28 inches. Untreated in either children or adults, Lyme disease may trigger chills, fever, general feelings of malaise, fatigue, and attacks of arthritis that may last weeks or months to years. Heart and nerve abnormalities may appear. Penicillin is used to bring Lyme disease under control in pregnant women and children.

Less prevalent than Lyme disease, Rocky Mountain spotted fever usually produces a rash on the soles of the feet and the palms of the hands. Prompt medical attention is essential to prevent possible complications. See ROCKY MOUNTAIN SPOTTED FEVER and LYME DISEASE under RASHES.

Intelligence and IQ

Intelligence is a quality, not a quantity. It therefore cannot be measured as precisely as height or weight; nor can it be exemplified as definitely as mechanical skill or athletic ability or musical talent. Although child development authorities and educators may disagree about how to assess intelligence, they generally agree on the following premise: no matter what is inherited and what is instilled by experience, children function best in later life if their earliest years of nurture bring out and develop their inborn capacities.

Encouragement and Enrichment

Beginning with proper prenatal diet and care, a healthy baby is born, and from then on, her intellectual capacities are shaped by experience. Loving and attentive parents give her the self-confidence to explore and learn. She is encouraged to express herself in language. She is exposed to a variety of experiences that will stimulate her curiosity and interest: plants, drawing materials, pets, picture books, outings to the beach. Her efforts to use her intelligence by asking questions are respected and encouraged rather than minimized and ignored.

IQ Tests

Once a child gets to school her capabilities may or may not be measured by a standard IQ test. Such tests, which have been abandoned in some states, assess specific areas of intelligence and are graded according to a statistical norm. Newer techniques for measuring intelligence are designed to compensate for a cultural bias that some authorities believe exists in the standard tests.

Jealousy

See BROTHERS AND SISTERS, NEW BABY.

Kidney Diseases

For a discussion of kidney diseases, see Ch. 17, *Diseases of the Urinogenital System*, and Ch. 18, *Cancer*.

Learning

See CURIOSITY, INTELLIGENCE AND IQ, READING, SCHOOL.

Lead Poisoning

Lead poisoning in children is usually associated with the ingestion of paint and plaster flakes containing high levels of lead. This is a problem in city slums where old buildings are being leveled, or in cases where youngsters manage to gnaw on repainted cribs and other furniture originally covered with lead-base paint. In homes being renovated, the dust from removal of lead paint can cause an increase in lead levels in the blood.

Lead poisoning is a serious danger to the health of approximately half a million children in the United States. Irreversible brain damage and anemia can occur if the condition becomes chronic; convulsions and death may occur in an acute case. To lessen such hazards, legislation now requires new cars to use only lead-free gasoline.

Learning Disability

A child with a learning disability is one who, though otherwise normal, cannot acquire certain skills or assimilate certain kinds of knowledge at the same rate as most other children. Obviously, almost every child lags behind her peers at one time or another in certain subjects; but the difficulties of a learning disabled child are far more severe. A 16-year-old who suffers from a learning disability may, for example, be capable only of third- or fourth-grade math while functioning at her own grade level in other subjects. Some learning disabilities are attributed to minimal brain damage, but in most cases the cause is unknown. See also DYSLEXIA.

Leukemia

See CANCER.

Lying

See DISHONESTY.

Malnutrition

Poor nutrition or undernourishment can occur not only as a result of a faulty diet, but also because a child may have a metabolic defect that prevents her body from making proper use of a particular essential nutrient. Temporary malnutrition may also accompany a long illness in which the child's appetite wanes.

Although malnutrition is usually associated with poverty and child neglect, it can also occur because of ignorance, carelessness, or fanaticism. Children have been found to be malnourished by parents following a macrobiotic diet or a faddish type of vegetarianism. Using vitamins as a substitute for food can also cause certain types of undernourishment.

Older children, especially girls approaching puberty, may embark on starvation diets in an attempt to ward off inevitable body changes and end up seriously malnourished. The general signs of malnutrition are increasing physical weakness, vague and unfocused behavior, as well as the particular symptoms associated with anemia and vitamin deficiencies. See also Ch. 27, *Nutrition and Weight Control.*

Measles

Measles is by far the most dangerous of the common childhood diseases because of its possible complications, such as meningitis, encephalitis, and severe secondary staphylococcus infection. Fortunately, widespread protection is available in the live measles vaccine, which should be given to every child over one year of age.

Symptoms

Measles, a highly contagious disease caused by a virus, has an incubation period of one to two weeks. The most noticeable symptom is the rash that begins on the head and face within a few days after the onset of the disease, and gradually erupts all over the body, blending into big red patches. Other symptoms include fever up to 104° F or higher, a severe cough, sore throat, stuffy nose, inflammation of the *conjunctiva* (the mucous membrane on the inner part of the eyelid and extending over the front of the eyeball), sensitivity of the eyes to light, enlarged lymph nodes, and a generalized sick feeling.

Any child who has contracted measles should be seen by a physician and watched carefully for possible complications. Moreover, if he is of school age, the school should be promptly notified. This, of course, is true for any contagious disease.

Treatment

Measles can be treated only symptomatically. During the incubation period, an injection of gamma globulin will lessen the severity of the disease, or occasionally prevent it. If there are other children at home besides the affected one, they should also receive gamma globulin injections. Antibiotics are of no help unless there is a secondary bacterial infection.

It is now suspected that vaccinations given in the United States and Canada during the 1960s and 1970s were not triggering permanent immunity to measles. Anyone who has been vaccinated during that period should consult his or her physician about reimmunization. The number of cases, including adult cases, of measles has risen dramatically. This is partly because of the need for revaccination in adults; it is also because many parents are not having their children immunized. Measles can be fatal and vaccination can protect against needless deaths from this preventable disease.

All parents should make certain that their children are vaccinated against this potentially serious disease. See IMMUNIZATION.

Medication

New parents can save themselves time and trouble by getting into the habit of writing down a physician's instructions about medication when the child requires it. Although dosages are usually clearly indicated on labels prepared by the pharmacist according to the prescription, the physician may add comments about how or when to change the dosage.

How to Give Medicines to Children

As for administering medication, a calm and assured approach and a minimum of fuss are more effective than wheedling and urging. A very young child may need to be distracted by cheerful conversation as the spoon goes into her mouth; an older child can be given some factual information about the medication and what it will do. No matter what the youngster's age, parents should never trick or fool her about what she's being given, nor should candied medicine be used under any circumstances. Setting up this type of confusion in a young mind can lead to an overdose of "candy" serious enough to require emergency hospitalization.

Overusing Medication

As a child gets older, she will become increasingly conscious of the medication her parents take. Families that are constantly swallowing one or another kind of pill—diet pills, sleeping pills, tranquilizers—might give some thought to their attitude towards drugs and how these attitudes are affecting their children. Generally, it's a good idea to refrain from medicating a child unless the pediatrician recommends it.

Old Medicines

Once the illness for which a particular medication has been prescribed is definitely over, the remains of the bottle or the leftover capsules should be flushed down the toilet. Old, outdated pills can be dangerous. For safety's sake, parents should review the contents of the medicine cabinet on a regular basis and get rid of any medications left over from a previous illness. Basic medications that are essential for occasional emergencies should be reviewed for continuing effectiveness. Some of these might have a limited shelf life and be completely ineffective should they be needed.

Meningitis

Meningitis is an inflammation of the *meninges*, the thin membranes that cover the spinal cord and the brain. The inflammation, which may be caused by a virus or by bacteria, is more common among children than adults, and may occur in epidemics. This is especially true if the infectious agent is meningococcal (*meningococcal meningitis*), because the meningococcal bacteria are also found in the throat and are transmitted by coughing, sneezing, and talking. This type occurs mostly in young adults. Another type of meningitis that commonly occurs among young children during the spring and summer is caused by such organisms as the mumps virus and the coxsackievirus.

Symptoms

Whatever the cause, the symptoms are generally the same: headache, fever, vomiting, and stiff neck. If untreated, the child may go into delirium and convulsions. Drowsiness and blurred vision may also occur, and if the disease develops in an infant, the pressure on the brain caused by the inflamed meninges will create a bulge on the soft spot (fontanelle) of the baby's head. No time should be lost in calling the physician about any of these symptoms.

Meningitis was almost always fatal before the availability of antibiotics, and although it is no longer the threat it once was, it must be treated promptly if irreversible consequences are to be avoided.

Mental Illness

Behind the search for the causes and treatment of mental illness in children is the current research in the relationship between that mysterious entity called the mind and that palpable physical organism called the brain. Parents of children diagnosed as mentally ill are themselves caught up in this distinction, often preferring to call their youngsters "emotionally disturbed." It is now estimated that about one-and-a-half million youngsters under 18 require some kind of treatment for mental illness, and this figure does not include the one million children diagnosed as hyperkinetic. The two most serious forms of childhood mental illness are autism and schizophrenia.

Autism

The term "early infantile autism" was coined in the 1940s to describe babies and young children who show unpredictable deviations in development. Some never learn to speak; others refuse to look anyone directly in the eye. Autistic children may have one or two extraordinary skills and be incapable of remembering their own names. In spite of a tendency on the part of a few specialists to ascribe autism to a rejecting mother's refusal to love the infant, most authorities now describe this mysterious disorder as an organic condition caused by neurological rather than by psychological abnormalities. The same conclusions are more or less being reached about schizophrenia.

Schizophrenia

In schizophrenia, a child is likely to exhibit any of the following symptoms: confused speech and thinking; lack of emotional responsiveness; withdrawal into fantasy; and, occasionally, hallucinations. There are indications that genetic inheritance plays some role in this disorder, and that environmental influences are also involved.

Studies suggest that symptoms originate in abnormalities of brain chemistry that may be corrected by the proper medication. Over the past twenty years, many special schools, both day schools and residential ones, have been established for training autistic and schizophrenic children. The most successful enlist the cooperation of parents as cotherapists. The National Society for Children and Adults with Autism was organized to initiate schools, offer counseling to parents, and foster research. The Society operates a National Information and Referral Service that can be addressed at 1234 Massachusetts Ave., NW, Ste. 1017, Washington, DC 20005. See also HYPERKINESIS.

Mental Retardation

An estimated six million people in the United States are in some degree mentally retarded—almost three percent of the population. Mental retardation occurs among all nationalities, races, and religions, and among the children of those in the highest social and economic groups as well as the lowest.

What Is Mental Retardation?

Mental retardation is a developmental disability in which the individual's rate of development as a child is consistently slower than average. Learning cannot be acquired at the usual rate, and the child encounters difficulties in social adjustment.

Degrees of Mental Retardation

Mentally retarded children (and adults) are classified into four categories depending upon the degree of retardation.

Mildly retarded children—those with IQs roughly between 50 and 70—belong to by far the largest category; nearly 90 percent of all retarded people fall into this group. IQ scores by themselves can be misleading, but they are a convenient guide to probable learning and development patterns if understood properly—that is, simply as one of the criteria by which the degree of a child's disability can be estimated. The retardation of mildly retarded children is usually not apparent until they are of school age. With special educational help, such children can achieve satisfying progress in school and, as adults, will be capable with proper training of handling any of a wide variety of regular jobs. They may be indistinguishable from nonretarded people and can be expected to take their places in the life of their community.

Moderately retarded children— those with IQs somewhat below 50— belong to a group that comprises about 6 percent of all retarded people in the United States. The retardation of these children is usually apparent before they begin school, often during the child's first year, in the form of delayed developmental landmarks— for example, late sitting, late standing, late walking, and delayed talking. Many children with Down's syndrome (Mongolism) fall into this group. These children require a more sheltered environment than the mildly retarded, but can be trained as adults to do productive, satisfying work.

Severely and profoundly retarded children often have other handicaps, such as impaired motor coordination or defective vision or hearing. The great majority of these children can be taught to care for their basic needs, and many can do useful work under supervision.

Causes

There are numerous causes of mental retardation. Some cases are specifically caused by congenital factors (conditions existing at or before birth). Among these are the following: deprivation of oxygen to the brain of a baby during the birth process; the mother's contraction of rubella (German measles) during the first three months of pregnancy; complications resulting from Rh factor blood incompatibility between mother and baby; a grossly inadequate prenatal diet of the mother; syphilis; hydrocephalus (accumulation of spinal fluid in the brain); or any other pressure or injury to the brain of the fetus.

Some forms of retardation result from hereditary factors, the genetic makeup of the parents. Down's syndrome and phenylketonuria (PKU) fall in this category.

Mental retardation can also occur as a result of disease. Inflammation of the brain is a possible complication of measles—now wholly preventable by the administration of the measles vaccine. Other causes are brain injuries that result from a severe blow to the head, as from a fall. Some of these injuries are deliberately inflicted, usually by parents. (See CHILD ABUSE AND NEGLECT.) Among environmental hazards, lead and mercury poisoning are of particular importance. Lead-based paint chips have been eaten by unattended children. (See LEAD POISONING.)

If retardation is suspected by parents, medical advice should be sought immediately and a thorough evaluation of the child conducted. Some types of retardation can be greatly benefited by medical and educational treatment. It should be emphasized that all retarded children can learn and that many can be helped to the extent that they can become productive citizens. Parents would like further information about mental retardation or who are in need of counseling should write to the Association for Retarded Citizens, P.O. Box 6109, Arlington, TX 76005. See also DISABLED CHILD.

Money

Money may not be the root of all evil, but it certainly is the cause of a lot of family quarrels. To communicate to children the value of money and how to use it, spend it, save it, borrow it, lend it, and earn it, parents should try to clarify their own attitudes and settle their own differences.

Young children hear money talked about all the time: "We can't afford it," "That's a bargain," "That's a waste of money." What does it all mean to a preschooler?

The Weekly Allowance

The best way for a child to get first-hand experience in dealing with "I need" and "I want" in terms of cash on hand is to give her a weekly allowance. There isn't any point in doing this until she has mastered addition and subtraction. If the prospect of getting an allowance is motivation for improving her number skills at school, so much the better. The amount of the allowance should be calculated in terms of what it's supposed to cover. These details should be spelled out so that there's no confusion about who is responsible for paying for what. As the child gets older, the amount is adjusted for increasing needs—social occasions such as a ten-year-old might enjoy when she and her friends stop for an ice-cream cone on the way home from school.

Saving

If the family feels that a child should be required to save part of her allowance, a piggy bank and a brief talk about the virtues of saving are essential. Some children get so anxious about money that they turn into misers. When this occurs, it may be advisable to point out that the money is not meant to be hoarded but to be spent on needs and treats. Children who receive birthday or other special presents in the form of money from relatives can open a bank account and learn about interest accrual. Although the money is rightfully theirs, they might be encouraged to consult the family before they spend it all on a passing enthusiasm.

Mumps

Mumps, a mild disorder in most children, is caused by a virus and has an incubation period of from two to three weeks. The most familiar symptom is swollen glands involving the jaw. The glands usually affected are the *parotid glands*—large salivary glands below and slightly in front of the ear—although other glands may be affected, too. Other symptoms include fever and a general sick feeling. No rash is present. Mumps lasts about five days; then the swelling disappears.

In an adolescent boy, the disease sometimes causes an inflammation of the testes (called *orchitis*) and may be very painful. In addition, if it involves both testes, there is a possibility—fortunately only a very slight one—that sterility will result.

In older children mumps occasionally produces the complication called *mumps meningoencephalitis*. The signs of this more serious disease are headache, fever, and extreme debilitation. Finally, there may be an inflammation of the pancreas, which can cause severe abdominal pain and vomiting.

Because mumps is now preventable, every boy and girl should be given the mumps vaccine. Boys should be given the vaccine before puberty.

Muscular Dystrophy

See Ch. 8, *Diseases of the Muscles and Nervous System.*

Nausea and Vomiting

Nausea, the signal that vomiting may occur, is often described as feeling sick to the stomach. The feeling is experienced when irritated nerve endings in the stomach and elsewhere send messages to the vomiting reflex in the brain. When the nerve irritation is acute, vomiting occurs.

Physical Causes

Although nausea and vomiting are usually associated with a child's upset stomach or the sudden onset of a high fever and an acute infection, many youngsters feel nauseated and throw up because of motion sickness in a car or plane, or as the result of severe pain occasioned by a bad fall or other accident. A physician should always be consulted when nausea and vomiting are accompanied by fever, cramps, or diarrhea. For the child who feels sick in a moving vehicle, the physician can prescribe suitable medication. For a youngster who has swallowed a toxic substance, vomiting must often be induced. See Ch. 35, *Medical Emergencies*, for further information on poisoning.

Emotional Stress

Chronic nausea may result from emotional stress. A child who doesn't want to go to school because of some threatening situation, or who is always too anxious before a test because of pressures to do well, or who is fearful about some athletic challenge but ashamed to admit it—children under these pressures are likely to develop symptoms of nausea. However, instead of dismissing the recurrence of nausea and vomiting as typical of an oversensitive child, parents should try to find out the source of the problem and, if necessary, arrange some family therapy sessions with the child.

Nervous Habits

Nervous habits both express and release inner tension, and because growing up isn't an easy process, it's inevitable that most children have one or another way of dealing with their fears, anxieties, and emotional pressures. There's no point in parental scolding or ridicule or punishment, because any of these approaches simply adds yet another pressure to those that exist already. After all, most adults have nervous habits too—whether it's smoking, or picking at a cuticle, or tooth-grinding—and no amount of nagging is likely to put a stop to any of them.

Some nervous habits can be unhealthy, and some can be socially unacceptable but essentially harmless. All are unconscious, and most eventually disappear with age. Among the habits that may need looking into in order to decide that they have no basis in a physical disorder are squinting and throat-clearing. Hair-twirling and foot-shaking can be entirely ignored. Nail-biting may persist for years, or it may yield to vanity or the comments of friends.

Thumb-sucking, abandoned at two, may recur at three because of the arrival of a new baby or because of the stresses of going to nursery school. Many school-age children continue to suck their thumbs when they're going to sleep. There's no need to worry about this habit unless the dentist notices the beginning of an orthodontic problem, in which case, the dentist and not you should discuss it with the child. Nose-picking in public is almost always abandoned when a child enters school. If a big fuss has been made about it, he may continue the habit at home as a gesture of defiance—or because it really is unconscious. When done in private, it's completely harmless.

Masturbation bothers many parents more than it should. In and of itself, there's no harm in it, but as a chronic expression of anxiety, it might be dealt with tactfully and indirectly by trying to get to the source of the tension rather than by punishing or humiliating the child.

New Baby

It's a good idea for parents to talk about the anticipated arrival of a new baby with their child or children before the pregnancy is really obvious. Conversations can be casual, and questions should be answered simply and factually. If any basic changes are to be made—especially if a child is to be shifted to a bed so that the new arrival can have the crib—this transition should be accomplished before the infant appears. Adults should refrain from asking such questions as "Would you like a little brother or a little sister?" or "Isn't it wonderful that there's going to be a new baby in the family?" Preparations made in advance of going to the hospital should, if possible, consider whether the child would prefer to stay at home or with a relative during mother's absence. When the baby is brought home and well-wishers arrive with presents, it's comforting for the first-born to sit in mother's or daddy's lap while visitors coo over the infant in the crib. Thoughtful baby-present givers will always include a little present for the baby's older siblings, too. Parents should do their best to make baby's big brother or sister feel that the new baby is his or hers no less than mother's or father's. See also BROTHERS AND SISTERS.

Nightmares

See DREAMS AND NIGHTMARES.

Night Terrors

See DREAMS AND NIGHTMARES.

Nosebleeds

Children are likely to have nosebleeds more often than adults, and they are usually no cause for alarm. A blood vessel near the nostril may be injured by energetic noseblowing, the presence of a foreign object, or by an accidental blow or an intentional wallop.

Apply Pressure

A minor nosebleed is most effectively stopped by applying pressure over the bleeding area. A child old enough to follow instructions should be told to sit down, hold the head slightly forward, and compress the soft portion of the nose between thumb and forefinger, maintaining the pressure for about five minutes and breathing through the mouth. Application of an ice pack to the outside of the nose is usually helpful. Fingers should be

withdrawn very slowly in order not to disturb the clot that should have formed.

Packing the Nostril

If this method doesn't stop the bleeding, a small twist of sterile cotton can be inserted gently into the nostril so that some of it protrudes. Light pressure should be applied once again for five minutes and the cotton allowed to remain in place for a while. Should the bleeding continue in spite of these measures, the child should be taken to a hospital emergency clinic.

Nutrition

Children's nutritional requirements are not the same as adults. Although that may seem like an obvious statement, the fact is many parents do not take it into account when planning meals.

Infants are incapable of digesting many products. Introduction of new food to an infant should be done one item at a time. If the baby has an allergic reaction, the parent then knows what it is in response to. If the baby has eaten two or three new items, it isn't possible to tell without another feeding which one the child is allergic to.

Children can outgrow some intolerances to food. A baby that could not properly digest citrus fruit may be able to handle it well a few months or years later. Some allergies, though, get worse with each exposure. Common food allergies and intolerances include nuts, berries, milk, eggs, and fish.

Children do not require the same quantity of food as an adult. Small children will eat less at a meal, but may need to eat more frequently during the day. Their stomach holds less so they get hungry more frequently.

Children also do not require the same quantity of minerals and vitamins as adults. Childrens' vitamins are available but should not be used to replace a healthy diet. Good eating habits in children establishes a pattern that they are likely to follow for the rest of their lives. Also, children should not become adapted to the idea of taking a pill every day.

Several studies show that children who are obese can diet effectively and that they are more likely to keep the weight off than adults are. Overweight children who diet for a period even as short as 10 weeks are less obese than overweight children who never diet at all. One study demonstrated that dieting in childhood does not completely prevent obesity but it does limit the amount of weight gain to less than half that gained by those who never dieted as children.

Weight is an extremely sensitive subject to children. Adolescents in particular are susceptible to negative self-images based on weight, and to criticism by others. Disorders related to eating are covered in *The Teens* under Anorexia and Bulimia.

Weight gain can commonly be traced to the amount of television a child watches. Obesity and television viewing are related through two habits. The first is that for every hour the child is plopped in front of a television is an hour the child is not playing and exercising. The other is that television watching is usually accompanied by snacking on high-fat, high-salt or sugar pre-processed food.

Orthodontics

Orthodontics is the branch of dentistry that specializes in the correction of *malocclusion* (an improper alignment of the upper and lower teeth at the point where they meet) or to irregularity of tooth positioning. Emphasis is now being placed on the prevention of malocclusion before it can occur. General practitioners of dentistry, *pedodontists* (specialists in children's dentistry), and orthodontists now believe that the need for expensive, time-consuming, and emotionally unsettling orthodontics can sometimes be avoided by beginning treatment as early as the age of four.

The positioning of the permanent teeth is the result not only of inheritance, but of other variables, such as lip-biting and thumb-sucking. Premature loss or partial disintegration of primary teeth also has a strong influence on whether the permanent teeth will be properly positioned.

Preventive Orthodontics

By the time the child is five, an X ray will show exactly how all the permanent teeth are situated in the gums. In some cases, it may be possible to guide these teeth as they erupt. If potential overcrowding and eventual crookedness are indicated, some baby teeth may be pulled to make room for the permanent ones. Normal positioning may also be accomplished by establishing a different balance of muscular forces.

Corrective Appliances

Corrective orthodontics uses many different types of appliances for the repositioning of permanent teeth, all of which operate on the same principle of applying pressure to the bone. Widening the arch of the upper jaw, for example, is accomplished by the use of a screw appliance fixed to the upper teeth so that the two halves of the hard palate are slightly separated along the middle suture, permitting new bone to fill in the space. Specialists point out that a bonus of this orthodontic correction is increased respiratory ease for youngsters who were formerly mouth-breathers.

Parents who have been advised by the family dentist that an orthodontic consultation is advisable for a child, and who are concerned about the eventual economic burden that prolonged treatment might represent, should get a second opinion from the clinical staff of a dental school associated with a university. See also DENTAL CARE.

Pacifiers

Some parents can't stand the sound of a baby's crying; others can't stand the sight of a baby sucking on a pacifier. Whatever the preference, what the baby needs during the early months is satisfaction for the sucking impulse. For most babies, this need seems to taper off at about six months; with those babies in whom the need re-

mains strong, the thumb seems to be a convenient substitute for the pacifier. Whatever decision is arrived at between you and your physician, the important thing to keep in mind is that the pacifier is no substitute for holding and cuddling the baby when she wants comforting, and that sometimes a parent is more dependent on a pacifier than the baby is.

If pacifiers are used regularly, more than one should be available, and they should be inspected periodically to make sure that bits and pieces of rubber haven't been chewed so loose that they may be swallowed and lodge in the windpipe.

Pets

Rural children usually have their own pet animals even if the animals aren't allowed in the house. Suburban families are likely to own a dog that's a pet as well as a discouragement to prowlers. It's the city child who may have to wage a persistent campaign before his parents capitulate to the idea of a pet. Yet even the smallest apartment can accommodate a pet bird or a small fish tank; a cat and a litter box won't cause extra crowding. Of course, dogs offer the greatest companionship but also impose the greatest responsibility; they do have to be housebroken and walked in all weathers at least twice a day. If a child brings a stray animal home, the dog or cat must be checked by a vet before it becomes a household member. Once a youngster can read, the acquisition of a pet hamster or a guinea pig or a pair of gerbils will provide the incentive for trips to the library for books on care and feeding.

Choosing a Dog

When a dog is to be the choice, it's often cheaper and more satisfactory to select one from the litter of a healthy dog you know than to buy one in a pet shop or from a commercial kennel. The Anti-Cruelty and other animal shelters can provide pets at little or no charge to families. The breed chosen should be suitable in terms of size, temperament, and cost of feeding. Relative advantages and disadvantages should be checked out at the library by the child whose responsibility the pet will be.

For an only child, a pet animal is almost a must, not only for companionship, but so that there's a being in the house who's smaller and more helpless than she is. In families where allergies are a problem, the physician should be consulted about the type of pet that will cause the least discomfort to a vulnerable member of the household.

Pica

Pica is the technical term for an abnormal desire to eat substances that are not fit for food, such as clay, earth, plaster and the like. This tendency is not to be confused with the tendency of babies and toddlers to put unsuitable things into their mouth. Pica is habitual and compulsive, and may result in serious disabilities. Because the phenomenon is especially conspicuous among poor and neglected children, some authorities associate it with nutritional deficiency, others with unsatisfied emotional needs. Signs of pica should be brought to the attention of a physician or a social service agency that can provide guidance on how the child's circumstances should be altered even if the total environment cannot be changed. See also LEAD POISONING.

Pills

See MEDICATION.

Pinworms or Threadworms

See Ch. 11, *Diseases of the Digestive System.*

PKU

PKU stands for *phenylketonuria*, an inherited metabolic defect. Approximately one baby in 10,000 is born with this disease, in which the body is incapable of producing certain enzymes that are essential for the metabolic conversion of the amino acid phenylalanine. The disorder causes the amino acid and some of its by-products to accumulate in the bloodstream to a dangerous degree. If the condition goes undetected and untreated, irreversible brain damage and mental retardation are the result.

PKU babies are characteristically blond and blue-eyed, with sensitive skin and faulty muscle coordination. In many parts of the United States, state laws require that three days after birth, all babies be given the blood test that detects the presence of PKU so that treatment can begin at once if necessary. Supervised treatment usually continues for several years, and in some communities is available at special therapy centers. Parents or prospective parents who would like to find out whether any member of the family is a carrier of the recessive gene that transmits the PKU disorder can arrange for diagnostic testing and genetic counseling based on the results.

Play

See FANTASIES, TOYS, SAFETY.

Pneumonia

See "Pneumonia" in Ch. 12, *Diseases of the Respiratory System.*

Poison Ivy, Oak, and Sumac Rashes

Poison ivy and poison oak are two plants readily found across the United States. Poison sumac is found in marshes in the southern and eastern states. Children frequently come in contact with the plants while playing, hiking, or camping. The oils from the surface of the plant brush against the skin and usually, within hours, a itchy painful rash appears on the skin.

If contact with poisonous plants is suspected, the first thing one should do is wash the area of skin thoroughly with soap and water as soon after exposure as possible. Removing the poisonous oils can eliminate or reduce the inflammation. Care should be taken not to spread the oils from the infected skin to other skin. Particular care should be given to not touch or rub your eyes after contact with one

of these plants. You should also be cautious of rubbing your eyes after scratching infected or exposed skin.

The rash is an itchy red group of small blisters. Cold water dressings can help reduce the itching. Use clean cotton cloth soaked in a solution of one teaspoon of salt per pint of water. Antihistamine medication can help reduce the itching and rash. If the rash persists, becomes infected, is severe, or covers a large part of the child's body, consult a physician immediately.

Poisons and Poisoning

Every year, hundreds of thousands of children swallow some poisonous substance—in too many cases with fatal results—because of parental carelessness, or because the child hasn't been given clear and unequivocal instructions about the difference between "candy" and medicine. Poisoning because of the ingestion of sugar-coated aspirin is a continuing problem; iron-containing multiple vitamins that seem to be a gourmet treat to some children also present a problem because iron in excess doses is a stomach irritant.

Safety Measures

Toddlers can do themselves damage because they're curious about everything, and their sense of taste isn't all that discriminating. Thus it's an absolute necessity to see that all household cleansers and strong chemicals are kept on high shelves rather than on the floor. Many bottles containing medicines come with safety caps that presumably cannot be opened by children—for instance, because pressure must be applied—but can be opened by adults. The experience of many parents, however, is that whereas their children can often open such caps, *they* frequently have a great deal of difficulty. Suffice it to say that the perfect childproof bottle cap has yet to be designed.

Because it's practically impossible for anyone except an expert to know what substances are poisonous to children in what amounts, or which seeds of which plants are harmful if swallowed, many authorities feel strongly that parents should immediately call the closest Poison Control Center for first-aid information rather than try to cope with antidotes or emetics on their own. The Centers are available by phone on a 24-hour-a-day basis. See Ch. 31, *Medical Emergencies*, to find the Poison Control Center nearest you. Make a note of the telephone number and make sure it's available to baby-sitters as well as to all responsible family members.

Poliomyelitis

Until the Salk vaccine was developed in the 1950s, there was no protection against polio (or, as it was then popularly called, *infantile paralysis*). The disease caused paralysis of the extremities and could cause death by paralyzing the muscles used in breathing.

The Salk vaccine utilizes doses of killed virus and is given by injection. Although it is still widely used in many parts of the world, in the United States the Sabin live virus vaccine, which is given orally, has virtually supplanted it. Repeated series of booster shots are unnecessary because the immunity persists for years.

It is advisable that a child receive three doses of the Sabin vaccine, six to eight weeks apart, starting at about the age of two months. One method employs *trivalent* vaccine, in which each dose contains three kinds of vaccine—to give protection against three strains of polio. Three separate doses are necessary, however, to insure full protection. The other method employs *monovalent* vaccines, in which each dose insures protection against a different type of polio.

Posture

"Stand up straight" is an order that many parents issue to their children with the regularity of drill sergeants. Actually, most youngsters tend to slump and have a potbellied look until they're about nine years old. This inelegant posture is not necessarily the sign of any disorder.

Youngsters who are regularly checked by a physician and given a good bill of health are not in any danger of developing a permanent curvature of the spine because they slouch. However, certain kinds of chronically poor posture may be an expression of some disorder that should be checked. Among these are flat feet, nearsightedness or astigmatism, or a hearing loss.

Emotional problems may also be expressed in a child's bearing. Anxiety can lead to carrying one shoulder higher than the other as if warding off a blow. Shyness or insecurity may cause a hangdog stance. For pubescent girls, embarrassment about burgeoning breasts may result in a round-shouldered slump. Some of these causes of poor posture should be discussed with a physician; others may be temporary and shouldn't be turned into major problems by incessant and unproductive nagging. A better corrective is participation in a dancing class or an exercise class. Sports such as ice-skating and bicycle-riding are good posture correctives, too.

Prejudice

The A student (female) who avoids studying mathematics because "girls aren't supposed to be good in math" and the black boy who goes out for the track team even though he'd rather be in the science club "because blacks are better at sports than at brainwork" have unconsciously accepted the prejudiced views of other people about them. What a waste for themselves and society!

Children who are raised in an atmosphere of contempt for and fear and mistrust of Catholics, Jews, Italians, blacks, women, men, are likely to spend the better part of their lives alternating between apprehension and arrogance. It's difficult to believe that adults can have a prejudice such as, "All Orientals are sneaky," which is supposed to describe millions of human beings, or "She's only a girl," which makes a judgment about one-half of the human race.

Being the Object of Discrimination

Parents who have themselves been discriminated against have to prepare their children for the reality of discrimination and how to cope with it. A child raised in an atmosphere of love and respect will have enough self-esteem to refuse to accept anyone else's false notions about him.

Privacy

Every child has a right to a certain amount of privacy even when he's very young. If, for instance, a parent or older child doesn't allow anyone into the bathroom when he's using it, a four- or five-year-old should be given the same option. When children share the same room, or even the same furniture, each one should have a drawer of his own and a shelf of his own for his things. Respecting his private property will lead him to respect other people's. A youngster does like the privacy of playing with his friends without having a parent hovering around all the time, and he certainly doesn't want anyone listening in on his phone conversations by the time he's nine or ten.

Parents have a right to privacy, too! Children should be led to understand—pleasantly but firmly—that some adult conversations are private and not meant for their ears. They should also be taught that when an older member of the family is behind a closed door, it's rude to barge in without knocking.

Puberty

See Ch. 3, *The Teens.*

Punishment

Severe physical punishment should be avoided. Ideally, punishment should be carried out because it has an instructional value for the child rather than because it helps a parent relieve his or her feelings of anger or frustration. Severe physical punishments—for example, the use of sticks, belts, or hard blows to the body—are extremely frightening and may even be permanently injurious to the child. They are also illegal actions, constituting child abuse. Frequently, this kind of discipline can evoke even further anger on the part of the child and lead to further misbehavior.

Duration

Punishments should not be long and drawn out, but should be as immediate as possible and last only a reasonable length of time. For example, withdrawal of television privileges for a month for a seven-year-old's misbehavior would be excessively long, because at the end of the month it would be difficult for her to remember what she had done that was wrong. Excessively long punishments are also difficult to enforce. If possible, a punishment should be related to the misbehavior for which the child is receiving the punishment.

Immediacy

Punishment "when father gets home" or a day later frequently has little meaning for the child and is unlikely to help her stop misbehaving. Rewards for good behavior should also be immediate; affection and approval for most children are often more powerful rewards than candy and money.

Rashes

Rashes of one kind or another are among the most common occurrences of childhood. Whether it's the discomfort of diaper rash soon after birth, the childhood markings of chicken pox, or a case of poison ivy, most skin eruptions aren't too serious and are usually of brief duration.

The First Six Months

Skin rashes are especially common during the first six months. They may result from overheating or overdressing, or to the use of detergents, powders, perfumes, and oils which cause *contact dermatitis.* In addition, certain foods may make the baby break out in facial rashes. Prolonged contact with wet diapers causes *diaper rash*, from the ammonia produced by urine.

Skin rashes can usually be prevented or controlled by:

- Control of temperature

- Proper clothing

- Avoidance of irritating perfumes, powders, and detergents in laundering baby clothes

- Avoidance, in certain circumstances, of milk or other foods, as suggested by your physician

- Avoidance of rubber pants over diapers

- Applications of ointments to rashy areas

If a disturbing skin condition persists or gets worse, your physician will check for special infections like impetigo or fungus, and, should they exist, recommend proper treatment. During the early years, most children develop the characteristic rashes of the contagious childhood diseases, and at these times, a physician's care is usually essential for the prevention of complications.

Eczema

Some children suffer from intermittent eczema that has a tendency to run in families. Eczema can be extremely uncomfortable, because the more it itches, the more it is scratched, and the more it's scratched, the more it itches. This cycle may be triggered by an allergy to a particular food or pollen; it may be a contact dermatitis caused by a particular fabric, or it might flare up because of emotional tension created by family arguments or anxiety about schoolwork. Eczema should be treated by the family physician who may be able to discover its source and prevent further attacks.

Other Allergic Rashes

Other rashes that are essentially allergic in origin are those resulting from contact with poison ivy, oak, or sumac. For information about these and other skin conditions, including hives, see "Disorders of the Skin," in Ch. 21, *Skin and Hair*.

The discomfort of many rashes can be eased by ointments or salves. Plain cornstarch is helpful for prickly heat. Rashes that are bacterial in origin, such as impetigo, or parasitic, have to be treated by a physician with antibiotic or fungicidal preparations.

Roseola

Among the more common rashes of early childhood is the one known as *roseola infantum*. It is believed to be caused by a virus. It begins with a high fever that subsides in a few days. There are no other specific signs of illness, and the end of the disorder—when the fever is usually gone—is signaled by the appearance of a body rash of red spots that disappear overnight. The one aspect of roseola that requires medical attention is the fever. Because high temperature can produce convulsions in infants and babies, efforts should be made to reduce it by sponging and nonaspirin medication. Antibiotics are not indicated unless there's some sign of a secondary infection.

Pityriasis Rosea

A long-lasting rash thought to be viral in origin is *pityriasis rosea*, easily identifiable because the onset of this infection is preceded by one large raised red scaly eruption known as the herald patch. The rash itself appears symmetrically and in clusters on the trunk, arms, and legs, and in some children on the hands and feet as well as the face. Unfortunately, this rash may last for more than a month. There is no treatment for it, and, although it leaves without a trace and almost never recurs, it can cause severe itching that should be eased with a salve or ointment. Soap is very irritating and should be avoided.

Rocky Mountain Spotted Fever

Among the diseases caused by organisms known as rickettsiae and transmitted to people by the animal ticks that are infected with them is *Rocky Mountain spotted fever*, also called *tick fever*. In addition to rising temperature, headache, nausea, and malaise, this disease produces a characteristic rash that starts on the ankles, lower legs, and wrists, and then spreads to the rest of the body. Children who wander about in the woods during the summer or whose pets run loose in tick-infested areas should be watched for the presence of a tick on the skin and the ensuing rash. Rocky Mountain spotted fever is a serious disease against which youngsters should be protected by wearing the proper clothing.

Lyme Disease

A rash may be the first visible symptom of Lyme disease, which had been reported in 34 American states by the late 1980s. Caused by a tick-carried bacterium, the disease can produce symptoms similar to those of arthritis, multiple sclerosis, and heart disease. The initial rash can extend over an area 28 inches across. Antibiotics including tetracycline and penicillin may be used in treatment. The risk of infection may be reduced by frequent inspections of skin areas and prompt removal of the pinhead-sized ticks. If not embedded, ticks can be brushed off; if embedded, they can be lifted out with a tweezers. The skin should be washed carefully with an antiseptic such as rubbing alcohol.

Reading

Children who see their parents reading or who've heard an older sibling say, "Don't interrupt me when I'm reading" are much more likely to want to learn how to read than those who have never seen an older person absorbed in a book or magazine.

Reading Difficulties

No matter how much the world changes, the child who can't read easily is handicapped. Where a true reading problem exists, parents should confer with the school about a practical solution. If a learning disability appears to be the explanation, tutoring or a special class may be essential. See DYSLEXIA.

Reading for Information

Many youngsters who don't see the point in reading for pleasure when there are so many other things they'd prefer to do may dash off to the library if they want information about horses or sailing ships or sewing. Families who would like their youngsters to read more than they do have the responsibility of providing a quiet corner, a decent reading light, and an occasional hour of uninterrupted leisure and privacy. Parents who object to their ten-year-old daughter's habit of "always having her nose in a book" instead of "getting some fresh air and exercise" should withhold their criticism unless the physician recommends a change in the child's activities.

Retardation

See MENTAL RETARDATION.

Reye's Syndrome

Reye's Syndrome is a childhood disease that affects the nervous system and the liver and can result in death. The symptoms normally occur after the child has suffered from the flu or a respiratory illness. The symptoms include vomiting, rash, and disorientation or confusion. If not immediately treated, seizures, respiratory arrest, and coma follow shortly. There is no cure but the dangerous manifestations of the disease can be treated to avoid complications, permanent damage, or death.

The syndrome is believed to be linked to treating the child with aspirin or aspirin-containing medication during the initial illness. Cases of Reye's Syndrome have decreased sharply since 1980, with the increase in public awareness of the link between the disease and the use of aspirin for children.

Given the risk of Reye's Syndrome, it is highly recommended that parents avoid aspirin for children during any illness with fever, flu, diarrhea, or respiratory symptoms. If symptoms persist or if aspirin was given just before the onset of symptoms, please notify a physician. Reye's Syndrome is diagnosed symptomatically.

Rheumatic Fever

Once called growing pains, rheumatic fever is actually a disease of the connective tissues, a secondary manifestation of a primary infection by streptococcus bacteria of the throat or tonsils. Its chief symptoms are pains and tenderness in the joints and sore throat.

Rheumatic fever may be mild enough to escape attention or it may be disabling for a period of months. The insidious aspect of the disease is that it may damage the child's heart in such a way that tissue is permanently scarred and function is impaired in the form of a heart murmur. Acuteness of symptoms varies. Any time from a week to a month after the occurrence of strep throat, the child may complain of feeling tired and achy. Fever usually accompanies the fatigue, and pains in the joints may precede swelling and the development of nodules under the skin in the areas of the wrists, elbows, knees, and vertebrae. The pediatrician can usually detect an abnormal heart finding. The sooner treatment begins, however, the less likely the risk of permanent heart damage.

Close supervision of the affected child may be essential over a long period. Antibiotics, aspirin, hormones (cortisone), and other medicines control the course of the disease and protect the child from its potentially disabling effects. See also "Rheumatic Fever and Rheumatic Heart Disease" in Ch. 10, *Heart Diseases*.

Roseola Infantum

See under RASHES.

Rubella (German Measles)

Rubella was once thought of as a benign disease. Then it was discovered that it could have serious consequences if it were contracted by a woman during the first three months of her pregnancy. The virus that causes rubella is transmitted from the infected woman to her unborn baby, and has been linked to birth defects of the heart, eye, ear, and liver, and to mental retardation.

In addition, a baby who has been exposed to the disease in utero may infect others even though he himself is not affected by it and shows no symptoms. (In fact, most babies are immune to rubella during their first year.) The rubella virus is highly contagious and spreads rapidly.

Rubella has been on the increase in recent years, largely due to the number of young adults who have never been vaccinated. Although it can be a mild illness, it can also cause severe birth defects if contracted by a pregnant woman. Because of the risk of miscarriage and birth defects, pregnant women are advised against getting the immunization during the course of their pregnancy. Anyone who suspects that they or their children were not vaccinated should seek immunization immediately.

The incubation period for rubella is two to three weeks. Symptoms include earache, swollen glands behind the ears, a low-grade fever, and a usually mild, blotchy rash that erupts over the body but lasts only a few days.

Runaways

In growing numbers children and youth ran away from home in the early and middle 1980s. The runaways left home for various reasons. Some were escaping physical or sexual abuse while many others had severe long-term psychological and other problems. A smaller percentage faced temporary or less severe home or school difficulties. Other reasons include "status criminal offense problems"—minor violations of the law that would not be violations at all if committed by an adult—and "poor communication" with parents. Truancy is an example of a status offense. Many children who leave home are not technically "runaways." Professionals call these children *throwaways* because they have in fact been thrown out of the parents' home.

Social service professionals believe many young persons leave home to escape from "dysfunctional families." In such families, parental separation or divorce, poverty, unemployment, and high mobility have, separately or in combination, made the home ineffective as a nurturing environment. The young person may become labeled as a "failure" or "troublemaker"; and a lack of warmth may characterize parent–child relations. In other cases delinquency among a youngster's friends may exert a powerful influence.

The runaways represent diverse age and economic groups. They come from a variety of racial backgrounds. A large proportion are in the 15 to 16 age group. But runaways range in age from 10 or younger to 18.

Parents faced with the fact that a child has run away have to make difficult choices. The child who stays away overnight or for two or more nights has usually not traveled more than 10 miles from home. He or she is usually staying with friends. Only about one in five ventures more than 50 miles from home. The parent or parents of a runaway, considering such facts and not wishing simply to wait, can:

- Look for the youngster themselves. Recommended by many social workers as a logical first step, such a search may involve calls to relatives or the child's friends, checks on favorite haunts, and "driving around" in areas that the young person knows and frequents.

- Report the runaway to police. A "first impulse" alternative, calling the police may not be in the child's best interest. For one thing, the police, especially in large cities, are

swamped with such reports. Parental searches actually succeed in finding runaways more frequently than police do. As a second consideration, once reported to police the youngster may be drawn into the juvenile-justice system. In some states, that could result in incarceration with adult offenders or delinquent juveniles. Other states provide that a runaway cannot be held—or cannot be held more than a brief, specified period.

- Contact a local branch of the National Network of Runaway and Youth Services. A private, nonprofit organization with more than 500 community-based shelter programs, the Network serves runaway, homeless, and other "problem" young people. It offers shelter and hotline services 24 hours a day, seven days a week. While not a search operation, the Network also provides crisis and long-term individual and family counseling, outreach, advocacy, referrals for medical, legal, and mental health assistance, and followup services.

- Contact the National Communications System. Supported by the U.S. Department of Health and Human Services, the system operates a nationwide toll-free telephone hotline. Services provided center on referral and crisis intervention aid.

Some national or local services have been established primarily to help runaways obtain clothing, shelter, and food. These organizations also try to mediate between parents and children and to bring families together. Three such groups operate the Runaway Hotline (800/231-6946), the National Runaway Switchboard (800/621-4000), and the National Center for Missing and Exploited Children (800/843-5678).

What happens after a child returns home may determine whether he or she will run away again. Family counselors suggest that parents remain calm. No matter how stressful the runaway incident may have been, parents should try to accept their child as a person. Many runaways, counselors say, are "testing the waters," or experimenting, or seeking a sense of self and identity. If the family can discuss what has happened, the problems that caused the young person to run away may be resolved.

In difficult situations, counseling may be necessary. More and more parents are turning also to inpatient psychiatric services. Usually, these parents have tried other solutions before turning to psychiatry. Contributing to the trend toward hospitalization and professional treatment is the increasing availability of insurance to cover the expected costs.

Safety

See "Accident Prevention" in Ch. 36, *Voluntary Health Agencies.*

Scarlet Fever

Scarlet fever used to be a disease that everyone dreaded. It is highly conta-gious, and can result in severe after-effects like rheumatic fever, or the kidney disease known as nephritis.

It is now known that scarlet fever is simply a streptococcal infection—a strain of a specific organism that also causes a diffuse red rash. It can be dealt with quite simply by your physician, the usual treatment being a ten-day course of penicillin, which cures the streptococcal infection and prevents most complications.

Schizophrenia

See under MENTAL ILLNESS.

School

In the United States, an elementary school is a place where children are taught not only how to read, write, handle numbers, and correlate sets of facts, they are also taught how to get along with children different from themselves, how to express themselves creatively, and how to become responsible citizens of a democratic society. If the reality of education falls short of these goals, parents are supposed to exert influence on the proper authorities to see that they are in fact accomplished.

Nursery School

For a child, leaving the protection of the family if only for a half-day in a nearby nursery school is a big step forward. The step is likely to be taken with eagerness if parents present the school as a pleasurable place to be, and not as a dumping ground for a youngster who's in the way of a new baby or a working mother.

Elementary School

The elementary grades represent a major change in many different ways, but most importantly because new authority figures begin to displace parents as the source of all wisdom. Adults and older siblings can help a child make a happy and productive adjustment to school by talking about it with interest and respect. Wherever possible, one or another parent should be present at parent-teacher meetings and participate in the activities of the child's group, such as class trips, visiting days, and the like.

Homework

When youngsters come home with school assignments that they find baffling, parents should feel free to ask the teacher for clearer instructions. If the child is at fault through inattention or ignorance, it might be pointed out to her that whether or not she gets a good education depends on how hard she's ready to work and not how efficiently the teacher can spoon-feed her.

Private Schools

Some families feel that the local public school is not the best place for their children to learn during the lower grades. Alternative private schools, whether denominational, discriminatory, or for gifted children, may have advantages that are less apparent to the child than to the parents, especially if attendance isolates the youngster from her friends in the neighborhood.

Staying Home from School

It's not unusual for a child to avoid going to school once in a while by saying she's sick. She may actually need a rest from the routine every few months. This is quite different from truly getting sick at the thought of facing school. A child who is nauseated in the morning, or who throws up, or who has a stomachache at breakfast, is probably experiencing feelings of anger, resentment, or anxiety beyond her ability to cope with them. Whatever it is in the school situation that's worrying her, she should be given the opportunity to talk about what's going on and the reassurance that efforts will be made to help straighten things out.

For children with disabilities, special facilities are often provided within the structure of the local school so that they can spend at least part of their day with their own age group.

Sex Education

Children need and deserve to have access to correct information about sexual functioning. If there is a natural openness in a family about questions of all types, children first start asking questions about sex when they are three or four; it is then that parents can begin describing sexual functioning to their children.

Questions about Body Parts

The first questions about sex usually have to do with the functioning of body parts. For example, children want to know where urine comes from, what happens to food when they eat it, where feces come from, and where babies come from. Explanations should be given in a straightforward, unembarrassed manner. Children should not be overloaded with information that they do not understand, but parents should be willing to answer questions to the best of their ability.

With older children, particularly 11- and 12-year-olds, it is often helpful for sexual questions to be answered by the parent of the same sex. Reading a book on sexual development together with the child can be a good experience for both parent and child. Parents frequently wonder if sex education may not lead children to engage in experimentation. Most of the evidence on this question indicates that children are more likely to experiment sexually when they are ignorant than when their questions about sex are reasonably and accurately answered.

Sexual Abuse and Incest

Of all the forms of child abuse (see CHILD ABUSE), sexual abuse, including incest, is the most common. Estimates of the number of sexual assaults on children in the United States range as high as five million annually. As many as 80 percent of these assaults occur within families. In many cases the adults reside outside the family but are closely acquainted with their victims.

Child sexual abuse takes many forms. While tens of thousands of children and young people are sexually attacked or molested, thousands of others are filmed, photographed, or otherwise exploited for the private recreational purposes of abusers. An estimated 50,000 children disappear annually; most of them are never found. Experts say many of these lost children are forced into a kind of sex-slavery, becoming victims of the "kiddie porn" (child pornography) trade. Within the home, sexual abuse may include rape, inappropriate fondling, exhibitionism, sexual intercourse, sodomy, and other acts.

Who are the victims of child sexual abuse? They are both males and females; they range in age from a few months to 16 years or older. The mean age at which a child experiences sexual abuse is nine. The victims represent all socioeconomic groups, all races, all geographic regions.

Protecting Your Children

Parents have the delicate task of maintaining a loving, touching family relationship while also teaching their child or children to recognize and reject "bad touches." Parents do not want to instill in their child fear, hysteria, or paranoia. But they should want their child to know how to escape or avoid abuse within or outside

---

Safety Tips for Parents

1. Know your children's friends.

2. Never leave your child unattended.

3. Be involved in your child's activities.

4. Listen when your child tells you he or she does not want to be with someone.

5. Pay attention when someone shows greater than normal interest in your child.

6. Have your child fingerprinted and know where to locate dental records.

7. Be sensitive to changes in your child's behavior or attitudes.

8. Take a photograph of your child each year (4 times each year if under age 2).

9. Be prepared to describe your children accurately—including clothing, visible identifying marks, or special characteristics.

10. Develop a set procedure should you and your child become separated while away from home.

11. Do not buy items that visibly display your child's name.

12. Be sure your child's school or day-care center will not release your child to anyone other than you or someone you officially designate.

13. Instruct the school to contact you immediately if your child is absent or if someone other than you arrives to pick up him or her without advance notice from you.

---

a pinch, hard slap, or a touch in a body area normally covered by a bathing suit. One exception, of course, is a physician's examination. Parental approval makes such an examination acceptable.

Children can and should learn to say "no" to an adult, psychologists tell us. Having said "no," whether the would-be abuser is a friend, relative, or stranger, your child should leave the scene quickly. Then he or she should report the incident to a parent. "Be sure to emphasize that if someone asks them not to tell that they should immediately tell," advises one authority. Parents should make it clear that they will not be mad if they receive such a report.

Parents need to instruct children periodically in the ways to respond appropriately to abusers' approaches. But then they have to listen if the child wants to talk. Children have to be sure both of the parents' love and their willingness to pay attention.

Symptoms to Watch For

A child encountering molestation or sexual abuse of any kind is undergoing an emotionally stressful experience. But the young person may be too shy to reveal what has happened. If a parent suspects that a son or daughter has been molested, one authority suggests, asking directly if anything has happened.

What symptoms might cause suspicion? As published in "Child Protection Alert," a publication of the American Christian Voice Foundation,

the home. Without dwelling on the details of what *could* happen, show what a bad touch involves—generally, there are at least 25 symptoms that you should watch for:

1. Explicit (sometimes bizarre) sexual knowledge

2. Precocious sexually related experimentation or speech

3. Toilet training relapses

4. Smearing of feces or urine

5. Gagging and unexplained vomiting

6. Speech problems

7. Regressive behavior

8. Masturbation

9. Withdrawal from normal human contact

10. Stomach and head pains

11. Bedwetting

12. Suicidal depression and/or self-destructive tendencies

13. Excessive fear of selected individuals or locations

14. Loss of appetite

15. Unexplained bruises or injuries in genital areas

16. Blood spotting or unexplained substances on underwear

17. Abrupt or radical behavioral or attitude changes

18. Lack of self-esteem or self-worth

19. Ulcers, colitis, anorexia, or other stress related disorders

20. Alcohol or drug abuse

21. Frequent nightmares

22. Excessive passivity

23. Vaginal or urinary tract infections

24. Infections of the mouth, gums, or throat. (Be vigilant for venereal diseases of the anus or throat. Incidences are no longer uncommon in children.)

25. Unexplained gifts, extra money, or the presence of pornography in your child's possession

Sources of Help

Where does a parent seek help once it's certain that molestation or abuse has occurred? The recommended first stage is to notify the police or local rape crisis center, or (where incest is the crime) the state child protection agency. To avoid adding to your child's stress, parents should *not* confront the offender while the child is present. Make sure the young victim has a complete physical examination if only to reassure the boy or girl that no permanent physical damage has been done. Depending on need, you may also want to ensure that the child gets counseling. Resource centers that provide diverse kinds of aid include:

- CHILD HELP National Child Abuse hotline: 800/422-4453

- Child Find hotline: 800/A-WAY-OUT for mediation; 800/I-AM-LOST for abducted children or people identifying missing or abducted children.

- National Center for Missing and Exploited Children: 800/843-5678 or 202/634-9821

- The Adam Walsh Child Resource Center: 407/833–9080

- National Crime Information Center (F.B.I.): 202/324-2311

- National Runaway Switchboard: 800/621-4000

Sibling Rivalry

See BROTHERS AND SISTERS, NEW BABY.

Sickle-cell Anemia

See Ch. 9, *Diseases of the Circulatory System.*

Sisters and Brothers

See BROTHERS AND SISTERS.

Sleep

See BEDTIME, DREAMS AND NIGHTMARES, SLEEPWALKING.

Sleepwalking

Sleepwalking may be distressing to the parent who witnesses it, but it usually does the child no harm. If the child seems to be about to do something dangerous, it's a good idea to wake her up with a few reassuring remarks and guide her back to bed. In most sleepwalking incidents, the child goes back to bed by herself and gets up the next day without the slightest recollection of her nighttime prowl.

Parents shouldn't tease or scold or make the child feel peculiar about walking in her sleep. It can be ignored unless it continues over a long period, and then it might be mentioned to your physician.

Smallpox

Smallpox has been eradicated everywhere in the world. Vaccination against smallpox has therefore been discontinued in the United States.

Smoking

Young children who see older children in the family or at home smoking cigarettes are going to equate smoking with being grown up even if their parents don't smoke. A ten-year-old who sneaks off to experiment with a cigarette shouldn't be treated like a criminal, but he should be told that he is harming himself. Parents who smoke and wish they didn't should concentrate on their own efforts to stop and hope that their offspring get the message. In any event, it might help to emphasize how hard it is to stop smoking once one has acquired the habit.

Sore Throat

"It hurts when I swallow" is a common complaint of childhood. It may be connected with a cold or tonsillitis, but if there is tenderness at the sides of the neck and a rise in temperature, the physician should be called promptly so that tests can be made to see whether the child has strep throat. Often a throat culture is necessary. A streptococcus throat infection that is undiagnosed and untreated can have serious consequences. See also STREP THROAT, TONSILLITIS.

Speech Impediments

Among the more common speech defects are *lisping* (the substitution of *th* for *s* and *z* sounds); *lallation* (the inability to pronounce *l* or *r* correctly), and stuttering. Although many children do outgrow their speech disabilities, a considerable number do not.

Therapy

Corrective therapy should be undertaken without too much delay. There have been many advances in the techniques used by speech pathologists, including the audiovisual devices and feed-back systems that promote self-correction. A list of certified speech pathologists can be obtained from the American Speech-Language-Hearing Association, 10801 Rockville Pike, Rockville, MD 20852. See also STUTTERING.

Stealing

See DISHONESTY.

Stepchildren

See Ch. 5, *The Middle Years*. See also ADOPTED CHILDREN.

Stomachache

A wide variety of disorders begins with some kind of abdominal pain, but in most cases, a stomachache is temporary and unaccompanied by any other symptoms. Digestive upsets are frequent in infancy, becoming rarer as the baby approaches the fourth month. See COLIC.

After the baby's first year, a stomachache may signal the onset of a cold or some other infection. The physician should be called if any of the following conditions occurs:

- When the stomach pain is accompanied by fever, vomiting, or diarrhea

- If moderate pain lasts for a considerable time—several hours, for example

- If the pain is obviously acute—the child is doubled over

- If the location off the pain shifts from one place to another

Never give a child a laxative or an enema except on a physician's orders.

A youngster who complains regularly of stomachaches without any other symptoms, and who might also complain of headaches or constipation shouldn't be dismissed as a worrier. The problem should be discussed with your physician so that an investigation can be made of possible causes. In many cases, constipation is the source of stomach pain. When the constipation is cleared up, the stomach pains cease.

Stomach pain may also be of psychosomatic origin, in children as well as in adults. If the pain cannot be explained after a physical examination and tests have been made, parents should consider how they can lighten some of the stresses and tensions in the child's life.

Strabismus

See CROSSED EYES.

Strep Throat

Streptococcal infections, commonly called strep throat, are caused by bacteria that inflame and infect the tissues in the throat. Symptoms include sore throat, swollen glands, redness or blotchy white spots on the throat and tonsils. Severe throat pain may occur for three to four days of the two-week run of the illness. Strep infections should be treated immediately after diagnosis by a physician with antibiotics such as erythromycin or penicillin.

Strep throat poses several risks to the health of both the adult and child sufferer. If left untreated, strep bacteria may produce the toxin that triggers scarlet fever, which also requires treatment with penicillin.

Strep can also lead to rheumatic fever. Rheumatic fever can develop into rheumatic heart disease, leaving the child with a heart murmur. Also treated with penicillin, the disease leaves little damage if caught and treated early.

The last serious problem to arise from a strep infection is relatively new. There a new strep type produces the same symptoms as toxic shock syndrome. The rare form of streptococcus causes low blood pressure, rash, high fever, and rapid organ and blood destruction. It ends in death in 20 percent of the cases. It

affects children and adults. Due to the rapid onset of serious and deadly symptoms, it is essential that medical treatment be sought immediately if you or your child suffers any one of the signs of this disease.

Stuttering

Stuttering, or stammering, is a speech dysfunction where the words are spoken with hesitation, repetition, prolongation, or stumbling on one or more syllable of a word. Parents should bear in mind, though, that many children stutter when they are learning to speak. At this stage it is not a permanent problem, and the child will usually outgrow it as ease with language increases.

For a child who continues to show hesitation in speech after the age of four or five, the parents should consider getting professional guidance of a physician, speech therapist, or counselor as recommended by the child's pediatrician. The speech problem may be related to cerebellar disease or a neuromuscular defect or a problem with the voice box. There is also some research being done on hearing problems with stutterers. Some patients respond well to speech therapy when the sound of their voice is played back on a delay through earphones. The slight delay allows them to speak without hesitation. Why this works is not fully understood.

Stuttering can also be related to emotional or psychological problems. Stress from early childhood speech impairment may create a psychological block to speaking. Other problems may enter into the reason for stuttering. It is not uncommon for there to be both emotional and physical reasons for stuttering.

For more information, please call the toll-free hotline for the National Center for Stuttering at 800/221-2483. They will provide information and guidance to parents.

Sudden Infant Death Syndrome

Sudden Infant Death Syndrome, sometimes referred to as SIDS and generally known as *crib death*, claims about 10,000 babies every year. It is the chief single cause of fatalities in infants, usually occurring between the ages of one month and six months. Although there are a number of plausible theories being investigated, its cause remains unknown. In some cases, autopsies indicate a hidden infection or an unsuspected abnormality, but in 80 percent of the deaths, no obvious explanation can be found. One cause appears to be an inherited heart irregularity, and another is respiratory distress, discussed under HYALINE MEMBRANE DISEASE. Improved hospital facilities for the care of premature babies who are considered to be at higher risk than those born at full term, as well as prenatal tests and ultrasonic alarm systems that monitor breathing are expected to reduce the number of SIDS victims.

Parents of infant SIDS victims often suffer intensely, apart from their natural grief, from feelings of guilt, as if they were somehow careless or negligent. They must be reassured that they could not possibly have foreseen the susceptibility of their child to this affliction and that there is therefore no way they could have averted its tragic result. They will have suffered enough without the wholly unwarranted feeling that they were somehow responsible.

Swallowed Objects

Babies in a crib or playpen can certainly be depended on to put anything within reach into their mouths, so it's a good idea to make sure that surfaces are cleared of anything that would cause a crisis if it were swallowed. Plastic toys and rattles should be inspected for loose parts. Pins, buttons, and small change should be kept in drawers. It's no serious matter if a child swallows a cherry stone or a plum pit or a small button, because these are not likely to cause problems in their passage through the digestive system. They will be disposed of in regular bowel movements.

Emergencies

Emergencies occur when the object is stuck in the windpipe or when it goes into the bronchial passage. If it is in the windpipe and isn't coughed up right away, use the first aid maneuver for "Obstruction in the Windpipe," Ch. 35, *Medical Emergencies* without delay. If is doesn't work the first time, do it again—and again. You must clear the windpipe. If all efforts fail, rush the child to a hospital.

Swearing

Sooner or later most children learn swear words, either from hearing their parents use them or from their peers. Young children may use curse words without knowing what they mean or without appreciating how offensive they may be.

Nowadays it is virtually impossible for children to avoid hearing words in everyday use that were strictly taboo when their parents were growing up. However jolting it may be to hear foul words issuing from their angelic-looking children, parents should be neither surprised nor unduly upset if this happens occasionally, especially if they themselves use curse words. They might well point out to the child, however, that many people object strongly to such language, and if they want to be treated courteously by adults, they had better watch their language.

Swimming

Every child should learn to swim, and the earlier the better. Families fortunate enough to have their own large pools can accomplish this in their own backyards; others may spend summers near a suitable body of water.

Although there's nothing like the ocean for water play, it's not a good place to try to teach a small child how to swim. There are too many extraneous hazards, such as undertow, waves, and unexpected depths. Many communities have outdoor public pools; most large cities have indoor and outdoor pools where professional instruction is available. Even when a child can swim moderately well, she should not be allowed to do so alone, and she shouldn't be allowed to go out in a boat by herself either. Rubber floats, rafts, and the like shouldn't be made available to youngsters until they can swim. A nonswimmer depending on such a device is in trouble if it should drift away from her in deep water.

Talking

The ability to speak is part of the human heritage. How soon and how clearly a child begins to do so depends on several factors. First and foremost is the ability to hear.

Hearing and Speech

Any illness or infection in infancy that has caused even a small hearing loss will interfere with the baby's perception of sounds. This in turn will prevent the normal development of those parts of the brain that govern the imitative aspect of speech.

A Stimulating Environment

How much attention and stimulation the baby gets from his environment and the people around him will have a great effect on how much he tries to say and the age at which he begins to say it. Being listened to and automatically corrected instead of being ignored or teased is the indispensable feedback process that enriches the learning of language. The clarity of the child's speech depends to a large extent on the examples before him; what his ears hear his brain will order his vocal equipment to imitate. Parents who want a child to outgrow baby talk should avoid responding to the baby in kind. Normal adult speech should become the norm toward which the child is constantly striving. See also HEARING, SPEECH IMPEDIMENTS, SWEARING.

Tantrums

See ANGER.

Tay-Sachs Disease

Tay-Sachs disease is an inherited disorder of the nervous system. It causes degeneration of the nerves, starting after six months of age. Infant development through pregnancy and the first six months is normal, but the disease can be detected through genetic testing. The first symptoms to appear are subtle, becoming more obvious with motor deterioration. They include a slowing of development, loss of vision, and eventually convulsions. A cherry-red spot develops on the retina of the eye. The child will lose the motor coordination that he already had, and will deteriorate to the point where he will be unable to lift his head. The child will not normally survive past the age of four.

Tay-Sachs is found with higher prevalence among the following populations: Ashkenazi Jews, Eastern European Jews, and French Canadians. Testing is recommended to anyone from these populations, and test-

ing is also recommended for all Jews to determine if one is a carrier of the disease.

Tay-Sachs is a form of cerebral sphingolipidosis. It is the infantile onset of the disorder. The others are Jansky-Bielschowsky disease (early juvenile), Spielmeyer-Vogt and Batten-Mayou disease (late juvenile), and Kufs' disease (adult onset). Symptoms are similar and include blindness within two years of the onset of the disorder.

Teething

Babies of four to six months drool a great deal and put their fingers in their mouth. These habits, and the telltale small bumps you may detect on the baby's gums, are the signs of teething. But they don't necessarily mean that the first tooth is about to erupt. That may not happen until he is nearly one year old, although it usually happens earlier.

Teething may or may not be painful. If the baby does fret, medication is available to alleviate the pain. (A little whisky rubbed on the gums is a home remedy that often helps.)

Tetanus

Tetanus (also called *lockjaw* because it causes spasms of the jaw) can occur at any age as the result of contamination of a simple wound. The causative organism is usually found in soil, street dust, or feces.

The disease is preventable by immunization. The triple vaccine DTP should be started at two to three

months of age. See also IMMUNIZA-
TION.

When a child suffers a puncture
wound, dog bite, or other wound that
may be contaminated, ask your physician to give the child a booster dose
of tetanus toxoid if she has not had a
shot within one year.

Tick Fever

See "Rocky Mountain Spotted Fever"
under RASHES.

Toilet Training

During the toddler stage parents begin to teach their child how to control
his bowel and urinary functions.

When to Start

A simple question parents always ask
is, "How do I know when my child is
ready to be toilet trained?"

Generally, children do not have
muscular control over their bowel
movements and urination until about
the age of two, so attempting to
toilet-train a child much before this is
usually wasted effort. If it is accomplished, the result is usually a training
of the parents rather than of the infant. Toilet training should usually
take place some time between the
age of two and three and one-half.

A child is emotionally ready when
he understands what is meant by toilet training and is willing to perform
toilet functions without expressing
fear of them. This may occur at any
age, but is perhaps most apt to start
between the ages of 18 and 24
months. With a first child it is usually
later than with a second or third child,
because the first child has no siblings
to emulate. But a first child should be
trained, usually, by the time he is
three. Training the child to stay dry
through the long night hours may take
even longer.

Resistance to Toilet Training

Early toilet training—training that is
begun during a child's first year—may
work, but as a child develops and as-
serts his personality and independence, he will resent any insistence
on manipulating the control of his bodily functions. He may get even by refusing to empty his bowels when put
on the potty. Worse yet, if another
baby has entered the scene, the
early-trained child may develop constipation, or may revert to wetting
and having bowel movements in his
training pants.

When you feel the child is ready for
training, establish the fact that going
to the bathroom is a normal part of
daily life. If the child expresses fear,
don't struggle with him. Don't fight
about it. Take him right off the potty
and let him know that you are not concerned or displeased. A genuine complication can arise if the child connects
his fear of toilet functions with your
displeasure at his failures.

Training can usually be facilitated
by praise from the parents for putting
the bowel movement and the urine in
the proper place, rather than by punishment. Excessive punishment or
the threat of it usually results in anger
on the child's part and increasing
stubbornness and resistances to toilet
training. Praise immediately following

the proper performance of the act is far more effective in encouraging compliance with the parents' goals.

Tonsillectomy

See "Tonsils and Adenoids" in Ch. 20, *Surgery*.

Tonsillitis

The tonsils are two masses of soft spongy tissue that are partly embedded in the mucous membrane of the back of the throat. Bacterial or viral infection of this tissue is known as tonsillitis. It used to be considered advisable to remove the tonsils if they became enlarged—which they normally do in the process of filtering out mild infections.

Nowadays, an occasional bout of tonsillitis isn't considered sufficient reason for surgical removal of the tonsils, especially because they're likely to be less prone to infection as the child gets older. However, even a mild case of tonsillitis should be called to a physician's attention. Acute symptoms such as swollen tonsils, sudden high fever, swollen neck glands, and severe pain when swallowing must be treated promptly since they might be an indication of a strep throat. The proper antibiotics are always effective in controlling this infection so that it doesn't turn into rheumatic fever or involve the kidneys. Tonsillitis caused by a virus usually responds to aspirin, bed rest, and a soft diet. See also ADENOIDS. For a description of tonsillectomy, see "Tonsils and Adenoids" in Ch. 20, *Surgery*.

Toy Safety

Toys come with a recommended age of use. It is important that parents heed the information. Some toys are unsuitable for certain ages, not only because of an inability to use it correctly, but because there may be pieces of the toy that are harmful. These are just a few examples of toys that can be safe at one age and not another; games may have small pieces can be swallowed by little children; electrical toys should only be handled by children old enough to understand the danger. Toys hanging in the crib should not be used by infants old enough to pull themselves up to a standing position because they may strangle on cords and strings of the toy. It should be noted that it is not always the case that only younger children should avoid older children's toys. Toys that are safe for younger children may tip, break, or pinch with the increased size and weight of an older child.

Not all toys come with recommendations or fulfill the safety standards set up by the U.S. government. Cheap imitations may not meet the rigid standards of the more established companies' toys. Several hundred toys are recalled each year, and more may have not yet been tested. It is important that a parent take responsibility for evaluating the safety of any toy to be given to a youngster.

For detailed and important information on age recommendations for toys (*Which Toy for Which Child*) and for a listing of products recommended for their reliability and safety, please write to U.S. Consumer Product Safety Commission, Washington, DC 20207 or call 1-800-638-CPSC. *The ABC's of Toys and Play* is also a worthwhile publication on how to select toys for children. It is published by Toy Manufacturers of America, Inc., 200 Fifth Avenue, New York, NY 10010.

Tuberculosis

See Ch. 12, *Diseases of the Respiratory System.*

Twins and Triplets

Multiple births may be *identical*—that is, the result of the splitting of a single egg fertilized by a single sperm—or they may be *fraternal*, which means that they developed from different eggs fertilized by different sperm. Most multiple births are fraternal; except for their birthdays, most twins and triplets are no more alike than other brothers and sisters of the same family.

Although there is no ready explanation for the occurrence of multiple births, the tendency is thought to be genetically determined through the mother. Twins occur about once in every 86 births, triplets once in every 8,000. Multiple births can be anticipated by a physician at least a month before delivery. They usually arrive about two weeks early, and if they give any indications of prematurity, they receive special hospital attention.

Urinary Infections

Urinary infections of either viral or bacterial origin are more common among girls than boys, especially during the preschool years. Such an infection is sometimes the explanation for a fever unaccompanied by other symptoms. Any inflammation that creates a burning sensation during urination should be cultured and treated promptly because it can spread from the bladder to the kidneys and create a major problem.

Girls can be spared frequent infection if tactful suggestions are made at an early age about their toilet routines. Fecal matter is high in bacterial content, so little girls should learn to wipe their bottoms from front to back. This procedure reduces the possibility of contaminating the urethra after a bowel movement.

Vaporizer

A vaporizer is a device similar to a humidifier that moistens the air with steam and thus alleviates some of the discomfort of respiratory congestion. During the winter months when heated interiors are likely to be especially dry and when colds are more common, children and grown-ups can benefit from moist air that keeps the throat and nasal and bronchial passages from feeling like sandpaper. Medication shouldn't be added to a vaporizer except at the physician's recommendation. If the device is used near a child's bed throughout the night, it should be placed on a surface high enough to prevent bumping into it accidentally should the child wake up in the middle of the night to go to the bathroom.

Vomiting

See NAUSEA AND VOMITING.

Warts

See Ch. 21, *Skin and Hair.*

Water Beds

Because of the softness and the motion of a waterbed, infants up to *at least* twelve months of age should never be left unattended on a waterbed. Infants left even briefly on a waterbed have suffocated. The risks are that the infant will become trapped between the mattress and the frame or wall, or become wedged between a sleeping adult and the mattress, or sink face first into the mattress and be unable to push himself up. Several infant deaths originally attributed to SIDS are now considered suffocation due to a waterbed. At least 24 infants have died while left to nap on the parents' waterbed in the last decade.

Whooping Cough

Whooping cough (also called *pertussis*), like diphtheria a bacterial dis-

ease, occurs more frequently than diphtheria because immunity to it wears off, especially in the older child in whom the disease may appear as a severe bronchitis.

Whooping cough can be very serious in young babies because it can cause them to choke and be unable to catch their breath. If your child does contract whooping cough, call your physician immediately. He or she may give a specific drug against the organism that causes the disease as well as a specific antitoxin against the poison that the bacillus releases.

It is advisable to immunize children against whooping cough as early as possible. The effective triple vaccine known as DTP provides immunization not only against whooping cough, but against diphtheria and tetanus as well.

Worms and Parasites

See Ch. 11, *Diseases of the Digestive System.*

they may be *fraternal*, which means that they developed from different eggs fertilized by different sperm. Most multiple births are fraternal; except for their birthdays, most twins and triplets are no more alike than other brothers and sisters of the same family.

Although there is no ready explanation for the occurrence of multiple births, the tendency is thought to be genetically determined through the mother. Twins occur about once in every 86 births, triplets once in every 8,000. Multiple births can be anticipated by a physician at least a month before delivery. They usually arrive about two weeks early, and if they give any indications of prematurity, they receive special hospital attention.

Typhoid Fever

See Ch. 11, *Diseases of the Digestive System.*

Urinary Infections

Urinary infections of either viral or bacterial origin are more common among girls than boys, especially during the preschool years. Such an infection is sometimes the explanation for a fever unaccompanied by other symptoms. Any inflammation that creates a burning sensation during urination should be cultured and treated promptly because it can spread from the bladder to the kidneys and create a major problem.

Girls can be spared frequent infection if tactful suggestions are made at an early age about their toilet routines. Fecal matter is high in bacterial content, so little girls should learn to wipe their bottoms from front to back. This procedure reduces the possibility of contaminating the urethra after a bowel movement.

Vomiting

See NAUSEA AND VOMITING.

Warts

See Ch. 21, *Skin and Hair.*

Whooping Cough

Whooping cough (also called *pertussis*), like diphtheria a bacterial disease, occurs more frequently than diphtheria because immunity to it wears off, especially in the older child in whom the disease may appear as a severe bronchitis.

Whooping cough can be very serious in young babies because it can cause them to choke and be unable to catch their breath. If your child does contract whooping cough, call your physician immediately. He or she may give a specific drug against the organism that causes the disease as well as a specific antitoxin against the poison that the bacillus releases.

It is advisable to immunize children against whooping cough as early as possible. The effective triple vaccine known as DTP provides immunization not only against whooping cough, but against diphtheria and tetanus as well.

Worms and Parasites

See Ch. 11, *Diseases of the Digestive System.*

3

The Teens

Puberty and Growth

The bridge between childhood and adulthood is a period of growth and change called puberty. There seems to be no standard pattern for the physical changes of puberty. Two boys of the same age who have been nearly identical throughout childhood may appear to set off along entirely different paths of physical development as they enter the teenage years. One may quickly shoot up to a height of five feet eight inches within a couple of years while his companion lags for a while at preteen size, then begins growing into a six-footer. One may develop a heavy beard in his early high-school years while the other boy will have no use for a razor until he is in college. However, both boys are normal youngsters, and each will eventually attain all of the physical attributes of adulthood.

Similarly, one girl may begin menstruating in her 11th year while a classmate will not experience her first menstruation until she is 16. One girl may need a bra while still in grammar school but her friend will fret about a small bustline for many years. But both girls can look forward to normal womanhood. Each has an individual pattern of development, and if there is any rule of thumb about puberty it is that each youngster has his or her own time schedule for the transformation into a mature man or woman.

Puberty: Changes in Girls

The physical changes that occur in the female body during puberty probably are more dramatic than those associated with a boy progressing into manhood. One definite milestone for the girl is her first *menstruation*, commonly regarded as the first sign of puberty. Actually, the first menstruation, known as the *menarche,* is only one of several signs of puberty, along with the slimming of the waist, gradual broadening of the hips, the development of breasts, the appearance of hair about the genitals and in the armpits, and a change in the rate of growth.

The Menarche

The age at which a girl first experiences menstruation generally varies over a period of ten years and depends upon the structural development of the youngster, her physical condition, the environment, and hereditary factors. Menarche can occur as early as the age of 7, and most physicians would not be overly concerned if a girl did not begin to menstruate until she was approaching 17.

The age range of 9 to 16 usually is considered normal. The median age for the start of menstruation is around 13½ years, which means that 50 percent of all females are younger than 13 years and 6 months when they reach the menarche, and half are on the older side of that age when they first menstruate. In general, the pubertal experiences of a girl follow a pattern like that of her mother and

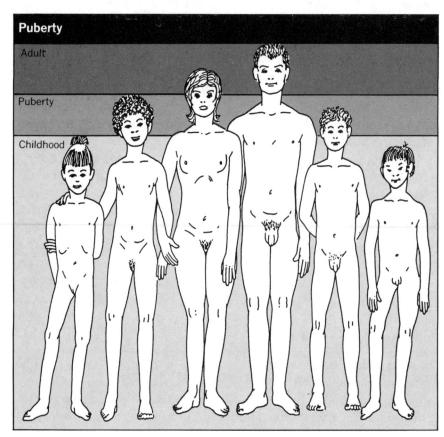

Puberty

Adult

Puberty

Childhood

sisters; if the mother began menstruating at an early age, the chances are that her daughters will also.

If the girl has not reached the menarche by the age of 18, she should be examined by a *gynecologist,* a physician who specializes in problems related to the female reproductive system. A medical examination also should be arranged for any girl who experiences menstruation before she reaches the age of eight or nine years.

When menarche occurs on the early side of childhood, the condition is sometimes called *precocious puberty.* The child may suddenly begin menstruating before her mother has told her what to expect, a situation that can prove embarrassing to both child and parents. It may first be detected by a teacher at school; occasionally, a young girl may be aware of bleeding from the vagina but because of fear or false modesty does not report the event to her mother or teacher. For this reason, parents should be alert for changes associated with early puberty and be prepared to explain the facts of life to their children. Also, in the case of precocious puberty, parents should arrange for medical consultation to be certain the bleeding actually is the result of first menstruation and not the effects of an injury or tumor.

Growth Spurt before Menarche

During the year or two preceding the menarche there is a growth spurt of two or three inches. This is because of the hormone changes of puberty. The *hormones* are chemical messengers secreted by glands in various parts of the body and carried rapidly through the bloodstream to organs or other glands where they trigger reactions. The spurt in growth preceding menarche results from the secretion of a growth hormone that is produced by the pituitary gland, and androgen, a hormone secreted by the adrenal glands. They produce rapid growth of the bones and muscles during puberty. The girl who is first among her classmates to menstruate often is larger than those who are of the same age but have not yet reached the menarche.

From numerous research studies of the menarche, it has been learned that poor nutrition and psychological stress sometimes delay the onset of menstruation, that girls reared in cities tend to menstruate earlier, and that climate is a factor, although both tropical and arctic climates seem to be related to early menarche. The first menstrual periods also are likely to occur during the school year, September to June, rather than during the summer vacation.

The First Menstrual Cycles

The first menstrual cycles tend to be very irregular and have been known to be as short as 7 days and as long as 37 weeks. Even when regularity becomes established, the adolescent menstrual cycle usually is longer than the average for adult women. The typical menstrual cycle of a young girl may be about 33 days, compared to an average of 28 days for an adult woman. About three years elapse before the menstrual cycles become regular. In the meantime, irregular menstrual patterns can be considered as normal for girls during puberty.

The first menstrual cycles also are *anovulatory*. In other words, the young girl's ovaries have not matured sufficiently to produce an *ovum*, or egg cell, that can be fertilized by the sperm of a male. There are, of course, the exceptions that make newspaper headlines when a little girl gives birth to a baby. But anovulatory menstruation generally is the rule for the first few months after the menarche.

Delayed Puberty

Delayed puberty probably causes as much anguish as precocious puberty. The last girl in a group of childhood chums to develop breasts and experience the menarche may feel more self-conscious than the first girl in the class to menstruate. If the signs that usually precede menarche have not appeared by the age of 17 or 18, a medical examination should be considered, even though the girl may be a late-late-bloomer at the other end of the spectrum from the 7- or 8-year-old child who has menstruated.

The absence of menstruation after a girl is 18 can be the result of a wide variety of factors. The cause sometimes can be as simple as an *imperforate hymen,* a membrane that blocks the opening of the vagina. It can be the result of a congenital malformation of the reproductive organs, such

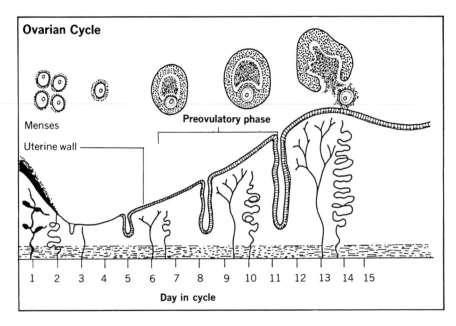

Ovarian Cycle

Menses

Uterine wall

Preovulatory phase

Day in cycle

1 2 3 4 5 6 7 8 9 10 11 12 13 14 15

as imperfect development of the ovaries. Accidents, exposure to carbon monoxide gas, or diseases like rheumatic fever or encephalitis in earlier years can result in brain damage that would inhibit the start of menstruation. The relationship between emotional upset and delayed menarche was vividly demonstrated during World War II when some girls who suffered psychological traumas also experienced very late signs of puberty.

Preparing Your Daughter for Menstruation

A mother's main responsibility is to convince her daughter at the beginning of puberty that menstruation is a perfectly normal body function. The mother should explain the proper use of sanitary napkins or tampons and encourage her daughter to keep records of her menstrual periods on a calendar.

The mother also should explain that menstruation usually is not a valid reason to stay in bed or avoid school or work. The girl should be advised that bathing and swimming should not be postponed because of menstruation. There are many old wives' tales about menstruation that are not true. But there may be some truth to stories that loss of menstrual blood can be weakening, particularly if the girl's diet does not replace the body stores of iron which may be lowered during menstrual flow. Iron is a key element of the red blood cell, and if iron-rich foods are not included in the meals of women during their years of menstruation they can eventually suffer a form of iron-deficiency anemia.

Postovulatory Phase

Menses

16 17 18 19 20 21 22 23 24 25 26 27 28 1 2 3

Hormone Activity: Becoming a Woman

Although the sex hormones are the key to what makes girls grow into women and boys into men, both sexes appear to receive secretions of male and female sex hormones in approximately equal amounts for about the first ten years of life. But as puberty approaches, the adrenal glands of girls seem to increase production of a female sex hormone, *estrogen*. Meanwhile, a nerve center in the hypothalamus area of the brain stimulates the pituitary gland, the master gland of the body, to secrete another kind of hormone, *gonadotropin*. Gonadotropin in turn activates a *follicle-stimulating hormone* that causes a matu-ration of the ovaries, which are part of the original equipment girls are born with but which remain dormant until the start of puberty.

During the second decade of life, the hormone activity stimulates the development of body tissues that not only grow in size but give a girl more womanly contours. However, the fully mature contours of a woman usually do not appear until after the ovaries are functioning and still another female sex hormone, *progesterone*, has been introduced in the system. The ovaries, uterus, Fallopian tubes, and vagina gradually mature as the menarche draws near.

Female Reproductive Organs

Ovary
Fallopian tube
Bladder
Uterus
Rectum
Cervix
Urethra
Vagina

Puberty: Changes in Boys

The appearance of male sexual characteristics during puberty is also influenced by hormonal changes. But the manifestation of male puberty is somewhat more subtle. The pituitary gland in a boy also secretes a gonadotropic hormone that stimulates maturation of *gonads.* In the male, the gonads are the *testicles,* the source of *sperm.* But whereas maturation of the ovaries in females leads to the menarche, there is no obvious sign in the boy that *spermatozoa* are being produced.

However, the secondary sexual characteristics, such as the growth of a beard and pubic hair, the spurt of growth of bones and muscles, the increase in size of the sex organs, and the deepening of the voice, are all indications of puberty. The changes in a boy's characteristics during puberty are usually spread over a period of two years, beginning with an increase in the size of the penis and testicles and reaching completion with the production of spermatozoa in the testicles. During the two-year period there usually is a noticeable increase in the chest size of a boy, with the broad shoulders of manhood appearing during the peak of bone and muscle growth. Generally, the appearance of pubic and facial hair, as well as hair in the armpits, follows the growth of the shoulder and chest area and precedes the change in voice.

The Testicles

The testicles are contained in a walnut-size sac of skin called the *scrotum.* It is held outside the body by a design of nature in order to maintain a temperature for spermatozoa production that is less than internal body temperature. Muscle fibers in the scrotum hold the testicles closer to the body for warmth in cold weather and relax to allow the sperm-producing organ to be farther away from the body when surrounding temperatures are warm.

In some cases, one or both testicles do not descend from the abdomen during the male child's early years. The result is that the undescended testicle or testicles will not produce sperm. An *incompletely descended testicle* always lies somewhere along the normal path to the scrotum. An *ectopic* testicle has deviated from that path and lies somewhere near the inguinal canal, at the junction of the thigh and the lower part of the abdomen. In a third departure from normal development, a *retractile testicle* has stopped short of the scrotum. It can be manipulated into the normal position or may descend to that position at puberty.

The danger of malignant change— of tumor development—usually warrants surgical removal of the incompletely descended and the ectopic testicle. A testicle trapped in the inguinal region may become inflamed because of the pressure of larger body parts in the area. In some cases, physicians are able to assist the de-

The Male Reproductive System

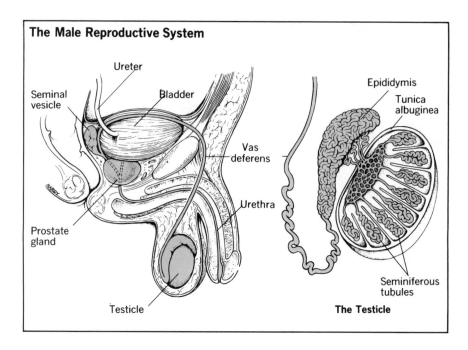

Ureter

Seminal vesicle

Bladder

Epididymis

Tunica albuginea

Vas deferens

Urethra

Prostate gland

Seminiferous tubules

Testicle

The Testicle

scent into the scrotum through administration of hormones or by surgery. At some point during puberty, a medical examination should include a check on the condition of the testes.

Genital Size

Many boys are as sensitive about the size of their genitals as girls are about breast size. In the case of an empty scrotum because of undescended testicles, it is possible to have the scrotum injected with silicone plastic for cosmetic or psychological reasons so the sac appears less flaccid or larger. The size of the penis may become the subject of discussion in the school shower room. If a boy appears sensitive about the subject, he should be assured that there is a wide variation in normal sizes and that like ears, noses, and other body parts the dimensions have little to do with function.

Nocturnal Emission

Another cause for concern by adolescent boys is the *nocturnal emission.* The nocturnal emission, sometimes called a *wet dream,* is the automatic expulsion of *semen* through the penis while the young man is asleep. The semen is secreted by the *prostate gland,* the *seminal vesicle,* and other glands that open into the *urethra.* The opalescent white fluid carries spermatozoa during intercourse and if the young male does not engage in sexual intercourse or does not masturbate, the semen simply accumulates until it overflows during a nocturnal emission. It is a harmless, normal occurrence.

Bone Growth

As the growth spurt subsides in the late teens, the *cartilage plates,* or *epiphyses,* in the long bones of the body close. Until the growth plates become filled in with calcium deposits, each long bone is in effect three bones—a central shaft separated from the ends by the cartilage growth plates. The growth plates are not completely replaced by bone until a female is about 20 and a male 23 years old. But the rate of growth begins to taper off as sexual maturity is achieved. After that, young women tend to retain fatty tissue and young men gain in muscle mass. It is a time to begin weight watching so that the hazards of obese adult life can be avoided. But the ravenous appetites developed during the period of rapid body growth and intense physical activity can easily evolve into bad eating habits during the teen years.

Skin and Hair Problems

Hereditary influences may determine many of the physical and psychological traits that an individual first becomes aware of in the teen years. Because of the various crossovers of the 23 sets of *chromosomes* and the nearly infinite combinations of *genes,* it is not always easy to predict how a child is going to appear as a young adult. But some features, such as hair color and eye color, usually can be identified with one or both parents; other traits may seem to be those of uncles, aunts, or grandparents. Heredity and hormones frequently are involved in the distribution of hair on the body and the oiliness of the skin, both of which can cause concern to teenagers who are plagued by an overabundance or lack of these cosmetic traits. An example of hereditary influences on hair patterns can be seen in early baldness. A receding hairline is not a trait of the parents but rather an influence of the genetic makeup of a grandparent—the trait skips a generation.

Removal of Excess Hair

While not much can be done about baldness that is hereditary, there are ways of handling the problems of excess hair. If a woman has excess hair on her face, arms, and legs, it can be removed by shaving, with wax, by electrolysis, or depilatories. Shaving is the most direct but not always the most satisfactory method of hair removal because it is intended only as a temporary measure. An alternate shortcut is bleaching with diluted hydrogen peroxide; the hair is still there but it is not as noticeable. Another method involves the use of hot wax spread on the skin and allowed to harden. When it is removed quickly, the hair is pulled away.

Depilatories are chemicals that destroy the hair at the skin line. Both hot wax and depilatories have longer-lasting effects than shaving, but they must be repeated at intervals of several weeks.

Depilatories, too, can produce unpleasant allergenic reactions. The only permanent method of removing excess hair is *electrolysis,* which is a time-consuming technique. Each hair root has to be burned out individually with an electric current. Electrolysis is recommended only for small areas and because of the time and expense involved would not be feasible for removing excess hair from regions other than the face.

Acne

There is some evidence that *acne* is partly hereditary. But it is such a common problem among teen-agers—it has been estimated that up to 90 percent of all youngsters endure some degree of acne—that it must have been inherited from a mutual ancestor like Adam or Eve. In fact, one of the deterrents to effective control of the skin disorder is that acne is so common that it is neglected by many youngsters. Waiting to outgrow acne can be a serious mistake, because the pimples, blemishes, blackheads, and boils that make life miserable for so many teenagers can be eliminated or considerably reduced. They can also cause scarring. A physician should be consulted in cases of severe or especially persistent acne.

Overactive Oil Glands

Acne can be seriously disfiguring at a time of life when most young people are sensitive about their appearance. It can occur at any time from puberty into early adulthood, and it is caused by poor adjustment of the skin to secretions of sebaceous glands. The imbalance resulting from hormones in the bloodstream will correct itself eventually. But to prevent permanent scarring, a program of simple skin care must be followed faithfully.

Acne is caused by overly active oil glands in the skin. When the oil glands become clogged, blackheads and pimples appear. (Blackheads are caused by a chemical change in the secretions of the oil glands.) To treat acne, a person should wash the skin to clear the pores and oil glands. The skin should be dry enough to peel away soiled layers and remove dirt from the pores. Most topical medications seek to keep the skin sufficiently dry to enhance peeling.

Skin Care

The face should be washed several times a day with warm water and mild soap. It should be dried thoroughly and gently with a clean towel. Careless handling of blemishes, such as squeezing blackheads, and picking at pimples and scabs can result in scarring. Teenagers also should avoid touching their faces. If the condition of the skin is worse than a few mild blemishes, a dermatologist will be able to prescribe topical medication, antibiotics, or hormones to treat the problem. Treatment often takes several months before there is noticeable improvement.

Other Precautions

Young women should not use cold creams or cosmetics unless they have been approved by a physician. Young men who shave must be careful to avoid cutting pimples. A physician also should be consulted about how diet can help control acne. Although the skin disorder is not a dietary disease, there is some evidence that certain foods tend to aggravate it. However, there is a lack of agreement among physicians as to whether chocolate, carbonated beverages, nuts, sweets, and other specific snack items may be the culprits. Because each youngster develops along an individual path, a food item that causes one teenager's face to break out with blemishes will not affect a sibling or classmate in the same way.

Diet

It is no surprise that many American teenagers have poor eating habits. A survey by the Food and Nutrition Board of the National Research Council recently showed that 40 percent of boys between 13 and 19 years of age and 60 percent of the girls in the same age group subsisted on diets that were substandard. Generally, the young people surveyed had abandoned the healthy eating habits of their families. They habitually skipped breakfast and failed to make up the nutritional loss during other meals.

There are several reasons for this phenomenon. Perhaps the most prominent reason is that teens are anxious to break away from their home. They therefore rebel against any form of convention or parental advice. The popularity of fast food institutions and snack shops is a also great contributor to the problem. Such places have become frequent hangouts for teenagers after school and on weekend evenings. With social gatherings in these surroundings, teenagers begin to develop poor eating habits. Frequently, they fill themselves up with non-nutritive foods and have no appetite later for balanced meals. At home, teenagers are great snack-eaters, and much snacking occurs while they are watching television. The combination of inactive television-watching and munching on junk foods leads to an unhealthy physical condition in teenagers.

Calories and Nutrition

A calorie is a unit of energy, and the human body requires a certain amount of energy each day in order to sustain life and continue normal physical activity. The amount of caloric intake varies according to the individual. Much of it depends on physical activity, size, and metabolic rate.

Calories in themselves are not bad. However, excessive intake of calories can lead to severe weight and health problems. Often the problem is not calories but the consumption of "empty calories" from foods high in fat or sugar that are of little or no nutritive value; such as sugary sodas, candy, and potato chips.

To maintain the proper balance between foods consumed and energy used in work and play, a teenager must regulate his or her caloric in-take. Much of the regulation occurs naturally. For example, when a person eats a lot, he or she is not hungry for a longer period of time than usual. Often, people crave foods that have been lacking in their diet. Thus, without conscious effort, most people are able to limit their consumption of foods to normal levels.

Nonetheless, teenagers should learn healthy eating habits and be aware of the potential of gaining weight. Regularly checking one's weight on a scale is not a good idea because it may foster unhealthy obsessions that can lead to skewed images of a teenager's physique and perhaps serious eating disorders. It is more important that a teenager monitor weight through the fit of his or her clothing.

Calcium and Phosphorus

Among the important minerals in teenage diets are calcium and phosphorus, which are required for the development of strong bones. Calcium also is required for the effective contraction of muscle tissues and is vital for normal heart function. Milk is the most easily available source of calcium and phosphorus. The recommended daily intake of milk for teenagers is four eight-ounce glasses. It can be served as fluid whole milk, as skim milk, buttermilk, evaporated milk, or as nonfat dry milk. Cheese or ice cream can be substituted for part of the fluid milk allowance. One cup of ice cream is equivalent in calcium to one-half cup of milk. A one-inch cube of cheddar cheese is equal to two-thirds of a cup of milk, which also is equivalent in calcium to one cup of cottage cheese. Two ounces of cream cheese are equal to one ounce of milk.

Iron

Iron is needed for the formation of hemoglobin, the substance that gives red blood cells their red coloration and is responsible for the transport of oxygen and carbon dioxide in the bloodstream. Hemoglobin has such an affinity for oxygen that without it humans would require 60 times as much blood to transport oxygen from the lungs to tissues throughout the body. Girls are five times as likely to need additional supplies of iron in their diets because of blood loss through menstruation. Recommended sources of iron are liver, heart, kidney, liver sausage, meat, shellfish, egg yolk, dark molasses, bread, beans and other legumes. If basic food lists seem dull, the teenager might think of the iron sources in terms of a peanut butter sandwich or two hamburgers; either choice would provide the daily iron needs for a girl. Other minerals that are important to a teenager's diet include the following:

● Sulfur is needed by the body for hair, skin, nails, and cartilage, and is available by eating nearly any protein-rich food.

● Iodine is needed for normal thyroid control of body metabolism and is supplied in the form of iodized table salt.

● Potassium is a tonic for the nervous system and the muscles and is available in adequate amounts in most kinds of meats, as well as bananas, orange juice, and milk.

● Magnesium collaborates chemically with calcium and phosphorus for normal muscle and nerve function, and is found in most forms of protein.

Note: Many of these nutrients are readily available in a normal diet. In most cases, it is not necessary to supplement a teenager's diet with these minerals. Children and teens should not rely on vitamin pills to make up for an unhealthy diet. It is better to eat nutritionally.

Weight Problems

Teens who are seriously overweight or who are contemplating radical weight reduction programs should be examined by a physician. Otherwise, unfair comparisons with other persons of the same age and height may lead to wrong conclusions about the need to gain or lose weight. The weight–height standards are based on averages, and there are many youngsters who are above or below the average but quite healthy and normal.

Another reason for a medical exam is to check the possibility of disease as the cause of the weight problem. The exam will also indicate whether the youngster has some other disorder that could be aggravated by a sudden weight loss.

Achieving optimum weight is only one step toward proper physical conditioning. A youngster who has been able to avoid physical activity by living in an elevator apartment, riding a bus to school, and watching TV after school hours instead of working or playing could be right on the button as far as weight for his age and height are concerned, but his muscular development and heart and lung capacity could be at the same time at a very low ebb.

Anorexia Nervosa

One of the most common eating disorders is anorexia nervosa, which occurs most often in teenage girls. It is a psychological disorder that in extreme cases results in death. The victims starve themselves in an exaggerated attempt to lose weight.

The most obvious trait is unnatural thinness. Other symptoms include the development of downy hair, called lanugo, obsession with exercise and "healthy" eating habits, emphasis on self-control and discipline, high achievement in school, alternative periods of strict fasting and binging, and rituals surrounding food preparation and eating.

Anorexics may weigh themselves several times a day and avoid eating when they are hungry. Most, according to experts, are usually preoccupied with their appearance or bodily "image" as a result of personality or ego problems and social insecurities. Anorexics frequently suffer from amenorrhea–cessation or delay of menstruation. Amenorrhea can have serious physical consequences.

Treatment of anorexia nervosa involves psychiatric counseling and, sometimes, hospitalization to ensure weight gain.

Bulimia

When binges become "gorge and purge" sessions—stretches of overeating followed by self-induced vomiting—the condition is called bulimia. Purging can involve vomiting, using laxatives, or taking diuretics. Bulimia may exist in conjunction with anorexia nervosa or it may afflict people who are of normal size or are slightly overweight. Like anorexics, most bulimics are female, who perceive themselves as larger and fatter than they really are. Studies have shown that 11 percent of high school females and 10 percent of female college students suffer from anorexia nervosa and/or bulimia.

Much of the problem stems from a poor self-image, some social insecurities, and a lack of self-control. Treatment involves psychiatric counseling. Physical damages may include a ruptured esophagus, dental caries, and hypoglycemia. For more information, or guidance to resources in your community, please contact the National Association of Anorexia Nervosa and Associated Disorders, Box 7, Highland Park, IL 60035; 312/831–3438.

Physical Fitness

Good physical conditioning is as important as weight control during the teen years. While not everybody can be an athletic champion, almost anyone who has time, discipline, determination, and patience can improve his or her heart, lungs, and muscles. Participation in school teams, intramurals, or independent exercise should be encouraged.

Exercise Goals

One of the goals of physical conditioning for teenagers is to tone and develop muscles. Muscles that are exercised regularly will grow in size and strength. Those that are not will atrophy (shrink in size).

Exercise increases the number of individual muscle fibers as well as the number of blood capillaries that supply the muscle tissue with nutritive substances. Consequently, the muscles become more efficient and more toned.

Physical conditioning should also include optimum cardiopulmonary fitness. The increase in heart activity and oxygen consumption is the basis for aerobic workouts. Aerobic means, literally, "with oxygen." Aerobic training involves maintaining a steady rate of physical activity so that the heart, lungs, and muscles work together at a level that is more demanding than a body's state of rest. Jogging, running, and rapid walking are common examples of aerobic training.

Exercise Precautions

The individual goals should be kept within sensible limits to avoid injury or impaired health. Overexertion can cause dizziness, nausea, and hyperventilation. Teenagers should avoid excessive exercise during severely hot and humid weather. To avoid dehydration, drink plenty of water before and after exercising.

Choosing Proper Equipment

When exercising, it is essential that a teenager use proper athletic gear to avoid injuries. The knees are one of the most vulnerable body parts. As such, a teenager must be fitted with high-quality athletic shoes, which should be replaced as soon as they wear out. A podiatrist can provide in-soles for proper foot balance for pavement or grass field. Protective gear, such as a mouth piece, shin guard, or riding helmet, is also important.

The Use of Steroids

Recently a substantial number of teenagers have been illegally abusing steroids in the hopes of developing bulky muscles. Considerable physical risks are involved with taking steroids at such a young age: stunted growth, acne, vomiting, enhanced breast development (for boys), and the development of permanent facial hair and deepened voices (for girls). For all users, there is a risk of long-term dependence or addiction to the drug. The psychological effects are equally serious. They include irritability, violent behavior, depression, mania, psychosis, and in some cases suicide.

Care of the teeth

During the teen years, careful supervision by the dentist and cooperation from the teenager are especially necessary. The poor eating habits of many teenagers are reflected in their cavity rate, which is usually higher during adolescence than in later life.

Conscientious oral care can help avoid a high cavity rate and bad breath, problems that are really caused by the same thing—*dental plaque*. For more information on this subject, see Ch. 22, *The Teeth and Gums*.

Need for Frequent Checkups

During adolescence, the dentist will often recommend more frequent checkups. Small cavities are treated before they become deeper and infect the pulp, the inner chamber of the tooth containing nerves and blood vessels. Should the pulp become infected, the tooth may need a root canal or require extraction.

The dentist also treats tooth decay, or *caries*, more popularly known as cavities, to prevent their spread. Cavities begin as a break in the tooth surface, which later enlarges. Food debris can become lodged in the cavity, be attacked by bacteria, and cause a cavity on the next tooth. The only way to avoid such a problem is to have the affected tooth treated immediately.

Front teeth often decay for the first time during this period. They are restored with a silicate or plastic filling close in color to the tooth. Unfortunately, these materials are not permanent and will need to be replaced in time. As a result, neglect of diet and oral cleanliness by an adolescent may mean that he may need many replacement fillings in the same cavity over his lifetime.

Orthodontic Treatment

The development and growth of teeth is completed during the adolescent period. When oral growth is improper, the adolescent needs treatment by an *orthodontist,* a dental specialist who treats abnormalities of the bite and alignment of teeth and jaws. Correction of such conditions as buck teeth, which mar a person's appearance, is a major reason for orthodontic treatment. But there are also major health reasons for orthodontic care. If teeth, for example, come together improperly, efficient chewing of food is impossible. The digestive system is strained because chunks of improperly chewed food pass through it. Orthodontic treatment will, therefore, result in lifelong better health and appearance. For more information, see Ch. 22, *The Teeth and Gums.*

Stimulants and Alcohol

Initial exposure to caffeine, tobacco, drugs, and alcohol usually occurs during adolescence. Teenagers should be fully educated regarding their physical effects and potential danger. They should learn how to use them, if at all, sensibly and in moderation, and to resist peer-group pressures.

Caffeine

Caffeine, which is naturally present in coffee and tea and is used in many carbonated beverages and medications, stimulates the central nervous system to overcome fatigue and drowsiness. It also affects a part of the nervous system that controls respiration so that more oxygen is pumped through the lungs. In large amounts, caffeine can increase the pulse rate, but there are few long-range effects because the substance is broken down by the body tissues within a few hours and excreted. Because of the action of caffeine in stimulating an increased intake of oxygen, it sometimes is used to combat the effects of such nervous system depressants as alcohol.

Nicotine

Nicotine is one of nearly 200 substances in tobacco. It affects the human physiology by stimulating the adrenal glands to increase the flow of adrenaline. The blood vessels become constricted and the skin temperature drops, producing effects not unlike exposure to cold temperatures. When comparatively large amounts of nicotine are absorbed by the body, the pulse becomes rapid and the smoker has symptoms of dizziness, faintness, and sometimes nausea and diarrhea. The release of adrenaline, triggered by nicotine, will produce temporary relief from fatigue by increasing the flow of sugar in the blood. However, the effect is transient, and the feeling of fatigue will return again after the increased blood sugar has been expended.

Other Properties of Tobacco

The nicotine in tobacco can be absorbed simply by contact with the mucous membranes of the mouth; the tobacco does not have to be smoked to get the nicotine effects. Burning tobacco produces a myriad of substances found in the smoke of many plant materials when they are dried and burned. More than 50 different compounds are known to occur in concentrations of one microgram or more in each puff of tobacco smoke. Again, laboratory tests have demonstrated that the substances in burning tobacco do not have to be inhaled; most of the chemical compounds can be absorbed through the mucous membranes while a puff of smoke is held in the mouth for a few seconds. At least ten of the substances in tobacco smoke have been shown to produce cancer in animals. Other chemicals in tobacco tars are known as *cocarcinogens;* although they do not produce cancer themselves, they react with other substances to produce cancers.

Smoking and Disease

The relationship among tobacco smoking and cancer, heart disease, and emphysema-bronchitis is well established, even if some of the cause and effect links are missing. Large-scale studies of the death rates of smokers and nonsmokers have been carried on for more than 20 years. One group, consisting of nearly a quarter-million war veterans, yielded results indicating that smokers are from 10 to 16 times as likely to die of lung cancer as nonsmokers. (The higher ratio is for heavy smokers.) Similar results have been obtained from studies of smokers and nonsmokers with heart disease and lung ailments.

Buerger's Disease

One of the possible, although rare, effects of smoking is the aggravation of symptoms of a particularly insidious circulatory disorder known as *Buerger's disease.* As noted above, one of the effects of nicotine is a drop in skin temperatures. Smoking a single cigarette can cause the temperature of the fingers and toes to drop as much as 15 degrees Fahrenheit; the average is a little more than a 5-degree drop. The temperature change results from constriction of the blood vessels at the extremities. Blood clots may develop in the vessels that have been constricted, cutting off the flow of blood to the tissues of the area. When there is numbness or pain in the extremities, the condition should receive swift medical attention to prevent serious consequences.

Carbon Monoxide Accumulation

Another little publicized effect of smoking is the accumulation of carbon monoxide in the blood. Carbon monoxide is one of the lethal gases emitted in automobile exhaust. It is also produced by burning plant materials such as tobacco. It is a dangerous gas because of its strong affinity for the hemoglobin of red blood cells. Unlike oxygen and carbon dioxide, which become temporarily attached, then released, from the hemoglobin molecule, carbon monoxide becomes permanently locked into the red blood cell chemistry so that the cells are no longer effective for their normal function of transporting oxygen to the body tissues. With the oxygen-carrying capacity of part of the red blood cells wiped out, brain cells and other tissues suffer a mild oxygen starvation and the results are a form of intoxication.

A strong whiff of carbon monoxide can be fatal. Smokers, of course, do not get that much of the substance into their blood, but they do pick up enough carbon monoxide to render up to eight percent of their red blood cells ineffective. Experiments at Indiana University show that pack-a-day smokers have the same level of carbon monoxide in their blood as subjects who inhale an atmosphere of one-fourth of one percent carbon monoxide. That level of carbon monoxide increases the shortness of breath during exercise by approximately 15 percent, and, the study shows, about three weeks of abstinence from smoking are required to permit the oxygen-carrying capacity of the blood to return to normal. It is the carbon monoxide of burning plant materials that produces most of the "high" associated with the smoking of many substances.

Alcohol

Alcohol usually is not considered a potentially dangerous drug because it is easily available at cocktail lounges and liquor stores and is served generously at parties. Alcohol has been used by man for thousands of years, at times as a sedative and anesthetic, and when used in moderation has the effect of a mild tranquilizer and appetite stimulant. But when consumed in excess amounts, alcoholic beverages can produce both psychological and physical dependence. It can produce illusions of being a pick-me-up, but studies indicate that this is due to a letdown of inhibitions and the weakening of some functions of the central nervous system, particularly in the cerebral cortex.

Parents and teachers share an important responsibility to educate young people about the use and misuse of alcohol. Like marihuana, the effects of alcohol on human beings are not thoroughly understood. Some users develop a tissue tolerance for alcohol so that their body tissues require increasing amounts. When alcohol is withdrawn from such users, they develop tremors, convulsions, and even hallucinations. However, there are many varied reactions to the use of alcohol, and an individual may react differently to alcoholic drinks at different times. See Ch. 29, *Substance Abuse*.

Drugs

During the 1960s there was an alarming increase in drug use among teenagers—a problem that deservedly received nationwide attention. Education concerning the hazards and occasional tragedies accompanying drug use is imperative.

Marihuana

Marihuana affects the central nervous system, including the brain, after it enters the bloodstream. According to some researchers, the substance accumulates in the liver. Some of the effects of marihuana are not unlike those of tobacco. The rate of the heartbeat is increased, body temperature drops, and blood sugar levels are altered. The drug user also feels dehydrated, the appetite is stimulated, coordination of movements becomes difficult, there are feelings of drowsiness or unsteadiness, and the eyes may become reddish. Taken in higher strengths, marihuana can cause hallucinations or distortions of perception.

Varying Effects

Scientists are uncertain about the pathways of the drug in the central nervous system and its effects on other body systems. The drug's effects seem to vary widely, not only among individual users but also according to the social setting and the amount and strength of the marihuana used. The effects, which usually begin within 15 minutes after the smoke is inhaled and may continue for several hours, vary from depression to excitement and talkativeness. Some users claim to experience time distortions and errors in distance perception. But others sharing the same marihuana cigarette may experience no effects at all.

Although marihuana is not addictive, in that users do not develop a physical dependence upon the substance and withdrawal of the drug produces no ill effects, there are dangerous results from the use of marihuana. Marihuana users find it hard to make decisions that require clear thinking, some users develop psychotic reactions or an emotional disorder called "acute marihuana panic," and there is some evidence that the active ingredient is transmitted by expectant mothers to their unborn children.

Hallucinogens

Marihuana sometimes is described as a *hallucinogen* because of visual hallucinations, illusions, and delusions reported by users after they have inhaled the smoke from a large number of "joints" or "sticks" of the drug. But marihuana should not be confused with the true hallucinogenic drugs such as *mescaline* and *LSD* (lysergic acid diethylamide) which are known by doctors as *psychomimetic* drugs because they mimic psychoses.

LSD and Mescaline

LSD and mescaline have marked effects on perception and thought processes. Teenagers usually become involved with the use of LSD because they are curious about its effects; they may have heard about its purported "mind-bending" properties and expect to gain great personal insights from its use. Instead of great insight, however, the user finds anxiety, depression, confusion, and frightening hallucinations. The use of LSD is complicated by the reappearance of hallucinations after the individual has quit using the drug; the very possibility of repeated hallucinations causes a sense of terror.

Morphine and Heroin

Besides the hallucinogenic drugs, there are *opium* derivatives, *morphine* and *heroin*. Morphine is one of the most effective pain relievers known and is one of the most valuable drugs available to the physician. Morphine and heroin depress the body systems to produce drowsiness, sleep, and a reduction in physical activity. They are true narcotics, and their appeal is in their ability to produce a sense of euphoria by reducing the individual's sensitivity to both psychological and physical stimuli.

Addictive Properties

A great danger lies in the ability of the body tissues to develop a physical dependence on morphine and its derivative cousin, heroin. The degree to which heroin's "desirable" effects are felt depends in part on how the user takes it. *Sniffing* is the mildest form of abuse, followed by *skin-popping*—subcutaneous injection—and then by *mainlining*—injecting directly into a vein, which is the method used by almost all those dependent on heroin.

The body adjusts to the level of the first doses so that increasingly larger injections of the drug are required to produce the same feelings of euphoria. The ability of the body to adjust to the increasingly larger doses is called *tolerance*. And with tolerance goes *physical dependence,* which means that when heroin or morphine is withdrawn from the user he experiences a violent sickness marked by tremors, sweating and chills, vomiting and diarrhea, and sharp abdominal pains. Another shot of heroin or morphine temporarily ends the withdrawal symptoms. But the user, now dependent upon the drug, must continue regular doses or face another bout of the withdrawal sickness. Heroin has no value as a medicine and is available only through illicit channels at a high price. The heroin addict usually is unable to hold a job because of effects of the drug and often turns to crime in order to finance his daily supply of the narcotic.

Shortened Life Span

The health of a narcotics addict declines so that his life span is shortened by 15 to 20 years. He usually is in continual trouble with the law because of the severe penalties for illegal possession of narcotics. If he sells narcotics, as many heroin addicts are driven to do to get enough money to support their habit, the punishment is even more severe.

Amphetamines and Barbiturates

Other commonly abused drugs are *amphetamines,* also known as *uppers* or *pep pills,* and *barbiturates,* sometimes called *downers* or *goof balls.* Amphetamines are used by physicians to curb the appetite when weight reduction of patients is needed and to relieve mild cases of depression. However, some physicians doubt that amphetamines should be used as a weight-control medication because of the risks involved; other experts have questioned whether the drugs are actually effective for that purpose.

Amphetamines stimulate the heart rate, increase the blood pressure, cause rapid breathing, dilate the pupils of the eyes, and produce other effects such as dryness of the mouth, sweating, headache, and diarrhea. Ordinarily, amphetamines are swallowed as tablets, but a more extreme form of amphetamine abuse involves the injection of the drug, usually Methedrine, directly into the vein.

Dangers of Amphetamines

The danger in the use of amphetamines is that they induce a person to do things beyond his physical endurance, cause mental disorders that require hospitalization, and, in large doses, can result in death. Although they do not produce the kind of physical dependence observed in the use of narcotics, amphetamine withdrawal for a heavy user can result in a deep and suicidal depression.

Barbiturates

Barbiturates are sedatives used by physicians to treat high blood pressure, epilepsy, and insomnia, and to relax patients being prepared for surgery. They slow the heart rate and breathing, lower blood pressure, and mildly depress the action of nerves and muscles.

Dangers of Barbiturates

Barbiturates are highly dangerous when taken without medical advice. They distort perception and slow down reaction and response time, contributing to the chances of accidents. Barbiturates are a leading cause of accidental poison deaths because they make the mind foggy and the user forgets how many pills he has taken, thus leading to overdosage. They also cause physical dependence with withdrawal symptoms that range from cramps and nausea to convulsions and death. See also Ch. 29, *Substance Abuse.*

Adolescent Suicide

Suicides among teenage boys and girls increased greatly in number during the middle 1980s. Health experts termed the phenomenon an "epidemic of self-destruction." In some areas suicides or suicide attempts took place in clusters. Often, groups of close friends were involved. In some cases of cluster suicides or attempts, it appeared that a suicidal attitude was contagious.

Suicide became the second leading cause of death among adolescents. In the nearly 30 years beginning in the late 1950s, the suicide rate among teenagers tripled. Preadolescents also began to take their own lives more frequently: public health personnel reported suicides among children as young as three.

Risk Factors

As educators, social workers, psychiatrists, and others became involved in community efforts to prevent teenage suicides, a number of "risk factors"—signs of an intent to take one's life—were isolated. Changes in a teenager's behavior, whether in peer relationships, school activities, or academic performance, were said to be primary indicators. So were emotional shifts, particularly toward anger or irritability. Depression and withdrawal, experts said, might accompany the emotional changes. Sadness, changes in eating and sleeping habits, and preoccupation with death were other signs.

Young people considering suicide showed other symptoms. Many reported headaches, stomachaches, and other ailments. Some talked about taking their own lives. A young person who had lost a close friend through suicide was at unusual risk, according to studies. Family histories of suicide and parental depression were cited as indirectly contributing factors.

Parent Involvement

For parents concerned about the possibility of a child's or teen's suicide, such clues are only clues. The parent still has the task of trying to resolve the potential suicide. Authorities make the following suggestions.

Act at Once

Where a preadolescent or adolescent gives clear signals—usually risk factors appearing in combination—that suicide might be contemplated, parents should seek help immediately. Local suicide hotlines or suicide prevention centers should be contacted; counseling may have to be started.

School Help

Many schools cooperate in efforts to prevent suicides. The schools may sponsor group meetings at which students talk out their feelings about suicide, and such meetings may be appropriate as a first or second step. A representative of the community crisis or prevention center normally takes part in such meetings. Many schools have special counselors, psychologists, and others who can serve as direct lines to sources of help.

Out-of-School Contacts

Group meetings provide all teenage participants with the names and locations of out-of-school contact persons who may be able to help them in a crisis. Most crisis agencies operate 24 hours a day, seven days a week, providing aid during the "danger hours" between late afternoon and midnight. Parents may want also to contact clergy, trusted friends or relatives, or others.

Peer Support

Where possible, peer support should be mobilized in the effort to prevent a suicide. Many young people, especially the friends of a depressed or otherwise suicidal teenager, can help—and will do so rather than hear later that a suicide has taken place. But parents should, according to experts, remember that a youngster with high status among his or her peers may influence those peers. Committing suicide, the high-status young person may convince others that "life isn't worth it." Surviving boy- or girlfriends are especially at risk.

Social and Sexual Maturation

The Prospect of Adulthood

As a youngster passes from childhood into adolescence, it is the psychological adjustments rather than the physical changes that are most likely to produce difficulties. The emotional problems, of course, are related to the hormonal activity of the developing body. However, the conflicts that frequently are upsetting to both the adolescent and other members of his family are the result of adjustments that must be made between the young person and the society in which he must live.

In our own culture, the teenager must continually adjust to a complex set of rules and regulations. He frequently may feel that he must accept the responsibilities of adulthood before he is entitled to the privileges of being treated as an adult. Childhood is only a step behind, but he has learned to suppress or ignore childhood relationships. He can easily forget the point of view of children and even resent the ability of his parents to recall the "cute" incidents of his earlier years. At the same time, he may be startled by the suggestion that within a few short years he and his teenage friends will face the selection of a career, marriage, establishment of a home, and a lifetime of responsibilities he may feel ill-prepared to assume.

Future Outlook for Teenagers

While a teenager may feel competent enough to handle adult responsibilities and decisions, he or she may have misgivings about what the future holds. Fear and uncertainty of the unknown can cause anxiety in teenagers, though they may not express it. They are aware that the choices they make—what college or vocational school they select, what profession they choose, who they marry, where they decide to live—can affect their entire lives.

An abundance of educational opportunities and careers choices is available for any teenager. It is the parents' responsibility to expose teenagers to all of the options and to guide them toward attainable goals. Parents should recognize a teen's strengths and weakness and direct him or her to the most appropriate educational institution or profession. Career and college guidance counselors at high school are very helpful.

In the past few decades, the outlook for males and females has become nearly identical, and the career options and lifestyles that teenagers may select are seemingly endless. Traditional social conventions are changing. Many marriages occur after both spouses have established careers, allowing for arrangements that were not possible for many parents of current teenagers. Given the professional opportunities for women, many families are dual-income, or, in some cases, the men choose to stay at home. Much of this depends on the economic needs of a particular family, but the options are there for nearly any kind of work situation and lifestyle.

Advanced Education

The educational requirements for current jobs place an added strain on the pace of growing up. Many teenagers must have some vague professional goals in order to choose the proper means of attaining them. All professions require a certain level of education and expertise. While much of the experience is learned on the job, many professions require college degrees and even graduate degrees. In many blue-collar professions, training is essential. It can be obtained through vocational schools, apprenticeships, or training programs.

Need for Independence

Adolescence is a time when a child slowly develops into an adult. With physical changes come psychological changes as well. As such, a teenager wants to be treated like an adult, not a child. These demands are often manifested in rebellious actions and disdainful remarks.

In a desire to act independently, a teenager may exhibit reclusive behavior in order to avoid contact with parents. He or she may be reluctant to divulge information. Sneaking out of the house is a common gesture. These are distinct attempts to dodge unsolicited advice from parents who are only too anxious to give it.

Parents should not be offended by these actions, rather they should allow their child to explore the world independently. Such an education will make them more confident and well-adjusted as adults. Teenagers who are not allowed much freedom are often more difficult to control and can cause more damage out of spite.

Conflicts between Parent and Teenager

Some conflicts between the generations are avoidable. The parents may be protective and slow to cut the apron strings because they love their children and want to prevent them from becoming involved in unhappy situations. The teenager resents the overprotective actions of the parents, regarding them as evidence that they do not trust their own children.

What parents should try to make clear to their children is that they make offering their years of experience as guidelines. Teenagers should value the counsel of more experienced members of the family; they should cooperate by listening to the adult viewpoint. If, after serious consideration of the parents' point of view, the youngster still wants to make his own decision in the matter, it should be understood that he may have to accept the responsibility for the consequences. A keystone in the training for adulthood is the concept that being an adult entails more than just privileges and the authority to make decisions; along with decision-making goes a responsibility to the family and society for the consequences of one's decisions.

Few parents, of course, would refuse to bail out a teenage son or daughter in real trouble. And even when a youngster is rebellious enough to leave home, he should know that the door will always be open to him when he decides to return. Again, limiting the options available to a teenager can lead to a snowballing of bad decisions and resulting complications.

In many cases, the conflicts between parents and teenagers derive from the illusion that a younger child has more freedom of choice. A small child may actually seem to have a freer choice of friends he can bring into his home and the games he can play with them. But there are always limitations to a child's choices, and parents are more understanding of the bad choices by attributing mistakes to the fact that "he's only a child."

Older youngsters become involved in situations in which the decisions are more important. A boy and girl at the age of five can "play house" together in an atmosphere of innocence. However, the same boy and girl could hardly suggest to their parents that they intended to play house at the age of 15. If the boy and girl, although next-door neighbors, are of different social or ethnic backgrounds, they may become aware of parental prejudices in addition to new rules of propriety as they grow into their teenage years.

Decisions of the teen years can involve the use of tobacco, alcohol, owning an automobile, handling of money, overnight trips with friends, association with friends who use drugs illegally, and relationships with members of the opposite sex. The consequences of all alternatives should be outlined for the adolescent.

Search for Identity

Part of the youngster's struggle for independence will involve what sometimes is described as a search for identity. A child accepts without much questioning that he is a member of a certain family and lives in a certain neighborhood. But as he grows older, he becomes aware of his status in the family as well as the status of his family in society. A seven-year-old could not care less about the background of his family or that of his second-grade friends. As he becomes a teenager he learns that such subjects may be matters of concern to parents and their circle of friends. He may imitate the attitudes of his family or disregard them, perhaps inviting criticism that he is rebellious.

More important to the youngster, however, is a growing concern about his position and role in life and where it may lead. He is still in the so-called formative years and is sensitive to countless influences in the world about him. Teenagers become concerned with approaching education and career decisions. It is natural for them to identify with older members in the family, teachers, and celebrities.

Need for Privacy

For the teenage girl, party invitations, dances, and diaries are important and an increasing amount of privacy is required. Even if she must share a room with a sister, there should be a part of the room that is her territory. She should have personal belongings that are not shared by a parent or sibling. If she has her own room, everything in the room probably will be regarded as her property. Even her mother should respect her privacy by knocking on the door and getting permission to enter her private world.

Although sometimes less sensitive about such matters, boys also are likely to insist on a certain amount of privacy as they grow older. They may share a room with a brother but they need trunks or other containers with locks in which they can keep personal possessions. Proof that such desire for privacy is not a passing fad for young men is found in their adult compulsion for private offices and a den or workshop area at home.

Contacts with Older Friends

Young teenagers, through part-time jobs as babysitters or errand boys, usually come in contact with young adults outside the family circle for the first time. The young adults may accept the teenagers as peers, which is flattering to the youngsters, who may in turn admire and imitate the young adults. If the teenager has been able to identify closely with his family's sense of propriety, the contacts can be a good social experience. But if the youngster has not been able to identify effectively with his parents and family members, he may be vulnerable to misguiding influences. Because of the urge for adult status, the teenager may find a premature outlet for testing his abilities to live the adult life in the company of young adults. He (or she) can absorb a lot of information—and misinformation—about sex, alcohol, drugs, and other subjects.

Teenagers certainly should not be cautioned against contacts with all young adults, but they should also have a reliable older person aside from their parents with whom they can discuss matters they would not discuss with a mother or father. The alternate adult might be a clergyman, the family physician, a teacher, or even a favorite aunt or uncle. Such an arrangement provides the youngster with a means of learning a bit more about life in an independent manner and from a different point of view than could be obtained within his own immediate family circle.

Relationships with the Opposite Sex

First teenage contacts with the opposite sex tend to be awkward and sometimes embarrassing despite the best efforts and intentions of parents. The meetings may be at school dances or movie dates, perhaps in the presence of a chaperon who is a teacher or parent.

Overcoming Insecurity

Some youngsters will feel more secure than others in social gatherings; those who feel insecure may not participate at all when such opportunities first arise. As the youngsters grow older, however, they find that more and more of their friends are dating or going to dances or parties to meet members of the opposite sex.

Some boys or girls who feel insecure may find that they are more gregarious or less ill-at-ease if they fortify themselves with a couple of drinks of an alcoholic beverage, or with drugs, before they join their friends. Youngsters who feel the need for stimulants or depressants in order to enjoy parties usually can be helped with psychological counseling to overcome their fears of inadequacy.

Young people should be assured that getting together at parties of mixed sexes is a natural thing to do. It has been going on for generations and although an individual youngster may feel ill-at-ease at his first few dances or parties, he probably will survive. As the boy or girl attends more parties the chances increase that he or she will meet a person of the opposite sex who is particularly attractive. If the feeling is mutual, the acquaintanceship may develop into more or less steady dating.

Going Steady

Steady dating, which leads to a formal engagement and marriage in many cases, should not be encouraged at an early age or before a young person has had an opportunity to date a number of prospective partners. At the same time, it should not be discouraged to the point of producing a rebellious reaction. As was pointed out earlier, some girls admit going steady with a boy for no other reason than to demonstrate their independence of judgment.

Controlling the Sexual Impulse

Teenagers who spend a lot of time together at parties, in their homes, or at recreational meetings such as beach outings are likely to be physically attracted to each other. It may begin with kissing, dancing, holding hands, or simply a natural urge to neck or pet. In more primitive societies, the couple might simply indulge in sexual intercourse without any concern for the possible consequences. But in our own society, young people are expected to control their natural urges.

Influence of the Mass Media

Complicating sincere efforts of a teenager to make the right decisions in relations with the opposite sex is the constant exposure of youngsters to movies, magazine articles, books, and other media suggesting that sexual relations between unmarried couples are not only acceptable but a common practice. Compared to the image of young love as displayed in movie promotion advertising, a teenage boy and girl may believe that a few ardent hugs and kisses in a secluded spot may be as innocent as making a plate of fudge together in the girl's kitchen.

Some girls, but not all, are as easily aroused as boys by close bodily contact with the opposite sex. Physical contact for most boys arouses sexual desire, partly because of the physiological makeup of the male.

The Sex Drive in Boys

Males are so constituted that during periods of abstinence from intercourse, their sperm builds up. During periods of sperm buildup, the male sex drive increases in strength. There are no standards or averages for the male sex drive; instead there is a wide variety of sexual appetites and abilities.

A girl who cuddles too closely to a boy may trigger a response she did not expect and may not want. Depending upon the boy and the status of his sex drive at that time, he might accept the girl's approaches as a suggestion that she is willing to have intercourse or is at least interested in petting. If the girl is simply being friendly, the results can be embarrassing to one or both of the youngsters. If the boy is the type who likes to discuss the details of his dates with friends, the girl may discover a sudden and unwelcome change in attitude by other boys of the group.

Walking hand-in-hand, or with an arm around the waist, and kissing that is not too passionate, usually are acceptable ways for young teenagers to display affection. And there are activities such as hiking or bicycle riding that afford a boy and girl a chance to be together and apart from the rest of the world. There also are picnics, ball games, movies, and concerts that permit togetherness without setting the stage for hard-to-control sexual impulses.

Masturbation

Another manifestation of the natural sex drives of young persons is masturbation. Discouraged by the rules and standards of society from fulfilling sex urges in the same manner as married couples, teenagers discover they can find sexual satisfaction in masturbation. Despite the stories that warn of physical or mental decay for youngsters who masturbate, the practice is not harmful unless the parents make an issue of it.

If there are dangers in masturbation, they are likely to be the isolation and loneliness associated with the practice and the confusion and anxiety that can result if the young person feels guilty or is punished or criticized for masturbating. Masturbation is such a natural reaction that most youngsters discover it by themselves even if the subject is never discussed by friends or family members. But for many young people, masturbation may violate religious or other beliefs or values. These youngsters may want to discuss the practice with a physician, understanding clergy, or some other trusted person.

Sex Education

Because boys and girls in their teens may be capable of producing children and are known to have strong sexual urges, they should be provided with authoritative information about human reproduction and birth control. It is up to the parents to make decisions regarding the proper sources of such information, how much information should be given, and at what age.

One of the reasons for the popularity of sex education in the schools is that teachers can get the parents off the hook by explaining the facts of life to youngsters. However, by forfeiting their prerogative to explain sex and human reproduction to their own children, parents must depend upon the teacher to make an acceptable presentation to the youngsters. The likely alternative is that youngsters will obtain a considerable amount of misinformation from friends and acquaintances at street-corner seminars or by experimentation.

In the days when the majority of the population lived on farms or near rural areas, children learned a few things about sex and reproduction simply by working with farm animals. They learned that cats produced kittens, dogs produced puppies, cows produced calves, and so on. This on-the-job type of sex education also provided farm youngsters with a smattering of genetics, because cross-breeding strains of animals frequently had economic consequences. It was not too difficult for the rural youngsters to relate their barnyard education to human experience.

Children enrolled in sex education classes in the urban areas of America today receive similar information—dogs have puppies, cats have kittens, etc.—by watching movies and reading books. However, the lessons may be superficial or incomplete, depending upon the teacher and the prescribed curriculum. For example, the children in one eastern school were taught that the baby develops in the mother's abdomen, which led some youngsters to believe the baby lived in the mother's stomach until born. "Why isn't the baby digested by the stomach acid?" asked one confused girl. And when asked how the baby gets out when it's time to be born, the teacher told the students that such questions should be answered by their parents. The point here is that parents should establish some rapport with their children to be sure they are learning a practical set of facts about adult love, sex, and reproduction, including the possible emotional and physical consequences of premarital sexual intercourse.

Although parents may find it difficult or embarrassing to explain the facts of life to their own children, it is one of the most important contributions that can be made to a maturing youngster. At the present time, at least one out of six teenage girls in the United States will have an unwanted pregnancy. Obviously, thousands of parents and teachers are not providing adequate instruction in sex education subjects.

The Male Reproductive System

Any instruction in the facts of life should begin by use of the proper names for the body parts involved. In the male, the external sex organs are the *penis* and the *testicles,* or *testes.* The penis contains a tiny tube, the *urethra,* through which urine is eliminated. Much of the fleshy part of the penis is composed of spongy tissue. When the penis is stimulated sexually, the spongy areas become filled with blood, which makes the penis larger and firm, a condition called an *erection.* The testicles contain male *sperm cells,* also called *spermatozoa.*

The sperm travel up tubules inside the abdomen to a storage organ, or reservoir, the *seminal vesicle.* The sperm storage area also contains a thick white fluid called *semen* that is secreted by glands that open into the urethra. One of the glands, the *prostate,* serves partly as a control valve to prevent urine from mixing with the semen, since both are discharged through the urethra. The semen, containing millions of sperm, empties periodically in a more or less automatic action, being squeezed out of the seminal vesicle by pulsating contractions. The contractions and ejection of semen are called *ejaculation.* During the sex act, or *intercourse,* with a female, the semen is ejaculated into the woman's vagina.

The Female Reproductive System

The *vagina* is the proper name for the tubular female sex organ. At the end of the vagina is an opening, called the *cervix,* which leads into the *uterus.* The uterus, or *womb,* is shaped somewhat like an upside-down pear.

When a baby develops within the mother's abdomen, it grows inside the uterus. The uterus also is the source of the bloody discharge that occurs periodically during the fertile years of women. When the blood is discharged it is called *menstruation,* or the menstrual period. The menstrual blood passes out through the vagina, which stretches to become the *birth canal* when a baby is being born. The urethra of a female empties outside the vagina.

The Menstrual Cycle and Conception

Unlike the male reproductive organs, which produce perhaps millions of spermatozoa each day, the female reproductive system ordinarily releases only one germ cell, called an *ovum* or egg, at a time. An ovum is released at an average frequency of once every 28 days. It should always be remembered that the 28-day figure is only an average; the actual time may vary considerably for reasons that are only partly known. The cycles are more likely to be irregular for teenage girls than for mature women. An ovum is released from one of the two *ovaries,* or sex glands, comparable in function to the male testicles, located on either side of the uterus. The ovum, or egg, is transported from the ovary to the uterus through a *Fallopian tube.*

If the ovum encounters male sperm during its passage from the ovary to the uterus, there is a good chance that fertilization, or *conception,* will occur through a union of a spermatozoon and the egg. The fertilized ovum, called a *zygote,* soon divides into a cluster of human tissue cells that become the embryo of a baby. For further information about pregnancy, see under Ch. 4, *The Beginning of a Family.*

During the time that the egg is maturing in the ovary and passing into the uterus after its release, the membrane lining of the uterus becomes thicker because it accumulates blood and nutrients. If the ovum is fertilized, it finds a spot in the membrane where it becomes attached and develops rapidly into an embryo, gaining its nourishment from the blood and nutrient-enriched lining of the uterus. If the ovum is not fertilized, it passes through the uterus, and the blood-rich membrane sloughs off. The blood and some of the cells of the membrane become the discharged material of menstruation. The unfertilized ovum could pass through undetected because it is nearly microscopic.

After menstruation has begun, the female reproductive cycle starts over again. The lining of the uterus once more builds up its supply of blood and nutrients to support a fertilized ovum. Ordinarily, the next ovum will be released about 14 days after a menstrual period begins. If a female does not have intercourse, or avoids intercourse during the time the ovum is released, or in some other manner is able to prevent sperm from reaching an ovum, she will not become pregnant but will experience a menstrual period at intervals that average around 28 days.

When fertilization of an ovum occurs, menstruation ceases and no further egg cells are released until the outcome of the pregnancy has been determined. In other words, the cycles of ovulation and menstruation start anew after the baby is born or the pregnancy has been terminated.

Contraception

The first rule of birth control is that no method is guaranteed to be 100 percent effective. Sexual intercourse nearly always is accompanied by some risk of pregnancy, and the teenagers who try to beat the odds should be willing to take the responsibility for the results. Teenagers should be provided with the basic facts of birth control as soon as they are capable of producing children themselves. But the emphasis should be on the relative unreliability of the techniques which do not require a visit to a physician's office. Many birth control devices and substances can be purchased without a physician's prescription. But if young men and women were aware of their chances of effecting a pregnancy while using such methods, they probably would have second thoughts about taking the risk. See under "Marriage and Parenthood" in Ch. 4, *The Beginning of a Family,* for a full discussion of birth control methods.

Venereal Disease

Equally important in the education of teenagers is a knowledge of the hazards of venereal disease. A poster prepared for a New York campaign against venereal disease carried the words "If your son is old enough to shave, he's old enough to get syphilis." The American Social Health Association estimates that 300,000 teenagers each year become infected with one or more forms of venereal disease. Most insidious has been the recent increase in gonorrhea, partly because girls who carry the infection may show no symptoms. A girl may have a slight but seemingly unimportant vaginal discharge. She may not be aware that she has gonorrhea until she is contacted by health officials after her boyfriend has reported to a physician for treatment. For more information on venereal disease, see Ch. 17, *Diseases of the Urinogenital System.*

Two reasons for the rising incidence of gonorrhea after it was once thought to be virtually eliminated by antibiotics are that condoms, once used as a mechanical barrier by males, have become less popular since teenage girls have obtained the use of oral contraceptives, and that new strains of the bacteria are resistant to the antibiotics. Some boys delay treatment when they realize they are infected with VD; they believe it makes them appear "tough" to be able to go without medical treatment even when it endangers their health.

4

The Beginning of a Family

Infertility, Pregnancy, and Childbirth

The decision of a young couple to begin a family is usually a happy event, with overtones of great responsibility for the parents-to-be. Although parenthood does bring fulfillment, happiness, and great rewards, it can also involve anxiety and heavy responsibility. Therefore, the decision to have a child should not be made lightly. Before increasing the family unit and thereby complicating it, the husband and wife should have a strong, good marriage, one based on love, understanding, and the ability to compromise and share.

Infertility

Once the decision to have a child has been made, a new set of problems can arise. Though the majority of women are able to conceive within a year after ceasing all methods of birth control, a large number of couples are faced with the problem of infertility. Old census reports and records show that in the early 1800s about one in six marriages was childless—the same proportion as today. However, because of improved medical and sur-gical techniques, the modern woman has a much better chance of overcoming a condition of infertility. For a description of the female reproductive organs and of the processes of conception and fertilization, see "Social and Sexual Maturation" in Ch. 3, *The Teens*. For a full treatment of women's health concerns other than those relating to pregnancy and childbirth, see Ch. 25, *Women's Health*.

Strain and Fatigue

There are many causes of infertility, and an equal number of cures. Nervous strain and mental fatigue can interfere with reproductive capacity, as can fatigue from physical work. If a woman has worries or fears about financial security or other matters, she may fail to conceive. It is believed that nervous tension can suppress human ovulation cycles through the relationship of the hypothalamus, a part of the brain, and the pituitary gland, which controls the flow of sex hormones. Recommended treatment for a wife under strain might include a vacation, a temporary interruption in her business or professional goals, or a reorganization of her living pattern to relieve tension.

A similar tension problem can challenge the potential fatherhood of the husband. He may appear to lose his sex drive or suffer from impotency because of stress related to his job. The solution may be a second honeymoon to remove the couple from a stressful environment, or a willingness to accept a lower standard of living until financial security is truly established. Keeping up with the Joneses may put an extra car in the garage, but the penalty might be an empty crib in the nursery.

Timing Ovulation

Occasionally, the reason for infertility may be something as basic as timing. Because of misinformation or misapplication of the correct information, husbands and wives may time their intercourse so the husband's sperm does not enter the female reproductive organs during the 24 hours or so of the menstrual cycle in which the ovum is most likely to become fertilized. The wife's menstrual cycle must be watched with extreme care so that the time of ovulation can be judged. Ovulation takes place 14 days before menstruation. In women with a 28-day cycle, ovulation would occur approximately 14 days after the previous period. Women with longer cycles ovulate later in the cycle. For a more accurate method of calculating ovulation, see "Basal Body Temperature" later in this chapter.

If the couple is in the habit of having rather frequent intercourse, including at the time of ovulation, they should abstain for a few days before the expected day of ovulation so the sperm count in the husband can build up to a higher level. Then, at the time of ovulation, the couple should have intercourse at least twice with an interval of six to eight hours between. For further assurance of success, the wife should lie on her back with her legs flexed following intercourse so that a pool of sperm will remain near the cervix.

Reproductive Incompatibility

Still another factor that can interfere with normal fertility is that of reproductive incompatibility, or an immune reaction, between sperm and ovum. This reaction between the male and female cells is similar to an allergic one and may happen in one of two ways. In the more complicated case of reaction between the sperm and the egg cell, the ovum may treat the sperm as a bit of foreign tissue, which it will reject. There is at present no foolproof remedy for this problem, but medical scientists are investigating it.

In the second type of situation, there can be an incompatible reaction between the acid environment of the female reproductive tract and the alkaline male sperm. Although the lining of the vagina usually is acid, it normally becomes alkaline at the time of ovulation to facilitate the survival of the sperm on its way to the cervix. But in some cases, the vagina remains acid enough to kill or immobilize the sperm. In cases of couples unable to have children for this reason, chemicals can be introduced into the vagina to neutralize its acidity.

The Fertility Examination

Although it has been popular for centuries to hold the female partner responsible for childless marriages, the male is just as likely to be the infertile one. But the ego of the man is often such that he may refuse to admit that he is infertile until it has been proved that the wife is indeed capable of bearing children. The easiest way to check out the causes of infertility is to submit to a series of tests by a physician.

The physician giving the tests may be a general practitioner or a specialist. There are two types of specialists who concentrate on the female reproductive system—the *gynecologist* and the *obstetrician*. The gynecologist is a

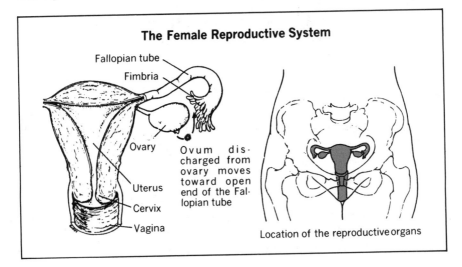

The Female Reproductive System

Fallopian tube
Fimbria
Ovary
Ovum discharged from ovary moves toward open end of the Fallopian tube
Uterus
Cervix
Vagina

Location of the reproductive organs

physician who specializes in the care and treatment of women, especially of the reproductive organs; an obstetrician specializes in the birth process. Because the areas of responsibility frequently overlap, the same physician often handles both specialties and is referred to as an *Ob-Gyn* physician.

Fertility examinations usually require a series of at least four visits by the wife over a period of about three months, and a similar series of visits by the husband. Both husband and wife usually attend the first meeting, when the physician explains some of the common causes of infertility and outlines the rules for the tests to be performed.

Next, the physician schedules separate conferences with the marital partners so that he can obtain information that husband and wife might be reluctant to discuss in each other's presence. This discussion might touch upon possible venereal diseases of earlier years, previous marital experiences, possible illegitimate pregnancies, and so on. The medical records also will include information about general health, diet, surgery, or diseases such as mumps (which might affect fertility), sex interests and practices, family histories of miscarriages or abnormal children, and contraceptive methods used.

Basal Body Temperature

The physician will often suggest that the wife begin the BBT, or basal body temperature charts. Using a special thermometer, the BBT is taken each morning at the same hour, before getting out of bed or having a first cigarette, which would alter the results. The BBT record is a remarkably accurate way of determining the day of ovulation, because ovulation causes a sudden rise in temperature. If there is no sudden rise in temperature dur-

ing the menstrual cycle, it is an indication that no ovum was released by the ovary. If the temperature rises to indicate ovulation and remains elevated for more than two weeks, it suggests that a pregnancy has begun. There are factors that can distort the readings, such as a fever or a mistake in reading the thermometer, but in general the BBT charts provide a reliable guide to the fertility cycles of the female partner.

Semen Exam

On the second visit to the physician, the husband is usually asked to bring a sample of semen in a corked bottle. The husband is generally advised to avoid intercourse for at least 48 hours before collecting the semen. The glass container of semen must be protected from heat and cold, and for this

reason should be carried in a paper bag to help insulate it from external temperature variations. A condom should not be used to collect or carry the semen because most rubber prophylactics contain chemicals that are harmful to spermatozoa.

The sperm examination should be

Male Ejaculation

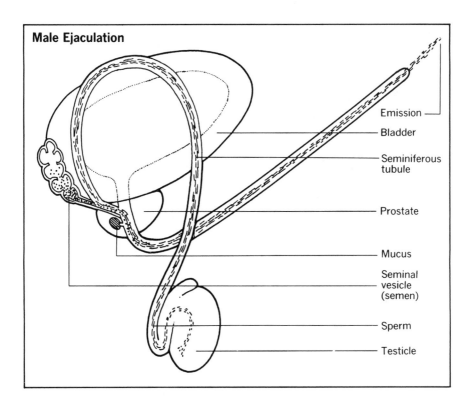

Emission

Bladder

Seminiferous tubule

Prostate

Mucus

Seminal vesicle (semen)

Sperm

Testicle

made within an hour or so after it is collected so the spermatozoa will be nearly as alive and healthy as they are at the time of intercourse. If for some reason the results are not conclusive, the husband will be asked to bring another sample of semen when he accompanies his wife on her third visit, which will be scheduled about four weeks later.

During the second visit, both husband and wife may be given physical examinations, with emphasis on the pelvic and genital areas. Laboratory tests of blood and urine are made, and the examining physician may decide to make a study of thyroid function.

Tubal Insufflation

The physician generally tries to schedule the third visit to coincide with the 12th day of the wife's menstrual cycle. The examination at that time may include a *tubal insufflation* test. Also known as *Rubin's test,* tubal insufflation involves the injection of carbon dioxide gas, or sometimes ordinary air, into the uterus. Normally, the gas passes up through the uterus and Fallopian tubes and exits into the abdominal cavity. This would be a sign that the tubes are not obstructed. A pressure gauge shows a drop in pressure as the gas passes into the abdominal cavity, and the physician may listen through a stethoscope for sounds of gas escaping through the

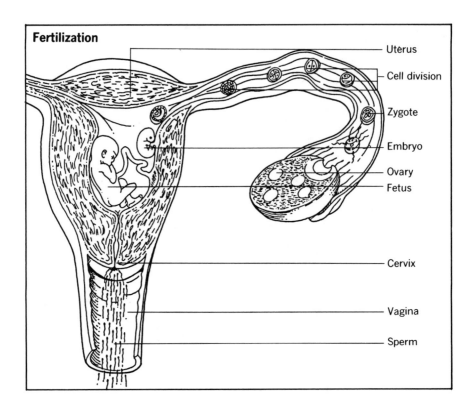

Fertilization

Uterus
Cell division
Zygote
Embryo
Ovary
Fetus
Cervix
Vagina
Sperm

tubes. The tubes are very narrow, and even a mild infection or scar tissue from a past infection can block them. Sometimes, forcing gas through the tubes is all that is needed to open them again so that chances of pregnancy will be enhanced.

A fourth visit, scheduled about four weeks after the third, should occur just before normal ovulation time. The couple may be instructed to perform intercourse about six hours before the visit. The tubal insufflation test may be repeated if the results of the earlier test were not satisfactory. In addition, a study of the cervical mucus may be made. In this study, the mucus is stretched into thin fibers or strands, which is possible only at the time of ovulation. During most of the reproductive cycle, the mucus is thick, dense, and jellylike. But the presence of estrogen hormones at the time of ovulation changes the mucus so that it makes a fibrous, fernlike pattern when placed on a glass slide.

The cervical mucus is also studied for the presence of active sperm. By using a high-power microscope, the examining physician can tell whether the cervical secretions are hostile to sperm. This would be the case if an adequate number of sperm are present, but are inactive or dead. The tests can be verified by placing a bit of semen on a microscope slide next to a sample of cervical mucus.

Hysterogram

If the tests up to this point have not revealed the cause of infertility, the physician (or a recommended radiologist) can inject a special oil into the uterus and tubes and follow its path through the reproductive organs by an X-ray procedure called a *hystero-* *gram*. If there is an obstruction or even a kink in the tubes that might interfere with the movement of an ovum, it should appear in the X-ray photographs, and the physician can then treat the problem accordingly.

Fibroids

The hysterogram may also reveal the presence of *fibroids,* benign tumors composed of fibrous tissue that usually attach themselves to the walls of the uterus. Fibroids come in varying sizes—from smaller than a pea to larger than a fist—and are present in varying degrees in about 30 percent of all women. Depending on where they occur, they may block conception, in which case they can be removed by surgery.

Other Procedures

Depending on what cause of infertility is suspected, the physician may recommend that the wife undergo a *culdoscopy, peritoneoscopy,* or *laparotomy.* The culdoscopy and peritoneoscopy require only a local anesthetic and a brief hospital stay. In the culdoscopy procedure, tubes are used to examine the pelvic organs without making a surgical incision. In the peritoneoscopy, a small incision is made just below the umbilicus. A laparotomy refers to any procedure involving an incision in the abdominal wall. Depending on the nature of the problem, a laparotomy and, to a lesser extent, the other two procedures, allow the gynecologist latitude to make some on-the-spot corrections.

The physician may also decide to do an examination of tissue cells from the vagina or the testicles of the husband in an effort to find out what is causing infertility.

In general, the chances of success in the treatment of infertility vary with the severity of the abnormality and the length of time the disorder has gone untreated. Most minor problems can be treated by surgery, restoring normal hormone balance, proper diet, psychotherapy, or other methods, such as a change in the techniques or frequency of intercourse.

Reproductive Technology

The science of *reproductive technology* offers other ways of achieving fertilization and parenthood. In all cases the new methods require that a third party enter, at least indirectly, into the reproductive relationship. The following techniques range from the very simple to the very complex.

In vitro fertilization (IVF) is the process that produces test-tube babies. A physician removes an egg from the woman's ovary and places it in a shallow dish filled with a special nutritional "bath." Some of the husband's sperm is added to the bath. If the egg becomes fertilized it is allowed to grow for a few days, then implanted in the woman's uterus to complete the gestation process.

Artificial insemination by donor (AID) is the injection by syringe of a donor's sperm into the woman's vagina. Injection takes place shortly before the woman is scheduled to ovulate. In such cases the husband's sperm, for one reason or another, cannot be used.

Surrogate motherhood occurs when a woman carries to term and delivers a child for another woman. The surrogate mother is first inseminated with the sperm of a husband whose wife cannot, for health or physical reasons, conceive and bear the child. After delivery, the surrogate mother signs for adoption by the husband and wife.

Egg donation involves removal of an egg from one woman for implantation in another. In some cases the transferred egg can be fertilized by the husband's sperm in natural intercourse. Following gestation, the baby is delivered through normal childbirth or caesarian section.

In *artificial embryonation* (AE) an infertile wife agrees to carry to term the embryo developed briefly in another woman's womb. In artificial embryonation, the childless couple form an agreement with the second woman, who is then inseminated with the husband's sperm. The embryo is allowed to develop for four or five days; physicians then try to flush out the growing embryo for implantation in the wife.

Embryo adoption (EA) is a procedure similar to artificial embryonation. But in EA the sperm of a donor, not that of the husband, is used to fertilize the volunteer "mother." Again the embryo is flushed out after a few days; the embryo is then implanted in the wife for gestation and delivery.

Many couples have specific personal reasons for using one of these methods of reproducing. The wife may, for a variety of physical reasons, be unable to conceive or carry a child. One spouse or the other may have inherited genetic defects that the couple do not want to pass on to their children. Two such defects are Huntington's chorea and hemophilia, for example.

The Expectant Mother

In most marriages there is no problem of infertility. A majority of women between the ages of 20 and 25 become pregnant during the first year of marriage. And that includes a substantial number who have tried to prevent conception with various birth control methods. The fertility prospects usually continue to be satisfactory for women up to the age of 35, but the chances decline for women in their late 30s.

When pregnancy does occur, it should be regarded as a natural process rather than a confining illness. Although some of the bodily functions are altered by approaching motherhood, it should be remembered that women have been bearing children for thousands of years, and the chances for a safe and successful delivery were never better than today.

The expectant mother can look forward to hearing a variety of old wives' tales about the hazards of pregnancy from well-meaning friends. But unless there are complications, there is no reason for anxiety. And many of the complications can be prevented or corrected with good medical care. The woman preparing for motherhood generally can relax and enjoy the state of pregnancy if she follows basic rules of health and hygiene.

Drugs and Cigarettes

Many obstetricians recommend that women refrain from taking any medications, including patent medicines such as cold remedies, during the first three months of pregnancy unless the medicine is essential for the preservation of the mother's health. There are a number of chemical substances in drugs which may or may not affect the development of the embryo. An example of the unfortunate results of drug use during the early months of pregnancy was that of thalidomide, used by a number of women in 1961–1962. The drug was one of the safest sedatives ever developed. But when used by pregnant women, thalidomide caused physically deformed babies.

Should an expectant mother smoke? A study of more than 16,000 pregnancies shows that mothers who smoke cigarettes are more likely to have stillborn babies, premature babies, and babies who are below average in weight than nonsmoking mothers. Other researchers have found that cigarette smoking stimulates contractions of the uterus, which could lead to premature birth. Mothers who smoke are also more likely to have spontaneous abortions or miscarriages.

Diet and Digestion

Acute dietary deficiencies also can affect the development of an unborn child. As the fetus develops, its growth rate is tremendous—the weight gain is as high as 650 percent per month after the unborn child has passed the third month in its mother's uterus. All of the nutrients needed for fetal growth must be taken from the mother's own diet and transmitted through the placenta. If the food eaten by the mother is not sufficient to sustain both mother and child, it is frequently the child who suffers.

This does not mean, however, that an expectant mother should eat double-sized meals because she has to feed two bodies. Obesity can be nearly as great a hazard to normal pregnancy as not eating enough.

Overweight women should curb their food intake with such dietary shortcuts as drinking skim milk and eliminating as many fats and carbohydrates as possible. Meals should include a high level of proteins and all the essential minerals and vitamins. The number of total calories should not be less than 1,800 per day, unless the physician recommends otherwise.

The rule of thumb on weight gain for a pregnant woman is that she should be about 20 pounds heavier at the end of the nine months than she was before conception. The rate of gain is important. It should be held to around one pound per month during the first three months, and between two and three pounds per month during the last six months.

Throughout the pregnancy, cravings for such foods as strawberries, ice cream, pickles, or whatever are usually caused by psychological reasons rather than physical ones. However, if the food items craved are nutritious and low in calories, there is nothing wrong with satisfying the whim. Pickles, incidentally, are lower in calories and richer in vitamin C, iron, and other nutrients than most other snack foods.

Heartburn

Many mothers experience heartburn during pregnancy, and investigators have found that the treatment should be related to the length of time the mother has been carrying the unborn child. Heartburn during the first trimester, or three-month period, is usually due to anxiety and tension. If the symptoms are severe, the physician may prescribe antacids or tranquilizers. Heartburn during the last six months is usually due to the crowding of the enlarged uterus within the abdomen, which lessens stomach capacity. The solution in such cases is to eat a number of smaller meals during the day rather than three large ones. Expectant mothers with heartburn should also use additional pillows so they sleep with the head and shoulders higher than the rest of the body, avoid tight clothing that squeezes the abdominal area, and not stoop or bend over after eating.

Morning Sickness

Morning sickness, characterized by nausea and vomiting, is one of the most common complaints of mothers-to-be. Although it is unpleasant, morning sickness rarely becomes so serious that special medical treatment is needed. While friends and relatives may try to convince the expectant mother that the sick feeling is all in her mind—and she certainly may feel some anxiety about her pregnancy—there is good evidence that there is also a physical cause. The level of gastric acid in the pregnant woman's stomach declines during the first trimester of pregnancy. Also, stomach activity during that period is at a low ebb, and digestion is one to two hours slower after a meal than before pregnancy.

In most cases of morning sickness, the mother is unable to hold down her breakfast. The feeling of nausea usually subsides by lunch time, and does not appear again until the following morning. For the majority of women, the feeling fades away entirely by the 12th week. If it continues into the last two trimesters, the condition may not be related to the pregnancy.

Food for periods of morning sickness should include crackers and dry toast, lemonade or soft drinks served at cold temperatures, and hot soup, tea, or coffee. Items to be avoided are greasy foods and liquids that are only lukewarm.

Toxemia of Pregnancy

The expectant mother should visit her physician as often as recommended and follow instructions carefully. She should report any signs of puffiness of the hands and face, headaches, or visual disturbances that she experiences. Such signs and symptoms, especially in the last trimester of pregnancy, suggest *toxemia*. It is one of the most serious complications of pregnancy, and it affects about five percent of all expectant mothers.

Toxemia of pregnancy is a catchall term that covers *hypertension,* or abnormally high blood pressure, and *edema,* or swelling of tissues due to fluid accumulation. Other symptoms are weight gain, *proteinuria,* or excretion of protein, and, in severe cases—when the disorder is sometimes called *eclampsia*—convulsions and loss of consciousness. Toxemia in late pregnancy is called *preeclampsia.*

Weight gain can amount to more than two pounds a week and may be due almost entirely to fluid retention. Proteinuria usually does not appear until after high blood pressure and weight gain have appeared. But even these clinical signs may develop before the mother-to-be knows that she has toxemia. As the problem progresses, she may have visual disturbances, puffy eyelids, headaches, and abdominal pains. When the latter symptoms occur the disease is rather well established.

The cause of toxemia is believed to be a failure of the mother's body to adjust to the metabolic and physiological stresses of pregnancy. With careful management, toxemia can be controlled with the help of drugs, regulation of weight gain and fluid intake, bed rest, and in some cases by early delivery of the baby. The fact that delivery of the child seems to resolve the problem of toxemia reinforces the theory of metabolic–physiologic relationships in the stresses of pregnancy in some women.

During pregnancy a number of complex changes take place in the mother's body—a different pattern of hormone activity, alterations in the glands secreting hormones, increased blood supply with greater demands on the heart, and a rapidly growing parasitic human in the uterus, which also grows and presses against other organs within the body. Each woman reacts somewhat differently to these changes, and toxemia is one of the reactions.

Backaches and Other Disorders

Some expectant mothers are concerned about whether the baby should be carried high or low. There is a belief among some women that a baby carried high will be a boy. The truth is that no single pregnancy is either high or low for the entire nine months. Some babies seem to be carried higher at certain stages of pregnancy while at other times they seem to be carried low. The position has nothing to do with the sex of the child.

Where the baby is carried also has nothing to do with a common complaint associated with pregnancy—backache. Backache in pregnant women is usually caused by changes in posture, and only rarely by abnormality of the organs within the pelvis. Usually it is due to bending, lifting, or walking without properly compensating for the added strain of the weight of the child, especially in the later stages of pregnancy. Generally, backache responds to rest, heat, and drugs, which relax the muscles—although the drugs should be used only on a physician's recommendation. The physician also may recommend that a lightweight maternity girdle be worn to help minimize the strain.

Improper posture in the final weeks may also be responsible for numbness and tingling or crawling sensations in the hands and arms. The hand-and-arm complaints frequently are related to what is called the *lordotic posture,* where shoulders are slumped, the spine curved forward, and the neck bent forward. The tingling sensations usually vanish when the posture is corrected. Exercises are used to help change the lordotic positioning of the spine and shoulders.

The mother-to-be must be careful about the use of seat belts when traveling by automobile or airplane. In the final months of pregnancy the belt should be fitted snugly around the lower third of the abdomen to protect the uterus from the steering wheel or dashboard in the event of an accident or sudden stop.

Pelvic X Ray

Occasionally, a physician will want to have X rays made of the pelvis of the mother to determine whether it is adequate to permit an uncomplicated childbirth. There is little hazard in a brief diagnostic X ray if modern equipment is used. Nevertheless, the mother should avoid exposure to unnecessary X rays, particularly during the first three months of pregnancy. Embryonic tissue is highly sensitive to radiation because the cells have not reached the degree of differentiation found in the fetus in the later months of pregnancy. In other words, the embryo's tissues are much more likely to be adversely affected by radiation.

Infection of the Urinary Tract

Urinary tract disturbances are not unusual during pregnancy, and may be recurrent in women who were treated for kidney or bladder infections before pregnancy. It is not unusual for women to void as frequently as once an hour or oftener and half a dozen times during the night. The disorder may be accompanied by fever and a burning sensation while voiding the urine. But most cases respond to the medications and special hygiene instructions prescribed by the physician.

Leg Cramps and Varicose Veins

Leg cramps and varicose veins affect a significant number of pregnant women. Leg cramps are the most common problem, and probably 85 percent of expectant mothers experience an occasional spasm of the calf muscles while carrying a child. The leg cramps may occur suddenly and be quite painful; at other times, the cramp may feel more like a simple kink in the muscles. The cramps occur more frequently in the last three months of pregnancy and are more likely to be experienced during a second or third pregnancy than during the first. Sluggish blood circulation and a dietary deficiency of calcium are thought to be the causes of leg cramps. The treatment consists of applying heat to the legs, massaging them, and sitting or lying down with the legs elevated. Drinking fortified milk will add calcium and vitamin D to the diet. In severe cases, muscle-relaxing drugs may be prescribed.

Varicose veins are more likely to appear during the second or third pregnancy, and tend to disappear after the birth of the baby. They are caused by a pooling of blood in the veins of the legs. Normally, the contraction of the leg muscles during walking has the effect of pumping blood from the legs back up toward the heart. But just the strain of standing can produce varicose veins even in normally active people who are on their feet for long periods. The strain of pregnancy also can upset the normal return flow of blood in the legs, so the veins become dilated. As with leg cramps, some relief can be had by sitting or lying with the feet raised. Additional relief can be obtained by wearing elastic stockings. If the varicosities remain after pregnancy, they can be treated by drugs or surgery.

Immunization

There are certain facts about immunization that a woman should know if she contemplates pregnancy. One is that the mother's reaction to smallpox vaccine can be transmitted through the placenta to the fetus. The disease can be fatal to an unborn child. Fortunately, smallpox has been eradicated from almost all areas in the world, and vaccination is no longer routinely required for travel abroad.

If the mother plans to be pregnant

during the winter months, she should arrange to receive a series of influenza shots beginning in September and ending by mid-December. If she has been immunized against influenza within the past two years, a booster shot should be sufficient.

Rubella, or German measles, can be a serious threat to the normal development of a baby if contracted during the first 12 weeks of pregnancy. The rubella vaccine normally given to children should be given to women of childbearing age only with caution. Some medical scientists believe that the virus can be transmitted by the vaccine to the fetus if conception occurs within two months after the vaccine is given. If the virus infects the unborn child, particularly during the first trimester, the child may be af-flicted with cataracts, deafness, or damage to the heart and nervous system.

Immunizations should also be obtained for diphtheria, malaria (if in an area where this is common), and mumps. If these diseases occur during pregnancy they result in spontaneous abortion in about one-third of the cases.

Tetanus is regarded as one of the most serious complications of pregnancy. The period of incubation for tenanus is shorter in pregnant than in nonpregnant women. It is particularly hazardous during the period immediately after abortion or childbirth. But the threat can be avoided by receiving proper tetanus immunization before pregnancy.

The Rh Factor

Blood incompatibilities between the mother and father can be another complication of pregnancy. The condition is caused by a blood protein known as the *Rh factor*. A person whose blood contains the protein is called *Rh-positive; Rh-negative* people lack the blood factor. Approximately 85 percent of the population is Rh-positive. The term *Rh* is derived from the first two letters of the name of the Rhesus monkey, a laboratory animal which was used for much of the basic research on the blood incompatibility problem.

About ten percent of all marriages in the United States involve an Rh conflict. If both husband and wife are either Rh-positive or Rh-negative, there is no problem. But if the wife has Rh-negative blood and her husband Rh-positive, the child of such a union may be threatened by death or mental retardation, particularly after the first pregnancy.

The Rh factor is inherited, and if the unborn offspring inherits the Rh-positive factor from its father while the mother has Rh-negative blood, the mother's blood may develop antibodies that destroy the baby's blood. The threat to the unborn child can be modified by a blood transfusion to the newborn infant or to the fetus before birth. The mother can also in effect be immunized against the development of antibodies by the injection of a gamma globulin blood fraction rich in passive Rh antibodies.

Usually, the first child is not affected by Rh blood conflicts. The red blood cells of the fetus can cross the placenta and trigger the reaction in the mother's blood system. But they do not reach their peak of entry into the mother's blood supply until the time of delivery. Thus, to prevent sensitization of the mother, physicians must eliminate the fetal red cells around the time of delivery—before the buildup of antibodies can begin. Once the antibodies have developed in the mother's blood, all future Rh-positive babies will be threatened un-less preventive steps are taken.

If the husband of an Rh-negative woman has Rh-negative blood, or if he carries genes for both Rh-negative and Rh-positive, the baby will probably inherit the Rh-negative factor, and there will be no blood conflict. In nearly every case of Rh conflict today the baby can be saved and the production of antibodies suppressed in the mother. But the blood of both parents should be checked at the start of pregnancy plans, and arrangements made to protect the fetus if there is a threat of blood incompatibility.

Genetic Counseling

The genetic background of each marital partner has an influence on the fetus, since hereditary factors have a tendency to show up in the offspring. In addition to desirable hereditary traits, over 1,200 congenital defects have been catalogued. However, genetic factors do not always appear in a new generation, and environmental influences do not always affect mothers in the same manner. During the thalidomide episode of the 1960s, for example, only 20 percent of the pregnant women who used the drug had deformed babies; the other 80 percent had normal offspring.

While the expectant mother should take all normal precautions and follow her physician's orders faithfully with regard to diet, hygiene, and exercise, if she and her husband have normal family histories she should not be concerned with congenital birth defects. However, there are cases where there is cause for legitimate worry about the chances of an inherited disorder. If there are cases of cystic fibrosis, phenylketonuria (PKU), sickle-cell anemia, or other genetic diseases in the background of either prospective parent; if the prospective mother is over 40 (at which age there is an increased chance of giving birth to a child afflicted with *Down's syndrome* or Mongolism); or if the parents or others in the family have previously given birth to a mentally retarded child, then it is recommended that the couple seek the advice of a *genetic counselor.*

Genetic counseling is available through a network of genetic counseling and treatment centers which were set up to help couples who are planning a family but are troubled by the possibility that their children may be born with a genetic disorder. When the wife gets pregnant a prenatal diagnosis is made. This procedure, known as *amniocentesis,* involves obtaining a small sample of the amniotic fluid that surrounds the fetus by inserting a hypodermic needle through the abdominal wall. The sex of the fetus can also be determined by this method, and because many inherited disorders are sex-linked (for example, transmitted only from mother to son), this information can be critically important. If the fetus is found to be affected with the suspected disorder a therapeutic abortion is performed, if so desired by the parents. Those interested in consulting a genetic counselor should write to the National Genetics Foundation, 555 W. 57th St., New York, NY 10019.

Physicians can also use *chorionic villi sampling* (CVS) to determine the sex of a fetus before birth. Where amniocentesis cannot be performed before the fifteenth or seventeenth week of pregnancy, CVS can be done as early as the ninth week. The sampling process involves removal of genetic material for analysis. Like amniocentesis, CVS also indicates whether a fetus has any of the approximately 350 genetic abnormalities. As one advantage to parents who want to avoid giving birth to a severely handicapped child, early CVS provides the option of a first trimester abortion.

Miscarriage

About ten percent of all pregnancies end in a *miscarriage,* often called a *spontaneous abortion.* A miscarriage can occur for a variety of reasons, many of which are related. Some of the reasons may be hormone malfunction or deficiency; a faulty sperm or ovum, which would, in the vast majority of cases, result in a cruelly malformed child or one incapable of staying alive if the pregnancy were carried to term; a poor *endometrium,* or lining of the uterus, in which the ovum is implanted; changes in the mother's body chemistry; or other factors that interfere with normal development of the child within the uterus.

Hormone Deficiency

Hormone malfunction is responsible for many spontaneous abortions. Once the placenta is established on the inner wall of the uterus, it ordinarily produces sufficient hormones to maintain the pregnancy. But the condition of the endometrium at the time the embryo becomes implanted in the uterine wall affects the later development of the placenta. That situation, in turn, may affect the secretion of the hormones needed to continue the pregnancy. The level of one hormone, called the human chorionic gonadotropic hormone, is frequently used as a barometer of the condition of the uterus. When the amount of that hormone excreted in the urine suddenly decreases, it is a warning signal that spontaneous abortion may be imminent.

Other physiological barometers are thyroid function and the rate of excretion of a substance known as sodium pregnanediol. Normally, there is a rise in thyroid activity when a woman becomes pregnant. The level remains elevated as long as the pregnancy continues, declining when the pregnancy is terminated either by delivery of a child or abortion. The expectant mother who has an underactive or overactive thyroid gland needs special medical attention because the hormone secreted by the gland seems to influence both the ovaries and the pituitary gland. Thyroid dysfunction is associated with infertility and the tendency toward spontaneous abortions.

Hormone deficiencies can contribute to the failure of the ovaries to produce thriving ova. In younger girls, the ovaries may be too immature to yield ova that are capable of continuing life after they are fertilized. In older women, the egg cells may be faulty because of approaching menopause. Even if the egg cell is perfect, defective sperm from the husband may be responsible for failure of the egg cell to develop into a healthy embryo after fertilization.

Still another cause of spontaneous abortion related to unfavorable hormone levels is the infantile or underdeveloped uterus, which may not have the capacity to maintain the fetus as it grows toward normal size for delivery. The undersized uterus can be treated with a hormone, estrin, to make it large enough to sustain a full-term pregnancy.

Other Causes of Miscarriage

Fibroid tumors or polyps in the uterus can interfere with both conception and pregnancy. Congenital malformations, such as a divided uterus, may also result in miscarriage. These problems can usually be corrected by surgery. A retroverted, malpositioned or tipped uterus can also be corrected to make carrying to term possible if this situation has caused a spontaneous abortion. An abnormality of the uterus called incompetent cervix used to be the cause of many spontaneous abortions in the last half of pregnancy, but in recent years a simple operation has been devised to correct the defect. See Ch. 25, *Women's Health,* for further information on gynecological problems.

Symptoms of Miscarriage

Spontaneous abortions usually are classified as threatened or inevitable. Generally, an abortion is considered to be of the threatened type when there is bleeding or cramps or both. Even when bleeding and cramps seem to be severe, it is possible that they will stop, or can be stopped, and the pregnancy will continue. If the bleeding and cramps become progressive and there is dilation of the cervix with the passage of tissue, the abortion is considered inevitable. Physicians sometimes can estimate the length of time that a spontaneous abortion has been progressing by examining the blood. If the blood is dark brown rather than bright red, it suggests that bleeding may have started at some time in the past. The longer the bleeding continues, the less chance there is that the fetus will survive.

Ectopic Pregnancy

Bleeding and cramping are not always signs of spontaneous abortion. Bleeding may be caused by a polyp or a malignant growth on the cervix. Cramps or bleeding can also occur if there is an *ectopic pregnancy,* a pregnancy outside the uterus. For example, the fertilized egg may become implanted in a Fallopian tube or even in the abdominal cavity instead of in the uterus. Many cases of ectopic pregnancy go undiagnosed because the symptoms are quite similar to those of a threatened abortion. Most ectopic pregnancies end in miscarriage when the pressure of the growing fetus causes the tube to rupture. In rare cases, the fetus may lodge in the abdominal cavity after rupture and continue to grow and develop. Such a fetus can be delivered by caesarian techniques, but is thought to be extremely dangerous for the mother. Most physicians prefer to perform a therapeutic abortion if this situation occurs.

Trophoblastic Disease

In about one of every 1,500 to 2,000 pregnancies in the United States, the placenta degenerates into a *hydatidiform mole,* a benign tumor consisting of a mass of grapelike cysts. This condition is known as *trophoblastic disease,* in reference to the *trophoblast,* a layer of cells that develops around the fertilized ovum and contributes to the formation of the placenta.

Signs and symptoms of a hydatidiform mole generally appear one to two months after conception. They include nausea and vomiting, persistent bleeding from the uterus, and an increase in uterine size more rapid than normal. X rays fail to show a developing skeleton and there is no fetal heartbeat perceptible at the usual stage of pregnancy. X-ray arteriograms and ultrasound scanning of the uterus also reveal signs of the mole. Spontaneous abortion commonly threatens and often occurs. Laboratory analysis of chorionic gonadotropic hormone levels in serum and vaginal smears are among other tests used to verify the presence of a hydatidiform mole.

The mole must be removed as soon as feasible after it has been identified, to decrease the chances of its invading the uterine wall and becoming cancerous. It is removed by surgical methods, such as suction curettage, or occasionally surgical excision. In those few cases in which the mole invades the uterus, the uterus is removed. Following a molar pregnancy that is neither invasive nor cancerous, a woman should be examined regularly for a year or so. Subsequent pregnancies are permitted and have every prospect of being successful. If the mole is invasive or cancerous, antitumor chemotherapy is essential. Occasionally, radiation therapy also is used.

Habitual Abortion

Among some women, spontaneous abortion occurs repeatedly and is known as habitual abortion. Habitual abortion usually threatens at the same stage of each pregnancy, and the measures needed to prevent a repetition of the miscarriage should be started as soon as the expectant mother knows she is pregnant. The usual prenatal care should be followed conscientiously, including the rules about nutrition and exercise. Cigarette smoking should be curtailed or eliminated because, among other reasons, tobacco use seems to affect the carbohydrate metabolism of smokers, and pregnant women are particularly sensitive to changes in carbohydrate balance. The cells that form the placenta and fetal membranes require large amounts of carbohydrates that can be assimilated easily. Even before the fertilized egg cell becomes implanted in the lining of the uterus, the cells of the endometrium demand unusually large quantities of glycogen, or body starch, that has been converted to simple sugar molecules. Other nutrients are also needed, of course, but the demand for them is not as critical as that for carbohydrates.

Induced Abortion

Not all abortions are involuntary. The induced abortion is a deliberate interruption of the development of an embryo or fetus because of therapeutic or nonmedical reasons. Such an abortion, usually performed in a hospital or clinic, requires antiseptic conditions. Local anesthetics are used if needed. In the procedure called *dilation and curettage,* or *D and C,* the physician enlarges the opening of the uterus to permit entry of the surgical tools used to scrape the lining of the uterus. The tissue is removed from the lining with a *curette,* a surgical instrument resembling a scoop with sharpened edges. Another method often used, called *vacuum aspiration,* employs suction to pull the embryonic tissue from inside the uterus. These techniques—the D and C and vacuum aspiration—can be used only during the first trimester of pregnancy.

If the abortion is delayed beyond the first three months, more complicated surgery may be required. An alternative method called *salting out* (medically, *saline amniocentesis*) involves the injection of a saline solution into the amniotic fluid. The salt water kills the fetus and induces labor, and the fetus is delivered, thus terminating the pregnancy. This method involves somewhat greater risk of complications than the other methods.

If an induced abortion is performed

by a physician in a hospital or clinic equipped with facilities to cope with possible complications the procedure is safe, with very low risk of complications. The notion that women are rendered sterile or more likely to have spontaneous abortions or pre-mature deliveries of wanted children in later years can be true; but this is usually so only in those cases where women had the procedure performed under unsanitary conditions or by someone who was medically incompetent.

Approaching Delivery

When all is going well with a pregnancy—and it does in the vast majority of cases—a favorite guessing game becomes the prediction of delivery day. There are several ways in which to estimate the approximate birth date of the new addition to the family. One is to calculate 267 days from the date of conception. Another approach is to count 280 days from the first day of the last menstrual period. This method is easier, because women are more likely to know the date of the last menstrual period than the last time they ovulated. Still another method commonly used is to

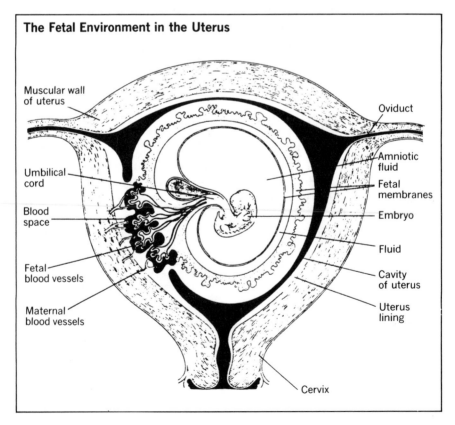

The Fetal Environment in the Uterus

Muscular wall of uterus

Oviduct

Umbilical cord

Amniotic fluid

Fetal membranes

Blood space

Embryo

Fluid

Fetal blood vessels

Cavity of uterus

Maternal blood vessels

Uterus lining

Cervix

Birth Sequence

Dilated cervix
During the first stage of labor the cervix dilates to form a passageway into the vagina, the birth canal. Contractions of the uterus may occur at intervals of approximately 5 to 15 minutes, with brief periods of rest in between, which permit oxygen to flow to the fetus.

Ruptured amniotic sac
Ruptured amniotic sac ordinarily signals the onset of the second and generally shorter stage of labor. Contractions during this stage occur in more frequent succession and are more intense. The so-called *bag of waters*, which contains the amniotic fluid, is ordinarily discharged during a strong contraction but may even rupture before labor begins.

Delivery
As the fetus moves into the lower pelvic region the mother naturally experiences a conscious impulse to bear down and help its entry into the world. She may feel a few moments of increased pressure or pain as the infant's head gradually appears and is followed by the rest of its body.

Placental stage
Placental stage is the third stage of labor and is characterized by the expulsion from the womb of the placenta, or *afterbirth*, to which the baby is connected by the umbilical cord. This cord is not cut until all the placental blood has pulsed into the baby's body.

count back three months from the first day of the last menstrual period and add seven days. No matter what method is used it will probably be wrong, since surveys show that fewer than five percent of all babies arrive on the day they were expected. However, the majority of babies are born within five days of the anticipated date.

As delivery day approaches, the physician usually wants to make some last-minute studies of the position of the child and its general condition. He may also want to check the size of the bony area of the mother's pelvis in an effort to determine in advance whether there will be any complications in delivery. During the examination, the physician usually looks for varicose veins around the vulva and vagina; they are a common occurrence among pregnant women, and some women claim they can tell when they are pregnant—even before a period is missed—by the appearance of these varicose veins.

By pressing the abdomen with the palms of his hands and his fingers, the physician can determine the position of the unborn child in the uterus. He also can get a fair idea of the size of the fetus and can tell how low it is in the pelvic region. The physician listens to the heartbeat of the fetus and, if labor is near, he may mark the position of the fetus on the skin of the mother's abdomen so that he can tell later if it has moved and in which direction.

In about half of all pregnant women, reddish streaks appear on the skin of the stretched abdomen. The streaks sometimes have the appearance of broken skin fibers because of stretching, but most physicians agree that the streaks are the result of hormone activity. It is another sign of a successful pregnancy.

In the final days before delivery, the physician usually makes an estimate of the space through which the baby must move to reach the outside world. He also must make a rough guess about the weight of the baby at birth. If the baby weighs less than five pounds at birth it is *premature* by definition and may require special care, which the physician would want to schedule.

Lightening

The phenomenon of *lightening* is a sign that pregnancy is approaching an end and that birth can be expected within about three weeks. When lightening occurs, the mother feels less pressure on the upper part of the abdomen and more discomfort in the pelvic region as the head of the fetus descends toward the birth canal. Lightening may be accompanied by strong contractions of the uterus, which may be mistaken for labor pains. If lightening does not occur during the final weeks, the physician may conduct further examinations to learn if the delay is due to a large fetus, twins (though a possible multiple birth is usually discovered earlier in the pregnancy), or another reason such as an unfavorable fetal position.

When lightening does occur on schedule, the physician usually assumes that the head of the fetus is low in the pelvic region and can pass through the birth canal without difficulty, since it has already completed the first part of the obstacle course to the outside world.

Fetal Position

With X rays and fetal electrocardiograms, it can be determined whether the unborn baby is upside down or in some other position in the uterus. A fetal electrocardiogram is made by placing electrodes on the mother's abdomen while she is lying on an examination table. The electrical impulses of the fetal heart muscle will produce a pattern revealing the direction of the heart which, in turn, tells which way the head is positioned. If the pattern indicates the head is toward the top of the abdomen rather than the bottom, a *breech presentation* can be expected in the delivery room.

Although 95 percent of all babies are in the head-downward position

Abnormal Presentations during Delivery

Breech

Buttocks presentation

Retroflexed uterus

Abnormal Shoulder-arm presentation

when labor begins, about three percent are in the more difficult breech presentation. Some physicians believe that a breech presentation is more likely if the fetus is delivered before term, since nearly 40 percent of the fetuses are in the breech presentation at the 20th week of pregnancy. However, this percentage declines as delivery day approaches, because the growing fetus finds it more comfortable to move its feet and bottom into the widest part of the pear-shaped uterus while the head fits into the narrow lower part.

Labor

The contractions of labor pains are something of a mystery. They are independent of the will of the mother. Women who are paralyzed or who feel no labor pains because of severed nerves can have a normal delivery. The uterus may even continue contractions automatically after it has been removed from the body.

First Stage of Labor

The first stage of labor is characterized by regular pains, which may occur at intervals of 5 to 15 minutes. During this stage the cervix becomes dilated and forms a passageway into the vagina. There is a rest period between the labor pains that lasts at least a minute and gives the mother a brief respite while permitting the flow of oxygen to the fetus by way of the placenta. (If the uterine contractions were continuous they would cut off the baby's oxygen supply.) During uterine contractions, the uterus rises in the abdomen; the change in shape can be observed at the start and end of each labor pain.

The so-called *bag of waters,* which actually is the *amniotic fluid* within the membrane, may be discharged at almost any time during labor. Sometimes the bag of waters ruptures before the labor pains begin, but this usually occurs during one of the strong contractions. The fluid generally comes out with a gush, but it may also be discharged in small amounts with each contraction. The term *dry labor* is used to describe contractions that begin after the bag of waters has ruptured. Ordinarily, the contractions become stronger and more frequent and the cervix dilates more rapidly after the amniotic fluid has been discharged.

Occasionally, the baby is delivered with the amniotic membrane still intact about its head. The membrane in such a case is known as a *caul.* At one time, a caul was regarded as a symbol of great superstitious value; midwives sold cauls to sailors who carried them for good luck on voyages.

Second Stage of Labor

Rupture of the bag of waters frequently climaxes the first stage of labor, which may last more than 12 hours if it is the first pregnancy. The second stage of labor is considerably shorter and can be expected to last around 2 hours in a first pregnancy, 30 minutes for a woman who has had children previously. The second stage may begin with rupture of the bag of waters if the amniotic fluid was not released earlier. The contractions are more intense and frequent, occurring at intervals of 2 to 3 minutes rather than the 5- to 15-minute intervals of the first stage. There also is a conscious desire on the part of the mother to help expel the fetus. She may feel additional pains, pressures, or irritations because of the presence of the fetus in the lower pelvic area.

During this series of labor pains the baby gradually makes its appearance outside the mother's womb. At first a bit of the scalp shows, then recedes as the labor pain subsides. With the next labor pain more of the head appears. Finally, the entire head is outside the mother's body, followed by the shoulders, trunk, and lower extremities.

Anesthetics and Drugs

Although it is standard practice to refer to the uterine contractions as labor pains, the amount of actual pain varies, and there are numerous methods for reducing the pain. True painless labor is rare, and when it occurs it is sometimes attributed to an abnormality of the nervous system.

The physician is as concerned about the welfare of the mother and baby as the mother herself, and this concern is reflected in the approach taken to provide relief from labor pains. The drug or anesthetic the physician chooses to use will be one that gives optimum relief to the mother without creating an environment in the womb that would threaten the life of the baby. A number of rather common drugs that could be used to relieve pain without harm to the mother could very easily be fatal to the infant, who would share through the placenta substances injected into the mother's bloodstream.

The type of anesthetic or drug administered to the mother is usually one that affects only the part of the nervous system associated with pain. If the substance also affected the motor nerves, the delivery would become stalemated. On the other hand, it would be very simple to handle the childbirth in a satisfactory manner as far as the baby is concerned if the mother were given no relief from pain.

Drugs used as aids in childbirth include analgesics, tranquilizers, barbiturates, and the type of drugs used in so-called twilight sleep—scopolamine and morphine. They can be given orally or by injection. In nearly all cases the drugs are used with caution, and they are frequently administered in combination with a gas anesthetic.

The gases frequently used during delivery are nitrous oxide, which provides intermittent relief from pain during the second stage of labor, and cyclopropane, which may be administered for caesarian section or cases of delivery in which there are complications requiring unconsciousness or deep analgesia (incapacity to feel pain). Nitrous oxide sometimes is provided during labor pains on signal from the mother. When she wants relief for a few moments or when she feels a pain starting, the mother signals the anesthetist, who places the mask over her face so she can take a few deep whiffs. The procedure is repeated when the next labor pain begins. Nitrous oxide may also be used in conjunction with ether or one of the other standard anesthetic gases. When properly administered, ether is safe and reliable for producing deep anesthesia or relaxation.

Still another anesthetic commonly used during delivery is a drug injected either for local anesthesia or for putting the mother to sleep for the period of delivery. Sodium pentothal is injected intravenously in many cases, particularly when forceps are used to assist in delivery. However, the physician has to work fast in these cases, because this is one of the drugs that can be transmitted through the placenta in a short time.

A caudal anesthetic can be used to block pain in the entire pelvic area. In this case, a drug is injected into the area at the bottom of the spinal column. Most women who have had a caudal anesthesia like it as a means of obtaining relief from labor pains, but it requires the presence of specially trained personnel.

When delivery can be timed rather precisely, a spinal anesthetic, sometimes called a *saddle block,* is injected into the region of the spinal cord in the lumbar area while the mother is in a sitting position. After the injection, the mother lies on her back and, in most cases, is free of pain for the remainder of labor and delivery.

Natural Childbirth

Natural childbirth methods are preferred by some women who want to participate as consciously as possible in the act of bringing a child into the world. Others, by contrast, want to go into the delivery room completely anesthetized—to enter a pregnant woman and awaken as a mother. In natural childbirth, most women receive a local anesthetic for the *episiotomy* incision, to make the vaginal area large enough for passage of the baby, drugs to relieve tension when requested, and *oxytocin*. Oxytocin is a hormone naturally secreted by the pituitary gland to help the muscles of the uterus contract normally.

Lamaze Method

A woman who chooses the natural childbirth technique developed by Dr. Ferdinand Lamaze conditions herself for labor pains by substituting a dif-

Natural Childbirth

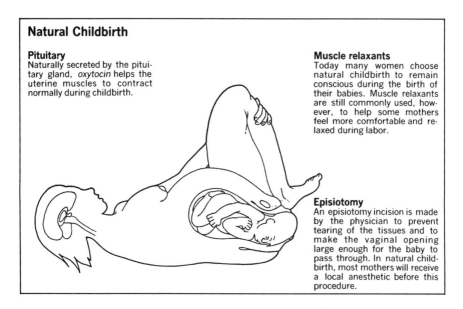

Pituitary
Naturally secreted by the pituitary gland, *oxytocin* helps the uterine muscles to contract normally during childbirth.

Muscle relaxants
Today many women choose natural childbirth to remain conscious during the birth of their babies. Muscle relaxants are still commonly used, however, to help some mothers feel more comfortable and relaxed during labor.

Episiotomy
An episiotomy incision is made by the physician to prevent tearing of the tissues and to make the vaginal opening large enough for the baby to pass through. In natural childbirth, most mothers will receive a local anesthetic before this procedure.

ferent response. Instead of crying out, for example, her response is a pattern of rapid, shallow breathing which she begins at the first sign of a uterine contraction. The conditioning exercises take about 30 minutes a day and should be started two months before the expected delivery date. Although some women who start natural childbirth training lessons are not able to complete the course for various reasons, most agree that they were better prepared for labor because of what they learned about the control of muscles and breathing.

Fathers-to-be are encouraged to participate in preparations for natural childbirth by coaching their spouses in breathing exercises and timing their contractions. Many hospitals now permit husbands to be with their wives during the second stage of labor in the hospital and even to be present in the delivery room.

Hypnosis sometimes is used instead of drugs or anesthetics for childbirth. But only a minority of women are able to accept the long period of training for the effective deep trance required, some applicants are not susceptible to hypnosis, and few obstetricians are adequately trained to control the hypnotic situation during delivery. Many physicians feel that the type of woman who would be a good subject for child delivery while hypnotized would get along just as well with the natural childbirth method.

LeBoyer Method

"The infant is like one possessed," writes Dr. Frederick LeBoyer of the moment preceding birth. "Mad with agony and misery, alone, abandoned, it fights with the strength of despair. The monster drives the baby lower still . . . The baby is now at the height of its travail. The effort required is too great. The end is surely near. Death seems certain. The monster bears down one more time, and it is then that . . .

"Then that everything explodes! The whole world bursts open. No more tunnel, no prison, no monster. The child is born."

In such terms Dr. LeBoyer focuses on the trauma that the child experiences at birth. The LeBoyer method seeks to train the mother to concentrate on that trauma while delivering her child. A form of natural childbirth, the technique also requires that silence or near-silence be maintained in the delivery room—to protect the newborn infant's ears and sensitivities.

"Relaxing, accepting the slow pace [of birth], letting it take command"— these responses on the mother's part lie at the heart of the LeBoyer method. When birth proceeds in this way, Dr. LeBoyer notes, the child enters the world relaxed and already adjusted. The painful aspects of birth have been eliminated; both mother and child enter on the new relationship outside the womb with calm acceptance.

Like other approaches to natural childbirth, the LeBoyer method requires the full understanding and cooperation of the mother-to-be. The benefits of natural methods are said to be shorter periods of labor and reduced birth trauma. Natural childbirth is also said to reduce morbidity and mortality rates among newborn babies.

Caesarian Section

A caesarian section may be performed in cases of diabetic mothers with rapidly growing fetuses, when delivery is complicated by breech or shoulder presentation, if the uterus is weak due to previous surgery or other reasons, or when the mother has a history of losing the child after carrying it to the time of delivery. There are several variations in caesarian techniques, some requiring a general anesthetic and others using local anesthetics and other medications. But all approaches are directed toward the same goal of saving the lives of both mother and baby. In nearly all instances, the uterus is closed after the baby and placental material are removed. Only in extremely rare cases is it necessary to remove the uterus. Most mothers who have caesarians can have more children in the future if they so desire.

Third Stage of Labor

After the baby is delivered through the normal birth canal, the placenta is expelled by the same route. This is called the third, or placental, stage of labor. The placenta, also known as the *afterbirth*, is connected to the baby by the unbilical cord. The cord is not cut until the blood has drained from the

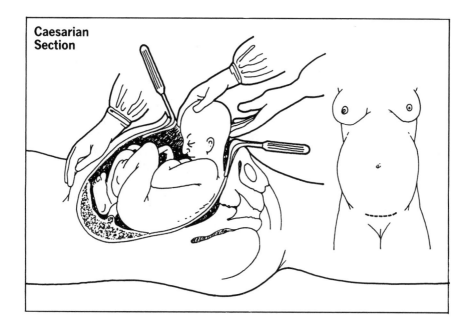

Caesarian Section

placenta into the baby's body; to help the flow the placenta is held above the level of the baby to get an assist from gravity.

Before the infant leaves the delivery room, it is examined for a normal heartbeat, possible abdominal distention or evidence of fluid in the abdominal region, possible abnormalities of the ears, and possible deformities of the mouth area, such as cleft palate or lip. The health of newborn babies is scored by the *Apgar system* when the baby is 60 seconds old. Five items of physical condition are noted and scored on a scale of 0 to 2. They are heart rate, muscle tone, respiration, nerve reflexes, and skin color. Babies that score 8 to 10 points are considered in excellent condition and are given routine postnatal care. If they score 7 points or less, additional measures are taken to get the infants off to a normal start in life. Since the system was started, nearly three-fourths of all newborn babies tested have passed with 8 points or more.

Breast and Bottle Feeding

Whether the infant is to be breast fed or bottle fed is usually a personal matter to be decided by the new mother. For the average healthy baby, there are no obstacles to breast feeding if the mother desires it and is able to produce and deliver milk. A few women are unable to produce a sufficient supply of milk and most supplement their output with bottle feedings. In a few cases, babies are allergic to mother's milk, but in such instances the allergen can be identified and removed from the mother's diet.

Feeding problems are sometimes fewer and less serious among breast-fed babies. The mother's milk contains most of the necessary nutrients and is available when needed at the proper temperature. It also is more likely to be fresh and free of infectious bacteria than bottled milk.

The mother's milk during the first few days after birth is yellowish in color and rich in proteins and minerals. It is called *colostrum,* and is replaced gradually by regular human milk by the fourth week. Mother's milk is low in iron and may lack vitamins C and D. However, the baby arrives in the world with enough stores of iron in its tissues to last through the first few months of life. Compared to cow's milk, human milk is richer in carbohydrates, but cow's milk has a greater proportion of proteins and minerals. The vitamin content of both mother's milk and cow's milk varies with the vitamin intake of each.

Mother's milk generally is more easily digestible in the baby's stomach than cow's milk, because the curd of mother's milk is fine and more rapidly metabolized. On the other hand, mothers who breast-feed sometime suffer from fissuring or cracking of the nipples, *mastitis* (breast inflammation) or diseases that require temporary or permanent discontinuance of breast feeding.

Surveys indicate that more than three-fourths of babies today are bottle fed. Many mothers avoid breast feeding because they feel it is socially unacceptable, that it interferes with employment or social life, that it will affect their physical attractiveness, or because of fear of failure. For mothers who select bottle feeding over breast feeding, the procedure is much simpler today than in previous years. Many of the differences in nutritional values of mother's milk and cow's milk have been reduced or eliminated by improved formula development. Equipment for preparing the bottled meals is superior to that used in previous generations. And there is less danger today of bacterial infection from cow's milk because of improved dairy sanitation methods. New mothers who choose not to breast-feed are usually given hormones, along with ice packs and analgesics, to relieve any breast discomfort that may appear during the first few days.

If the mother wants to breast-feed the baby, plans should be made in advance of delivery. The first feeding can be started as soon after delivery as is feasible for both mother and child, usually within hours after birth. Although the first breast feeding can be delayed for several days, because of the stimulation of milk secretion immediately after delivery, the first ten days to two weeks are crucial in the establishment of a breast feeding program. The sucking reflex of the baby at the mother's breast triggers release of the hormone oxytocin, which in turn influences the release of another substance of the pituitary gland, prolactin, needed for the production of milk in the mother's breast. See also "Feeding the Baby" in Ch. 2, *The First Dozen Years.*

Family Planning

When and How to Plan

Planning a family basically means figuring out when you want children, how many you want, and how long you choose to wait between pregnancies. It is always recommended that you discuss these things before marriage. It is going to be a major sticking point in a relationship if you want four children and your partner's idea of family is a parakeet.

When to have a family is also important. If you are in your twenties or early thirties and wish to have children, you have several years for doing so. If you are in your late thirties or older, having children may be an immediate priority. This is true for both men and women. Although most men are physically capable of fathering children throughout their lives, they should be young enough to participate actively in the raising of the children. If you father a child when you are 51 years old, you will be 72 when the child graduates from college. This is something to consider when you make the decision to become a parent.

Almost no couple expects problems with fertility or conception when they plan a family. Yet approximately 10 percent of all couples have enough difficulty conceiving that they require fertility testing or treatment. See the beginning of this chapter for a thorough discussion of infertility.

For those whom infertility is not an issue, planning pregnancies involves decisions about birth control and spacing of pregnancies.

Timing Between Pregnancies

The minimum time a couple should leave between pregnancies is set by the period of time the baby is breastfed. Breastfeeding and pregnancy tax the mother's and the fetus's health. It is recommended that any mother who is breastfeeding a child, and is pregnant, wean the child.

For the recovery of the physical health of the mother, two years is the average recommended wait. This puts the children almost three years apart in age.

The length of time between children should take into consideration the age and health of the parents, the number of children the couple wants, and the difficulty they have in conceiving. For a couple that suffers through a miscarriage for every successful pregnancy, a long wait may not be recommended. It should also be noted here, though, that a good gynecologist/obstetrician will be able to recommend what is in the mother's best health interest in spacing of pregnancies. For any couple that experiences difficulties with pregnancies, a doctor's advice on their particular situation should be the primary source of information.

Once physical considerations are understood, it becomes a matter of personal priority for the parents. Some parents prefer to wait until one child is in school, or at least out of diapers, before having another child. Having two toddlers can be quite trying on a parent's energy and patience. Having children close in age may help in arranging the parents' schedule around the children. The problems of day care may only be extended a year or two if the children are close in age. For children five years apart, working parents have at least one child in day care for ten years. For more discussion on child care and day care, see the end of this chapter.

Birth Control

Spacing of pregnancies can be controlled by birth control. Several options are available to couples who wish to prevent pregnancy either permanently or temporarily. Temporary measures means that, once the method of control is stopped, the woman can become pregnant. Permanent birth control is surgically achieved by cutting or removing part or all of the reproductive system. Once a permanent surgical procedure has been done, it is extremely difficult or impossible to reverse.

In the discussion of different types of birth control, a failure rate is given. The failure rate is determined by the number of people who conscientiously use the birth control and still get pregnant. The rate is per year, not per use. So if one person in one hundred has a failure, that means that one woman in hundred gets pregnant during one year of use.

Oral Contraceptives

The birth control pill comes in various types. The main ingredient in all of them is synthetic estrogen. Synthetic estrogen has two common types: mestranol and estradiol. The quantity of estrogen in a pill can vary from .03 milligram to .1 milligram for the average dosage. The pill will also contain synthetic progestogen, of which there are several types. Commonly used progestogens are norgestrel, norethindrone, and ethynodiol diacetate. Levels of progestogen can vary from .15 milligram to 2 milligrams.

The two hormones work in combination to prevent ovulation. Pills with the hormones are taken every day for 21 days. Some pill packages come with seven extra pills containing inactive ingredients. The cycle is 28 days, so the schedule will either be 21 days on pills, 7 days off, or 21 days on hormone pills, and 7 days on placebos (pills with no effect). The reason doctors prescribe the 21/7 set of pills is that the patient is less likely to forget a pill if one is taken every day without exception.

After the 21st pill with hormones is taken, the level of estrogen drops as the placebo (or no pill) is used. After 24 to 48 hours, the menstrual cycle will begin. It will usually be lighter in flow and take fewer days than previous periods. The pill may also eliminate cramping.

The effectiveness rating of the pill is less than one pregnancy for 100 women (a year) for pill doses of .35 milligrams or higher of estrogen. For pill doses of less than .35 milligrams of estrogen, there is a very slightly higher pregnancy rate.

Some women experience side effects. These side effects may be minor, from headaches to weight gain, or they may be major, from blood clots to strokes. The increase in risk is directly affected by the patient's age and smoking habits. Women over the age of 35 or smokers increase the risk of heart attach, stroke, and blood clots considerably by taking the pill. The pill does not have any linkage to uterine cancer, cervical cancer, or breast cancer. If a woman already has cancer, taking the pill is not recommended because it may stimulate tumor growth, but it is not linked to beginning cancerous development.

Oral contraceptives can only be obtained through prescription by a licensed physician. Dosage is insufficient if the woman experiences bleeding during the 21 day cycle, heavy menstrual flow, or other unusual symptoms. Consult with your physician if you experience problems. Occasionally switching from one type of synthetic estrogen to another, without increasing dosage, can remedy a problem.

Once on the pill, women who decide to get pregnant should stop taking the pill. Restarting ovulation may take a few months so it may be a while before the woman becomes pregnant. *It is not dangerous* for a woman to become pregnant immediately after stopping oral contraceptives. It is not a major health concern if pill taking overlaps pregnancy slightly. It may cause some problems if pill taking continues past the first trimester.

It was once believed that a woman should cease pill taking for a period of months, either every year or every ten years. Neither has proved to be of medical benefit.

The Mini-Pill

The mini-pill is the nickname of the progestin-only oral contraceptive. For women who run higher health risks by taking estrogen, the progestin pill may be an alternative. The risk of pregnancy is at least 1 percent higher than for the combination pill, and missing a day increases the likelihood of unwanted pregnancy (a higher risk than missing a combination pill). The risk of ectopic pregnancy (the fetus develops outside the uterus, usually in the fallopian tube) is also greater. Ectopic pregnancy can be an extremely painful, serious complication with the risk of sterility to at least one fallopian tube. Any woman on the mini-pill who suffers from lower stomach pain should be tested immediately for an ectopic pregnancy.

IUDs

Intrauterine devices (IUDs) are small pieces inserted semi-permanently into the woman's uterus. Barring complications they remain in place for one to two years. One type sold in the United States is a form called the Copper T. It is made of copper and is t-shaped, measuring less than 1 inch in length. The other is a double s-shape. Two small threads descend from the tail of the device, through the cervix into the vagina. These threads are used to check position of the IUD and to withdraw the IUD after the prescribed period of time.

IUDs are recommended only for women who have already had one successful delivery, are active in a mutually monogamous relationship, and who do not plan on getting pregnant for a few years. The device is inserted at the doctor's office after verification that the woman is not pregnant, has no current pelvic infection or disease, and has never had an ectopic pregnancy.

Because of the problematic history of the IUD, most of the devices were taken off the market. The Dalkon Shield was associated with a number of serious problems and triggered numerous lawsuits against the company. Since then, research and testing of IUDs has improved. However, there are still serious potential complications from using an IUD. The side effects are too numerous to list here, but the major ones are septic or spontaneous abortion, perforation of the uterus or cervix, ectopic pregnancy, or fetal damage during pregnancy. Common minor complaints are cramping, heavy menstrual flow, anemia, or amenorrhea (no period).

Pregnancy rate for IUDs vary from less than 1 pregnancy for 100 women using the device, to 8 pregnancies per 100. Individual devices have varying rates and their effectiveness is also determined by the size of the woman's uterus. The larger the uterine cavity, the less likely she will conceive while using the IUD. Some women accidently expel the IUD; this occurs less frequently with the large size IUDs inserted into larger width uteruses.

Condoms

Condoms are rubber or natural material sheaths that fit over the glans and shaft of the penis. Natural material condoms are usually made from sheep intestinal tissue and will protect against unwanted pregnancy but may allow the AIDS virus to pass through. For this reason, rubber condoms are preferred for both protection against pregnancy and disease.

Several types of condoms are available to the general public. They are purchased without a prescription at a drug store, pharmacy, or other general merchandise shop. They come with or without lubrication on the rubber, and with or without a reservoir tip. The reservoir tip is intended to hold the semen after ejaculation.

Similar to the male-worn condom is the female-worn condom—a rubber sheath inserted into the vagina. The physical appearance of the female-condom is a tube, with a sealed ring at the top. The plastic ring, similar to a diaphragm ring, fits against the cervix at the top of the vagina.

Condoms, even without the use of a spermicide, have a low failure rate. When used correctly, the rate is 2 pregnancies for every 100 users. In actuality, the pregnancy rate is closer to 10 percent, since the condom is frequently used incorrectly. One of the more common errors is placing the tip of the condom too close to the glans of the penis, leaving no room for the semen after ejaculation. Other reasons are tearing or mispositioning of the condom during intercourse, although this is extremely rare. Another, more common problem is the use of petroleum jelly for lubrication. Petroleum products deteriorate rubber material. Only water-based lubricants should be used. Also, the penis should be withdrawn while still erect, to insure that the condom remains in place throughout intercourse. Correct storage of the condom, away from heating sources, helps keep the condom in good condition.

Condoms, when used with spermicides, have an even lower failure rate, at less than 1 percent. Spermicides also help protect against venereal disease. Condoms, and condoms with spermicides, offer the best protection against contracting a venereal disease during intercourse.

Spermicides

Spermicides come in creams, foams, and jellies. They may be inserted by the female with a plastic applicator, or by suppository or tablet. The spermicide should surround the cervix. The specific requirements vary from type to type, but usually the spermicide must be applied within 30 minutes before intercourse. It must be reapplied for each episode of intercourse.

Spermicides are most commonly used with diaphragms, condoms, or other barrier methods of birth control. On their own, spermicides have an estimated failure rate of 15 percent. The two most common ingredients in spermicides are nonoxynol and oxtoxynol. The percentage of the spermicide in the cream, jelly, or foam will vary from 1 percent to more than 12 percent. Some people may have allergic responses to the higher percentage spermicides, but the higher concentrations are more effective in preventing pregnancy.

Diaphragms and Other Barriers

Barrier methods of birth control work by placing a physical barrier, usually of rubber, over the cervical opening to the uterus. The barrier remains in place for at least several hours after intercourse to prevent sperm from entering into the uterus. Barriers are used in conjunction with spermicidal creams, foams, or jellies to enhance protection against sperm passage.

The single-most common form of barrier is the diaphragm. The diaphragm is prescribed by a physician after sizing a women for the dimensions of the diaphragm. If a woman loses or gains more than ten pounds, or becomes pregnant, she should be checked to see if the diaphragm size has to be changed.

The rim of the diaphragm is coated with a spermicidal agent and then is put in place before intercourse. Another application of spermicide is required for each episode of intercourse. The diaphragm should be removed 24 hours after the last episode of intercourse and should be washed thoroughly before reuse.

The failure rate for diaphragms when used with spermicides is 3 percent, when used correctly. The diffi-culty in using a diaphragm is in positioning of the diaphragm and sizing of the diaphragm. Different brands of diaphragms, combined with experience of the woman in using it and whether she has had children, can increase the failure rate to as high as 20 percent.

Cervical caps are smaller types of rubber barriers. They are currently unavailable in the United States, except for those women participating in the initial pre-FDA studies on their effectiveness. One of the reasons they are not currently marketed in the U.S. is because the failure rate can be extremely high on them, as high as 44 percent.

A contraceptive sponge is also available as a barrier method. The contraceptive sponge works something like a diaphragm, but is thrown out after use. The sponge is moistened before placement against the cervix, and it releases spermicides for 24 hours after intercourse. It must be removed after 24 hours. The failure rate is almost 18 per 100 users for women who have never had children. It becomes much higher with women who have had children, at 28 percent failure.

Natural Birth Control Methods

Natural birth control is called that when it requires no outside prevention method for pregnancy. Natural methods include rhythm method, withdrawal, and abstinence.

Rhythm method involves determining the woman's ovulation cycle and avoiding intercourse during the days before and after ovulation. Ovulation occurs *on average* fourteen days before the next period. This is only reliable for a woman who has an exact 28 day cycle with the normal ovulation timing. Many women ovulate earlier or later in the menstrual cycle, and many cycles are longer or shorter than 28 days. To determine ovulation, vaginal body temperature are charted and physical characteristics of vaginal secretions are monitored for changes over a period of several months to determine regularity and time of ovulation. If a couple chooses to use rhythm method for birth control, it is recommended that you consult with a doctor for specific details of monitoring temperature and secretions patterns. It is a relatively complex procedure and requires a great deal of commitment by both partners to make this effective. Rhythm method has as high as a 20 percent failure rate when used correctly. It is much higher when used by couples inexperienced in monitoring ovulation.

Withdrawal method refers to the withdrawal of the penis prior to ejaculation, during intercourse. The risk in this method is that preejaculative liquids can contain enough sperm to impregnate a woman. Also, semen on the exterior of the vagina, or the labia, can also travel back into the uterine cavity and fertilize an egg. Timing on withdrawal is essential and should be done prior to any ejaculation. Because of this, withdrawal is often considered an inadequate form of birth control. It can be emotionally and physically dissatisfying. It also has an exceedingly high failure rate, estimated between 20 and 40 percent. This is only slightly better than no birth control at all.

Permanent Birth Control

Hysterectomy

Hysterectomy is the removal of the uterus and, perhaps, the cervix. This procedure is completely irreversible. Chances of pregnancy following the procedure are none.

A *subtotal hysterectomy* is the removal of the uterus, leaving the cervix, fallopian tubes, and ovaries in place. A *total hysterectomy* is the removal of the cervix as well as the uterus. *Oophorectomy* and *ovariectomy* are both used to describe the surgical removal of one or both of the ovaries. *Ovariohysterectomy* is the removal of the ovaries, fallopian tubes, and uterus. The quantity of tissue removed will be determined by the patient and the doctor, based on the

reasons for the operation. For removal of cancerous tissue, all the organs may need to be removed. For sterilization, only a subtotal hysterectomy may be necessary.

Hysterectomies have become increasingly used to correct problems that may be remedied by medication, or which may be temporary in nature and not warrant surgery. To recommend a hysterectomy solely for birth control is unusual. It should only be done in cases where some underlying physical problems require surgery. Although hysterectomies are common, they are still considered major surgery and should be approached as such, by both the doctor and the patient. Recoveries can take six weeks or longer.

Tubal Ligation

Tubal ligation is the surgical blocking of the fallopian tubes. The fallopian tubes transport the egg from the ovary to the uterus. By blocking the path that the egg travels, the egg is no longer capable of making contact with the sperm. Tubal ligation is done by cutting, tying, banding, cauterizing, or removing a section of each tube so the path is no longer continuous. Depending on the surgical method used to block the tube, the ability to reverse the procedure (should you decide later to have chil-

dren) may be nearly impossible. Also depending on the method used to tie off the tubes, the number of women who become pregnant after a tubal ligation is, at the highest, 2 in 1000.

Tubal ligation can be done immediately following childbirth, if the doctor is briefed on the decision well in advance of the delivery. It can also be done by scheduled surgery at any time. 15 percent of all women over the age of 45 have elected to have a tubal ligation.

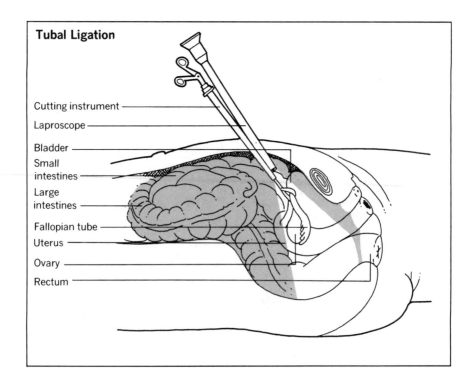

Tubal Ligation

Cutting instrument

Laproscope

Bladder

Small intestines

Large intestines

Fallopian tube

Uterus

Ovary

Rectum

Vasectomy

Vasectomy is sterilization of the male by cutting the vas deferens, the tubes that transport the sperm. The surgery is normally performed in the doctor's office with local anesthesia. Incisions are made either on each side of the scrotum or on the center midline of the scrotum. The tubes are then cut, and tied or cauterized on each end. Pain following the procedure is usually responsive to non-aspirin painkillers. Heavy lifting or strenuous exercise should be avoided for a week.

Vasovasotomy is the surgical procedure that attempts to reconnect the vas deferens after a vasectomy. This operation is done for men wishing to reverse the surgical sterilization. Success at this procedure can vary from 30 to 75 percent, depending on the type of initial sterilization procedures, and on the skill of the surgeon.

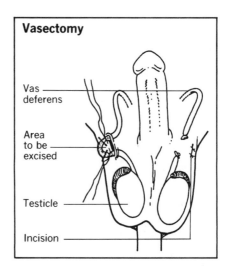

Vasectomy

Vas deferens

Area to be excised

Testicle

Incision

Conception

Once you decide that you would like to have a child, planning the pregnancy involves two basic schedules. The first is deciding when you want the child to arrive. This includes deciding when pregnancy would be convenient. The second is discovering when fertility occurs each month in the woman's cycle.

When to Get Pregnant

In deciding when the best time of the year to have a baby arrive, several things should be taken into account. If you plan on taking time off from work, for the child, you should consider the work you do and when a break in the work load would prove easiest to pull away.

Weather may also help you decide when you wish to get pregnant. Buy-ing winter clothing for the last stage of pregnancy can be costly. Getting a winter coat, and sweaters, and longjohns to fit during the eighth and ninth month of pregnancy may require buying clothes you won't ever wear again. Getting summer dresses and cotton pants for the last trimester of the pregnancy may be cheaper. Some women, however, cannot bear the thought of being eight months pregnant in the August heat.

Each family works on a slightly different schedule than the next. Planning can help ease the burden of time off and child care that may be essential to making a family work.

How to Get Pregnant

Once you have decided on starting or continuing a family, planning the pregnancy involves calculating the fertile period in the menstrual cycle. For some parents, this requires no effort at all. Some women get pregnant immediately after stopping birth control. For others, months of timing ovulation may be required for successful conception.

The best method to figure out an ovulation cycle is to work with your physician. There are some things you can do in advance to help, though. Write down the starting and ending date of your period, for several months. If anything significant happens during the month that may have changed the cycle, such as an illness, note it in your calendar.

Your physician can give your specific information on physical characteristics and signs of ovulation that you should watch for. Basal body temperature fluctuates just before ovulation. If you chart your temperature every day at the same time, usually first thing in the morning, you should notice a slight change in the body temperature approximately two weeks before your period. The rise in temperature of about .4 to .8 degrees Fahrenheit appears normally within 24 hours of ovulation. It should last a few days and then the temperature should return to a normal level.

Some women do not get a sharp increase in temperature. It may be more subtle, more gradual, or even may drop in temperature slightly. It is important that you chart more than a couple months to get a better general view of your own body's rhythm.

Checking the viscosity of mucous production can also give some signs of ovulation. Cervical mucous production becomes more transparent and more elastic as ovulation occurs. There are also physical changes that can be noted under a microscope.

By establishing and keeping a calendar for these changes, a woman should be able to, with the help of her obstetrician or gynecologist, determine when she is fertile. If, after several months of intercourse during periods of fertility, the couple still has not conceived, the physician will recommend testing for egg and sperm production.

The Menstrual Cycle

The menstrual cycle runs, on average, every 28 days. As many women have cycles longer than 28 days as have cycles shorter than 28 days.

Some women's cycles are not always the same length. Cycles may vary each month, with no true regularity.

Some women have a lower abdominal pain midway through their cycle that accompanies ovulation. Called *mittelschmerz,* the pain can vary from a dull ache lasting hours to a sharp pain that only lasts minutes. The pain is believed to be caused by the release of the ovum from the ovary.

A new cycle is marked from the first day of menstruation. On the first day after menstruation stops, the body's hormonal levels are at their lowest for estrogen and progesterone. The uterine lining is at its thinnest. As the level of estrogen rises the blood-lined wall of the uterus builds. The wall prepares for the embedding of a fertilized egg. For the average cycle (28 days) the wall continues to build for two weeks.

While this is occurring, at least one egg is developing in an ovary. The ovary that develops the egg may alternate from left side to right. How this is controlled by the body's hormonal system is not yet understood. After approximately two weeks, the body releases luteinizing hormone (LH), triggering the release of the ripe egg from the ovary.

The egg travels down the fallopian tube. This may take from one to five days. While the egg is in the fallopian tube, the body continues to prepare the uterine wall for implantation of a fertilized egg.

If intercourse takes place during this period of time, the egg and the sperm meet up in the fallopian tube. One sperm will penetrate the egg wall and the egg immediately produces a barrier that prevents a second sperm from penetrating. The fertilized egg,

called the blastula during that stage of development, continues to travel down the fallopian tube to the uterus.

If the egg implants on the tube wall, or lodges against something and cannot continue on to the uterus, it will continue growing in the fallopian tube. It will only take a matter of days for the embryo to outgrow the size of the tube. Spots of blood will be the first sign of an *ectopic pregnancy,* or a pregnancy that develops outside the uterus. The accompanying pain will continue to get worse until treatment is sought. After a few days of spotting and pain the fallopian tube will rupture, producing tremendous pain and blood flow. This is an extreme emergency and medical attention should be sought immediately.

If the embryo successfully makes the journey to the uterine lining, it will usually implant against the blood-filled wall. The embryo will develop a cord attachment to the wall, establishing the placental link between the mother and the embryo. Though this cord flows the blood that will keep the embryo alive.

Some eggs will not successfully lodge against the wall. They may pass undetected with the menstrual blood. They may also temporarily lodge against the wall, delaying menstruation, but then be dispelled by the body. One in ten pregnancies is estimated to end in some form of miscarriage. See the section on Miscarriage, earlier in this chapter, for information.

If the embryo successfully attaches, it will usually continue to develop normally through to completion of pregnancy. The embryo triggers hormonal signals that shut off the menstrual cycle. This prevents further development of eggs in the ovaries, keeps the uterine lining intact, and seals the cervix to prevent infection and allow amniotic fluid to fill the uterus.

If the egg is unfertilized during its passage through the fallopian tube, it will either pass into the uterus and then wash out with the menstrual blood or will deteriorate before leaving the body.

Approximately a week past ovulation the ovary will trigger an increase in progesterone production. This, in turn, will cause the deterioration of the uterine wall's blood lining. The deterioration takes about seven days before menstruation begins.

Menstruation is the passing of the blood from the uterine wall. The blood is shed, on average, two weeks after the day of ovulation. Menstruation lasts from three to seven days.

The flow of blood will vary during the course of menstruation, with the heaviest flow occurring early on after onset.

Extremely heavy periods, called *menorrhagia,* may occasionally occur during one's lifetime. If it is a persistent problem, consult with your gynecologist. Painful periods or, *dysmenorrhea,* is the technical term for periods with cramps. As anyone who has had cramps can testify, they can be quite painful. There are several medications that can be taken to ease or relieve the pain of cramping with menstruation. Most require a physician's prescription. Some over-the-counter medications, such as ibuprofen, can also help. Cramps are the contractions of the uterus that force the lining to be shed. Many women stop having dysmenorrhea after the birth of their first child. Other women who previously had no problem suffer from cramps only after childbirth. Birth control pills can also eliminate or reduce menstrual pain.

Child Care and Day Care

Once you have a child, you make a choice about how that child is to be cared for during the years before school. The majority of families in the United States can no longer afford to have one parent stay home to raise a child. This means that, for at least part of the week, the child will be cared for by someone other than a parent.

For children with only one primary caretaker, and this counts for more than one quarter of American children, time in day care is essentially the same amount of time as the average adult full-time employee. The quality of the care is as influential on the child's upbringing as the quality of the parental care received during nonwork hours. Because of this, child care selection is extremely important to the safety and well-being of any child entrusted to someone else.

Child Care in the Home

Nannies, au pairs, child care workers, and babysitters, are people who come to, or live in, the homes of the child for whom they care.

Few families can afford the salary and the living space required of the live-in nanny. For those who can, the nanny provides a registered, reliable, trained caretaker who will supervise the child for as many years as the parents deem necessary. Au pairs are much the same type of worker, except they usually do not have educational training for child care. They tend to be younger workers, less likely to stay for more than a year or two in the same position. Many au pairs are foreign students seeking a chance to live abroad for a while.

Child care workers and babysitters may come to take care of the child during assigned hours. They may work for one family, or a few families may pool together resources and use one caretaker for several children. One child care worker should care for no more than four or five children at a time, to provide the best safety and education for the children.

When hiring someone to come watch your children in your home, several things should be considered. The most important is to check the personal history of whomever is being considered. This now means going beyond personal recommendations. Check for police records, work papers, history of employment, and any other documentation that the person can provide to show stability, reliability, honesty, and integrity *while working with children.* In most situations, the caretaker will be unsupervised while working with your small children. Children's versions of events may not fully explain events you should know about, or may exaggerate problems with the caretaker that are not important. You have to have complete faith that this person is delivering the service you expect in a manner that meets with your full approval. If you have the opportunity to observe at least one full day of activity under the care of the worker, you should take it. This gives you a sample of how your child will spend important hours of his development. It also allows you to watch how a worker deals with the frustrations and problems that come up every day when dealing with youngsters.

Child Care Centers and Programs

Many states are now requiring registration of child care centers. Even for individuals who run informal-style child care in their own home, licensing may be required. The state will set up rules of how much space is needed per child, how many staff employees per child, what kind and variety of food is to be served, what activities are allowed, and what type of insurance is needed to cover for accidents while at the center. Check to see if your state has a licensing program, and what the licensing requirements are. If your state does have such a program, you should only use licensed facilities for your child. If there is no mandatory licensing, find out if there is a voluntary licensing program for day care. You should check references thoroughly for programs that have no governmental inspection. Even with licensing, you want to ask the same types of questions that the licensor asks:

- How many staff per student?
- With whom is a sick staff member replaced?
- What food is provided for the children?
- What activities are provided for?
- What instruction and education is the child given?
- What are the age ranges of the children enrolled?
- How many children does the facility accommodate?
- How many children per classroom or room?
- Are any activities off the center grounds? Is permission obtained in advance to take the child off the grounds?
- What is the policy for sick children? Are they allowed in the classroom? If a child is brought to the center, obviously sick, what procedures are followed by the day care staff?
- If a child gets sick or injured while at day care, what procedures are followed?
- What is the policy of allowing children to leave with someone other than a parent? Is advance notice required? Is the parent the only acceptable guardian to be picking up a child? (Although it may seem initially that you would only want a

parent picking a child up, you may wish to carpool, or have a babysitter or a relative pick up a child. You want to make absolutely sure, though, that the child cannot leave with anyone who walks in and asks to take the child home.)

- What are their hours? What are their pickup times? If you are late, what do they do with the child?
- What is the discipline policy of the center? (This is of fundamental importance that the policies be explained in advance of enrollment.)
- Do they expel children? For what reasons?

Look around the facilities. Are they clean, well kept, and brightly lit? Are there appropriate types of toys for your child's age? Are there any safety violations or dangerous aspects to the room's design (such as an open staircase without guardgates).

Attend the facilities while day care is in session. Observe the interaction of the children to see if they are well cared for, occupied in a manner you find suitable, and playing or interacting positively. Get references from parents whose children are the same age as yours and are currently using the day care program.

Once you have enrolled in the program, continue to monitor the classroom atmosphere. Occasionally drop by early before picking a child up to watch the activities. Continue to talk to other parents who have children in the same program. And, above all, continue to talk to and listen to your child about how he has spent his day.

5

The Middle Years

Maintaining good health over the years is far simpler, less expensive, and more comfortable than restoring health that has become poor. Because some diseases cannot be cured after they are contracted, it is only logical to try to prevent all possible health problems. The techniques of modern preventive medicine are available to Americans of every age.

All people are not beautiful or handsome, but nearly everyone can have the kind of attractiveness and vitality that comes from good health. The health of an individual depends upon the kind of body he inherits and the care he gives it. Good health can be thought of as a state of social, physical, and mental well-being, a goal virtually everybody can attain—if the responsibility for maintaining one's own health, with occasional help from the health experts, is accepted.

Keeping Fit

Physical Changes

Physically, middle age should be a pleasant plateau—a time to look back on a vigorous youth, enjoy an active present, and prepare for a ripe old age.

Middle age should not be measured by chronological age but by biological age, the condition of various parts of the body. You might say that the middle-aged body is like a car that has been driven a certain number of miles. It should be well broken in and running smoothly, but with plenty of reserve power for emergencies, and lots of mileage left.

Biological age should be measured by the state of the heart, arteries, and other essential organs, the length of life and comparative health of parents and grandparents, temperament and outlook on life, and outward appearance. The way you have fed or treated yourself is important. Eating the wrong kinds of food, being overweight, smoking too much, or worrying too much can add years to biological age.

However, no one should be surprised if he is not in quite the shape he was when he was 25 or 30 years old. At age 40 to 50 it is perfectly normal to have only 80 percent of the maximum breathing capacity, 85 percent of the resting cardiac output, 95 percent of the total body water, and 96 percent of the basal metabolic rate. These factors, however, should not slow anyone down very much.

There is one difference, though, that can be anticipated in middle age. Reaction time and decision-making processes may be a bit slower. This is because the nervous system is one of the most vulnerable to aging. The cells of the central nervous system begin to die early in life and are not replaced, while other organs are still growing and producing new cells. Specific response to input is delayed because it takes a greater length of time for an impulse to travel across the connections linking nerve fibers.

Thus, though you may function as usual under normal conditions, you may find it a little harder to respond to physical or emotional stress. However, if you have followed a sound health maintenance program, including good nutrition, enough mental and physical exercise and rest, and moderate living habits, you should respond to unusual physiological or emotional stress quite adequately.

The Importance of Checkups

Physical disabilities associated with chronic disease increase sharply with age, starting with the middle years. While more than half (54 percent) of the 86 million persons who have one or more chronic conditions are under age 45, the prevalence of disability from illness is greatest in the 45 and older age group. Of those under 45 who have chronic conditions, only 14 percent are limited in activity as compared with almost 30 percent of the 45 to 64 age group. And only 1 percent of those under 45 with chronic illness are completely disabled, as compared with 4 percent in the 45 to 64 age group.

These figures suggest that it is wise to have an annual checkup so that any disease process or condition can be nipped in the bud. Further evidence of the value of medical checkups comes from the Aetna Life Insurance Company, which compared two groups of policyholders over a five-year period. Those who did not have checkups and health counseling had a death rate 44 percent higher than the group who did. Regular checkups will not only help prolong life, they will also help you to live it more comfortably.

Here are some other good reasons for having a physical checkup:

- If an organ has been attacked by serious disease in youth, it may deteriorate at an early adult age.

- Heredity may play an important role in determining the speed at which various organs age. If your parents and grandparents had arteriosclerosis, there is a chance you might develop this condition in your middle years.

- Your environment (smog, poor climate, etc.) might affect the rate at which your body ages, particularly the skin.

- Individual stresses and strains or abuses or overuse (of alcohol, for example) may create a health problem in middle age.

- The endocrine glands (pituitary, thyroid, parathyroids, adrenals, ovaries, testicles) play important roles in aging. Serious disease of one or more of these glands may lead to premature aging of an organ dependent upon its secretions.

- At middle age you are more likely to be beset by emotional strains at work or at home that could make you an early candidate for heart disease, arteriosclerosis, and other degenerative disorders.

- The earlier a chronic disease is detected, the better the chance that it can be arrested before permanent damage is done. This is especially true in the case of glaucoma, diabetes, heart disease, cancer of the lung or breast or other cancers—all of which could have their onset in middle age.

To help detect disease and other debilitating conditions, many physicians utilize automated medical screening, which combines medical history with selected physiological measurements and laboratory tests to give the physician a complete health profile of the patient. This profile should indicate the probability of any chronic condition, which the physician could then pinpoint with more thorough tests.

Also, annual checkups enable the physician to observe changes taking place over a period of time. For example, he is able to observe gradually changing blood chemistry levels or a progressive increase in eye pressure that could signal the onset of disease.

Don't Try To Be Your Own Physician

A panel of medical specialists from the University of California at Los Angeles recently found that many men of 40 years and older were dosing themselves with unnecessary pills and "conserving" their energy by increasing bed rest to the point that it actually became enervating.

These physicians point out that increasing dependence on pills can be harmful as well as expensive. Laxatives are a good example of a popular commercial medicine taken unnecessarily by large numbers of people. Perhaps only one person in 100,000 may have an actual motor disability of the bowels, and most constipation can be easily corrected through proper foods and exercise, without resorting to laxatives. Also, taking vitamin pills or avoiding all high-cholesterol foods is unnecessary—unless recommended by a physician.

But, most important, "conserving" energy through prolonged bed rest or avoiding exercise can be fatal. The panel members pointed out that before age 40, a person exercises to improve his performance, but that after age 40 he exercises to improve his chances of survival.

Physical Fitness and Exercise

In middle age most of us stop performing most forms of exercise other than those that we enjoy doing. In other words, we find it easier to bend an elbow than lift weights. This is unfortunate, because in middle age most of us need regular exercise to maintain both mental and physical fitness and to increase endurance, strength, and agility.

As noted earlier, in middle age there is some decrease in breathing capacity, cardiac output, and metabolic rate; yet exercise can improve these functions. The more often the normal heart and circulatory system are required to move blood to active regions of the body through exercise or movement, the more efficient they become. Protracted exercise also improves the work of the lungs by increasing their ability to expand more fully, take in more air, and utilize a greater proportion of the oxygen in the inhaled air.

While exercise alone cannot eliminate obesity, it can help prevent it by improving digestion and bowel movements and by burning up excess calories. Exercise can also make you feel, look, and think better. Some traditional formal exercises, however, like touching the toes while keeping your knees stiff, or doing deep knee bends, are potentially harmful in middle age; they put too much stress on weak parts of the back and legs.

Despite protests about not having enough time, everyone has time to exercise, particularly if it is worked into the daily routine—for example, walking instead of riding to the train, office, store, or bus stop. You might find you'll get there faster, especially in traffic-clogged metropolitan areas, and you'll save money as well. More important, those minutes of "stolen" exercise accrue over the years in the form of improved health.

Sports and Games

If you don't like formal exercise, you can get exercise informally—through a favorite sport, whether it be golf, tennis, swimming, jogging, skiing, cycling, or whatever. Many sports and games are stop-and-go activities that do not provide helpful, rhythmic exercise, but here's how you can make them more beneficial.

Golf

Instead of riding in a golf cart between shots, walk—in fact, stride vigorously, lifting your head and chest. And don't make golf a cut-throat competition or business pursuit. Relax and enjoy it—count your blessings rather than your bogeys.

Tennis

Like golf, tennis can be a cut-throat competitive sport or a pleasant pursuit. If it's played with muscles tied in knots from nervous tension, it will not provide any fun or healthful exercise. Also, players over 30 are well-advised to play more doubles than singles and to avoid exhausting themselves in the heat of competition.

Swimming

Along with fast walking and jogging, swimming is one of the best all-around exercises. When swimming, most of the muscles are exercised and lung capacity and cardiac output are improved. The exercise potential can be increased by doing pull-ups with the diving board or ladder and by bobbing up and down in the water.

Jogging

This popular sport can be combined with walking, done in a group or alone, either outdoors or indoors, and alternated with other exercises. Moreover, it doesn't require any special equipment and has been recognized by fitness experts as one of the best exercises for the heart and circulation. However, it is wise to get your physician's advice and approval before embarking on a jogging program.

Skiing

Skiing is healthful as well as fun. You can get in shape for skiing and improve your ability by jogging and by practicing some of the techniques needed in skiing—such as the rhythmic left-right-left-right twist of foot, knee, and leg in short turns. To do this exercise, stand up straight with your feet quite close together and flex your knees forward so that the weight goes onto the balls of the feet. Now, arms apart for balance, twist your feet and knees to the left without twisting your upper body. As you do this, try the modified half-bends of the traversing position that all ski schools teach. Then reverse the position to the right, and keep repeating.

Other Sports

Other worthwhile sports for healthful exercise include badminton, bicycling, canoeing, rowing, table tennis, skating, and squash. However, they should be sustained for at least 30 minutes at a time, ideally four times a week, and should be combined with supplemental exercises.

A Word of Warning

Everyone should beware of becoming a weekend athlete and punishing himself with an overdose of exercise or sports only on weekends. It makes as much sense as stuffing yourself on weekends and starving the rest of the week. It's far more sensible—and healthful—to engage in sports activities for an hour or so at a time on a daily basis.

Exercises

Participating in sports activities is not the only way to keep fit. Special exercises can help reduce tension and build muscles. For instance, one way to relax is to do rhythmic exercises, particularly for the trunk, that help to improve circulation. You can also try exercises that will relieve tense muscles and improve breathing. The exercises described below were developed by Dr. Josephine L. Rathbone of Columbia University.

Breathing to Relax

Lie on your back on the floor with knees bent and feet resting on the floor. Take a deep breath, letting both the abdominal wall and chest rise. Hold the air for a few seconds, then expel it through your mouth with a gasp. Repeat four or five times at regular intervals.

For Tense Arms

Standing erectly, swing both arms forward, then to the side, letting them drop during the swings so that your hands brush your thighs with each motion. Keep your shoulders low. Repeat a few times. Then, sit on the edge of a chair and clench one hand tightly. Swing your arm vigorously in large circles, keeping your hand clenched. Then repeat with other arm.

For Tense Legs

Sit on the edge of a table with lower legs hanging free. Then, alternately, swing them backward and forward. Try to keep your legs moving in rhythm.

For Stomach Tension

Kneel with your feet under your hips and swing your trunk down to one side and around, sweeping your arms in a wide circle, coming up again on the opposite side. Or stand with your hips supported against the wall, feet apart and a few inches from the wall. Bend your body forward, arms drooping, and let your body sway from side to side, with your arms and head loose.

Relaxing at Work or Home

Relieve tension while sitting by holding the spine erect, shoulders low. Turn your head so that the chin touches first one collarbone, then the other. Move slowly and rhythmically.

Yoga

You can also relax and become revitalized through various Yoga exercises. Courses are taught at many recreational centers. Some of the exercises require only a minimum of time, and can be done not only before and after the workday but in the office during the lunch hour.

Isometrics

Isometric exercises—pitting one muscle against another without moving—can also be practiced at odd moments. These exercises should, however, be done only by healthy persons, and not by anyone with a cardiac problem. To strengthen arm and shoulder muscles through isometrics, put the fist of one hand against the palm of the other and push without moving. Or push up with your arms from a chair or the edge of a table. Strengthen arm and neck muscles by grasping the back of the neck with laced fingers and pulling forward—again, without movement.

All of the above exercises and sports can put you on the road to physical fitness. Just remember, whatever form of exercise or sport you choose, make it fun and do not strain yourself unduly.

Rest and Sleep

Rest and sleep adequate for one's personal needs are another vital component of good health and good appearance. They also influence human relationships and mental alertness. Scientists believe that during sleep the body replaces tissue cells and eliminates waste products created by fatigue at a faster rate than when awake.

Sleep also rests the heart and blood system, because heart muscle contractions and blood pressure are slower then. Excessive fatigue from lack of sleep increases susceptibility to a number of ailments, including the common cold. If an individual gets an adequate amount of sleep (usually seven to eight hours for an adult), he will feel ready to meet the day's activities. If not, his memory may not be sharp, and he may be irritable because his nervous system has had inadequate rest.

A quiet, dark, ventilated room, a fairly firm mattress, and performance of a moderate amount of exercise during the day will aid sleep. When worry, frustration, or anxiety make it difficult to sleep, a conscious attempt to relax will help. Sedatives or sleeping pills should not be taken unless they are prescribed or recommended by a physician.

Personal Hygiene

Disease germs can enter the body only in a limited number of ways. One of the major ways is through the skin. The skin is a protective covering which, when broken, can admit harmful bacteria or viruses easily.

Simple precautions are very effective. The hands come into contact with disease germs more than any other part of the body. Therefore, they should be washed whenever they are dirty, prior to preparing food or eating, and after using the lavatory.

The rest of the body must also be kept clean, because adequate bodily cleanliness will remove substances that, by irritating the skin, make it more susceptible to infection. Bathing also improves the muscle tone of the skin. Hair should also be washed frequently enough to prevent accumulation of dust and dead skin cells.

Openings in the body are also paths by which disease germs can enter the body. The nose and ears should be carefully cleaned only with something soft, for instance, a cotton swab. Genital orifices should be kept clean by frequent bathing. Any unusual discharge from a body opening should be promptly reported to a physician. The problem can then be treated at its earliest stage—the easiest time to solve the problem.

Personal hygiene includes care of the nails. They should always be kept clean and fairly short. Hangnails can be avoided by gently pushing back the cuticle with a towel after washing the hands.

Care of the Feet

"My feet are killing me!" is a complaint heard more frequently in middle age, especially from women. The devil in this case usually takes the shape of fashionable shoes, where the foot is frequently squeezed into shapes and positions it was never designed to tolerate. Particularly unhealthy for the foot was the formerly fashionable spike heel and pointed toe.

Any heel two inches or higher will force the full weight of the body onto the smaller bones in the front of the foot and squeeze the toes into the forepart of the shoes. This hurts the arch, causes calluses on the sole of the foot, and can lead to various bone deformities.

The major solution to this problem is to buy good shoes that really fit. The shoes should be moderately broad across the instep, have a straight inner border, and a moderately low heel. To fit properly, shoes should extend one-half inch to three-fourths inch beyond the longest toe.

Avoid wearing shoes that have no support; also, avoid wearing high heels for long periods of time. Extremely high heels worn constantly force the foot forward and upset body balance. Changing heel height several times a day will rest the feet and give the muscles in the back of the legs a chance to return to their normal position. It's highly desirable to wear different shoes each day, or at least alternate two pairs. This gives the shoes a chance to dry out completely. Dust shoes with a mild powder when removed.

Shoes should not be bought in the morning. They should be tried on near the end of the day, when the feet have broadened from standing and walking, and tightness or rubbing can be more easily detected.

As to hosiery, socks and stockings should extend a half-inch beyond the longest toe. Stretch socks are fine in many cases, but plain wool or cotton socks help if your feet perspire a lot.

Foot Exercises

Exercise your feet by trying these simple steps recommended by leading podiatrists:

- Extend the toes and flex rapidly for a minute or two. Rotate the feet in circles at the ankles. Try picking up a marble or pencil with your toes; this will give them agility and strength.

- Stand on a book with your toes extended over the edge. Then curl your toes down as far as possible, grasping the cover.

- After an unusually active day, refresh the feet with an alcohol rub. Follow this with a foot massage, squeezing the feet between your hands. When you are tired, rest with your feet up. Try lying down for about a half-hour with your feet higher than your head, using pillows to prop up your legs.

- Walk barefoot on uneven sandy beaches and thick grass. This limbers up the feet and makes the toes work. Walking anywhere is one of the best exercises for the feet if you learn to walk properly and cultivate good posture. Keep toes pointed ahead, and lift rather than push the foot, letting it come down flat on the ground, placing little weight on the heel. Your toes will come alive, and your feet will become more active.

Foot Ailments

Doing foot exercises is particularly important in middle age, because the foot is especially vulnerable to the following problems.

Bunions

A bunion is a thickening and swelling of the big joint of the big toe, forcing it toward the other toes. There is also a protuberance on the inner side of the foot. Unless treated, this condition usually gets progressively worse. Surgery is not always necessary or successful. Often, special shoes to fit the deformed foot must be worn.

Stiff Toe

People suffering from this problem find that the big joint of the big toe becomes painful and stiff, possibly due to a major accident or repeated minor trauma. This condition usually corrects itself if the joint is protected for a few weeks, usually by a small steel plate within the sole of the shoe.

Hammer Toe

This clawlike deformity is usually caused by cramping the toes with too small shoes. The pressure can be eased with padding and, in some cases, the deformity can be corrected by surgery.

Ingrown Toenail

Cutting the nail short and wearing shoes that are too tight are major causes of ingrown toenails; the edge of the nail of the toe—usually the big toe—is forced into the soft outer tissues. In some cases the tissues can be peeled back after soaking the foot in hot water, and the offending part of the nail can be removed. To prevent ingrown toenails, the nails should be kept carefully trimmed and cut straight across the nail rather than trimmed into curves at the corners. For severe or chronic cases of ingrown toenails it is best to seek professional treatment.

Morton's Toe

This is the common name for a form of *metatarsalgia,* a painful inflammation of a sheath of small nerves that pass between the toes near the ball of the foot. The ailment is most likely to occur in an area between the third and fourth toe, counting from the large toe, and usually is due to irritation produced by pressure that makes the toes rub against each other. In most instances, the pressure results from wearing improperly fitted shoes, shoes with pointed toes, or high heel shoes, which restrict normal flexing of the metatarsals (the bones at the base of the toes) while walking.

Temporary relief usually is possible through removal of the shoes and massaging of the toes, or by application of moist, warm heat to the afflicted area. In cases of very severe pain, a doctor may inject a local anesthetic into the foot. Additional relief sometimes can be obtained by wearing metatarsal arch supports in the shoes. However, continued irritation of the nerves can result in the growth of a tumor that may require surgical removal.

Care of the Teeth

An attractive smile is often the first thing that one notices about others. In addition to creating an attractive appearance, healthy teeth and gums are a basic requirement for good overall health. The dentist should be visited at whatever intervals he recommends, usually every six months.

Neglect of oral hygiene and the forgoing of dental checkups are commonplace in the middle years. An often-heard excuse is that the eventual loss of teeth is inevitable. Years ago, loss of teeth really was unavoidable. Today, however, thanks to modern dental practices, it is possible for nearly everyone to enjoy the benefits of natural teeth for a lifetime.

Problems of Aging

When the human body reaches middle age, a number conditions that are the result of advancing years begin to make themselves felt. These include wrinkling of the skin, baldness, varicose veins, and the body's decreased ability to deal with nicotine, caffeine, alcohol, and excess calories.

Skin

The skin usually starts to show its age in the mid to late 30s. At that time it starts to lose its elasticity and flexibility, and becomes somewhat thinner. Little lines—not yet wrinkles—start to show up, usually crow's feet around the eyes.

Wrinkling takes place at different times with different people, and sometimes in different areas of the skin. Heredity may play a part.

Treatment for Wrinkles

While wrinkles do not hurt, many people want to do something about them. Experienced physicians and dermatologists have a number of techniques for removing or minimizing wrinkles. One accepted method is *dermabrasion,* or planing of the skin. The physician sprays on a local anesthetic, then scrapes the skin with a motor-driven wire brush or some other abrasive tool. The treatment usually takes one session, and no hospital stay is required. There will be some swelling and scab formation, but this should clear up in a week to ten days.

Another method is called *cryother-* apy, in which the physician freezes the skin with carbon dioxide. This induces peeling, which improves the appearance of flat acne scars and shallow wrinkles.

The use of retinoic acid, or Retin-A™, for the treatment of wrinkles has become popular in recent years. Retinoic acid was originally used for the treatment of acne and has not yet been studied for long-term use for wrinkles. The effect is temporary on wrinkles, and skin will return to original condition after discontinued use. Some side effects include heightened sensitivity to sunlight and skin irritation or rash.

Skin Texture Change

Besides wrinkling, the skin has a tendency in some people to become thinner, leathery, and darkened as they move towards the 40s and 50s. This effect can be minimized if the skin is toned with cold cream and other emollients that provide the moisture and oil the skin needs. Also, overexposure to the sun, likened to putting one's body in hot oven, is one of the prime agers of skin and should be avoided.

Cosmetic Surgery

Cosmetic surgery procedures include *rhinoplasty* (nose); *facial plasty* or *rhytidoplasty* (face lift); *blepharoplasty* (upper eyelids and bags under the eyes); breast augmentation and reduction; and as the dermabrasion and other methods mentioned earlier. See "Plastic Surgery" in Ch. 20, *Surgery.*

Baldness

Until recently, medical opinion on the causes of baldness cited three factors—sex, age, and heredity—and maintained that nothing could be done.

Other causes have since been found and include infections, systemic diseases, drugs that have a toxic effect, mechanical stress, friction, and radiation. Diet does not usually affect baldness, but chronic starvation or vitamin deficiencies can contribute to dryness, lack of luster, and hair loss. Also, excessive intake of vitamin A can cause hair loss.

In women, loss of hair is quite common toward the end of pregnancy, after delivery, and during menopause. A hysterectomy, crash dieting, severe emotional stress, high fever, a major illness such as thyroid disease or diabetes, certain allergies, and the use of systemic drugs such as steroids and amphetamines—all can produce hair loss.

There are two common types of baldness in men: male pattern baldness (*alopecia*) and patchy baldness (*alopecia areata*). The latter is more common in women.

Male Baldness

Male pattern baldness may begin as early as the early 20s or 30s. Hair falls out from the crown until a fringe of hair remains at the sides and along the back of the head. At the onset, a bald spot may appear on the crown of the head; balding spots in other areas may merge to form the fringe pattern.

In patchy baldness, hair may fall out suddenly in patches. In this case, hair usually returns after going through three growth periods. The new hair may be thinner than the original hair. Although patchy baldness is self-limiting and often self-curing, therapy is indicated for some patients. The therapy may consist of injections of soluble steroid suspensions directly into the scalp. Regrowth may begin in three to four weeks, but remains localized at the sites of injections.

Hair transplants remain the most dependable way to grow new hair—especially in men with male pattern baldness. The process involves cutting out *punch grafts,* small patches or plugs of hair and follicle-bearing tissue, from the back or sides of the head. The grafts are immediately inserted into recipient incisions that are slightly smaller than the plugs. In a two- or three-hour session a physician can transplant 60 to 80 plugs of hair. Adequate coverage of a balding crown usually requires 200 to 400 plugs.

Female Baldness

The hair on the crown of a woman's head may thin out, but women seldom become bald as men do. Progesterone, administered in careful, dose-regulated treatments, has been used successfully by some dermatologists. The progesterone is applied to the scalp as a cream or ointment.

Drug Treatments

Other forms of therapy have come into experimental use for both men and women. Many of them involve the use of drugs. In one treatment carefully monitored doses of cortisone are injected into the scalp. In another, the drug psoralen may either be applied to the scalp directly or taken internally. A combination of drugs including 8-methoxypsoralen and inosiplex may be used in conjunction with ultraviolet irradiation.

Most acclaimed of all the new drug therapies is minoxidil, a derivative of the blood pressure-reducing drug Loniten. Physicians simply order Loniten reformulated as a topical solution. Thicker than water, the minoxidil has been used generally by prescription as a gel. Visible improvement is never guaranteed, and in most cases results can take from four months to a year.

Minoxidil must be prescribed by a physician and requires medical monitoring about every four months. It must be used indefinitely to maintain new hair growth. Early findings suggest that the drug works best on men who have not been bald for a long time. Some dermatologists believe that patients with minoxidil-generated growths of hair can gradually, over time, switch to low-dose, modified use patterns.

Excess Hair

For some middle-aged women, the problem is too much hair in the wrong place, instead of too little. Excess hair can grow on the face, chest, arms, and legs. In some instances, unwanted hair may be a sign of an endocrine disorder that can be detected by a physician. In other cases, it can be caused by chronic irritation, such as prolonged use of a cast, bandage, or hot-water bottle; it can also be due to excess exposure to the sun, iodine or mercury irritation, or localized rubbing.

Excess hair can be bleached, shaved, tweezed, waxed, or removed by chemical depilatories and electrolysis. Only electrolysis is permanent. See "Hair Removal" in Ch. 21, *Skin and Hair.*

Varicose Veins

Another complaint of middle-aged men and women is *varicose veins.* About half the women over 50 years of age have these enlarged veins with damaged valves in their thighs and calves.

Varicose veins can occur in various parts of the body. They are, however, most common in the legs.

Varicose veins are usually caused by years of downward pressure on the veins, causing the valves to break down. This often happens to people who must stand for many hours at a time. The large, bluish irregularities are plainly visible beneath the skin of the thighs and calves, and they cause a heavy dragging sensation in the legs and a general feeling of tiredness and lack of energy.

Treatment

In most instances, the best treatment involves surgery to tie off the main veins and remove all superficial veins that lend themselves to this procedure (called *stripping*). In other cases, varicose veins can be relieved by wearing elastic stockings or compression bandages.

Varicose veins that remain untreated can cause *varicose ulcers,* which usually form on the inner side of the leg above the ankle. Treatment calls for prolonged bed rest, warm applications, and surgical ligation and stripping of the varicose veins responsible for the ulcers. Thus, it is wise to consult a physician if varicose veins appear.

Menopause

The permanent end of a woman's menstrual cycle is called *menopause.* The duration of time it takes for the body to change over to a non-menstruating hormonal structure varies. It may be as short as a year; some women may experience menopausal signs and occasional periods for up to ten years.

The average age bracket for menopause is between 40 and 50 years of age. However, about 12 percent of women reach menopause between ages 36 and 40; 15 percent between 51 and 55; and 6 percent either earlier than 40 or later than 55. What this basically means is that menopause can normally occur anywhere between 36 and 56 years of age.

The *premenopausal period* is the period of time before frequently irregular menstruation or cessation of menstruation. The body begins to undergo changes that may go unnoticed. Ovulation may be irregular and skip menstrual cycles. The estrogen and progesterone levels may lower.

Signs that accompany the premenopausal period include increasing or lessening menstrual flow, skipped or shortened periods, and occasional irregularly timed menstruation.

The *perimenopausal period* is the onset of noticeable changes. The menstrual cycle may abruptly cease, or become unpredictable and irregular. Hormone levels of estrogen and progesterone continue to decline. Egg production becomes increasingly irregular or ceases entirely. Egg production may or may not correspond to menstrual flow. A woman can continue ovulating without having a period, or may have periods without ovulation.

The most familiar signs of menopause occur during the perimenopausal period. These occurrences should be considered "signs" and not "symptoms" since they do not represent anything going wrong. They are not a sign of illness.

The one sign that everyone is aware of is the "hot flash." Referred to as flashes or flushes, this is a rapid increase in blood vessel dilation at the surface of the skin. The skin temperature can rise between four to eight degrees. The internal body temperature may drop with the increase of the surface temperature. A common hot flash pattern is a sudden feeling of extreme warmth, occasionally accompanied by heavy sweating, and chills following, as the internal body temperature cools. For some women, flashes occur daily; for others they may only occur once every several weeks. Some menopausal women never experience them. Many women experience flashes but are not disturbed by them.

Hot flashes at night, which produce heavy sweating and chills, are sometimes referred to as "night sweats." They may just be nighttime flashes. They can, though, lead to loss of sleep and thereby trigger fatigue, irritability, and insomnia. Problems with sleep should be discussed with your physician.

Dressing for fluctuations in body temperature may help reduce some undesirable side effects. Wear layers of clothing so when you are warm you can take off the top layer. The top layers are available, then, if you get cold later. It is commonly feared by some women that others can tell when one is experiencing a hot flash. This is rarely true; the usual physical response is a slight blush that goes unnoticed by others. Reassurance by friends can help relieve anxiety.

Other signs of menopause that may be problematic or startling when they occur include flooding. This is the sudden onset of a very heavy menstrual flow. It can occur without warning and normal amounts of menstrual protection may not be adequate. As with the hot flashes, this may never happen, or it may happen extremely infrequently, or it may be a recurrent problem. It is, however, usually only a problem in terms of hygiene and embarrassment. Flooding alone is not normally a symptom of an underlying problem. If there is no underlying disease, no surgery or treatment is required for this. If you are distressed by flooding and need reassurance, or *if it is accompanied by pain* please see a physician.

Vaginal changes that occur during menopause can include a thinning of the vaginal wall. This is normally associated with the reduction of estrogen production. The vagina will produce less lubrication and hold less moisture. The signs of this may include perceived dryness, itching, irritation from walking, and pain or discomfort during intercourse. Because the loss of lubrication may be the underlying cause, using douches and feminine hygiene sprays are not recommended. A water-based lubricant, such as K-Y Jelly™, is recommended for discomfort, particularly with intercourse. You should avoid oil-based lubricants, such as Vaseline™, as they are more difficult for the body to absorb and may create problems with infection.

Mood swings are also commonly cited as a sign of menopause. They may accompany the hormonal swings of the early stages of menopause or they may occur later. Many women do not have noticeable mood change at all.

The change of mood may be sudden or may be slow. Depression has been noted by some women, with its passing as the body adapts to the new hormonal levels. Knowing that it is caused by hormonal changes may help some women adjust to temporary shifts in mood. Debilitating or distressing changes should always be discussed with your doctor.

The *post-menopausal period* is the rest of one's life after menopause. The menstrual cycle has ceased entirely. The production of eggs has stopped. The body's production of estrogen and progesterone is very low. The body is back to a stable, predictable physical pattern.

Hysterectomies and Hormonal Supplements

When problems arise with the reproductive organs, or the body's response to the fluctuation in hormone production, there are a few methods of alleviating the problems.

Hysterectomy, the surgical removal of the uterus, and oophorectomy, the surgical removal of the ovaries, are medical procedures done to alleviate major medical problems or remove cancerous tissue. Cancer of the uterus, ovaries, or cervix are frequently treated with removal of the cancerous and surrounding tissue. Hemorrhaging that has not responded to hormonal or other surgical techniques (such as a dilation and curettage—D&C) may be corrected with a hysterectomy.

Other problems that can be alleviated surgically are noncancerous fibroid growths, endometriosis (the uterine tissue invades other tissues), and physical impairment or deterioration of the uterus or ovaries, as is the case with collapse of the uterus through the cervix.

There are several types of hysterectomies, differing in how much of the sexual reproduction system is removed.

A *subtotal hysterectomy* is the removal of the uterus, leaving the cervix, fallopian tubes, and the ovaries in place. A *total hysterectomy* is the removal of the cervix as well as the uterus. *Oophorectomy* and *ovariectomy* are both used to describe the surgical removal of one or both of the ovaries. *Ovariohysterectomy* is the removal of the ovaries, fallopian tubes, and uterus. The quantity of tissue removed will be determined by the patient and the doctor, based on the reasons for the operation. For removal of cancerous tissue, all organs may need to be removed. For sterilization, only a subtotal hysterectomy may be necessary.

Although hysterectomies are common, they are still considered major surgery and should be approached as such, by both the doctor and the patient. Recoveries can take six weeks or longer.

A physician may prescribe estrogen and progesterone supplemental pills to reduce or eliminate some of the adverse physical reactions to menopause. Hormonal treatment may reduce or eliminate hot flashes and vaginal wall thinning and drying. It can reduce heavy menstrual bleeding. However, hormone therapy increases a woman's risk for heart disease and strokes. It is also believed to increase the risk of breast cancer. The risks and benefits should be explained by and discussed with your physician before starting any treatment.

Male Sexuality and Aging

Most men are capable of having intercourse, and fathering children, throughout their lives. Aging can reduce some physical capacity in sexual performance, but the vast majority of men remain sexually capable through old age.

Physical problems that can be encountered, however, involve testicular failure and testicular cancer.

Testicular cancer is relatively rare, affecting less than 2 percent of the adult male population with cancer. Symptom include include a noticeable lump in the the testicle, swelling, and some alteration in the consistency of the affected testicle. The symptoms may also include dull aching from the lower abdomen, groin or scrotum. Men are now recommended to do monthly physical check for lumps, as women are recommended to do self-breast exams. The reason is that testicular cancer, when caught early, has a very high survival rate. If left unchecked until the yearly physical, the cancer has a chance to spread.

Testicular failure is when the body shuts off the functions of the testes. This may be caused by hormonal deficiency and can be cured through hormonal replacement therapy. Since hormonal therapy can lead to prostate problems, it is recommended that a physician closely monitor any medication for testicular failure.

Vasectomy

Vasectomy is the sterilization of the male by cutting the vas deferens, which are the tubes that transport the sperm. The surgery is normally performed in the doctor's office with local anesthesia. Incisions are made either on each side of the scrotum or on the center of the scrotum. The tubes are then cut, and tied or cauterized on each end.

Vasovasotomy is the surgical procedure that attempts to reconnect the vas deferens after a vasectomy. This operation is done for men wishing to reverse the surgical sterilization. Success at this procedure can vary from 30 to 75 percent, depending on the type of initial sterilization procedures, and the skill of the surgeon in reconnection of the tubes.

Drugs, Chemicals, and Alcohol

Most substances consumed in excess cause temporary problems at the least, and permanent damage to your health at the worst. One of the problems with excess is that as you age, you are able to tolerate less. Most people recognize that, as they grow older, they are less able to handle the rigors of exercise and stress. It is not expected, though, that they will tolerate less the effects of cigarettes, alcohol, and chemicals such as caffeine.

There are two basic risks that come from indulgence of these substances. One is from long-term use; the other is from individual instances of overindulgence.

● With the continued use of a substance such as nicotine over a long period of time, the cumulative effects on the body begin to take a toll. The body removes the substance less rapidly from the system. The delicate tissues of the kidneys, liver, lungs, or other vital organs may become damaged or destroyed from processing what the body basically responds to as a poison. The risk is that you will become one of those to suffer the consequences of long-term use. Some of the damage may be reversed if the habit is broken. Other effects may be permanent, risking scarred tissue, destruction of the organ, and, eventually, death.

● Binging in drinking, or taking drugs, always runs the risk of an overdose—forcing major trauma to the body and, perhaps, resulting in death. Binging on cigarettes, food, and caffeine may not result in such an immediate and dramatic response, but the short-term damage can also be substantial to the body. As you age, your body will tolerate such abuses less and less well.

Nicotine

Nicotine is thought to get into the system through the membranes of the mouth and related areas. Thus, a person who holds an unlighted cigar in his mouth may absorb nicotine.

While a little nicotine is not harmful, most steady smokers absorb too much nicotine for their own good. Lung cancer kills over 142,000 persons a year. Lung cancer only has a 13 percent survival rate, for living five years after diagnosis and treatment.

Also, cigarette smoking is believed to be a primary cause of *emphysema* (a disease that decreases efficiency of the lungs) which kills over 15,000 persons a year. Approximately 100,000 cigarette smokers die from heart attacks each year.

In their book *Vigor for Men Over 30,* the authors, Drs. Warren R. Guild, Stuart Cowan, and Samm Baker, suggest these tips on giving up smoking:

- *Try a program of enjoyable physical activity.* They suggest that if the urge to smoke becomes overpowering, the smoker should take a brisk walk, do a set of invigorating exercises at home or in the office, or engage in an enjoyable sport.

- *Don't use antismoking drugs or other nostrums without a physician's advice.* Such devices may do more harm than good. Your physician is the one who can advise you on the best way to cut down on smoking, and he can help you cope with any withdrawal symptoms such as nervousness, dizziness, or insomnia.

- *Don't try to cut down on too many things at the same time.* Concentrate on cutting down on your smoking, and relax about cutting down on diet and drinking, too. One reduction at a time is best.

- *You've got to quit completely.* Like the alcoholic, you've got to say, "This is my *last* cigarette"—and mean it.

- *Quit when there's a major break in your routine.* The recovery from an operation or illness is a good time to stop. After you have established the habit of *not* smoking, make that habit a part of your daily life.

- *Try something different to throw desire off the track.* Take a shower—you can't light a match under water. Also, you can't hold a cigarette if you're playing table tennis or practicing your golf swing.

Caffeine

Laboratory studies show that caffeine appears to work on the central nervous system: fatigue and drowsiness fade while mental activities quicken. But too much caffeine can produce headaches, irritability, and confusion.

Although tea leaves contain almost twice as much caffeine as an equal weight of coffee, smaller amounts of tea are used to make a cup of tea, thus lessening the per-cup intake rate. Cola and chocolate also contain caffeine. Although these drinks are not addictive, abstaining from them is no easy matter, as anyone who has tried to give up coffee drinking can attest.

Ordinarily, drinking a few cups of coffee or other caffeine beverage is not harmful—unless your physician tells you to cut down. But if you find that you need a caffeine beverage to keep going, you might be better off taking a rest instead.

Alcohol

Many physicians feel that a person's capacity to handle liquor diminishes after age 40, and that alcohol intake should be cut down after this age. Also, some people seem to develop an allergic reaction to alcohol—an allergy that can be fatal. One physician described the extra dry martini as "the quick blow to the back of the neck."

Drinking too much and too fast can jar the whole system. It tends to make the drinker nervous and on edge instead of providing calming relief from tensions. The hard-pressed executive is especially vulnerable to the quick, fast drink he takes to provide instant relaxation when he is fatigued.

"The key to the real value of alcohol is intelligent drinking," says Dr. Harry J. Johnson, of the Life Extension Institute. Dr. Johnson says that he sometimes recommends a drink or two before dinner, which he says is the best time to indulge. However, Dr. Johnson suggests a tall, well-diluted highball taken in a peaceful, quiet setting.

How to Avoid Drinking

If you find that drinking is a problem at business luncheons, conventions, and cocktail parties, Dr. Warren R. Guild recommends the following commonsense ways to pass up drinks:

- Say "no thanks" if you do not like the taste or effect of alcohol. Order a juice or nonalcoholic beverage just to have something to sip. Actually, many more jobs and clients have been lost through drinking too much than by not drinking at all.

- Wait for others to order drinks. If someone else refuses a drink, you can decline too. Or, you could say, "I'm not having one but you go ahead." This usually sets the pace for drinking.

- Instead of a powerhouse martini, try vermouth on the rocks, beer, wine, or a well-diluted highball.

- Use dieting as a reason to cut down or out on drinking. You have a good excuse—a drink has 100 or more calories.

- Make arrangements with your favorite restaurant or bar to serve you "your usual." You could make this a nonalcoholic drink.

Remember that alcohol definitely decreases your ability to concentrate, absorb, or produce thoughts or ideas. After drinking you will not be as efficient at writing, drawing, handling objects, or driving. If the level of alcohol in your blood exceeds 0.05 percent—which, depending on weight, is approximately the equivalent of two ounces of hard liquor or two bottles of beer at one session—*you are not a safe driver.*

Treating a Hangover

What if you do drink too much and have a hangover? Is there anything you can do about it? Dr. Harold T. Hyman, formerly of the Columbia University College of Physicians and Surgeons, recommends calling a physician if the case is particularly bad. You should keep in mind that alcohol is toxic, and can be deadly in large quantities. It is not unheard of to have people die of alcohol poisoning, when they have ingested too much alcohol in one evening. Blacking out, passing out, and vomiting are all signs of severe overindulgence and should not be treated lightly.

Less acute sufferers should, on awakening after a binge, take warmed fluids (tea, consommé, clam broth). As soon as your stomach feels in shape, eat warm, soft foods at frequent intervals—poached egg, milk toast, pureed soup, mashed potatoes. Despite your craving for cold, carbonated fluids, avoid them; they may cause stomach cramps.

To prevent a hangover as you drink, Dr. Guild recommends taking *fructose.* Fructose, or *levulose,* is a crystalline sugar, the sweetest of the sugars. It increases the rate at which the body metabolizes and eliminates alcohol. It seems to work best when the alcohol is combined with something naturally high in fructose, as the tomato juice in a Bloody Mary, for example. Or just sip tomato juice between drinks.

Looking for quick panaceas in the medicine cabinet to cure a hangover or any other condition seems to become increasingly popular after age 40. Panaceas are all right up to a point, but indiscriminate self-treatment can do a great deal of harm, because it may mask a more serious illness or may prevent a condition from clearing up if left alone. In drinking, as in eating, the key is moderation.

Proper diet

Proper diet is an important contribution an individual can make to his good health, because foods build body tissues and provide energy for the body to work. Adequate diet planning is not difficult. The basic rules of good nutrition must be learned. See Ch. 27, *Nutrition and Weight Control,* for a full treatment of diet and nutrition.

Applying these rules to a daily diet will take only a few minutes of planning when the menu is decided upon, and will reap enormous rewards in good health and appearance. The hardest part of planning a balanced diet is to avoid selecting food solely on the basis of taste or convenience and ignoring nutritional value.

Vitamins

Eating a proper, balanced diet will fulfill vitamin and other nutritional requirements. Therefore, there is no need for a healthy person who eats nutritious foods to take vitamin pills. Vitamins and other food supplements should be taken only on the advice of a physician or dentist. If a person decides he is deficient in some dietary element and purchases a patent medicine to treat the problem, he may only make it worse. It is rare to find someone deficient in only one element, and by trying to treat himself, he may delay seeking the advice of a physician.

Breakfast

Many Americans neglect breakfast, an important contribution to good diet. Studies prove that men, women, and children need an adequate breakfast. A good breakfast can provide a start in obtaining the day's vitamin and mineral requirements. It is also a help to dieters and those trying to maintain a stable weight, since those who have eaten a good breakfast are able to avoid mid-morning snacks such as sweet rolls, cakes, and the like, which are usually high in carbohydrates and calories.

Weight and Health

Overweight is one of the biggest deterrents to successful middle age, and is also one of the greatest threats to health and longevity. As one physician said, "Consider how few really obese persons you see over 60 years of age." Unfortunately, in middle age most of us maintain the eating habits of our youth while we cut down on our exercise. The result: added weight that acts as a deterrent to our physical well-being.

The overweight person is more likely to develop arthritis, diabetes, heart disease, high blood pressure, kidney trouble, and many other disabling or fatal disorders. As the American Heart Association said recently: "Pity the fat man; the statisticians number his days."

As reported in *Nation's Business,* "If you are overweight by 10 percent, your chances of surviving the next 20 years are 15 percent less than if you had ideal weight; if you are 20 percent overweight, your chances are 25 percent less; if you are 30 percent overweight, 45 percent less." In other words, the odds are against the overweight.

If you do not know what your ideal weight should be, a physician can tell you. To check yourself, try the "pinch" test. Take a pinch of skin on your upper arm just below the shoulder. If more than a half-inch separates your fingers, you are too fat. Try the same test on your stomach when you're standing erect. And, of course, your mirror can reveal the tell-tale signs of middle-age fat—the double chin, sagging belly, flabby arms and legs.

Good Eating Habits

Is there any magic way to reduce? The only sure way is to *eat less,* and to continue this practice all the time. It will not help if you go on a crash diet and then resume your normal eating habits. And while exercise will help control weight and burn up excess calories, probably the best exercise is to push yourself away from the table before you've overeaten.

Calories do count, and usually the caloric intake of a person in the 40- to 55-year age bracket should be about one-third less than that of a person between ages 25 and 40. Again, your physician or a good calorie-counter can help you determine what to eat and how much.

Here are some additional tips from nutritionists to help you lose weight:

- *Cut down on quantity.* Eat just enough to satisfy your appetite— not as much as you can. Even low-calorie foods will add weight if you eat enough of them.

- *Eat less more often.* Spread your food intake over several meals or snacks. Some hospitals have been experimenting with five meals a day, spreading the recommended total food intake over two full meals a day (brunch and dinner) and three snacks (continental breakfast, afternoon snack, and evening). They find that the stomach handles small amounts of food better, that metabolism keeps working at a good pace all day, and that blood sugar levels (your energy reserve) do not drop between meals.

- *Avoid high-calorie foods.* Cut out breads, rolls, jellies, jams, sauces, gravies, dressings, creams, and rich desserts. These are the villains that add calories and are not as rich in nutrients.

- *Look for natural flavors.* Cultivate an interest in the natural flavor of what you eat. Try vegetables without butter, coffee and tea without cream and sugar. You might want to substitute a squeeze of lemon on your vegetables or noncaloric sweeteners in your beverages.

- *Serve only just enough.* Keep portions small and put serving dishes with leftovers out of sight. Taking seconds is often just a habit. Cultivate the idea of just one serving, and you will find it satisfies the appetite. Another idea: serve meals on smaller plates. the portion will look big if only in relationship to the size of the plate.

In order to maintain a healthy body and a youthful appearance while dieting, you must make sure you eat the necessary proteins and nutrients. This can be done by selecting foods from the four basic food groups. See Ch. 27, *Nutrition and Weight Control.*

As a panel of experts on middle age said in a recent interview: "Two factors are vital to successful middle age: physical activity and a variety of interests. Move around but don't rush around. Keep an open mind and a closed refrigerator. Remember that variety is more than the spice of life— it's the wellspring of life. The person who pursues a variety of activities will usually stay fit long after middle age."

Living Life to the Fullest

No wise man ever wished to be younger.   —JONATHAN SWIFT

Staying young is looked on by most of the rest of the world as a peculiarly American obsession. This obsession is certainly fostered and exploited by the advertising industry, but its causes have to be looked for elsewhere.

In many countries, it is the old who are venerated for their wisdom and authority. This point of view is likely to prevail in societies that stay the same or that enjoyed their greatest glories in the past.

America is another matter. Because of its history, it is literally a young country. It is also a nation built on the idea of progress and hope in the future. And to whom does the future belong if not to youth?

Keeping up with change is unfortunately identified by too many people with how they look rather than how they think or feel. To be young in heart and spirit has very little to do with wearing the latest style in clothes—no matter how unbecoming—or learning the latest dances. Maintaining an open mind receptive to new ideas, keeping the capacity for pleasure in the details of daily living, refusing to be overwhelmed by essentially unimportant irritations can make the middle years more joyful for any family.

A Critical Time

Nowadays, the average American can expect to reach the age of 70. Thus, for most people, the middle years begin during the late 30s. Ideally, these are the years of personal fulfillment accompanied by a feeling of pride in accomplishment, a deeper knowledge of one's strengths and limitations, and a growing understanding and tolerance of other people's ideas and behavior.

Emotional Pressures

In many families, however, the pleasures of maturity often go hand in hand with increased pressures. It's no simple matter for the typical husband and wife in their 40s to maintain emotional health while handling worries about money, aging parents, anxiety about willful teenagers, tensions caused by marital friction, and feelings of depression about getting older. To some people, the problems of the middle years are so burdensome that instead of dealing with them realistically—by eliminating some, by compromising in the solution of others—they escape into excessive drinking or into sexual infidelity. It doesn't take much thought to realize that those escapes do nothing except introduce new problems.

Physical Symptoms of Emotional Problems

For others, deep-seated conflicts that come to a head during the middle years may be expressed in chronic physical symptoms. Many physicians in the past intuitively understood the relationship between emotional and physical health, but it is only in recent years that medical science has proved that feelings of tension, anxiety, suppressed anger, and frustration are often the direct cause of ulcers, sexual impotence, high blood pressure, and heart attacks, not to mention sleeplessness and headaches.

Of course, there are no magic formulas that guarantee the achievement of emotional well-being at any time of life. Nor does any sensible person expect to find a perfect solution to any human problem. However, it is possible to come to grips with specific difficulties and deal with them in ways that can reduce stress and safeguard emotional health.

Sexuality during the Middle Years

In spite of the so-called sexual revolution and all its accompanying publicity, it is still very difficult for most people to sort out their attitudes towards sexual activity. It is a subject that continues to be clouded by feelings of guilt and anxiety, surrounded by taboos, and saddled with misinformation. For each individual, the subject is additionally complicated by personal concepts of love and morality.

Many people were shocked when the Kinsey reports on male and female sexual behavior appeared. More recently, militant efforts have been made in various communities to prevent the schools from including sex education in their courses of study. Yet marriage counselors, family physicians, ministers, and all other specialists in human relations can attest to the amount of human misery caused by ignorance about sex—all the way from the ignorance that results in a 15-year-old's unwanted pregnancy to the ignorance of a 50-year-old man about his wife's sexual needs.

Pioneering Work in Sexual Response

According to the research of Dr. William H. Masters and Mrs. Virginia E. Johnson, directors of the Reproductive Biology Research Foundation in St. Louis and authors of *Human Sexual Response* and *Human Sexual In-* *adequacy,* 50 percent of all married couples can be considered sexually inadequate. These authorities define sexual inadequacy as the inability to achieve sexual communication in marriage or insecurity about whatever sexual communication does exist.

In the intensive sexual therapy they offer to married couples professionally referred to the Foundation, Dr. Masters and Mrs. Johnson concentrate on the relationship between husband and wife. They stress the concept of sexual activity as communication between two human beings, each with unique needs and desires that must be fulfilled by the other. The basic attitude they hope to instill in those who come to them for help is that pleasure in sex is natural and can be achieved through an understanding of giving and receiving it.

Emotional Causes of Sexual Inadequacy

It is not unusual for a couple whose marriage began with a satisfactory sexual adjustment to find the relationship deteriorating as they approach their 40s. From the point of view of how the body itself functions during the middle years, there is rarely a physical reason for a decline in the ability to perform sexually. Almost always, male impotence or lack of female responsiveness is caused by psychological factors, some deeply buried, others superficial.

The Impotent Husband

Because of particular circumstances and differing personalities, many middle-aged men spend their days in a state of impotent anger. They may have suppressed feelings of hostility against an unreasonable boss; they may feel put down by a successful neighbor; they may be unable to deal effectively with a rebellious son. With such men, a chain of cause and effect sometimes develops that cannot be broken without professional help.

The tensions generated by impotent anger may result in impotence during the sex act. Because the underlying causes for sexual impotence are probably unknown to him, a middle-aged husband may develop deep anxieties about his waning sexuality. These anxieties in turn cause the sexual incompetence to continue.

There is also the husband who unconsciously builds up resentments against his wife because he thinks she is paying too much attention to the house and the children or to her career and too little to him. Their surface relationship may not be affected, but his body will express his feelings by withholding itself from her as a form of punishment.

Another typical cause of temporary impotence is a feeling of guilt about an adventure in sexual infidelity. Impotence with the marital partner under these circumstances is usually the husband's way of punishing himself for behavior that he considers wrong.

The Unresponsive Wife

Many men complain about their wives' waning interest in sex during the middle years. It is true that women sometimes give or withhold themselves from their husbands as a reward or a punishment, but more commonly, wives who are unresponsive are likely to be expressing resentment about the fact that the only time they get any attention is in bed, and even there, the attention is apt to be perfunctory rather than personally gratifying and meaningful.

When this is the case, the breach in a marriage is likely to widen unless there is a willingness on the part of both partners to confront the problem openly, if necessary with a marriage counselor, minister, or physician, so that a satisfactory solution can be found. Otherwise, the wife's resent-ment of neglect expressed in sexual coldness may lead her husband to look elsewhere for gratification.

Sometimes a woman seems unresponsive only because she feels she is being used as a sex object instead of having her needs satisfied. This unconscious feeling may express itself in the lack of responsiveness that is mistakenly called frigidity. As a result of their experience in helping many couples achieve good sexual relationships, Dr. Masters and Mrs. Johnson assert that the word *frigidity* has little meaning. There are very few women incapable of being physically aroused and satisfied by an understanding sexual partner.

Being Honest

In most cases of sexual inadequacy, insight and honesty about feelings are usually a more effective treatment than hormones, sex manuals, and so-called aphrodisiacs.

Any married couple whose sexual problems have become acute during the middle years should look for the causes in their own emotions about themselves and each other. They should also examine any persistent feelings of tension and anxiety that might be the result of practical matters in their daily lives, such as worry about money or children.

New Treatments

Where other approaches fail, the impotent male can either undergo a test for erectability or try one of the new treatments currently available. Conducted during sleep, the tests provide evidence indicating that impotence in any given case has physical or psychological causes. Physical causes may include such diseases as diabetes; some drugs or medication, including those used to treat high blood pressure; and alcohol abuse, hardening of the arteries, or testosterone or thyroid hormone deficiencies.

These tests have shown that physical causes underlie impotence in nearly half of all cases. As a result much research has been conducted into physical "cures." All of the tests operate on the accepted medical principle that "normal" men have approximately five erections during every sleep period. In what is called the *stamp test,* a strip of stamps is wrapped around the penis before the subject retires for the night. Fitted snugly around the shaft of the penis, the strip tears along one of the perforated edges if the subject experiences an erection while sleeping.

Two other tests are more reliable. In one, a *snap gauge band* made of elastic fabric and Velcro is wrapped around the penis; the band has three snaps designed to open at various stages of penile rigidity. A third test utilizes a *Nocturnal Penile Tumescence Monitor* to tell exactly when erections occur, with what rigidity, and for how long. Two circular elastic silicone bands are attached to the penis; sensor wires connect the bands to an apparatus like an electrocardiograph machine.

Of the prosthetic devices used to "cure" impotence, three can be implanted in the penis in operations that take one to three hours under local anesthetic. The simplest utilizes two semirigid rods that keep the penis permanently erect. A second implanted type, made of flexible, plastic-covered metal wire, also maintains the penis in a constantly erect state but can be bent into an erect or downward position. A third type works hydraulically to pump the penis into a naturally erect state. Two expandable metal tubes implanted in the penis function with an attached tiny pump in the scrotum and a water reservoir placed behind the muscles of the lower abdomen. Pressure on the pump causes the penis to erect; valves make possible penile relaxation.

Beyond Motherhood: New Goals

There are many women casting about to find ways of spending their newly found spare time, women who are bored by bridge and gossip, who enjoy being a wife and mother and grandmother but also want an outlet that is their very own, disengaged from their role in the family. Such women might do some thinking about unfulfilled aspirations and the interests of their younger years, abandoned because of practical pressures.

Each one must find a way of spending leisure time in a way that is personally meaningful. Never mind that the children think it's funny for their mother to be going back to school for a college degree; or that the husband doesn't understand why his wife isn't taking it easy instead of taking a part-time job in a department store; or that the neighbors make remarks about the easel and paints that have suddenly appeared on the back porch.

Returning to Work or School

More middle-aged, middle-class women are taking jobs after years of

housekeeping than ever before. Many companies are eager to hire them—

on a part-time basis if necessary—because they are usually serious, competent, and reliable. Colleges make special provisions for women who want to complete their education after a long absence from studies. Even in small towns, there are many fruitful avenues for earning money or engaging in a productive hobby.

A feeling of pride in accomplishment at a time when household chores and child-raising no longer require much daily attention is usually the best medicine for depressed spirits. Personally meaningful activities outside the home are also an excellent way to keep in touch with what's happening in the world. Nowadays there is no reason for a woman in her 40s or 50s to feel restless, bored, or useless. The opportunities for self-expression and personal fulfillment are sufficiently varied to satisfy anyone's individual needs. All it takes is the genuine desire to find them.

More Than a Breadwinner: Vocation and Avocation

Everybody knows that it takes money to maintain a household and raise a family, and there is no doubt that during the middle years financial pressures reach their highest point, what with sending children through school, helping to support aging parents, and meeting increased medical and dental expenses. At this time, even those men who truly enjoy their work often feel they scarcely have the time or peace of mind to enjoy anything else.

Need for Other Outlets

Just as most women need personal outlets for their individuality away from home and family, so most men can achieve better emotional health if they find avenues of self-expression unrelated to their job or their role as husband and father. This does not mean becoming so passionately involved in playing golf or going fishing that the family is constantly neglected. Nor does it mean spending excessive amounts of money on rare stamps at the expense of the family budget.

On the other hand, if a man chooses a hobby that doesn't include the family, such as singing in a choir or studying a foreign language, rather than choosing one that does—such as going on camping trips or taking pictures—there is no reason for the rest of the household to be resentful. Togetherness is a good thing to strive for, but it isn't a hard and fast principle to be applied to all activities.

It's healthier for a man to take an occasional fishing trip with his cronies, enjoy every minute of it, and come home relaxed and refreshed, than to take along a wife who will be bored and children who will be restless. In such far-too-frequent cases, no one has a good time. Nor should a father insist on teaching his son how to play chess so that they can share a hobby when his son would rather spend his time otherwise.

A Satisfying Hobby

The choice of a satisfying leisure-time activity is an entirely individual matter. Some men prefer a hobby that is sedentary, such as model-building. Others who have to sit in an office all day find the vigorous play of the handball court physically and emotionally exhilarating.

Some men, oppressed by constant association with other people, enjoy solitary hobbies such as long nature walks; others, whose jobs involve working alone, like to get together with a group for bowling or bridge playing. There are those who like competitive hobbies and those who want to escape the competitiveness of their work by puttering around in the basement or studying the fine points of the Civil War or experimenting in haute cuisine.

Many men as well as women find the idea of community service appealing as a productive way of using free time. The opportunities are endless: going into poorer neighborhoods and training athletic teams; starting a tutoring group as part of a church activity; getting involved in grass-roots politics and pressing for local reforms; organizing a block association for property maintenance and improvement.

Building a collection can be a gratifying hobby, and the collection need not involve much money. The pleasures usually come from finding a rare specimen—whether it's a matchbook cover or an old comic book—from satisfying a need to own something unique, and from learning in the process of looking for items of interest.

Flexing Mental Muscles

Healthy human beings, regardless of age, need a certain amount of intellectual stimulation to keep their spirits refreshed. The arteries of the body may harden slowly with age, but there are people whose minds remain young and limber in spite of their increasing years.

Housewives commonly complain that they do not get enough stimulation from their daily chores. Men talk about getting into a rut on their jobs—going stale. Yet stimulation for the mind is no farther away than the nearest library, if the mind is hungry for food for thought. There's plenty of mental exercise available for those in the middle years who are willing to review their old ideas and to examine some new ones.

Family Discussions

Having relaxed discussions with teenage children can be a fine source of intellectual refreshment if both generations can listen to each other with tolerance and mutual respect. Some parents get huffy and defensive if their views are challenged. This defensiveness—in some cases, downright hostility—results in closing the channels of communication.

This is not to suggest that every idea espoused by the young should be adopted by their elders. But opinions can be exchanged and challenges involving facts and figures can be met in the spirit of civilized discussion. There are areas in which parents can be educated by their children, and the areas can range all the way from trying out new recipes suggested by a venturesome daughter to getting a book on drugs from the library in order to answer a son who cheerfully calls his father a drug addict because he has to have three drinks when he comes home from work.

Community Resources

Some families find they need go no farther than their own home for intellectual activity. For those who want broader opportunities to use their heads, there are community resources that can be explored. Church organizations, parent-teacher associations, or social clubs can be used as forums. These might include public discussions, film presentations, and meetings on problems of current interest, such as drug addiction and slum clearance.

For those looking for enlightenment of a specific kind, the facilities of schools in the area should be investigated. Many colleges and universities offer adult education programs that cover a wide range of subjects—from real estate evaluation to philosophy. It's also possible to set up a study group composed of friends and associates who want to find out more about American history or the history of art, to study anthropology or the behavior of social insects, and to hire a lecturer to meet with the group once or twice a week.

Travel

Travel is a wonderful way of broadening interests, even if the trip means going to a nearby city or dairy farm. When children are in their later teens and can safely be left on their own for a few days—with some neighborly supervision—a husband and wife can enjoy going places of special interest to them rather than having to take younger tastes into account.

The destination needn't be another continent to provide fascinating new sights and information. People who live in Chicago will find the small seacoast villages of New England a totally new world; Bostonians will find a way of life strange to them if they drive through the Smoky Mountains; people who live in a small town or a farm can get a big lift out of wandering about in a big city.

In traveling abroad, the more advance planning that is invested in the trip, the greater the rewards. Every effort should be made to learn at least a little of the language of the country to be visited, and instead of settling for a group tour in which each moment is planned, there's much pleasure to be gained from exploring a particular enthusiasm, whether it be food, architecture, history, or a return to the village of one's foreign-born ancestors.

Separation and Divorce

Marriage in this country is based on the highly personal concept of love rather than on such traditional foundations as a property merger between two families or an arrangement determined by the friendship of the young people's parents. It is often assumed, therefore, that if mutual love is the basis for embarking on a marriage, its absence is a valid reason for dissolving it, either by legal separation or divorce.

The idea of divorce is not particularly modern; in practically every time and place where a form of marriage has existed, so has some form of divorce, with reasons ranging from excessive wife-beating to failure to deliver a piece of land mentioned in the marriage contract.

The High Rate of Divorce

What is new is the high rate of divorce. Figures now indicate that in the United States as a whole, approximately one in every four marriages is terminated by legal arrangement. However, these figures by no means indicate that the family as an institution is on the way out, because a constantly increasing number of people who get divorced get married again.

There are many reasons for the growing rate of separation and divorce:

- Over the last 50 years, a continually increasing percentage of the population has been getting married.

- Although the trend toward earlier marriages has leveled off in recent years, a significant number of people still marry at earlier ages than was common in the past. (The number of divorces is highest among the poorly educated group who marry under the age of 21.)

- The legal requirements for separation and divorce are less rigid than formerly.

- With increasing independence and earning capacity, women are less frightened of the prospect of heading a family.

- The poorer groups in the population, in which desertion was a common practice, are more often obtaining divorces.

Contrary to popular belief, there are more divorces among the poor than among the rich, and more among the less well-educated than among the educated. Also, most divorces occur before the fifth year of marriage.

Telling the Truth to Children

Most people with children who are contemplating a breakup of their marriage generally make every effort to seek professional guidance that might help them iron out their differences. When these efforts fail and steps are taken to arrange for a separation or divorce, it is far healthier for parents to be honest with each other and with their children than to construct elaborate explanations based on lies.

A teenager who is given the real reason for a divorce is less likely to have something to brood about than one who is told lies that he can see through. If the real reason for a divorce is that the parents have tried their best to get along with each other but find it impossible, the child who is in his teens or older can certainly understand this. If the marriage is coming to an end because the husband or wife wants to marry someone else, the explanation to the child should avoid assigning blame. When the rejected parent tries to enlist the child's sympathy by blackening the character of the parent who is supposedly the cause of the divorce, results are almost always unpleasant. Under no circumstances and no matter what his age should a child be called on to take the side of either parent or to act as a judge.

Nor should children be told any more about the circumstances of the breakup of a marriage than they really want to know. Young people have a healthy way of protecting themselves from information they would find hurtful, and if they ask few questions, they need be told only the facts they are prepared to cope with. Of course, as they grow older and live through their own problems, they will form their own view of what really happened between their parents.

After the Separation

Traditionally, in separation and divorce proceedings, the children have remained in the custody of the mother, with financial support arrangements and visiting rights spelled out for the father. Although an increasing number of fathers have been awarded custody of their children in recent years, it is still commonly the mother who must face the problems of single parenthood after divorce. Although teenage children may need some extra attention for a while, there is no need for a mother to make a martyr of herself, nor should she feel guilty when she begins to consider remarrying.

The father should be completely reliable in his visiting arrangements, and if he has remarried, should try to establish good relationships between the offspring of his former marriage and his new family.

Stepchildren

People who remarry during the middle years frequently find themselves in the role of stepparent. This is a role with many problems and many rewards; the chief requirements are patience and tact.

The stepchild has to deal with many complicated feelings: his sense of loss, either through death or divorce, of his own parent; his resentment against the parent who has remarried, and his hostility to the stranger who has become his new parent.

A stepparent should proceed affectionately but cautiously, and should not try to be accepted by the child as a replacement for the parent who has gone. If the child and stepparent have achieved a friendly rapport before the remarriage, they should build on the friendship rather than trying to transform it into a parent–child relationship immediately. When the child's trust has been gained, the stepparent can gradually assume some of the authority of a true parent, always waiting for the child to indicate a desire and need for it first.

A Death in the Family

When a husband or wife dies during the middle years, there is a general feeling that the death is unnatural because it is in all ways premature: the normal life expectancy has been cut short, the one who remains is prematurely bereaved, and the children are deprived of a parent too soon.

There are a few consolations in the presence of death: some people are sustained by their religious beliefs, others by the rallying of relatives and friends, and still others by happy memories of the years spent together in a fulfilled relationship.

The bereft parent should share his grief with the children, but they should not be thought unfeeling if they seem to be going about their business almost in the usual way. They may be dealing with a tangle of feelings that will take some time to come to the surface—feelings of guilt about past thoughtlessness, of confusion about wishing that the parent who remains had died instead, and of fear connected with the thought of their own death.

When the time seems right, young people can be encouraged to talk about the parent who died. Remembering funny incidents and times of anger, reliving shared experiences—these can act as a restorative to the living and make family ties closer.

As for remarrying, although the children and the deceased's relatives may consider such a step a disloyalty to the memory of the dead, it is actually a tribute, because it implies that the state of marriage was a happy one.

The Single Parent

When the job of being a single parent has to be faced, either because of death or divorce, the problems may seem overwhelming. Although they differ considerably depending on whether the parent is the father or mother, they are nonetheless difficult to sort out, particularly at a time when morale may be at a low ebb.

The Single Father

The single father with growing children often feels helpless in dealing with household tasks and gains some insight into the number of tasks involved in keeping things running smoothly at home. If he has a teen-age daughter or son, he can depend on him or her to do part of the job, but young people should not be burdened with all the responsibilities of housekeeping if some other arrangement can possibly be made. Perhaps a relative can be called on to help out part-time, or a professional house-keeper can be engaged for a few hours a day. Outside help is particularly important if the care of younger children is involved.

A motherless girl in adolescence may seek out the companionship and occasional guidance of an older woman who was a friend of her mother's, or she may spend more and more time at the home of a friend whose mother she likes and respects. Such a transfer of affection should not be considered as disloyalty.

The Single Mother

The mother who is a single parent usually has to cope with problems of earning and managing money. Fortunately, the job opportunities for middle-aged women are varied, and if the family finances can be worked out on the basis of a part-time job, this is a good transitional solution for making the adjustment of handling a job and running the household. A widow or divorcee may need to call on a friend or relative to help her with such practical matters as income tax, mortgages, loans, or investments. If these matters can be handled by a family lawyer without the fees being prohibitive, so much the better.

A widow or divorced woman should avoid concentrating too much on her children, nor should she give a son in his teens the understanding that he is now the head of the family. He is and must remain her son and nothing more. If an authority figure is needed as partial replacement for the departed husband, he should be sought among neighbors or relatives for whom the children feel respect.

In many communities, single parents have formed groups for discussion and mutual help. Such groups can usually be located through local social work agencies. Parents Without Partners, 7910 Woodmont Ave., Ste. 1000, Bethesda, MD 20814, specializes in the problems of single parents and publishes literature of interest to them.

6

The Later Years

Aging and What To Do About It

Growing older could mean growing healthier. In many ways you are as old as you think and feel. Consider these points:

- No disease results just from the passage of years.

- We age piecemeal—each organ separately rather than uniformly.

- In retirement you have less daily stress and strain, and you have more time to take care of yourself.

What, then, makes a person think and feel old?

The Aging Process

Physically, we mature at about 25 to 30, when the body reaches maximum size and strength. Then, body tissues and cells are constantly being rebuilt and renewed. Nutrition, rest, exercise, and stress influence the length of time that the body can maintain a balance between the wearing down and rebuilding of body tissues. When more cells die than can be reproduced, they are replaced by a fibrous, inert substance called *colagen*. The living process slows down to compensate, and we begin aging; strength and ability start to decline.

But this happens at various intervals. For instance, vision is sharpest at age 25; the eye loses its ability to make rapid adjustments in focus after age 40. Hearing is sharpest at about age 10, then diminishes as you grow older. Sensitivity to taste and smell lessens after age 60.

The decline in strength and muscle ability is long and gradual; there are even gratifying plateaus. At age 50, a man still has about four-fifths of the muscle strength he had when he was 25.

Although physical abilities may decline, mental abilities may actually improve during the middle years, and memory and the ability to learn can remain keen. Dr. Alfred Schwartz, dean of education at Drake University, was asked: "Can a 70-year-old man in reasonably good health learn as rapidly as a 17- year-old boy?" Dr. Schwartz answered:

> Indeed he can—provided he's in the habit of learning. The fact that some older people today are not active intellectually is no reflection on their ability to learn. There is ample proof that learning ability does not automatically decline with age.

Regardless of what you may have heard, organic brain damage affects less than one percent of those over age 65.

But in thinking about physical change, remember that this is just one aspect of aging. Age is determined by emotional and intellectual maturity as well as by chronological years.

Can a person do anything to retard aging?

Most *gerontologists* feel that the reason more people don't live longer is that they are not willing to follow a regimen of diet, exercise, rest, recreation—coupled with the exclusion of various excesses. And while there isn't anything you can do to set back the clock, you can keep in good health by making sure to have regular physical examinations, sufficient exercise, adequate rest, nutritious food, and a positive mental attitude.

A Positive Mental Attitude

Mark Twain once said: "Whatever a man's age he can reduce it several years by putting a bright-colored flower in his buttonhole." A lively, fresh outlook is essential for enjoyable living at any age. Most physicians believe there is a direct connection between one's state of mind and physical health. This is especially true when you are faced with the challenges of retirement. Plato said: "He who is of a calm and happy nature will hardly feel the pressure of age, but to him who is of an opposite disposition, youth and age are equally a burden."

Experts in the field of aging have found that most older people can relieve transitory depression by a deliberate shift of thought or by physical activity. If you look upon retirement as an opportunity to take better care of yourself and to pursue old and new interests, you'll go a long way toward better health.

The Annual Checkup

For peace of mind and to maintain and improve your health, make it a habit to see your physician at least once a year. To remind themselves, many people make an appointment on their birthday. An annual checkup is especially important in later years and should not be put off or neglected.

During a routine checkup, the physician pays special attention to enlarged lymph nodes of the neck, armpits, and groin, and the front of the neck. He also checks the condition of veins and arteries and looks at your knees and arches—which are of particular importance to older people.

He makes tests for arteriosclerosis, high blood pressure, diabetes, brain tumors, and other diseases. He can feel and tap your body to check your lungs, liver, and spleen, and he can take electrocardiographs to detect changes in your heart. Simple tests can note bladder and kidney conditions.

In addition, the physician usually asks about personal habits—smoking, drinking, eating. He also wants to know about any unusual symptoms you might have. Be completely frank with your physician, answer his questions as directly as possible, and give all information that might be helpful.

When explaining the nature of your ailment or symptom, tell him what part of the body is involved, what changes are associated with the symptoms, and whether symptoms occurred after a change of diet or medicine. Tell him about any previous experiences with this condition and what treatments you might have had.

It is extremely important to tell your physician about any pills you are taking—including aspirin, tranquilizers, and sleeping tablets. Even the most common drug can affect the potency of medication he might prescribe.

After he has taken your case history and after he has all the reports from your tests, the physician will want to talk with you, explain his findings, and perhaps make some recommendations. Take his advice; don't try to be your own physician.

If you have questions, don't be afraid to ask them. Have him explain the nature of your ailment, how long it may take for relief or cure, how the therapy or medication is expected to work, and the possible impact on your everyday activities.

Hopefully, by following his advice you'll stay healthy and well. However, if you are at home and feel ill, call your physician if:

- Your symptoms are so severe you can't endure them.

- Apparent minor symptoms persist without explainable cause.

- You are in doubt.

For more information, see "The Physical Examination" in Ch. 26, *Physicians and Diagnostic Procedures.*

Oral Health

It is especially important in later years to have regular dental checkups. After age 50, over half of the American people have some form of *periodontal disease*, and at age 65 nearly all persons have this disease.

Brushing teeth and gums regularly is a defense against periodontal disease. Use dental floss to remove all food particles and plaque from areas between the teeth, especially after each meal. See "Periodontal Disease" in Ch. 22, *The Teeth and Gums*, for more information on this subject.

Dentures

If you do lose some teeth, they should be replaced with bridges or partial or full dentures, because the cheeks and lips will otherwise sag and wrinkle and make you look older than you really are. Chewing ability and the clarity of speech are also impaired if missing teeth are not replaced. See "Dentures" in Ch. 22, *The Teeth and Gums*.

Diet and Health

Just what are your food requirements as you grow older? Basically you need the same essential nutrients that you have always needed, except that you face special problems. You need to:

- Select food more carefully to eat adequate proteins, vitamins, and minerals—while cutting down on calories.

- Get the most nutritious food for the least money and make the most of what you buy.

- Avoid bad eating habits—make mealtime a pleasure rather than a chore.

- Learn new techniques to stretch meals, use leftovers, and substitute lower-priced items with the same nutritional value for higher-priced foods. In other words, learn how to shop well.

Basic Requirements

How can you get the essential nutrients every day? A good rule is first to eat recommended servings from the Basic Four Food Groups (see below) established by the National Research Council. Then, eat other foods that you like, as long as they do not go over the recommended daily caloric intake. The average man in the 55-to-75-year age group should consume 2,200 calories a day; the average woman in the same age group, 1,600 calories a day. This is a drop of between 500 and 600 calories a day from what was needed at age 25. As you grow older, your physical activity decreases and your metabolism slows, causing body fats to build up at a much higher rate and making you more prone to hardening of the arteries and certain heart conditions.

Here are the Basic Four Food Groups:

Meat Group

Two or more servings from this group of foods are recommended daily. A serving is two to three ounces of cooked meat, fish, or poultry; two eggs; occasionally one cup of cooked dry beans or peas; one-half cup peanut butter; or one cup cottage cheese.

Dairy Foods

Dairy food requirements may be satisfied by two cups of milk or its equivalent in cheese, ice cream, etc. A one and one-third ounce slice of cheddar-type cheese or one scant pint of ice cream is equivalent to one cup of milk. Imitation ice cream or ice milk where vegetable fat has been substituted for butterfat has just as much protein.

Vegetables and Fruit

The daily vegetable and fruit requirement consists of four or more servings. A serving is one-half cup. Include one serving of citrus fruit each day and dark green or deep yellow vegetables every other day.

Bread and Cereal Group

Each day have four or more servings of whole grain, enriched, or restored products such as breads, cereals, rice, hominy grits, noodles, or macaroni. One serving is a slice of bread; one-half to three-fourths cup cooked cereal, pasta, or rice; one medium potato.

Use other foods such as sweets, baked goods, or desserts to complete meals and treat the sweet tooth. But remember to count calories. Nutritionists have found that skinny animals live longer than fat ones, and this seems to be true of people, too.

Beware of food fads and so-called health foods unless these are recommended by your physician. Also, do not buy vitamins and mineral tablets unless prescribed. When you obtain vitamins from food, your body uses the amount necessary to maintain proper health, appetite, and resistance to infection. Your body promptly eliminates excesses of vitamin C and the B complex, and stores an excess of vitamins A and D in your liver and other body organs. It may take up to seven years of practically complete deprivation for a previously healthy adult to show signs of a vitamin deficiency.

Some older people may go on low-fat diets because of fear of cholesterol caused by talk and advertisements for unsaturated fats. Get a physician's recommendation before curtailing your fat intake—too little fat and dairy products can be as harmful as too much.

Also, unless prescribed, do not take iron tonics or pills. Usually you'll get adequate iron intake if you eat meat, eggs, vegetables, and enriched cereals regularly. Adding more iron to a normal diet may even be harmful.

Eating Habits

If you find that mealtime is a chore rather than a pleasure, try these tips to enhance your meals:

- Try a two-meal-a-day schedule. Have a late breakfast and early dinner when you are really hungry. But be sure to get your Basic Four requirements in these two meals.

- Drink a glass of water as soon as you wake up to promote good digestion, weight control, and bowel movements.

- Try a walk or light exercise to stimulate appetite and to regulate body processes. Moderate exercise also will help regulate weight because it burns up calories.

- You might sip glass of wine before dinner. Recent research shows wine is very useful to older people in improving appetite and digestion. Port, a light sherry, and vermouth with a dash of soda are good appetite stimulators.

- Make meals interesting by including some food of distinctive flavor to contrast with a mild-flavored food; something crisp for contrast with softer foods, even if it is only a pickle or a lettuce leaf; some brightly colored food for eye appeal.

- Pep up your food with a judicious use of herbs and spices or flavor-enhancers like wine, bottled sauces, fruit juices, and peels.

- If some food causes you distress, eliminate it and substitute something else of equal nutritive value. Green salad may include too much roughage for the intestinal tract; ham or bacon may be supplying your body with too much salt, which increases water retention. Or you may be drinking too much coffee, tea, or soft drinks.

- Be realistic about your chewing ability. Food swallowed whole may be causing digestive problems. If your teeth are not as good as they were or if you are wearing dentures, try cubing, chopping, or grinding foods that are difficult to chew. Let your knife or meat grinder do part of the work.

- Try a different atmosphere or different setting for your meals. Use candlelight, music, and your best linen on occasion. Move outdoors when the weather is good; eat your lunch in the park and dinner on the patio.

- Occasionally invite a friend or relative to dine with you. It's surprising what stimulating conversation and an exchange of ideas can do to boost your mood and appetite.

- Try a new recipe or a new food. Thanks to modern transportation, foods are available in larger cities from many areas and other countries. Eat eggplant or okra, avocado or artichoke, gooseberry jam, or garbanzo beans in a salad. And why not have a papaya with lemon juice for breakfast?

Cooking Hints

Try these ideas for preparing food more easily; they are especially useful if you have only a single gas or electric burner:

- Combine your vegetables and meat—or some other protein food—in a single pot or pan. You can cook many hot, nourishing meals of this kind: Irish stew, braised liver or pot roast with vegetables, ham-and-vegetable chowder or fish chowder, a New England boiled dinner.

- Combine leftovers to make a one-dish meal. Leftover meat combines beautifully with vegetables, macaroni, or rice. Add a cheese or tomato sauce or a simple white sauce and heat in a baking dish. Chopped tomatoes or green onions or chives will give extra flavor and color to the dish.

- Round out one-dish meals with a crisp salad topped with cut strips of leftover cooked meat or poultry or another raw food, bread, a beverage, and perhaps a dessert.

- Mix leftover cooked vegetables with raw fresh ones, such as chopped celery, cucumber slices, tomatoes, green pepper, shredded cabbage, to make an interesting salad.

- Cream vegetables, meat, fish, or chicken. Or serve them with a tasty sauce. Use canned tomato or mushroom soup for a quick and easy sauce. If the dish is a bit skimpy, a hard-boiled egg may stretch it to serving size.

- Add a bit of relish, snappy cheese, or diced cucumber to a cooked dressing for meat or vegetable salad.

- If you cook a potato, an ear of corn, or some other vegetable in the bottom of a double boiler, you can use the top to warm rolls, heat leftover meat in gravy, or heat such foods as creamed eggs or fish.

The Value of Exercise

As you grow older, exercise can help you look, feel, and work better. Various organs and systems of the body, particularly the digestive process, are stimulated through activity, and, as a result, work more effectively.

You can improve your posture through exercise that tones supporting muscles. This not only improves appearance but can decrease the frequency of lower-back pain and disability.

Here are some other benefits of exercise: it can increase your ability to relax and tolerate fatigue; it improves muscle tone; reduces fat deposits; increases working capacity of the lungs; improves kidney and liver functions; increases volume of blood, hemoglobin, and red blood cells, leading to improved utilization of oxygen and iron.

Also, physically active people are less likely to experience a heart attack or other forms of cardiovascular disease than sedentary people. Moreover, an active person who does suffer a coronary attack will probably have a less severe form. The Public Health Service studied 5,000 adults in Framingham, Mass., for more than a decade. When any member of the group suffered a heart attack, his physical activity was reviewed. It was found that more inactive people suffered more fatal heart attacks than active members.

Walking for Exercise

Exercise need not be something you *must* do but rather something you *enjoy* doing. One of the most practical and enjoyable exercises is walking. Charles Dickens said:

> Walk and be happy, walk and be healthy. The best of all ways to lengthen our days is to walk, steadily and with a purpose. The wandering man knows of certain ancients, far gone in years, who have staved off infirmities and dissolution by earnest walking—hale fellows close upon eighty and ninety, but brisk as boys.

The benefits of walking were revealed in a recent Health Insurance Plan study of 110,000 people in New York City. Those who had heart attacks were divided into two groups—walkers and nonwalkers. The first four weeks of illness were reviewed for both groups. At the end of the time 41 percent of the nonwalkers were dead, while only 23 percent of the walkers were. When all physical activity was considered, 57 percent of the inactive had died compared to only 16 percent of those who had some form of exercise.

Walking is as natural to the human body as breathing. It is a muscular symphony; all the foot, leg, and hip muscles and much of the back musculature are involved. The abdominal muscles tend to contract and support their share of the weight, and the diaphragm and rib muscles increase their action. There is automatic action of the arm and shoulder muscles; the shoulder and neck muscles get play as the head is held erect; the eye muscles are exercised as you look about you.

Other Types of Exercise

Swimming and bicycling exercise most of the muscles, and gardening is highly recommended. The fresh air is beneficial, the bending, squatting, and countless other movements exercise most parts of the body.

Surprisingly, most games do not provide good exercise. According to a physical fitness research laboratory at the University of Illinois, the trouble with most games is that the action is intermittent—starting and stopping—a burst of energy and then a wait. The bowler swings a ball for two and one-half seconds and gets about one minute of actual muscular work per game. Golf is a succession of pause, swing, walk—or, more often, a ride to the next pause, swing, and so on. Also, you spend a lot of time standing and waiting for the party ahead and for your partners. Tennis gives one more exercise but it too involves a great deal of starting and stopping, as does handball. No game has the essential, tension-releasing pattern of continuous, vigorous, rhythmic motion found in such activities as walking, running, or jogging.

For formal exercises, you could join a gym, but you might find your enthusiasm waning after a few weeks. You could also exercise at home; there are many excellent books on exercise that provide programs for you to follow at home on a daily basis.

But everyone's exercise capacity varies. It is best to discuss any new exercise program with your physician, especially if you have some ill-ness or are out of practice. Then select an exercise which is pleasant for you and suitable to your condition.

It is most important always to warm up before any strenuous exercise. The U.S. Administration on Aging's booklet, *The Fitness Challenge in the Later Years*, states:

> The enthusiast who tackles a keep-fit program too fast and too strenuously soon gives up in discomfort, if not in injury. A warm-up period should be performed by starting lightly with a continuous rhythmical activity such as walking and gradually increasing the intensity until your pulse rate, breathing, and body temperature are elevated. It's also desirable to do some easy stretching, pulling, and rotating exercises during the warm-up period.

The booklet outlines an excellent program—*red* (easiest), *white* (next), and *blue* (the most sustained and difficult). Each program is "designed to give a balanced workout utilizing all major muscle groups."

A Word of Caution

You may be exercising too strenuously if the following happens:

- Your heart does not stop pounding within 10 minutes after the exercise.

- You cannot catch your breath 10 minutes after the exercise.

- You are shaky for more than 30 minutes afterwards.

- You can't sleep well afterwards.

- Your fatigue (not muscle soreness) continues into the next day.

Sensible, moderate exercise geared to your own physical capacity can help to give you a sense of all-around well-being. As Dr. Ernest Simonson, associate professor of physiological hygiene at the University of Minnesota Medical School, has said:

> Those who exercise regularly never fail to mention that it makes them feel better in every way. It's common logic if one feels better, his attitude towards others will be more congenial. When one is in a cordial, happy frame of mind, he will likely make wiser decisions, and his world in general will look better.

Weight Control

Importantly, both diet and exercise affect the individual's ability to control his weight (see Ch. 27, *Nutrition and Weight Control*; "Weight Problems" in Ch. 23, *Aches, Pains, Nuisances, Worries*; and Ch. 37, *Physical Fitness*). Healthy habits in both areas provide a complete answer for many older persons. For others, some additional effort is required.

The same diet rules that help the older person feel well and function adequately will make weight control simpler. But persons beyond middle age who have weight problems should make extra efforts to bring their weight down. Extra pounds of fat only make it harder for the vital organs to function; excess poundage also forces the heart to work harder. A variety of diets may be used to bring your weight back to where it should be. But the calorie-counter program may suffice for most persons.

Exercise provides the second key to weight control. Many physicians feel that older persons of both sexes should walk at least a mile daily. Other exercises acclaimed by physicians include golf, gardening, working on or around the house, and similar activities. Some other basic rules regarding exercise and diet should be noted:

- Avoid junk, or high carbohydrate, food where possible.
- Make certain you are eating foods that provide enough protein.
- Eat to assuage hunger, not to drive away boredom.
- Remember that appetite usually decreases with age, and act accordingly.
- Avoid vitamins unless they are prescribed by your physician, and use them accordingly.
- Try every day to eat foods in the four basic groups.
- Keep moving; walk daily—to the store, post office, church, around the block.
- If you exercise already, do it regularly; a little exercise daily is better than a lot on weekends.
- If you don't exercise but are thinking of starting a program of workouts of some kind, start slowly and build up—following your physician's recommendations.
- If stress gives you problems, find ways to relax without eating or drinking; consider light exercises, yoga, meditation, breathing exercises, or some other method.

Skin Problems

As a person grows older, his skin begins to wrinkle; oil and sweat glands slow down, causing the skin to become dry. Also, the skin may lack the elasticity and tone of normal skin, and this might cause changes in facial contours.

However, the skin, like other parts of the body, tends to age according to various factors. Among prime agers of the skin are exposure to sunlight and weather; the sailor and chronic sunbather may have older-looking skin than their years. Also, hereditary and racial factors influence skin age.

Itching

The skin often itches as one grows older. Itching usually stems from external irritations or internal diseases. External irritations may be more severe in winter because of lack of humidity and because the skin oil does not spread properly. Too many baths or wearing wool garments could also cause itching. You can correct this by cutting down on bathing, maintaining correct temperature and humidity, and applying skin creams.

If itching does not clear up in about two weeks, the trouble may be due to any of a number of internal diseases, some of them serious. Thus, it is wise to see your physician if itching persists.

Skin Cancer

Skin cancer can be easily diagnosed and treated. The two most common types are *basal cell* and *squamous cell.*

The basal cell type begins with a small fleshy *nodule,* usually on the face. It may take several months to reach one-half to one inch in diameter. In about a year it begins to ulcerate and bleed. Then it forms a crust, which it sheds at intervals, leaving another ulcer. If you notice anything like this, see your physician. He can usually remove the ulcer by a local operation.

Squamous cell cancer is often aided by smoking and exposure to the sun. The lesions may appear on the lips, mouth, and genitalia, and they tend to spread and increase in size. Horny growths in exposed areas—face, ears, neck, and scalp—may be forerunners of squamous cell cancer. Again, your physician can treat or operate effectively. See also Ch. 18, *Cancer.*

Vitiligo

Vitiligo, loss of pigment, is not caused by a disease, but it could be a hereditary problem. The affected area of skin has patches of whiteness throughout, but these can be masked by cosmetics.

Senile Purpura

Sometimes the skin develops *senile purpura* as one grows older. The characteristic hemorrhages of this condition usually appear on the extremities, and the purple color gradually fades and leaves mottled areas of yellow-brown. Generally, the skin is thin, fragile, and transparent in appearance.

Stasis Dermatitis

Sometimes in association with such conditions as varicose veins, the skin may develop *stasis dermatitis*, an acute, chronic condition of the leg, associated with swelling, scaling of the skin, and in some cases, ulcer formation. It may exist for years with or without ulceration.

If any of the above conditions develop, it is wise to consult your physician rather than try to treat yourself.

Other Skin Conditions

Other skin conditions that may develop in the later years may include an increase in coarse hairs on exposed places such as the upper lip or chin. The downy hairs in the ears and nose become become thicker and more apparent, and the eyebrows may become bushy. Graying hair is popularly associated with aging, but its onset often depends upon genetic factors and varies so much that it cannot be used as a reliable measure of age.

The earlobes may elongate as you grow older and the nails may become coarse and thickened or thinner and brittle.

Relieving Skin Conditions

As mentioned earlier, you can use some creams to relieve dryness and scaliness in older skin. The best of such creams are the water-in-oil emulsions (cold creams) such as Petrolatum Rose Water Ointment USP XVI, or oil-in-water emulsions such as Hydrophilic Ointment USP XVI. Wrinkle creams will not help much, but some conditions may be masked by regular cosmetic items such as powder, rouge, mascara, hair dyes, etc.

Sunscreens may aid in preventing acute and chronic overexposure to the sun's rays.

Various types of surgery may be performed to correct older skin conditions, but they won't work for everyone. Among some of the more common types of surgery are plastic surgery, dermabrasion (skin planning), chemosurgery (chemical cautery), cryosurgery (freezing of the skin), and electrosurgery (employing electricity). See "Plastic and Cosmetic Surgery" in Ch. 20, *Surgery*.

Hearing Loss

About three out of ten persons over age 65 have some hearing loss; at age 70 to 80 this percentage increases greatly.

Causes

While some hearing loss can be blamed on bad listening habits (tuning out people and conversation a person does not want to hear), the two major causes are conduction loss and nerve defects. A person with conduction loss hears high-pitched sounds best; a person with nerve impairment hears low sounds best. A combination of the two is called mixed deafness.

Conduction loss can be caused by wax, diseases of the ear, disturbances of the eardrum, or abnormalities inside the ear. It can also be caused by *otosclerosis*, a bony growth over the window to the inner ear. Most of these conditions can be treated by an ear doctor (*otologist*). He can remove wax from the ear, repair or replace eardrums, remove bony growths, and loosen or remove fixed ear bones.

Nerve defects may be another story. They are caused by wear and tear on the ear, disease, certain drugs, and blows and skull fractures, and usually cause permanent damage that cannot be helped by surgery or medical treatment.

Some persons complain about ringing in the ears (*tinnitus*) that may start without warning and vary in intensity and quality. What causes tinnitus in one person may not cause it in another, but often it is caused by wax in the ear, middle ear infection, arteriosclerosis, or certain drugs.

Hearing Aids

In most cases a hearing loss can be helped with a hearing aid or surgery. But if you think you have a hearing problem your first task is to see your physician. If your problem is not medically treatable, and if your physician believes a hearing aid will help you, you should see a dispensing audiologist. The American Speech-Language-Hearing Association, 10801 Rockville Pike, Rockville, MD 20852, will supply a directory of certified practitioners on request. If you have trouble finding an audiologist, an experienced hearing-aid dealer may be able to advise you on the device best suited to your needs. The National Hearing Aid Help Line (800/521-5247), a service of the National Hearing Aid Society, provides lists of dealers certified as dispensing audiologists.

A hearing test at a hearing aid clinic may be your next stop. Here trained audiologists will scientifically measure your hearing and assist you in trying on different kinds of aids. The audiologists do not sell hearing aids, but can tell you what kind is best for you. Basically, there are five kinds of aids:

- Body types that operate with a cord running to the receiver mold in the ear from a miniature microphone carried in a pocket, pinned to the clothing, or worn in a special carrier. These devices are about one to one and one-half inches long and weigh about two ounces.

- Behind-the-ear types that weigh only about one-half ounce and fit behind the ear. A plastic tube leads from the microphone to the receiver that fits in the ear.

- Hearing aids that fit inside the ear canal and weigh about one-sixth of an ounce. This model has become the most popular among hearing aid wearers.

- A type that fits in the outer ear.

- A "bionic ear" that requires surgery to make possible a *cochlear implant*. In the surgery a strip of 22 platinum electrodes is inserted into the inner ear, or cochlea (see "The Ear," in Ch. 1, *The Body*). A tiny cable connects the electrodes to a microchip planted under the skin behind one ear and to a microphone and transmitter attached to a headset.

A sixth kind of hearing aid, one that was built into eyeglasses, has virtually disappeared from use.

Buying a Hearing Aid

No single hearing aid is ideal for every hard-of-hearing person. Thus testing is essential if you are to find the right aid. You may want to bring a friend or relative when you are being fitted. A familiar voice serves as a yardstick to help you judge which aid is best.

It takes time to get used to a hearing aid. An aid amplifies all sounds—wanted and unwanted. It also changes most sounds, giving them an "electronic" character. Voices may sound unnatural and tinny. Normal noises may be harsh and grating. But special circuiting in many of today's aids limits the sound level reaching the eardrum. These *automatic gain controls* prevent discomfort but may distort speech. A still newer approach is to use filters to screen out background noises.

In addition to greatly reducing the sizes of many hearing aids, technological advances are expanding the usefulness of hearing aids continually. Noise blockers filter out sounds that do not fit with speech patterns. Tiny microphones reduce the buzzing noises picked up by some older hearing aid models. Treble and bass dials give the wearer a way to adjust sound quality to background noises. With the dials the wearer can also make adjustments to the hearing fluctuations resulting from bodily changes.

If you do not want to wear a hearing aid, or cannot adjust to one, you can try lip reading or speech reading. Each involves watching the lips and vocal chords to determine what another person is saying.

Talking to the Hard-of-Hearing

If you are talking to someone who has some hearing difficulty, he'll understand you better if you speak slowly and distinctly and use the lower range of your voice. Face him when you speak; let him see the movements of your lips. It also helps to point to visible objects.

Above all, don't shout. In fact, raising your voice sometimes pitches it into a higher frequency which a hard-of-hearing person may find difficult to understand.

Other Health Problems

The following health problems might also confront an older person. (Many of these conditions are discussed at greater length elsewhere in the book; in such cases, cross-references are supplied for your convenience at the end of the section.)

Heart Disease

The heart is the strongest, toughest muscle in the body. It is like an engine that could run 70 years or more without an overhaul. The heart has a complete maintenance and repair system, enabling many heart disease victims to continue long and useful lives.

While heart disease is not necessarily a product of aging, some heart and blood vessel problems become more acute as one grows older.

The following symptoms do not necessarily indicate heart disease, but it is wise to see a physician if you notice any of them:

- Shortness of breath
- A feeling of tightness in the chest or pain directly related to exertion or excitement
- Swelling of the feet and ankles
- Unusual fatigue

There is much that physicians can do to prevent heart conditions or to relieve them once present. But there is much that you can do to help yourself.

Weight

Extra pounds of fat mean more work for the heart.

Diet

The rules of sound nutrition apply to proper heart care.

Smoking

Heavy cigarette smokers suffer three times as many heart attacks as do pipe or cigar smokers. Nonsmokers are safest.

Exercise

Exercise improves the pumping action of the heart as well as circulation, digestion, and general health.

Worry

Worry increases tension and elevates blood pressure. Try to cultivate a philosophical approach to the daily ups and downs. See Ch.10, *Heart Disease*.

Strokes

Strokes are not hopeless; even severely paralyzed patients may make remarkable progress. A *stroke* occurs when the blood supply to a part of the brain tissue is cut off and, as a result, the nerve cells in that part of the brain can't function. When this happens, the part of the body controlled by these nerve cells can't function either.

Whenever the blood supply is cut off from an area, small neighboring arteries get larger and take over part of the work of the damaged artery. In this way nerve cells that have been temporarily put out of order may recover, and that part of the body affected by the stroke may eventually improve or even return to normal.

Once a stroke has occurred, a sound rehabilitation program can help the patient resume as many normal activities as possible. This program can be worked out in cooperation with the physician, patient, family, and local organizations. See Ch. 9, *Diseases of the Circulatory System.*

Arthritis

There are two main types of arthritis: *rheumatoid arthritis* and *osteoarthritis.*

Rheumatoid arthritis—which can cause pain and swelling in joints, nerves, muscles, tendons, blood vessels, and connective tissue in the whole body—can strike at any age, but it occurs mainly in the 25-to-40-year age group. The exact cause of rheumatoid arthritis is unknown.

Osteoarthritis is a degenerative joint disease that affects almost everyone who lives long enough; it is a product of normal wear and tear on the joints over the years. Poor posture and obesity are contributing causes, as are heredity and trauma.

Osteoarthritis is usually mild, and it seldom cripples. Pain is generally moderate. Unlike rheumatoid arthritis, which is inflammatory, spreads from joint to joint, and affects the whole body, osteoarthritis confines its attack locally to individual joints. Rarely is inflammation a problem.

Osteoarthritis is likely to develop in any joint that has been required to take a lot of punishment or abuse: the knee or hip joints of someone who is overweight; joints injured in an accident; joints injured or overused in sports; joints subjected to unusual stresses and strains in work or play; joints with hidden defects that were present at birth.

There is no specific cure for arthritis, but the pain and swelling can be controlled. In other than acute cases, common aspirin has proved the safest and most popular medication.

Adequate rest for both the body and the affected joint is a fundamental treatment. Heat, controlled exercise, hydrotherapy, and massage are all effective if done under a physician's supervision. See "Arthritis and Other Joint Diseases" in Ch. 7, *Diseases of the Skeletal System.*

Cancer

Cancer strikes at any age, but it does strike more frequently in the later years. Many factors are believed to contribute to cancer; frictional and chemical irritations like cigarette smoking, irritation of the skin and mouth (such as poor dentures), exposure to the sun, X rays, or radioactive elements. Common sites are the lips, mouth, stomach, intestines, rectum, liver, pancreas, lungs, breast, kidney, bladder, skin, uterus, and prostate.

Early detection and prompt treatment are the best protection against cancer. If any of the following seven danger signals lasts longer than two weeks, be sure to get a checkup.

- Unusual bleeding or discharge

- A lump or thickening in the breast or elsewhere

- A sore that does not heal

- Change in bowel or bladder habits

- Hoarseness or cough

- Indigestion or difficulty in swallowing

- Change in wart or mole

Great strides have been made in treating cancer through surgery, radiotherapy, and chemotherapy. See Ch. 18, *Cancer*. For cancers affecting women only, see "Cancers of the Reproductive System" and "Cancer of the Breast" in Ch. 25, *Women's Health*.

The Eyes

The eye does age. After age 40, failing vision is usually caused by natural hardening of the lens, making it difficult to see close objects. However, failing vision may also be the first symptom of a serious bodily disorder, or of glaucoma or of a cataract, which requires a physician's immediate attention.

Both glaucoma and cataract can be treated effectively. About 90 percent of glaucoma cases can be checked with eye drops and about 95 percent of cataracts can be removed by a painless operation.

Other diseases that may develop in later years affect the blood vessels of the eye. A common condition is *senile macula degeneration* which causes a blind spot to appear when the victim looks directly at something. The exact cause of senile macula degeneration is not known. See under Ch. 16, *Diseases of the Eye and Ear*.

Diabetes

Most likely candidates for diabetes are overweight persons past 40, particularly those who have a hereditary history of diabetes, and especially older women.

The exact cause of diabetes is not known, but it is a functional disorder in which the body cannot handle certain foods—mainly sugars and starches. Symptoms include increased thirst, constant hunger, frequent urination, loss of weight, itching, easy tiring, changes in vision, and slow healing of cuts and scratches.

Treatment and control consist of planned diet, exercise, and, in many cases, insulin shots or oral medication. Well-controlled diabetics can lead active lives. See Ch. 15, *Diabetes Mellitus.*

Constipation

There is no truth in the notion that a daily bowel movement is necessary for good health. A movement every day or twice a day may be all right for one person; for another every three or four days may be enough.

The two most common causes of chronic constipation are physical inactivity and poor food and water habits. Ironically, constipation may be caused by swallowing a cathartic nightly to induce a bowel movement. The habit eventually leads to chronic constipation because normal bowel movement ceases and bowel evacuation depends on using a cathartic.

To maintain proper bowel movement, try the following:

- Drink eight to ten glasses of water a day. Take two glasses of water on an empty stomach as soon as you get up.

- Drink more fruit juices and eat more dried and fresh fruits.

- Get at least one-half hour of moderate exercise daily. Walking, for example, is excellent, particularly if you relax while you walk.

- Give yourself enough time for normal bowel movement and set up a regular time for evacuation.

- If you are constipated, consult your physician to make sure it is simple and functional. See under Ch. 23, *Aches, Pains, Nuisances, Worries.*

Back Problems

As we grow older, the back muscles—weakened by inactivity, poor posture, and almost unavoidable wear and tear—start to complain.

Other causes of back problems are muscle and joint strain, changes in the spine, psychological tension, and internal diseases. Here are some tips to help avoid backache:

- Learn to lift correctly. Use your leg muscles, which are stronger than back muscles, by placing your feet closer to the base of the object, bending your knees outward, and pushing up with your legs.

- Avoid subjecting your back to any sudden, erratic motion.

- Try to improve your posture when sitting and walking.

- Sleep on a firm bed; a bed board may be helpful.

- Get regular exercise of a type that stimulates all your muscles rather than just a few.

- If you sit for a long period, get up and stretch occasionally.

- Beware of excess weight. Extra weight on the abdomen pulls on the vertebrae at the small of the back, increasing the spine's normal curve and causing pain.

- Try never to become overfatigued or exhausted, either physically or mentally. Emotional pressure, from work or personal problems, causes muscle tension. See "Backaches" in Ch. 23, *Aches, Pains, Nuisances, Worries.*

Because the feet are farthest away from the heart's blood supply, they are often the first areas affected by circulatory diseases. Also, arthritis and diabetes might first show up in the feet.

Warning signs include continued cramping of the calf muscles, pain in the arch and toes, and unusually cold feet—especially if accompanied by a bluish skin. Brittle or thickened toenails or burning, tingling, and numbness may also signal a circulatory disease.

Foot ulcers may be one of the first signs of diabetes. Some *bunions*—swollen, tender, red joints—are caused by arthritis. Swelling around the feet and ankles suggests a possible kidney disorder.

If you have these symptoms, go to a *podiatrist* (a foot doctor) or to your own physician. They are trained to recognize these symptoms.

Most older people, however, suffer from minor aches and pains in the feet that are caused by poor foot care or abuse. See "The Vulnerable Extremities" in Ch. 23, *Aches, Pains, Nuisances, Worries.*

Care of the Feet

To prevent these problems, treat yourself to daily foot care. Dry your feet thoroughly and gently after bathing and inspect the skin for abrasion, rough spots, or cracks. Dry carefully between the toes. If the skin is dry or scaly, lubricate it with lanolin or olive oil. Next, apply a medicated foot powder recommended by your podiatrist or physician over the entire foot, especially between the toes, as a preventive measure against athlete's foot.

When you cut your nails, do it with a strong light and be careful to cut straight across the nail to prevent ingrown toenails. Avoid the use of strong medications containing salicylate and strong antiseptics like iodine, carbolic acid, lysol, or bleach. Harsh chemicals that attack toughened skin can irritate normal tissue and cause infection. Avoid using hot water bottles, electric pads, or any form of extreme heat or cold. Diabetics should visit a podiatrist regularly.

The Prostate

Men over 50 may have an enlarged *prostate.* (This is not caused by sexual excesses or venereal disease.) The exact cause is not known, but it's estimated that some type of enlarged prostate is present in about 10 percent of 40-year-olds and 80 percent of 80-year-olds.

The prostate is a rubbery mass of glands and muscle tissue about the size and shape of a horse chestnut. It is wrapped around the urethra and base of the bladder at the point where they join. The prostate functions as part of a man's sexual apparatus, providing a fluid that transports and nourishes the spermatozoa.

Symptoms of an enlarged prostate include difficulty in urination. There might be an initial blocking of the urine, or the stream may lack force. You may feel that you can't empty the bladder, and you may have urgent needs to urinate. You may have pain or blood in the urine from straining.

If you have any of these symptoms, your physician can easily check for enlarged prostate by a simple rectal examination. If he discovers an enlargement, he can usually treat it in early stages with simple massage. But if it has progressed too far, he may have to operate.

An operation is usually performed through the urethra or by an incision in the lower abdomen. The choice depends upon the individual problems of the patient and the judgment of the surgeon. In either case, the patient usually recovers completely in a short time.

A rectal examination can also discover early stages of cancer of the prostate, which is not uncommon in men over 40. Some 20 percent of men over 60 have this condition, and it is most common in men over 70.

Unfortunately, this disease does not manifest itself early, so it is important that men over 40 have the diagnostic rectal examination. If the disease is detected early and treated—usually by surgery, hormonal therapy, and possibly radiation—the cure rate is very high. If found late, the cure rate is low.

When treatment is by surgery, the entire prostate and upper urethra may be removed. In some cases, the disease may be retarded or relieved by treatment with female hormones. (The male hormone is known to hasten prostate cancer.)

In both enlargement and cancer of the prostate, early detection is vital to a successful cure. That is why it is important to have a rectal examination. See also "Cancer of the Prostate" in Ch. 18, *Cancer.*

Alzheimer's Disease

Alzheimer's disease is a group of brain disorders marked by progressive deterioration and affects both memory and reasoning abilities. Victims of Alzheimer's, which is a form of dementia, or mental deterioration (see"Dementia" in Ch. 8, *Diseases of the Muscles and Nervous System*), undergo various behavioral changes. These include an inability to concentrate, anxiety, irritability, agitation, withdrawal, and petulance. Persons suffering from Alzheimer's may wander about and lose their way. They may have temper tantrums and engage in obsessional behavior, such as repeatedly washing dishes. Time and place disorientation may be accompanied by delusions and depression. In the later stages of the disease, sufferers often lose bladder and bowel control.

Diagnosing Alzheimer's in its early stages is difficult despite its numerous symptoms. Laboratory tests that could identify the disorder do not exist. Adding to the problems of diagnosis, various other disorders have similar symptoms. The best medical alternative, a complete physical examination, generally includes a review of any drugs or medications the patient has been taking as well as standard laboratory tests. The latter help to rule out other diseases or disorders that may be treatable. A clinical evaluation can include a CT (computed tomography) scan, an EEG (electroencephalogram), and assessment of evidence from family members and the patient regarding the latter's (or patient's) mental state.

Even when diagnosed with relative certainty, Alzheimer's disease cannot be cured. But some symptoms, including depression and delusions, can be treated. The effect is to slow the progress of the disorder. Where Parkinson's disease or heart problems accompany Alzheimer's, treatment can focus on alleviation of those conditions.

Theories regarding the causes of Alzheimer's abound. Because it is known that the disease leads to severe atrophy and distortion of the cerebral cortex, researchers have explored both genetic and physiological theories. On the genetic side, studies have indicated that persons with relatives who had or have Alzheimer's face three or four times the normal risks of becoming victims. On the physiological side, Alzheimer's patients have been shown to lack adequate supplies of *choline acetyltransferase* (CAT), a neurotransmitter, or chemical, that enables brain signals to travel from one cell to another. Such findings, it is hoped, will lead eventually to cures.

Meeting the Challenge of Leisure

Leisure Activities

In ten years of retirement, you will have the leisure time equivalent of working 40 hours a week for 21 years. You cannot fish this time away and you cannot rest it away. Whatever you do for long must have meaning—must satisfy some basic need and want. Certain needs remain constant throughout life:

- Security—good health, income, and a recognized role in society

- Recognition—as an individual with your own abilities and personality

- Belonging—as a member of a fam-ily, social group, and community

- Self-expression—by developing abilities and talents in new areas and at new levels

- Adventure—new experiences, new sights, and new knowledge

There are many activities that can satisfy these basic needs and wants to keep you mentally and physically in top shape.

Travel

Travel satisfies your need for adventure in many ways. If you travel off-season at bargain rates, you'll find that time truly is money. Most travel problems stem from rushing to meet a schedule. Making every minute count on a fast-paced European tour can be expensive and exhausting. For the same transatlantic fare, you can spend a full year in Europe at one-third the daily cost of a three-week vacation.

Wherever you travel, it isn't enough just to sightsee. Try to center your travel around an interest or a hobby. You can take art or music tours—tours that stress education, night life, culture, or special interests. You can travel on your own or with a group. But whatever you do, participate; don't just observe.

Doing things instead of just observing adds new dimensions to the pleasure of going places. For people who participate, travel means the adventure of enjoying exciting new places, people, and experiences. To help plan your trip, write to the government tourist offices of foreign countries (ask your library for addresses); to the National Park Service, Washington, DC; and to state or local chambers of commerce (no street addresses necessary).

Gardening

Gardening satisfies one's need for self-expression in many ways. Being outside in the fresh air and planting living things can bring satisfaction and peace of mind.

Gardening is a many-faceted hobby that offers many challenges. You can go into plant breeding, growing for resale, introducing new plants, collect-ing the rare and unusual, plant selecting, or simply cultivating what you find personally appealing and satisfying.

Your local library or bookstore has many books on the subject. There are local and national garden clubs that you can join to learn about your hobby and to meet other people who are interested in gardening. Write the Government Printing Office, Washington, DC 20401, for help and advice. In addition, state extension directors at state colleges and universities, county agricultural agents, and local plant nurseries can give expert advice and information.

Reading

Reading offers excitement, adventure, pursuit of knowledge, and an introduction to new people and places. Your local library is the best place to launch a reading program—and you may be surprised to find that it offers more than books. Most libraries have art and music departments, audiovisual services (films and microfilm copies), foreign language departments, periodical rooms (newspapers and magazines), writing classes, genealogy workshops, and special courses of general interest.

Hobbies

A hobby can be any physical or mental activity that gives you happiness, relaxation, and satisfaction. It should not be just a time killer—it should offer some tangible reward. Also, it should have continuity, not be too expensive, and not make undue demands on time and energy. Perhaps you would prefer a series of hobbies, some serious and some just for fun. They can be related to your work or completely unrelated. In any event, a hobby should be something you've always wanted to do.

Before selecting a hobby, consider these points:

- Do you like to do things alone? Consider arts, crafts, reading, sewing, fishing—activities that are not dependent on others, although you can enjoy them with others.

- Do you like groups? Seek hobbies that include other people—organizational, sport, game, or craft activities.

- Do you like to play to win? Try your luck in competitive or team games that stress winning.

- Do you have to be an expert? Too many of us are afraid to try new activities because we hate to fail or look clumsy. But be fair; judge your efforts in light of your past experience and present progress; do not compare yourself to someone who's been at it longer than you.

- Do you put a price tag on everything? Many people will not engage in an activity if it costs too much. Yet, many hobbies fail because they're tried on a shoestring without adequate equipment. Also, some people do not want to do anything unless it brings in money. If so, perhaps you should look for something that's an offshoot of the work or business you know best.

Creative Crafts

Creative crafts are difficult for most of us because we are conservative, afraid to make mistakes, sensitive because of buried and almost forgotten blunders. Yet creativity is essential to life. Without it we don't live fully; through creative skills we refurbish old interests and develop new ones.

Most of us are happiest with creative crafts that do not require intricate work or fine detail and that are not too demanding physically. Some crafts best suited to retirement years include weaving, rug making, sewing, ceramic work, knitting, plastic molding, woodwork, leathercraft, and lapidary.

You can learn these and other crafts and also market your products through senior centers, adult education classes, and senior craft centers.

Volunteer Work

Through community service and volunteer work, thousands are not only helping others but are serving themselves. Such activities keep time from hanging heavy, give purpose to retirement, and in some cases may lead to paying jobs and a second career.

Participating in community activities is not difficult. In some communities a call to the city clerk is enough to get started. In others, a letter to the mayor will bring faster results. In larger cities, call the Volunteer Bureau in your area; this is a United Fund agency that acts as a clearing house for volunteer jobs.

If you wish to have the type of volunteer job that leads to a second career, you might consider doing work for one of the government programs utilizing the skills of older people. All of these programs have been assembled under the umbrella of one organization called ACTION. For additional information about any of the following programs, write to ACTION, Washington, DC 20525.

- The Foster Grandparent Program hires low-income men and women over 60 to give love and attention to institutionalized and other needy children.

- The Peace Corps is seeking the skills of retirees. However, you must be skilled in some trade or profession, pass a tough physical examination, and complete a rigorous orientation and training program. For information, write to ACTION, Washington, DC 20525, and request a copy of *Older Volunteers in the Peace Corps*. It lists specific skills needed in the Peace Corps.

- Other programs within ACTION include the Retired Senior Volunteer Program, the Service Corps of Retired Executives, the Active Corps of Executives, and VISTA (Volunteer in Service to America). Many of the workers in these programs are paid.

There are other volunteer jobs that may not pay a salary, but do fill a basic need by allowing you to pass along your skills and ideals to younger people. You can do this through the Boy Scouts, Girl Scouts, Boys Clubs of America, YMCAs and YWCAs, hospitals, schools for the handicapped and mentally retarded, and many other organizations.

Continuing Social and Intellectual Activities

The one organ we can depend upon in old age is the brain. At 80, a person can learn at approximately the same speed he could when he was 12 years old. But like any organ, the brain must be kept active and alert by constant use.

One of the best ways to exercise the brain is through some process of continuing education. This does not have to mean going back to school or taking formal classes. Continuing education can take the form of participating in discussions in senior centers, "Y's," town meetings, or study courses. You can find out about educational opportunities and possibilities by contacting local, state, or national offices of education; state employment offices; the information service of your Community Council or Health and Welfare Federation; the Adult Education section of the U.S. Office of Education, Washington, DC 20202; the National Education Association, 1201 Sixteenth Street, NW, Washington, DC 20036; the State Commission on Aging (write to your state capital).

Your local library may have some suggestions (and perhaps offers some classes), and your local "Y" is probably offering some programs.

The federal government continues to be a prime source of educational literature. Each year the government prints about 50 million books, pamphlets, brochures, reports, and guidebooks on everything from astrology to zoology. For a free price list of specified subjects, write to the Superintendent of Documents, Government Printing Office, Washington, DC 20401.

Formal and informal learning situations can help you keep pace with change and the future. Continuing education prepares you to live contentedly with a free, independent spirit and mind—while providing you with the means for improved social integration, participation, and satisfaction.

Sexual Attitude and Activity in the Aged

We have come far since the Victorian era when talk about sex was taboo. Now science is taking a candid look at sex in the later years and is exploding old myths as well as exploring new truths. Such enlightenment can help reduce any remaining guilt in this area.

After Age 60

In one study to determine the pattern of sexual behavior after 60, researchers at Duke University quizzed 250 people aged 60 to 93 about their sexual activities. Of the 149 who were married, 81 reported they were still sexually active; even in the single group, 7 of the 101 questioned reported "some sexual activity."

Dr. Gustave Newman, who conducted the study, reported 10 percent of the couples over 60 as having sexual relations more than once a week, though couples over 75 unanimously reported less activity.

"No age is an automatic cut-off point for sex," claims the late Dr. Isadore Rubin in his study, *Sexual Life After Sixty*. "But," he continues,

sexuality cannot flourish in a climate where rejection of aging as a worthwhile stage of life leads inevitably to self-rejection by many older persons . . . the men and women who "act old" in their sexual activity before their bodies have really called a halt become sexually old long before their time.

Sexual Interest after Menopause

Actually, many women take a renewed interest in sex after menopause. Dr. William H. Masters and Mrs. Virginia E. Johnson in their study *Human Sexual Response* credit the tendency of many women to experience a second honeymoon in the early 50s to the fact that they no longer have to worry about pregnancy and usually have resolved most of the problems of raising a family.

On the other hand, they tell us:

Deprived of normal sexual outlets, women exhaust themselves physically in conscious or unconscious efforts to dissipate their accumulated and frequently unrecognized sexual tensions. Many demonstrate their basic insecurities by casting themselves unreservedly into their religion, the business world, volunteer social work, or overzealous mothering of their mature children or grandchildren.

Lessened Response of Men

While some women become more responsive as they grow older, Masters and Johnson point out, "There is no question that the human male's responsiveness wanes as he ages." They attribute this to attitudes arising from:

- Boredom—being taken for granted by his wife

- Economic pursuits—occupational competition becomes a demanding,

all-consuming activity

- Fatigue from unusual or excessive physical strain, such as that induced by sports; or mental fatigue induced by such factors as a "bad day at the office"

- Overindulgence in food and drink, usually alcohol

- Physical and mental infirmities

- Fear of failure

Myths about Sex

One common reason for an older person's termination of sex life is the often mistaken idea that continued sexual activity in middle and old age may adversely affect health. Although the old myths that sex is weakening or speeds the aging process have been largely dismissed by physicians today, some people still cling to them; what sexual activity they do have is troubled by fear.

Heart Patients

Cardiac patients are no longer admonished to lead sexless lives except in extreme cases. After a heart attack most are able to resume sexual activity within a few months, although patients with angina pectoris may be advised to proceed cautiously.

According to Dr. Philip Reichert, former executive secretary of the American College of Cardiology:

> We must get rid of the notion that every heart patient lives under an overhanging sword and that he faces the constant threat of sudden death. The congenial married couple, accustomed to each other and whose technique is habituated through many years of companionship, can achieve sexual satisfaction without too great an expenditure of body energy or too severe a strain upon the heart. . . .

Hypertension sufferers may sometimes indulge in a restricted form of sexual activity with medical supervision. And modern therapy and surgical methods can often prevent or delay impotence caused by prostate disease or diabetes.

Other Health Problems

But where any health problem is involved, it is best to analyze your sex needs and those of your partner; consult with your physician and partner as to how you can both attain satisfaction without harm to your health; see your physician regularly and report accurately distress symptoms and the conditions causing them.

Recent research has dispelled other long-held ideas about sex, too—among them the myth that masturbation is childish and harmful to health. Moreover, Rubin points out: "All studies of older persons have shown that autoerotic activity, while not as common as in the younger years, is far more prevalent in later years than most of us have imagined." He quotes a survey by *Sexology* magazine that showed that of 279 married men studied, 1 out of every 4 masturbated after age 60.

Dr. Lester W. Dearborn, marriage consultant, in pointing out the role masturbation plays in the lives of the single or widowed, comments:

> It is to be hoped that those interested in the field of geriatrics will . . . encourage the aging to accept masturbation as a perfectly valid outlet when there is a need and other means of gratification are not available.

The "dirty old man" myth has run

its course, too. Although society tends to picture both the child molester and the exhibitionist as older men, experts point out that both typically belong to much younger age groups. Donald Mulcock, child welfare specialist, in studying men who assaulted children sexually in England and Wales, found most offenses against boys were committed by men between the ages of 39 and 50, those against girls by men between 33 and 44. Only six percent of the men he studied were 63, and none was older.

Cellular Therapy and Hormone Treatment

To keep older people vigorous and active, some researchers have experimented with *cellular therapy* as a means of retarding aging. Dr. Paul Niehans, a Swiss physician, introduced the idea of cellular therapy in the 1930s with his theory that organs begin to deteriorate in old age when the body fails to replace the cells that compose it. He prescribed a treatment whereby a person is injected with cells from healthy embryonic animal organs. (He used sheep, pigs, and calves.) He believed that the animal cells from a particular organ would migrate to the same organ in the aging body and reactivate it. Thus, kidney troubles could be cured with cells from an embryonic animal kidney. Although such notables as Sir Winston Churchill, Pope Pius XII, Somerset Maugham, and Dr. Konrad Adenauer submitted to it, cellular therapy is not widely accepted in the United States today as an effective agent against aging.

More to the point, most researchers feel, are the current experiments with hormones. Hormones help women through the tension of menopause and are used to treat impotence and loss of sexual desire. However, some studies have linked estrogen hormone therapy statistically with uterine cancer. For this reason and because of side effects, hormones face many years of testing before they will be used extensively to retard aging.

Mental Outlook

Good health plus a romantic outlook promote sex appeal at any age. Being romantic and showing affection, whether sexually or not, keep you sparkling and lively no matter what your age.

A good wholesome attitude toward life, a hearty sense of humor, a sympathetic interest in other people—all help make up the indefinable something that makes us appealing to the opposite sex. Good grooming plays an important role, too. Cleanliness, neat suitable apparel, and good posture all add to the image we create of ourselves in other people's minds. So do the manners we reflect in the courtesies we show the people around us—the thoughtful little things we do for them, our reactions to the things they do for us.

If you're a woman over 65 who is

looking for companionship, you'll probably find a good personality uplift will get you farther than a face or bust lift. If you're a man who is hoping to find feminine companionship, you will probably find a good spiritual overhaul more image-enhancing than dyeing your hair. Also, a good night's sleep is the best aphrodisiac.

The Right Housing

Selecting retirement housing is like selecting a spouse; there are many possibilities, but few that are right.

Ideally, the right housing should take care of you rather than requiring you to take care of it. It should give you shelter, security, and privacy; allow you freedom; and keep you near friends, relatives, and a grocer who delivers.

To Move or Not to Move

What is the right housing for you— the one that you are in or some other place? The answer to this question depends upon the state of your pocketbook and the state of your health.

Advantages of Moving

Right now you might be in good health, but this could change. Would stairs become a problem? Could you keep up the house and garden? Would you want more adequate heat? Older people are more comfortable when the temperature is over 75° F. You might also need better lighting in several rooms.

If you are retired, you might find that you cannot keep up expenses on the old house. You might find that your larger, older house does not suit the reduced size of your family or your need for work or recreation. You could probably save money by living in a smaller place that requires less upkeep. You could also arrange to move nearer children and grandchildren, or into an area where you could find new opportunities for work and recreational activities.

Advantages of Staying Put

But by staying in your home you would remain in familiar surroundings and near old friends. You could maintain your comfortable routine and remain independent as long as possible. If you have unused space, you could move into the first floor and shut off the second floor to save on heat and maintenance. Or you could convert part of the house into apartments.

Where to Live?

Many older persons fulfill ambitions of long standing by moving to warmer climates after retirement. The question whether such a move should be undertaken should be considered with other questions relating to housing.

Moving to a different climate makes sense for many reasons. Many elderly persons feel threatened or restricted by cold winters and their usual accompaniments—snow, sleet, and high winds. Having more leisure time, older persons feel that warmer temperatures will make it possible to take part in more activities for more hours of the day than if they "stay put." Some persons move so that they can live closer to friends who have already moved—or to children or other relatives. Some move to play golf or tennis outdoors the year around.

An individual or couple considering a move to a warmer climate should look at a number of basic considerations. A key one relates to the cost of living in the new area or state. Living on incomes that may have been substantially reduced by retirement, older persons without special preferences may select that state that offers the cheapest living.

"Retirement to the sun" entails many other decisions. States like New Mexico offer a wide range of sites, from urban to desert, from high mountains to empty plains. Some of the states with favorable tax laws and cheap living costs have little to offer in the way of cultural attractions. Other states may lack recreational activities.

Psychological Trauma

Moving 100 or 1,000 or 2,000 miles to live in a warmer climate obviously involves some pain of separation and loss. The psychological trauma occasioned by a departure from old friends and familiar surroundings has caused major problems for some older persons. For that reason, the psychological challenge should be given deep consideration *before* any move is made.

How to alleviate the trauma of leaving the familiar for the unfamiliar? Some persons spend a year in the new locale, return home, and *then* make up their minds to move or not to move. Others, including those who cannot afford such trial living, at least visit the target region to "get a feel" for it and its way of life.

Requirements of Retirement Housing

Whatever you plan to do, your retirement housing should be located near or be easily accessible to shops and recreation centers by public transportation. To make living arrangements more pleasant, individual housing units should contain at least 400 square feet, and there should be two or more rooms.

The new dwelling unit should be equal to or better than the housing you have been used to in the past. It should be suitable for comfortable living in both health and sickness—easily adaptable to convalescent needs with either two bedrooms or a bedroom and sleeping alcove.

In addition, retirement housing

should incorporate the following:

- All rooms on one floor, and that floor reached by few, if any, steps

- No thresholds or tripping hazards

- Nonslip surfaces in hallways, bedrooms, and kitchens

- Handrails by all steps and inclines

- Adequate illumination in halls, near steps, and in other potentially hazardous areas

- Fully automatic central heating

- Doors and halls wide enough to accommodate a wheelchair

Public Housing

If you decide to move and to rent instead of buying, consider public housing projects. These projects are available to single men and women 62 or older, as well as to families whose head is 62 or older or has a spouse at least 62. Local housing authorities build, purchase, or lease the units and set entrance requirements and maximum income limits. Rents are comparatively low.

The Housing and Urban Development Agency also makes loans for nonprofit (and profit) sponsors that will build housing for senior citizens with moderate or higher incomes.

Retirement Hotels and Communities

You might also consider retirement hotels, which are especially numerous in Florida, California, and Texas. These hotels are usually refurbished former resorts that provide room and board at a fixed monthly rent.

Retirement communities offer housing of various types, usually apartments, cooperatives, and individual units. It usually costs about $450 a month or more to cover mortgage payments, living, and maintenance expenses.

Would you like retirement community living? It's usually the life for people who like people and who enjoy being active. For those who don't, it can be a bit tiring. Some couples do not like the closeness and activity found in a retirement community and prefer living in a less social environment.

Lifetime Care Facilities

In contrast to the emphasis on independent living in retirement communities, many projects sponsored by church, union, and fraternal organizations stress lifetime care (room, board, and medical care for life), with fees based on actuarial tables of life expectancy at age of entry. Housing alone costs from $10,000 to $30,000, depending upon age and type of living accommodation, *plus* a monthly charge of around $250 per person to cover meals, medical care (exclusive of Medicare), maintenance, and other expenses. In many cases, lifetime care for a couple could cost around $90,000.

Cooperatives and Condominiums

In addition to lifetime care facilities, many church, fraternal, and union groups offer other types of housing. In the case of church-sponsored housing, residence usually is not restricted to members of the sponsoring faith.

Some of these units are operated as *cooperatives;* others as *condominiums.* The major difference in the two is that condominium owners have titles to their units, while cooperative residents are stockholders in the cooperative association with occupancy rights to specific units. Condominium owners pay their own taxes; cooperative residents pay taxes in their monthly charges.

Mobile Homes

You might also want to consider a mobile home. A suitable one must be at least 10 feet wide and 50 feet long.

What is it like to live in a mobile-home park? Certainly, there is a closeness in these parks that you would not have in a normal neighborhood. Typically, the mobile home is placed on a lot 25 to 30 feet wide and 75 feet deep. This means that you could have 12 families within a radius of 100 feet.

Residents visit back and forth and hold frequent picnics, barbecues, and other social activities. This would not be the way of life for someone who did not enjoy group activities.

Be Realistic

To find out what type of housing is best for you, look around the area to see where you want to live. Each community is different, shaped by the people who live there. Talk to the residents and do some serious thinking before you move, not forgetting to carefully consider your financial position in regard to the new locale. Try to be realistic; don't expect to find the perfect climate for health and happiness. The nearest thing to it would be a place that encourages outdoor life, is neither too hot nor too cold, has a relative humidity of around 55 percent, and enough variety in weather, with frequent but moderate weather changes, to be interesting and not too monotonous.

If you have any doubts about the location as far as health is concerned, check with your physician.

When Faced with Ill Health

How can you help yourself or others when faced with a serious or terminal illness?

Alvin I. Goldfarb, M.D., former consultant on Services for the Aged, New York State Department of Mental Hygiene, notes the importance of self-esteem, self-confidence, sense of purpose, and well-being to a person who is seriously ill or dying. Supported by the idea, "I've led a good and full life," older people can face a serious or terminal illness with dignity. Sometimes this acceptance may be almost an unspoken and tacit understanding between the aging and society to help the separation process along.

When a person is terminally ill, the chances are that he is not in severe pain. With the increasing supply of pain-relieving drugs and the possibility of sedation, very few elderly patients suffer greatly with pain. While a fear of death probably exists in most people, when death is actually encountered the fear is seldom overwhelming, even though it may deeply affect others directly involved with the dying patient.

Most patients are at least aware of the possibility of dying soon; those with lingering conditions are particularly adept at self-diagnosis. But more often, they notice a change in social relationships with friends, family, and medical personnel.

Patient–physician relationships can be vital in helping the seriously ill patient retain peace of mind. It is the physician's responsibility to give compassion and recognize fear, even when it is hidden. Likewise, he should respond to a patient's hidden wish to discuss his illness. Of course, there is no set formula for communicating with seriously ill patients. Each individual needs a different approach, and most physicians are sensitive to this.

Many physicians report that death, except in unusual cases, is not accompanied by physical pain. Rather, there is often a sense of well-being and spiritual exaltation. Physicians think this feeling is caused by the anesthetic action of carbon dioxide on the central nervous system and by the effect of toxic substances. Ernest Hemingway wrote, "The pang of death, a famous doctor once told me, is often less than that of a toothache."

Stages of Death

According to physicians, people die in stages—rapidly or slowly, depending on circumstances. First comes *clinical death,* when respiration and heartbeat cease. The brain dies as it is deprived of oxygen and circulating blood, and *biological death* occurs.

Life can be restored in the moments between clinical death and brain death if circulation and respiration are continued through the use of medical devices that stimulate the heart and lungs.

After the brain ceases to function, cellular death begins. Life is not considered to be completely lost until the brain stops functioning. It is possible for surgeons to remove viable organs after biological death for transplant or other use.

Many clergymen and physicians insist that we need more honest communication about death, as such communication is probably the single most useful measure to avoid unnecessary suffering. Sound knowledge never made anyone afraid. And although death will probably always remain essentially a mystery, scientists will continue to search for a better understanding of its nature. By such means they may learn a great deal more about life.

The Autopsy

Family members adjusting to the death of a loved one may face the question of whether or not an autopsy should be performed. More and more, medical experts are underscoring the need for an autopsy as a means of confirming the cause of death. The postmortem examination may also "provide a reasonable context for accepting death," according to Daniel W. McKeel, director of autopsy pathology at Washington University School of Medicine. From a family and genetic point of view, the autopsy may reveal information about specific conditions or medical problems in the deceased that survivors can use to guide their own health practices and concerns.

Contrary to some reports, the autopsy need not delay funeral arrangements or disfigure the body so as to require a closed casket. Autopsies are generally mandatory in homicide, suicide, burn deaths, deaths resulting from on-the-job injuries, operating room deaths, and questionable or unwitnessed deaths.